Dramatic Identities and Cultural Tradition

STUDIES IN SHAKESPEARE
AND HIS CONTEMPORARIES

LIVERPOOL ENGLISH TEXTS AND STUDIES

General editor: PHILIP EDWARDS

Titles in this Series

Dramatic Identities and Cultural Tradition

STUDIES IN SHAKESPEARE
AND HIS CONTEMPORARIES

Critical Essays by
G. K. HUNTER

Professor of English Literature
Yale University

BARNES & NOBLE BOOKS · NEW YORK
(A division of Harper & Row Publishers, Inc.)

Published in the U.S.A. 1978 by
HARPER & ROW PUBLISHERS, INC.
BARNES & NOBLE IMPORT DIVISION

ISBN 0-06-493062-9

First published 1978

Set in Monotype Sabon 11D/12 pt by
The Lancashire Typesetting Company Limited, Bolton
and printed and bound in Great Britain by
R. & R. Clark Limited, Edinburgh, Scotland

This volume is dedicated
to the memory of
ERNEST SCHANZER
Colleague, scholar, friend
BORN 1922   DIED 1976

Io dico pena, e dovrei dir sollazzo

Preface

I am indebted to Professor Philip Edwards for the suggestion that Liverpool University Press publish a collection of my essays. When he first approached me I formed the ambition not only of integrating the essays chosen into a single continuous argument but also of recapturing wasted time and incorporating into revised versions all the second thoughts, answers to critics, and more recent information that was available.

But as soon as I began to work towards this end I discovered that it was beyond my reach; and that the choice before me was between the original essays, only superficially corrected, and (on the other hand) the dream of a perfected achievement never to be achieved. Within the modest limits of the possible I have done what I can to remove glaring inconsistencies and patent overlaps; but I have not endeavoured to secure textual consistency. I have not removed, for example, variation between the old-spelling quotations of one chapter and the modernized quotations of another. The variation quite well expresses my own divided mind on this question, and I do not believe that any reader will be misled.

I have also sought by selecting and ordering the essays (and by supplying some bridge passages) to create enough connection and continuity to define what is common to them all. The chosen essays all deal with Renaissance drama; and I have sought to narrow the focus still further by dividing the book into broadly defined sections. The essays in the first section are concerned with the theatrical definition of the Elizabethan audience's English identity, achieved by setting against that both meaningful alternatives and fruitful interactions. The essays of the second group show how traditions are modified when they impinge on the self-identity of the audience; they also show, conversely, how Shakespeare has to be re-invented to suit the interests of later and different traditions. The essays of the third part describe some structures used to predetermine meaning for its audience by unifying divergent material inside largely implicit cultural assumptions. The 'sections' thus overlap: they define predominant but not exclusive interests.

The book, of course, cannot wholly escape its origin in occasional publications; nor do I wish to smooth away the irregularity of its contours or the variousness of its materials. I can only hope that the variousness will remind readers of Cleopatra rather than Proteus.

Contents

STRUCTURES

Plates

Acknowledgements

Acknowledgement is gratefully made to the following:

The editor of *Shakespeare Survey* and Cambridge University Press for permission to reprint (with some changes) (1) 'Elizabethans and foreigners' from vol. 17 (1964); (2) 'Seneca and the Elizabethans' from vol. 20 (1967); (3) 'Shakespeare's earliest tragedies' from vol. 27 (1974).

The British Academy for permission to reprint (with some changes) 'Othello and colour prejudice', the British Academy Shakespeare Lecture for 1967, first published in *The Proceedings of the British Academy*, vol. liii (1967).

The Warburg Institute for permission to reprint 'The theology of Marlowe's *The Jew of Malta*' from *The Journal of the Warburg and Courtauld Institutes*, vol. xxvii (1964).

The editors of Stratford-upon-Avon Studies and Edward Arnold Ltd for permission to reprint (with some changes) (1) 'English folly and Italian vice' from vol. 1, *Jacobean Theatre*; (2) 'The heroism of Hamlet' from vol. 5, *Hamlet*; (3) 'Shakespeare's last tragic heroes' from vol. 8, *The Later Shakespeare*.

Renaissance Drama and Northwestern University Press for permission to reprint (1) 'Italian tragicomedy on the English stage' from New Series, vol. vi (1973); (2) 'Ironies of justice in *The Spanish Tragedy*' from vol. viii (1965).

Routledge and Kegan Paul for permission to reprint (with some changes) 'Seneca and English tragedy' from *Seneca*, ed. C. D. N. Costa (1974).

The English Association for permission to reprint 'A. C. Bradley's *Shakespearean Tragedy*' from *Essays and Studies*, vol. 21 (1968).

The editors of *Harvard Studies in English* for permission to reprint 'T. S. Eliot and the creation of a symbolist Shakespeare' from vol. 2 (1971), edited by Reuben Brower.

The editor of *The Review of English Studies* and the Oxford University Press for permission to reprint '*Henry IV* and the Elizabethan two-part play' from vol. v (1954).

'Five-act structure in *Doctor Faustus*' was first published in *Tulane Drama Review*, vol. viii, no. 4. Copyright 1964 by *Tulane Drama Review*. Reprinted by permission. All rights reserved.

IDENTITIES

I

Elizabethans and foreigners

The impact of foreigners on a community or a culture is affected, obviously enough, both by the opportunities for contact and knowledge that exist, and by the framework of assumptions within which information about foreign lands and customs is presented and received. The period with which we are concerned here—let us say the sixteenth and early seventeenth centuries—is well known as one in which the amount of scientific information about the world increased dramatically. In the Renaissance period England, like the rest of Europe, acquired modern-style maps; trade-contacts with Turkey[1] and Russia[2] became a commonplace feature of economic life; visitations of Red Indians, Eskimos, and Negroes,[3] an influx of refugees from Europe, plantations in the New World, and knowledge of other European ventures of a similar kind—all this might seem to give the average Englishman of the early seventeenth century almost as much expertise in physical geography as is possessed by his modern counterpart. But this is to reckon without the 'framework of assumptions'. It is probably true to say that by the early decades of the seventeenth century more scientific information was available than could be digested within the terms in which the world was traditionally conceived; and it is certainly true that the facts of physical geography which were accepted by sailors as useful in practice were very difficult to accommodate within the sophisticated and complex traditions that form the natural background to literature.

[First published in *Shakespeare Survey*, 17 (1964)].

1. The Levant Company was established in 1579.
2. The Russia Company had its first privileges confirmed in 1569.
3. See Sidney Lee, 'Caliban's visits to England', *Cornhill Magazine*, N.S. xxxiv (1913), 333–45.

What was the framework of assumptions concerning
foreigners? When we look at medieval writings seeking for
information that bears on the question, 'what attitudes to
foreigners were traditional in English literature?' we find
little evidence; and this very absence must be our starting-
point. Most medieval literature is located in a dimension that
cares little for the compass. It is true that Chaucer's Knight
had been

> At Alisaundre ... in Pruce.
> In Lettow hadde he reysed and in Ruce,
> No Cristen man so ofte of his degree.
> In Gernade at the sege eek hadde he be
> Of Algezir, and riden in Belmarye.
> At Lyeys was he, and at Satalye,
> Whan they were wonne; and in the Grete See.[4]

And of his Wyf of Bath he tells us,

> thryes hadde she been at Jerusalem;
> She hadde passed many a straunge streem;
> At Rome she hadde been, and at Boloigne,
> In Galice at seint Jame, and at Coloigne.[5]

But the interest of these journeys is not geographical; the
points mentioned are only important as points of connection
with the Divine.[6] The typical travellers of the Middle Ages—
the pilgrim and the crusader—often brought back information which the modern geographer sees to be of scientific
value, but this information was only a by-product (and they
saw it as a by-product) of movement on quite another plane.
There is no point in complaining that the sixth-century monk
Cosmas, 'should have known better'[7] (a phrase we shall often
meet in this study) than create a *Christian Topography*[8]
which Sir Raymond Beazley has stigmatized as 'systematic

4. Prologue, A. 51–59.
5. Ibid., A. 463–6.
6. Cf. C. R. Beazley, *The Dawn of Modern Geography* (1897–1901):
'Devotional travel was as little in sympathy with exploration for the sake of
knowledge as the theological doctrines of a scriptural geography ... were in
sympathy with the formation of a scientific theory of the world's shape' (i. 13).
7. B. Penrose, *Travel and Discovery in the Renaissance, 1420–1620* (Cambridge, Mass., 1952), p. 7.
8. Translated in Hakluyt Society, vol. xcvii (1897).

nonsense',[9] as a marvel of 'scientific supernaturalism'.[1] It is true that Cosmas Indicopleustes ('he who has sailed to India') was a notable traveller: he had travelled to Malabar and Ceylon, and then back again to Egypt before he settled to write his account of the world. And it is equally true that he did not use this geographical experience to influence his Bible-centred model of the world. But why should he? If the Bible gives the most important information about the world, then it is proper to avoid the snares of mere sense impression by clinging (so far as is possible) to biblical texts and intentions. It may be proper to remember here the famous scholastic exercise on the word Jerusalem:

Literally, it is the city of that name; allegorically it represents Holy Church; tropologically, it signifies the faithful soul of whosoever aspires to the vision of eternal peace; anagogically, it denotes the life of the dwellers in Heaven who see God revealed in Zion.[2]

What is, on a map, only a physical position (neither more nor less important than any other) acquires intensity of meaning by the superimposing of spiritual senses over the physical one; the undifferentiated physical fact has to aspire to spiritual meaning in order to become important. The medieval *mappa mundi* is an excellent demonstration of this view of geography. It details an image of the world as Christendom, centred on Jerusalem, not only because Ezekiel 5: 5 reads, 'Thus saith the Lord God; This is Jerusalem: I have set it in the midst of the nations and countries that are round about her', but because the Holy Land represents the natural hub of Christian experience, which spreads out from this centre to the fringe of circumambient waters (for 'God said, Let there be a firmament in the midst of the waters' [Genesis 1: 6]) where Pagans live, close to Leviathan (both whale and Devil), together with Negroes, apes, semi-homines, and others whose distance from full humanity could be measured by their geographical distance from that area where humanity had been most fully realized in the life of Christ.

9. Beazley, op. cit. i. 32.
1. Ibid., p. 252.
2. Gilbert de Nogent (Migne, *Patrologia Latina*, clvi, col. 25) quoted in Caplan, 'The four senses', *Speculum*, iv (1929), 283.

Other aspects of medieval geography and ethnography bear witness to the same basic assumptions.[3] That primitive view of the Ptolemaic 'threefold world'[4] which saw the continents as populated by the sons of Noah—Africa by the descendants of Ham, Asia by those of Shem, Europe by those of Japhet—*could* have been used as the starting point for a science of ethnography. But the interest of the medieval mind was less in exploring the racial differences than in categorizing theological statuses. In the medieval world, it was the scientific fact that was the sport, present but uncategorizable, and therefore meaningless. The *mappa mundi* in Hereford cathedral categorizes Europe and Africa by these names; but the words *Europa* and *Affrica* are interchanged: 'an "error"', remarks Denys Hay, 'which could scarcely have occurred if the words had meant anything'.[5]

The *mappa mundi* survived for longer than might have been expected.[6] Competent *portolani* or coastal charts exist from the end of the thirteenth century, and probably existed even earlier;[7] but though these might be useful to mariners, it

3. See, for example, the 'Beatus' maps, whose radical purpose was 'the delineation of the twelve apostles, their dioceses and their distribution over the habitable world as "sowers of the word"' (Beazley, op. cit. ii. 563).

4. R. R. Cawley, *Unpathed Waters* (Princeton, 1940), pp. 75 ff., traces the prevalence of this idea in English literature up to 1641.

5. Denys Hay, *Europe, the Emergence of an Idea* (Edinburgh, 1957), pp. 54 f.

6. See plate vii in the original printing of this article (*Shakespeare Survey* 17 [1964]), John Cayworth's Christmas masque of 1636, *Enchiridion Christiados* (B.M. Add. MS. 10311), is the latest use that I have found. The masque is illustrated by a T–O type map, showing Christ's descent through the world from Heaven (at the top of the map), his descent into Hell, and his re-ascension into Heaven. As Cawley remarks, 'Cayworth would have gone far to seek a design which would suit his purposes quite so perfectly' (*Unpathed Waters*, p. 76). It is clear that Cayworth intends his map-form to be spiritually effective, and this implies (what is more interesting there) that he expected it to be intelligible as a world-shape to his patron and to his generation. Another interesting volume, pointing to the late diffusion of these medieval notions is *S.T.C.* 17297—*Mappa Mundi: otherwyse called the Compasse and Cyrcuet of the worlde, and also the Compasse of every Ilande, comprehendyd in the same* [R. Wyer, 1535]. This is advertised in the colophon as *Very necessary for all Marchauntes and Maryners. And for all such, as wyll labour and traveyle in the countres of the worlde.* But in spite of much invocation of the name of Ptolemy, the image of the world provided is the medieval one, centred on Jerusalem (sig. A3ᵛ), with the Terrestrial Paradise in the East, and Hell 'in the myddes of Affryke under the earth'. Africa is the land 'of dyvers shape of people, and many great wonders' (sig. A4ᵛ), and America has no mention at all.

7. See M. C. Andrews, 'The study and classification of medieval mappae mundi', *Archaeologia*, lxxv (1924–5), 64.

did not follow that the learned would consent to take notice of them.[8] Indeed if we see the *mappæ mundi* as primarily 'emblems of man's spiritual world', there is no good reason why the two kinds of knowledge should conflict. As in the parallel case of Ptolemy and Copernicus, the two maps showed remarkable powers of coexistence, even though they were (seen on a single plane of 'truth') mutually exclusive.

The capacity of the individual mind to remain quite happy in the possession of incompatibles is a source of endless fascination when we read the Tudor voyagers and their propagandists. Dr John Dee, scientific colleague of Ortelius and Mercator, was at the same time a myth-bound and credulous charlatan.[9] Sir Walter Ralegh was a competent navigator and explorer; and yet he asserted his belief that there were headless people on the Caora river, 'with their eyes in their shoulders, and their mouthes in the middle of their breasts', giving as one reason for the belief that 'such a nation was written of by Mandeville'.[1] Sir John Mandeville's *Travels* was the most popular of all the travel books; Josephine Waters Bennett records twenty-five English editions before 1750.[2] Richard Hakluyt, a hero of modern geography, included Mandeville's *Travels* in the first edition of his *Principall Navigations* (1589), alongside more modern travellers and observers whose standards were quite different from his. John Stow, the painstaking and accurate antiquary, recorded in the margin of his copy of Norden's *Description of Hertfordshire* (1598), his opinion that Mandeville's 'travayles in forraine regions and rare reportes are at this time admired through the world'.[3] In the same way, when

8. 'None of [the early printed world maps] is influenced by the advances in geographical knowledge. . . . There is thus no group of printed maps based on Spanish, Portuguese or Italian portolans, notwithstanding their proximity in time' (Erich Woldan, 'A circular, copper-engraved medieval world map', *Imago Mundi*, xi [1954], 13].

9. On Dee's gifts to Geography see E. G. R. Taylor, *Tudor Geography, 1485–1583* (1930).

1. 'The discovery of Guiana', in Hakluyt, *Principal Navigations* (Glasgow, 1903–5 edition), x. 406.

2. Josephine Waters Bennett, *The Rediscovery of Sir John Mandeville* (New York, 1954).

3. Quoted in M. Letts, *Sir John Mandeville* (1949), p. 13.

Stephen Batman in 1582 reissued Trevisa's medieval translation of Bartholomaeus Anglicus's *De Proprietatibus Rerum*,
he included additional material from such painstaking modern observers as Sir Humphrey Gilbert, Stow, Gesner, and
Ortelius, seeming not to notice that the new patches tore
away the substance of the old, fabulous material.[4] The result
is a hotch-potch, neither entirely spiritual nor scientific, but
in a Limbo somewhere between. Geoffroy Atkinson, in his
survey of the French geographical literature of the Renaissance, has noted:

La survivance des idées de l'ancienne géographie et des 'Images du
Monde' côte à côte avec les vérités nouvelles est responsable d'une
partie de la confusion qui caractérise ce domain littéraire, surtout
avant 1560. Mais jusqu'en 1609 les ouvrages 'géographiques'
présentent, à nos yeux d'aujourd'hui, un mélange du croyable et
de l'incroyable.[5]

If anything, the confusion in France is more obvious than
that in England, though not different in kind. No English
figure focused as sharply the contradictions of the age as did
André Thevet, 'grand voyageur' and Cosmographer Royal.
Thevet's *Cosmographie Universelle, illustrée de diverses
figures des choses plus remarquables veuës par l'auteur* (1575)
is a wilderness of marvels. The work was criticized by the
geographers of the day, but the author won the acclaim of
Ronsard, Jodelle, and de Baif.[6]
    The learned did not come clearly to the aid of the practical
traveller, by establishing rational boundaries to assumptions
about foreigners; neither did the practical man use his experience to correct his frame of reference about what might
be expected. The travellers, as Wittkower has told us:

from the Dominican and Franciscan monks of the thirteenth
century to Columbus and Fernão de Magellan, went out to distant
countries with a preconceived idea of what they would find. Many

---

4. See especially Bk xviii, cap. 48, 'De Faunis et Satiris'.
    5. Geoffroy Atkinson, *Les nouveaux horizons de la Renaissance française*
(Paris, 1935), p. 14.
    6. See, for example, Gilbert Chinard, *L'Exotisme américain dans la littérature
française au XVIe siècle* (Paris, 1911), p. 10.

of the travellers were learned; they had a knowledge of classical authors, they knew their Christian encyclopaedias, their treatises on natural science, their romances, they had seen on their maps the wondrous nations in those parts of the world to which they were travelling—in short, their imagination was fed from childhood with stories of marvels and miracles which they found because they believed in them.[7]

Writers on early geography tend to be disdainful of this 'frame of reference', to be implacably progressivistic in their viewpoint. Penrose never tires of castigating Columbus for the 'curious medievalism' of his thought—elsewhere his 'perverse medievalism' or his 'warped medievalism[8]—but the interest of our period would seem to lie precisely in this overlap between the medieval world and the modern one, an overlap which allowed development and smooth progression rather than jarring disruption.

The new information which the English voyages of the sixteenth century brought to the national culture had to be fitted, as best it could, into a received image of what was important. This means that the facts were not received in quite the same way as they would have been in the nineteenth century. Historians of the last century were much taken with the idea of the Elizabethan imagination liberated by the voyagers. But there is little evidence of this outside the unhistorical supposition, 'that's how I would have reacted'. The voyages certainly did expand the physical horizon, but it is not clear that they expanded the cultural horizon at the same time. Englishmen became aware of India, Brazil, and the Spice Islands as possibly exploitable sources of wealth; to some they suggested possible avenues of imperial expansion (this we may take to be the master impulse in Hakluyt);[9] there was a small but influential circle interested in the technical (map-making, economic, astronomical) arrangements that had to be involved. But none of these were close to the traditional areas of culture; and to many of those who were close, it seemed that the new activities offered only new

7. R. Wittkower, 'Marvels of the East', *Journal of the Warburg and Courtauld Institutes*, v (1942), 195.
8. Penrose, op. cit., pp. 78, 86, 90.
9. See G. B. Parks, *Richard Hakluyt* (New York, 1928).

opportunities for baseness. George Buchanan spoke for many of the wisest minds when he declared that it was Avarice that had discovered America.[1] The image of man in his theological, political, and social aspects could not be much affected by the discovery of empty or primitive lands; the aim of travel in this period is usually stated to be the observation of courts, universities, and other sophisticated societies; and America could not offer anything of this kind. Atkinson has shown how small a proportion of French geographical literature in the period 1480–1609 was actually concerned with the New World.[2] In France in this period there were twice as many books published about the Turks[3] as there were about both the Americas, and four times as many about Asia in general. What is more, the proportion of books devoted to America actually drops as the period advances. The same balance seems to exist in Italian and Spanish literature also,[4] and there is no reason to suppose that the English figures are very different; the 'framework of assumptions' made the facts of physical geography seem uninteresting to the average cultured man of the period, a source neither of instruction nor of illumination.

Geographical exactitude was no part of the literary tradition, and even those writers who 'should have known better' show astonishing carelessness about place-names and modes of transport, using them for their associations, not for their reality. It may be that we can now 'exonerate' Shakespeare for shipwrecking Perdita on the sea-coast of Bohemia,[5] but it remains hard to find Helena a reasonable route from Rousil-

1. *De Sphaera*, i. 182, quoted by C. S. Lewis, *English Literature in the Sixteenth Century* (Oxford, 1954), p. 16. Cf. Atkinson, op. cit., 'L'idée maîtresse des voyageurs de la Renaissance fut sans doute l'ambition de faire fortune' (p. 135).

2. Ibid., pp. 9 ff.

3. The Renaissance period was fascinated by the Turkish Empire as combining the features of a diabolical portent with those of a remarkably efficient politico-military organization. Knolles's great *Generall Historie of the Turkes* (1603) nicely catches this ambivalence in his opening phrase about 'the glorious Empire of the Turkes, the present terrour of the World'.

4. See (on Spain) Angel Franco, *El tema de América en los autores españoles del siglo de oro* (Madrid, 1954), and M. A. Moringo, *América en el teatro de Lope de Vega* (Buenos Aires, 1946); on Italy see Rosario Romeo, *Le scoperte americane nella conscienza italiana del Cinquecento* (Milan and Naples, 1954).

5. See S. L. Bethell, *The Winter's Tale* (1947), p. 33.

lon to Compostella which goes via Florence,[6] or explain
Proteus's sea-journey from Verona to Milan.[7] But Shakespeare is not exceptional; this is only common form in the
period. Barnaby Rich's Don Simonides sails from Venice to
Genoa (possible, I admit) and only a few hours from Venice
is shipwrecked 'in a wilde deserte . . . onely inhabited with
brute and savage beastes'; there he wanders for seven days
before he meets another human being.[8] And yet Rich had
served abroad in Holland and France and had been at sea as a
privateer.[9] Henry Roberts was an author who spent most of
his energies recording voyages and singing the praises of
seamen. He was a sea-captain himself, and had been to
Algiers, to Brazil, and the Canaries.[1] But when he comes to
write a romance, such as *A Defiance to Fortune* (1590), he
makes his hero take ship from Siena,[2] while his *Haigh for
Devonshire* (1600) describes a journey from Bordeaux to
Rouen via the forest of Ardenne.[3] Thomas Lodge wrote his
A Margarite of America (1596) while at sea with Cavendish:

Touching the place where I wrote this, it was in those straits
christned by *Magelan*; in which place to the southward many
wonderous Isles, many strange fishes, many monstrous Patagones
withdrew my senses . . . so that as there was great wonder in the
place wherein I writ this, so likewise might it be marvelled. . . .

It is obvious enough from the tone of this description that it is
the legendary strangeness of the place rather than its factual
existence that, for Lodge, makes it worth literary mention.
The *America* of his romance has nothing to do with geography. The Empire of Cusco is no more Peruvian than that
of Mosco is Russian; both (as C. S. Lewis has remarked) 'are
conceived as high pagan civilizations in some undefined
period of the past'.[4]

---

6. *All's Well that Ends Well*, III. iv. 4 and III. v. 34.
7. *Two Gentlemen of Verona*, II. iii. 30.
8. *The straunge and wonderfull adventures of Don Simonides* (1581), sig.
M3ᵛ.
9. See Cranfill and Bruce, *Barnaby Rich* (Austin, Texas, 1953).
1. See L. B. Wright, 'Henry Robarts', *Studies in Philology*, xxix (1932),
176–99.
2. Sig. E4.
3. Sig. C2.
4. C. S. Lewis, op. cit., p. 424.

Marlowe is well known to have had a map.[5] He seems to
have written *Tamburlaine* with Ortelius's *Theatrum Orbis
Terrarum* open in front of him.[6] It was a trait of scholarship
to use the most scientific atlas for his thesaurus of names;
but he used it as a poet, not as a geographer, arbitrarily selecting quite unimportant towns to stand for the regions he
intended.[7] There is little or no sense of reality in the places
where Tamburlaine operates. Babylon, Natolia, Zanzibar,
the Terrene and the Euxene seas—these, the last enchant-
ments of the atlas, fitly convey the magic of 'the sweet
fruition of an earthly crown'; but it adds nothing to know
the physical reality of such places.

Sometimes, however, the new facts did cohere with
assumptions already existing, and already prepared for in
terms of emotional impact. The search for a Terrestrial
Paradise was one of the motifs which the early voyagers
caught easily from their fabulous predecessors.[8] And even the
facts of American life could not wholly disabuse the imagination of the dream of an ideal natural civilization:

the people most gentle, loving and faithfull, voide of all guile and
treason, and such as live after the maner of the golden age.[9]

. . . soo that (as wee have sayde before) they seeme to lyve in the
goulden worlde, without toyle . . . without lawes, without bookes,
and without Judges.[1]

The history of the New World seemed to give body and
reality to this old dream, especially where (as in England and
France) it provided a nationalistically attractive contrast
between the ideal innocence of the exploited Indians and the
corruption of the 'civilizing' Spaniards, who

in stead of spreading Christian religion by good life, committed
such terrible inhumanities, as gave those that lived under nature

5. M. E. Seaton, 'Marlowe's map', *Essays and Studies*, x (1924), 13–35.
6. Ibid., p. 28.
7. Ibid., pp. 27 f.
8. See G. Boas, *Essays on Primitivism and Related Ideas in the Middle Ages*
(Baltimore, 1948); Luis Weckmann, 'The Middle Ages in the conquest of
America', *Speculum*, xxvi (1951), 130–41.
9. Hakluyt (ed. cit.), viii. 305.
1. Peter Martyr [Anglerius], *The decades of the newe world or West India*,
tr. R. Eden (1555), sig. E1ᵛ.

manifest occasion to abhor the devily characters of so tyrannical a deity.[2]

To be fair to the Spaniards, one must note that the *History of the Indies* by Las Casas is one of the most radical documents in the whole of this literature; but Las Casas can hardly be taken as representative of the Spanish colonizers; and it is to the countries excluded from conquest that we must look for further development of this theme. Sir Thomas More's *Utopia*, Montaigne's *Essays* (especially that on the Cannibals), and Shakespeare's *The Tempest* all show a view of the 'savage' which is powerful, because they see him in relation to European sophistication, as an implicit criticism of European ways of life. In this respect the figure of the exotic foreigner is very like that of the pastoral shepherd; Gilbert Chinard has made this point in respect of Ronsard's *Isles Fortunées* (of 1553):

ses sauvages ne ressemblent pas plus aux vrais sauvages que les bergers de tout le XVIe siècle ne ressemblent aux pastours de l'Ile-de-France ou ceux de Sannazar aux pâtres italiens. Si la vie et l'observation avaient fourni quelques traits, un point de départ assez difficile à situer, l'imagination poétique n'avait pas tardé à tout embellir et à tout magnifier.[3]

The foreigner could only 'mean' something important, and so be effective as a literary figure, when the qualities observed in him were seen to involve a simple and significant relationship to real life at home. Without this relationship, mere observation, however exact, could hardly make an impact on men caught up in their own problems and their own destiny.

The image of the world as a Christian entity centred on Jerusalem, and awareness of foreignness only in the sense of devil-prompted infidelity—this was, it is true, a vision which bore little relation to the general hatred of 'strangers'—even Christian strangers[4]—and the mass persecution of them,

2. Fulke Greville, *Life of Sir Philip Sidney* (1652), ed. Nowell Smith (Oxford, 1907), pp. 116 f.
3. Gilbert Chinard, op. cit., pp. 123 f.
4. The word *foreigners* is not at all common in the sixteenth century; *strangers* is the normal expression. Indeed the first three examples of the former word in O.E.D. (that is, up to 1637) are all qualified by the latter word, as if to provide a clue to the meaning.

which went on all through the Middle Ages. But it is equally true that these eruptions of man's base nature were not canonized by theory, and so did not emerge in literary expressions. Europe retained a strong common culture well into the seventeenth century. Chaucer was widely read in at least three European literatures, but he shows little awareness of cultural distinctions, and he is probably right enough, in terms of his own time, in failing to do so. Erasmus and More do not seem to have thought of one another as 'foreigners', and even such later humanists as the Scaligers, or Lipsius, or Casaubon knew 'the foreigner' only in the sense of 'the boor', the man whose Latinity fell below an international standard of excellence, such as today applies only to hotel cuisine.

But this common culture seems to exist in the seventeenth century largely as a hang-over from the period of a common faith; the fragmentation of faiths in the period of the Reformation had its parallel (if not result) in the fragmentation of national cultures. The career which carried Isaac Casaubon (1559–1614) from international scholarship to Anglican apologetics[5] may serve as a model of the whole drift of interests. The national claim to represent a separate (and better) religious tradition—the development of 'God's Englishman' to set against Popish wickedness—made the old organization of the West as Christendom, centred on Jerusalem, seem unsuitable, even in theory. When Jerusalem is set

In England's green and pleasant land

it becomes obviously desirable to create another, England-centred, intellectual pattern of European races. But we should beware of supposing that a pattern of races emerged readily from the Europe that Christendom had become, a pattern capable of supplying moral discriminations rich and complex enough for literary use. There were, of course, intellectual patterns by which the main European nations could be related to one another. There was the ancient climatic contrast[6] which set Northern phlegm against Southern

5. Mark Pattison, *Isaac Casaubon* (1892).
6. J. O. Thomson, *History of Ancient Geography* (Cambridge, 1948), pp. 106 ff. Charron, *Of Wisdom* (tr. Samson Lennard; ent. S. R. 1606), has an interesting discussion of this (Bk I, cap. xlii). See also Waldemar Zacharasiewicz,

blood, and which was much invoked to contrast the grossness of the Teutons with the passionate conduct of the Latins. But this does not take one very far; more detailed relationships of place and temperament, such as John Davies of Hereford's 'never yet was fool a Florentine'[7] have the air of being climatic glosses on an existing cultural image. Surveys of the time are fond of making lists of French, English, Spanish, etc., national characteristics, such as we find in Portia's review of her suitors,[8] or at the end of Fynes Moryson's *Itinerary*,[9] as a mode of rhetoric in Thomas Wilson's *Art of Rhetoric*,[1] or as a poem in Turler's *The Traveller*.[2] But such lists hardly go beyond journalistic generalizations about superficial mannerisms (e.g. clothing, or eating habits):

> The Dutchman for a drunkard
> The Dane for golden locks,
> The Irishman for usquebaugh
> The Frenchman for the [pox].[3]

Here is material for caricature, but hardly for character.

Modern authors sometimes create profoundly revealing conflicts out of the clash of racial *mores*; for a modern author may see civilizations as representative of possible lines of development in human consciousness: Godbole, Aziz, and Fielding in Forster's *A Passage to India* or Lambert Strether and Mme de Vionnet in Henry James's *The Ambassadors* provide obvious examples of this. But the complexity of valuation and the withholding of immediate judgement that these works require is a rare gift at any time; the Elizabethan urge to moralize was normally served most easily by presenting the foreigner in terms derived from simple nationalism. The European foreigner appears in post-Reformation English

'Johannes Kepler, James Howell und Thomas Lansius: Der Wettstreit der eüropäischen Nationen im 17 Jahrhundert', *Johannes Kepler 1571–1971: Gedenkschrift der Universität Graz* (Graz, 1975).

7. John Davies of Hereford, *Microcosmos* (ed. Grosart, 1878), p. 32.
8. *The Merchant of Venice*, I. ii. 32 ff.
9. Fynes Moryson, *An itinerary, containing his ten yeeres travell* (1617), iii (Glasgow, 1907), 448 ff.
1. (1585), ed. G. H. Mair (Oxford, 1909), pp. 178 f.
2. *De Peregrinatione* (Strassburg, 1574); *The Traveiler of Jerome Turler* (1575).
3. John Marston, *The Malcontent* (1604), V. ii. 1–4.

literature, in fact, as part of a process of vulgarization (in both senses of the word). He comes into literary focus caught between the xenophobic poles of Fear and Derision, which had always operated where Englishmen and Foreigners came into contact, but which was new as a literary image. And this applies not only to plays like *Jack Straw* (> 1593) and *Sir Thomas More* (*c.* 1596) which take anti-foreign feelings as their subject-matter, but is inescapable in any work showing the foreigner living in England; in such a context the 'stranger' could be shown to be a villain or a clown, but little else.

William Haughton's run-of-the-mill comedy *Englishmen for my money: or, a woman will have her will*, which he seems to have written for Henslowe about 1598, may be taken as a fair example of stock attitudes (of the more genial kind) to foreigners who tried to live in England. It tells the story of Pisaro, a 'Portingale' usurer-merchant resident in London,[4] whose three daughters are (illogically enough) totally English in outlook. They are wooed on one side by three English gallants, and on the other by three foreigners, a Frenchman, a Dutchman, and an Italian. The daughters prefer the English suitors, the father promotes the foreigners; and the plot thus consists of the usual New Comedy type of intrigue and counter-intrigue. In the end the Englishmen (of course) win the girls and the foreigners accept this proof of superiority. What is interesting about this play in the context of a general consideration of foreigners is the superficiality of the colouring that their nationalities provide. We can recognize the plot of the usurer's fair daughter as a recurring stereotype. Usually the father's choice is rich and old, and ridiculous for these reasons; Haughton has added foreignness to the list of disqualifications, but it does not appear really different in kind from the other qualities of a standard pantaloon. Foreignness is no part of the moral structure, but is only an intriguing local colour.

Sometimes, though less frequently (as is understandable in

4. It is worth while noticing that this 'Portingale' seems to be a Jew, in fact, though the word 'Jew' is never used. He is called 'Signior Bottle-nose' (Hazlitt's Dodsley, x. 522) and elsewhere he is said to have 'a snout / Able to shadow Paul's, it is so great' (p. 481).

any literature that aims to be entertaining rather than disruptive) the foreigner living in England is shown as more malignant than comic. In such cases he is seen (as always) to be dangerously 'cleverer than us', as slick, devious, and lacking in integrity. In Robert Wilson's *Three Ladies of London* we meet Aritfex, an honest English tradesman, who cannot sell his honestly made wares, 'for there be such a sort of strangers in this country | That work fine to please the eye, though it be deceitfully'.[5] When Artifex has been brought near enough to starvation he succumbs to these foreign wiles and is instructed by the Franco-Scottish Fraud how to make trashy goods look attractive. In the sequel-play, Wilson's *Three Lords and Ladies of London* Fraud reappears, this time (dressed as 'an old French artificer') deceiving the honest English clown Simplicity.[6] The moral structure of these plays derives from a very different convention from that of *Englishmen for my money*, but the 'foreignness' of Fraud is as incidental as that of the suitors in Haughton's play. He is not wicked because he is foreign but foreign because he is wicked.

At the same time, however, as these prejudices were invading literature from the market-place, increased national separateness was making foreign culture more attractive. The sense that foreigners are 'cleverer than us' can also be taken to mean that we must learn from them; rustic integrity can also be seen as provincial backwardness. 'Home-keeping youth have ever homely wits', says Shakespeare,[7] and the vision of courtly culture that he gives us in his high comedies is always set abroad. The New Learning substituted classical for biblical Holy Places as points of pilgrimage (geography was only taught in the period as ancillary to classical History and Literature).[8] But the cultural image of Rome could not obliterate its politico-religious significance sufficiently to turn it into a second Jerusalem. Throughout the period there is a strong ambivalence in the attitude to travel. The obvious educational advantages are seen; yet (as S. C. Chew has

5. Hazlitt's Dodsley, vi. 279.
6. Ibid., pp. 438 f., 499.
7. *Two Gentlemen of Verona*, I. i. 2.
8. Foster Watson, *The Beginnings of the Teaching of Modern Subjects in England* (1909), p. 91. F. de Dainville, S.J., *La géographie des humanistes* (Paris, 1940).

remarked) 'It is difficult to discover in the literature of the period any whole-hearted and unqualified commendation of travel'.[9] The power of European and especially Popish corruption to mar the youth of England was much mulled over by moralists; and travel itself (even in the abstract) is seen as of doubtful spiritual utility;[1] it was dangerously close to *curiositas*—that spending of effort on matters no way essential to salvation. The bottom panel of the engraved title-page of Samuel Purchas's *Pilgrimes* (1625) (Pl. 1)[2] seems to provide a useful emblem of this ambivalence. Purchas was, of course, a clergyman as well as a propagandist for the voyagers, and the two roles were not entirely coherent. On one side the title-page tells us that 'soldiers and Marchants [are] the worlds two eyes to see it selfe'; in the middle it shows us Purchas reading verses from Psalm 39, 'for I am a stranger with thee, and a sojourner, as all my fathers were', and 'verily every man at his best state is altogether vanity', and from Hebrews 11, 'they were strangers and pilgrims on the earth'. We are still close to the medieval attitude, even here among the documents of the new geography.

I have suggested that the clear emergence of the foreigner in post-Reformation English literature was part of a process of *vulgarization*. Vernacular and popular prejudices invaded literature, to deprive those who were known from close contact with English life of any status save that of failed Englishmen. And the more intimately these strangers are known, the less their *strangeness* seemed intriguing, the more it seemed despicable. The Irish, the Welsh, and the Scots were normally seen as absurd deviations from an English norm; and the better-known Europeans acquired the same status.

The inhabitants of the Low Countries ('Dutch' and 'Flemings')[3] were the best-known strangers in Elizabethan

---

9. S. C. Chew, *The Crescent and the Rose* (New York, 1937), p. 29.

1. Foster Watson has a useful survey of attitudes to travel in the period (op. cit., pp. 128–35).

2. Cf. the MORS written round the Hereford *Mappa Mundi*.

3. *Dutch* simply meant (in this period) 'German-speaking' (distinguished when necessary into 'High-Dutch' and 'Low-Dutch'). Most of the refugees were, however, from the nearest area of Teutonic-speaking population, i.e. were 'Dutch' in the modern sense. But Elizabethan vagueness in these matters defies simple explanation. Thus in Dekker and Webster's *Northward Ho* the 'Hollander' has his home in Augsburg.

England. In the census of 1567 there were 2,030 Dutch in London out of a total of 2,730 aliens in all;[4] in Norwich at the same time there were about 4,000 Flemings[5] and there were considerable numbers distributed throughout East Anglia and the southern counties. In 1573 there were said to be 60,000 Flemings in England.[6] But neither the Low Countries nor their inhabitants appear to have much significance in the literature of the time. Of course there are plenty of 'butter-box' fat Dutchmen in the drama, characters with names like Hans van Belch,[7] usually drunk, and unable to speak English even when sober; but these waterfront humours do not add up to anything like a serious image of what it is like to be Dutch. Even Marston's 'Dutch Courtesan' (with the Venetian courtesan's name of Franceschina)[8] is little more than a villainess whose villainy becomes comic-grotesque when she cannot speak English properly.

The one exception here can be argued to be a 'proof' or refinement of the rule rather than an opposite. The exception I refer to is that dreary exhibition of depravity and torture, the anonymous *A Larum for London* (1602). This is a play about the sack of Antwerp by the Spaniards in 1576. Antwerp is here, however, more an example than a place. It serves the same function as Niniveh did in an earlier example of the same genre (Greene and Lodge's *A Looking Glass for London*, 1590) or as Jerusalem did in Nashe's pamphlet *Christ's Tears over Jerusalem* (1593)—as a model of urban self-centredness and deafness to the truth. The London audience are invited to let

> your proud eyes ... see
> The punishment of City cruelty:
> And if your hearts be not of adamant
> Reform the mischief of degenerate minds.
> (Prologus)

4. Huguenot Society Publications, vol. x, part i (1900), 365.
5. *Social England*, ed. Traill and Mann (1903), iii. 500.
6. E. Eckhardt, *Die dialekt- und ausländertypen des älteren englischen Dramas*, Teil ii (Materialien zur Kunde des älteren englischen Dramas, vol. xxxii) (Louvain, 1911), p. 48.
7. In Dekker and Webster's *Northward Ho* (1605).
8. I cannot even guess why Marston represented Franceschina as Dutch. It is entirely proper to her part that she should be foreign, a stranger to the bourgeois comforts of the Subboys and Freevills, but I do not know why Holland should be the foreign country chosen.

What Antwerp was yesterday London may well be tomorrow, for already, it is implied, the same mercantile selfishness and contempt for soldiership can be seen:

> No marvel then like misery catch hold
> On them, did fasten on this woeful town
> Whose bleeding fortune, whose lamenting cries,
> Whose streets besmeared with blood, whose blubbered eyes,
> Whose tottered walls, whose buildings overthrown,
> Whose riches lost and poverty made known,
> May be a mean all cities to afright
> How they in sin and pleasure take delight.   (Epilogus)

The soldier who is despised and neglected today will be sought for tomorrow; but by then the 'fat-pursed peasants' and 'swilling epicures' will have starved him out of existence. The 'burghers' and 'froes' of this play are Dutch (or Flemish or Belgian) by history rather than geography. Antwerp is no more racially defined than was Greene's Niniveh.

It seems as if the Dutch were too close to the eyes of the English beholders for anything more than detailed idiosyncrasies to be observable. France, whose Huguenot refugees soon began to rival the Dutch and Flemings in numbers, was not in very different case. In so far as the French fitted into the Southern climatic stereotype of hot-blooded, fiery-tempered, subtle, dandified, smooth-tongued, and Roman Catholic, their role duplicated that of the Italians (see below); but France as a country was too well known to be complex and divided in itself to provide a fitting background for the full development of these characteristics. The Elizabethans seem to have been aware of France as a great and complex polity, working out in its history approximately the same problems as beset England. Marlowe's *The Massacre at Paris* (1593) and Chapman's political plays are set in France, but are not 'foreign' in the sense that they are self-consciously un-English. France is in these cases a convenient locale for the pursuit of political and religious conflicts that could not be safely dealt with in an English setting. The locale and the history are real and so avoid the escapist emphasis of Ruritanian settings, but French national characteristics play little part in the effect. The casts of such plays have little or nothing in common with characters like Dr Caius (in *The Merry Wives of Windsor*) or the Dauphin in *Henry V*, who appear in contrast to the English and whose national characteristics are as superficial as those of the Dutchmen we have already discussed.

It seems to be the great virtue of Italy as a setting for literature of this period that everyday experience (and prejudice) supplied so little check and limitation to imaginative rendering. The number of Italians living in London was very small. In the census of 1567 there were only 140 Italians recorded;[9] and by 1580 the number had dropped to 116.[1] There was no traditional relationship between the countries, not even the relationship of war (as with France and Spain), and no strong economic links (as with the Low Countries and the Hanseatic ports). Italians are rarely mentioned in the petitions in which London merchants regularly complain of the unfair competition of aliens and strangers; and when Hand D (commonly supposed to be Shakespeare's) in the play of *Sir Thomas More* makes Sir Thomas speak of possible reprisals against English merchants abroad, he does not even mention Italy as a possible scene of such activity:

> go you to ffraunc or flaunders to any Iarman
> *p*rouince [to] spane or portigall nay any where.[2]

The absence of these varieties of knowledge gave all the greater strength to the cultural image of Italy as the land of wit, of pleasure and of refinement, the home of Petrarch and Bembo and Castiglione and Ariosto, of Machiavelli, Aretino, and Guicciardini. It was an image which could be turned various ways (like the word *wit* itself), towards romance or towards diabolism, for use in comedy as well as in tragedy. The absence of a clearly defined central government in Italy further increased the malleability of the image, for it was only in a cultural sense that Italy was a 'country' at all. There, the high life of courts could be portrayed without intruding questions of responsibility (as they could hardly be in France

9. Huguenot Soc. x (i), 365.
1. W. Besant, *London in the time of the Tudors* (1904), p. 80.
2. M.S.R., ll. 250 ff. Cf. the petition against Aliens printed in Besant, op. cit., Appendix iii, which lists those by whom the realm is pestered as 'Frenchmen, galymen, pycardis, flemings, keteryckis, Spaynyars, Scottis, Lombards'.

or Spain, let alone England), whether in a mood of elegant idleness (the Milan of Shakespeare's *Two Gentlemen*) or in one of criminal selfishness (the Venice of Marston's *Antonio and Mellida*). And in the conflicts between these states there was no question of aligning one side or another with the English way of life. Italy as an image was sufficiently remote from England not to enforce immediate and invidious comparisons of national detail; but its way of life was (especially in tragedy) strange enough to force comparison with English life at a general moral and social level. The ambivalence of which I have already spoken in relation to travel, the simultaneously held desire to know, and fear of knowing, operated at maximum pressure in relation to Italy. For here there was a plethora of imaginative material and very little of that practical experience which might have limited its use.

Below[3] I develop the view that the 'Italy' of Elizabethan and Jacobean tragedy is related to England in the same way as the abstract world of the Morality play (say Skelton's *Magnificence*) is related to real life (say the court of Henry VIII). That argument is concerned principally with the corrupt Italian courts which are so common a feature of Jacobean tragedy; but there is a parallel line of argument centred on the mercantile world of Venice which should make the relationship between England and the image of Italy sufficiently clear.

Robert Wilson's late morality, *The Three Ladies of London* (*c.* 1581), focuses neatly the observed relationship between Venice and London. This play shows the gradual domination of London by the Lady called Lucre (who may be taken to stand for the acquisitive instinct) and the exiling of her virtuous sisters, Love and Conscience. Among the new servants who flock to serve Lucre is one called Usury, and in conversation with him she reveals her genealogy:

LUCRE. But, Usury, didst thou never know my grandmother, the old Lady Lucre of Venice?
USURY. Yes, madam; I was servant unto her and lived there in bliss.
LUCRE. But why camest thou into England, seeing Venice is a city Where Usury by Lucre may live in great glory?

3. pp. 103–32.

USURY. I have often heard your good grandmother tell,
  That she had in England a daughter, which her far did excel.[4]

The point is then made that what Venice has been in the past
London is now becoming; and nowadays, Lucre concludes,

I doubt not but that you shall live here as pleasantly,
  Ay and pleasanter too, if it may be.

It is clear enough that Venice is here a type-name for 'the
commercial society' and represents an ethos which could
create a 'Venice' in London, by the same route as might establish 'Jerusalem' in England's 'green and pleasant land'.

It is the dynamism of this threat to life as it is that gives
force and propriety to the most rigorous development of this
morality image—to the Venice of Jonson's *Volpone*. Jonson
has painstakingly documented the topography of a real
Venice; but, as often with Jonson, the texture of physical
reality is only a surface. The social habit on which the plot
turns (legacy hunting) belongs to the Roman Empire, not
at all to the Venetian Republic. But it matches the Venetian
background, for it turns the acquisitive instinct into the sole
dominating force of social existence. Obsessed by their mania
for money, these characters achieve their Venice by losing
their humanity. At the level of achievement they are Magni-
ficos, Avvocatori, etc.; but beneath the Venetian robes lie the
predatory fur and feather and membrane of fox and flesh-fly,
raven, gor-crow, and vulture. The merchant as predator
today holds Venice in fee; but tomorrow (the moral seems to
run) it may be called London. As if to drive home this point
Jonson throws into his animal city an English innocent
abroad and his resolute tourist wife. This pair, Sir Politic and
Lady Would-be, measure not only the distance of Venice
from London, but also the ease with which it could be
annihilated. Their virtue is protected by nothing but their
ignorance, not even by their will to be virtuous, for what they
'would be' is Politic, that is, Italianate, that is, amoral.

  Shakespeare's *The Merchant of Venice* is clearly less
rigorous in the use of the Italian setting to focus the meaning
of the play. The Venetian world is here self-sufficient and
does not ask to be brought into relation to London. But the

4. Hazlitt's Dodsley, vi. 268 f.

setting is not without propriety for all that. What we have here (and in this the play is comparable to *Volpone*) is a world of Finance, where lovers, Christian gentlemen, friends, enemies, servants, daughters, dukes, fathers, Jewish usurers, all express themselves in terms of financial relationship; and where the differences between love and hate, bounty and selfishness, Mercy and Justice, Christianity and Jewry are all treated in terms of money and how it is handled. Shakespeare focuses his Venice, however, not by pointing it back to England, but by pointing it out to the remoter world of 'blaspheming Jews',[5] whose non-Christianity, like that of pagans, infidels, Moors, and Turks gave depth of meaning to 'foreignness' that mere difference of European race could hardly do.

I have suggested that the Elizabethan awareness of foreigners was closely conditioned by a traditional religious outlook on the world; and that much 'new knowledge' lay fallow or was treated in a merely superficial manner because of this. The European nations were inexorably emerging from the matrix of Christendom; but they did not yet stand distinct enough from one another to allow simple dramatic opposition. Even Italy supplied a distinct moral image only in the small areas of power-politics or commercial practice. These were hardly to be seen as the fruits of a deeper level of national wickedness; an Italian on the stage had to do more than announce his racial identity before his moral status was known. For such large-scale contrast the Elizabethan author had to go beyond Europe, and draw on oppositions that were older than ethnographic differences, on the conflict between God and the devil, between Christian and anti-Christian.

Shakespeare's *Merchant of Venice* treats its Italians as Christians (though merchants) and therefore 'like us'. For the opposition is with a figure who stands outside Christianity altogether, and whose commercial practice is seen as a part of his religious attitude: legalistic, obdurate, revengeful. In sixteenth-century England the threat of the infidel outsider still had the general effect of stilling internal European oppositions and stressing the unity of Christendom.

When Don John of Austria (Philip of Spain's half-brother) defeated the Turks at the battle of Lepanto, England was in

5. *Macbeth*, IV. i. 26.

the middle of a life-and-death struggle with Spain and the
Pope (this was the year of the Ridolfi Plot); Elizabeth might
treat the news with the wry awareness that the balance had
been tilted against France;[6] but the popular reaction was one
of rejoicing:

The ninth of November a sermon was preached in Paules Church
at London, by maister William Foulks of Cambridge, to give
thanks to almightie God for the victorie, which of his mercifull
clemencie it had pleased him to grant to the christians in the
Levant seas, against the common enimies of our faith, the Turks.[7]

Present at this service were the Lord Mayor with the alder-
men and the craftsmen in their liveries:

And in the evening there were bonefiers made through the citie,
with banketting and great rejoising, as good cause there was, for a
victorie of so great importance unto the whole state of the
christian common-wealth.[8]

Foulkes's sermon took as its text, Psalm 16, verse 4: 'Their
sorrows shall be multiplied that hasten after another god.'
The force of the old conception of the world is too obvious
on such an occasion to require comment. And throughout the
period, the glory of Lepanto did not fade. James I wrote a
famous poem on the subject. In 1593 Gabriel Harvey can ask
the very rhetorical question,

Who honoureth not the glorious memory and the very name of
Lepanto: the monument of Don John of Austria, the security of
the Venetian state, the Halleluia of Christendome, and the
welaway of Turky?[9]

And Thomas Randolph can sum up for us the general
nostalgia for Lepanto when he says (well into the next
century), 'The last valour show'd in Christendom | Was in
Lepanto'.[1]

6. C.S.P. (*Spanish 1568–1579*), p. 359.
7. Holinshed's Chronicle (1808 edn), iv. 262. Compare the response to the
Turkish attack on Malta in 1565, cited below p. 85.
8. Ibid.
9. *A new letter of notable contents* (1593) (*Works*, ed. Grosart, i. 262).
1. *The muses looking glass* (Oxford, 1638), Act III, scene iv (*Works*, ed.
Hazlitt, ii. 232).

Shakespeare in *The Merchant of Venice* uses the figure of the Jew rather than the Turk to represent the pressure of infidel forces on the Christian dispensation. This was necessary if the play was to turn on interpretations of a mode of social conduct, not on the tragical arbitrament of war. But the point of infidelity is the same. Congreve's Lady Pliant was picking up an old tradition when she pursued her husband with the string of names, 'heathen . . . Turk, Saracen . . . Jew'.[2] In medieval representations the Jew swears by Mahomet, and he does so as late as in Wilson's *Three Ladies of London*;[3] in Marlowe's *Jew of Malta* Barabas and Ithimore make a point of the common Jewish-Turkish interests:

> we are villaines both
> Both circumcized, we hate Christians both.[4]

The two catch phrases, 'to turn Turk' and 'I am a Jew if . . .' were making precisely the same point: of betraying one's baptism, or selling one's soul to the devil.

Modern scholars often labour to document the exact racial background of Shylock (or Othello); and certainly we can say that Shakespeare *could* have learned many true facts about these remote races. But the evidence of the plays suggests that the old framework of assumptions about Jews, Turks, and Moors—and this means theological assumptions —provided the controlling image in his mind. It is clear that few Elizabethans had met a Jew (or a Turk, or a Moor); Jews provided no economic threat to the country. And so a modern historian can legitimately wonder at the residual

2. *The double dealer*, Act IV, scene iv. Cf. Brandt/Barclay in the *Ship of Fools*, where in the section 'Of straunge Folys and infydels as sarasyns, paynems, turkes and suche lyke' we may read the following:

> The cursed Iewes despysynge christis lore
> For theyr obstynate, and unrightwyse cruelte
> Of all these folys must nede be set before
> The nacion of Turkes next to them shall be
> The sarrazyns next . . .
> The Scithians and also they of Sarmatyke
> And they of Boeme, by fendes fraudolent
> Ar led and blynded with an errour lyke . . .
> The owgly Mauryans ar also of this sect etc.
>   (1874 edn, ii. 188 f.)

3. Hazlitt's Dodsley, vi. 345.
4. Ed. Tucker Brooke, ii. 979 f.

prejudice through which 'Shakespeare could stir the blood of his audience by the spectacle of a Jewish usurer, three hundred years after there had been Jews in the land'.[5]

It is my argument below (pp. 65–75) that to the Bible-readers and sermon-attenders of the Elizabethan age there was no difficulty in recalling the nature of the Jewish threat, a threat which was never-ceasing, for as Christ himself had remarked of the Jews, 'Ye are of your father, the devil',[6] and between the devil and the godly no peace could be imagined. In the medieval English *Play of the Sacrament* the Jew Jonathas is depicted as a rich man; but his wealth is not directly involved in his sin, which is simply the ritual re-enactment (with a consecrated wafer) of the central and never-to-be-forgotten sin of Jewry—the betrayal and murder of Christ.

When in 1594 Dr Lopez was arraigned for attempting to murder the Queen, Sir Edward Coke did not fail to raise his Jewishness in the argument against him: 'This Lopez, a perjured traitor and Jewish doctor, worse than Judas himself, undertook the poisoning.'[7] It is the biblical sin that is still the key to the attitude. Again, when Lopez was at the gallows he 'declared that he loved the Queen as well as he loved Jesus Christ, which coming from one of the Jewish profession [= confession] moved no small laughter in the standers-by'.[8] What the audience could not forget was the relationship between the Jew and Christ; his activities in the world of the present could only be understood in the light of this. Shakespeare in *The Merchant of Venice* hardly mentions religion; but the contrast between the man who gives his life for his friend and the self-justifying legalist is squarely based on the traditional contrast between the Gospel and the Law, however glossed with economic and psychological probability.

5. Besant, op. cit., p. 239.
6. John 8: 44. Cf. Thomas Ingelend, *The Disobedient Child* (c. 1560) in which the Devil says:
> All the Jews and all the Turks,
> Yea, and a great part of Christendom,
> When they have done my will and my works,
> In the end they fly thither, all and some.
> (Hazlitt's Dodsley, ii. 310)
7. See G. B. Harrison, *Second Elizabethan Journal* (1931), p. 289.
8. Ibid., p. 304.

And Jewish usury itself was seen by Shakespeare's contemporaries as more than either economic or racial fact. A usurer
is a Jew whether he is racially (confessionally) Judaic or not.
Bacon uses the verb 'to Judaize' of usury in general.[9]
'Lombard-Jew' is a typical conflation of appropriate
nationalities, since (as Langland tells us)

> Lumbards of Lukes . . . lyven by lone as Iewes[1]

and in the Elizabethan period we find the same compound in
Nashe,[2] and in Beaumont and Fletcher's *The Laws of Candy*:
'an usurer or Lumbard-Jew'.[3]

The acceptance of the idea 'Jew' as a fairly blank norm of
villainy[4] gave authors an opportunity to play an effective
theatrical trick on the audience's expectations, dramatizing
the idea 'worse than a Jew'. In Wilson's *Three Ladies of
London* we meet Mercatore, a Christian merchant from Italy
who undermines English sturdiness by importing knick-
knacks, 'Musk, amber, sweet powders, fine odours, pleasant
perfumes, and many such toys, Wherein I perceive consisteth
that country gentlewomen's joys'.[5] Mercatore cheats Gerontus, a Jew, of the money for these imports, and when Gerontus meets up with him in Turkey, and asks for his money, the
Christian threatens to 'turn Turk' (quite literally) and so (in
spite of Turkish abhorrence) escape the debt. Gerontus,
rather than see such a shocking breach of Christian faith,
cancels the debt. This is wildly unrealistic, of course; but it
is a good indication of the extent to which the Jew in this
period is an idea or a norm rather than a person.

Another sophisticated use of the Jew figure can be seen in
Marlowe's *The Jew of Malta*, where Jew and Christian once
again (as in *Three Ladies*) face one another under pressure
from the Turks. This time, however, everyone is much more
realistic, and therefore much more unpleasant. The Jew has

9. 'Of Usury'.
1. C text. Passus v. i. 194.
2. 'Lenten Stuffe' (1599), in *Works*, ed. McKerrow, iii. 211.
3. IV. ii. 32 f.; *Works*, ed. Waller and Glover, iii. 283.
4. It is worth noting a correction in Jonson's *Every man in his humour*,
where the Quarto text (1601) reads *I am a Jew* (III. i. 40) where the Folio (1616)
reads *I am a knave* (III. iii. 48).
5. Hazlitt's Dodsley, vi. 330.

all the wickedness that was traditionally associated with his nation; but the Christian is almost without his expected virtue. The author again uses the expected opposition only as a ground plan or *canto fermo*, over which he works sophisticated inversions and variations.[6]

A pamphlet of the seventeenth century bears the curious title, *The blessed Jew of Marocco, or a blackamoor turned white*.[7] The two paradoxes in the title are obviously seen as parallel: and what I have already said about the attitude to Jews can be (in large part) applied to 'Moors' also. Indeed I wish to go further and point to *Othello* as the most magnificent specimen of the dramatic 'inversion of expected racial values' I have discussed above in relation to 'Jew' plays. In a subsequent essay I will be developing this idea at some length. All that is needed in the present context is to make the point that in Elizabethan drama before *Othello* there are no Moor figures who are not either foolish or wicked (or both). Eleazer in *Lust's Dominion* (*c.* 1600), Aaron in *Titus Andronicus*, Muly Hamet in *The Battle of Alcazar* (*c.* 1589) illustrate the normal dramatic expectation of a man whose colour reveals his villainy as (quite literally) of the deepest dye. We should have no doubt, of course, that Shakespeare's Othello, like the 'Moors' I have already mentioned, is not conceived of as a 'sheikh of Araby' kind of coloured man, but as 'the thick-lips', 'the devil', with 'collied' complexion: in short as a coal-black negro.[8] The central point to be made is that the Moor like the Jew (though with less obvious justification) is seen primarily in this period in religious terms. The

6. See below, pp. 60–102.
7. (1648); Wing, S. 545.
8. It is sometimes supposed that the Elizabethans made a regular distinction between a blackamoor and a tawny moor. Morocco in *The Merchant of Venice* is called a tawny moor, and the New Arden editor glosses this 'in contrast to a black one'. Portia, however, says that he has 'the complexion of a devil' and in any normal usage this would mean 'black' (see text below). The word *tawny* often seems to mean little more than dark. Thus in *King Leir*:

As easy is it for the Blackamoore
To wash the tawny colour from his skin.
(*M.S.R.* 1271 f.t)

Eleazer, in *Lust's Dominion* is clearly black; yet he is called *tawny* (ed. Brereton [Louvain, 1931], l. 231); he comes from Barbary (229), but is said to be an *Indian* (1819, 2316).

epithets that Jonson and Shakespeare apply ('superstitious Moor', 'irreligious Moor')[9] seem to me to be the basic ones. And the Moor had a very obvious advantage in the presentation of *a priori* wickedness: however large was the 'bottle nose' that Henslowe used to present the Jew of Malta on the stage[1] it could not have been as impressive as the total sable of the Moor, when seen as an emblem of Hell, of damnation, as the natural livery of the devil. It follows that the sophisticated dramaturgy which turns such assumptions on their heads, allows the audience its prejudice and then inverts it, is even more startling in *Othello* than in *The Jew of Malta*. It is worth noticing that in this play as in Marlowe's (and in Wilson's *Three Ladies*) the pressure on these issues is provided by the Turks, 'the general enemy Ottoman'. Under the threat of this real political terror Othello emerges as not only not the outcast his skin suggests but as the first gentleman of Christendom, in the last sense in which Christendom had any meaning.

Othello is thus a play whose meaning emerges from the matrix of the old assumption that 'strangers' are meaningful only because of their status in God's providence. Shakespeare here exploits with magnificent bravura what the older geography could give him—a freedom to concentrate on essential moral problems—where the new geography could only give him facts. There is enough 'Moorish' and 'Venetian' colouring to stop us losing our sense of the here-and-now in place and character; but this is only a starting-point for a demonstration of what such characteristics can imply. The 'overlap' in Renaissance geography of which I have already spoken, the coexistence of scientifically incompatible views of the world, allows Shakespeare to explore, swiftly and coherently, the image of the foreigner, the stranger, the outsider in a context which is at once terrestrial and spiritual.

9. Ben Jonson, *Sejanus*, v. i. 712; Shakespeare, *Titus Andronicus*, v. iii. 121. See Plates 2 and 3 for iconographical evidence.
   1. *Jew of Malta* (ed. Tucker Brooke), 1229.

2
Othello and colour prejudice

It is generally admitted today that Shakespeare was a practical man of the theatre: however careless he may have been about maintaining consistency for the exact *reader* of his plays, he was not likely to introduce a theatrical novelty which would only puzzle his audience; it does not seem wise, therefore, to dismiss his theatrical innovations as if they were unintentional. The blackness of Othello is a case in point. Shakespeare largely modified the story he took over from Cinthio: he made a tragic hero out of Cinthio's passionate and bloody lover; he gave him a royal origin, a Christian baptism, a romantic *bravura* of manner and, most important of all, an orotund magnificence of diction. Yet, changing all this, he did not change his colour, and so produced a daring theatrical novelty—a black hero for a white community—a novelty which remains too daring for many recent theatrical audiences. Shakespeare cannot merely have carried over the colour of Othello by being too lazy or too uninterested to meddle with it; for no actor, spending the time in 'blacking-up', and hence no producer, could be indifferent to such an innovation, especially in that age, devoted to 'imitation' and hostile to 'originality'. In fact, the repeated references to Othello's colour in the play and the wider net of images of dark and light spread across the diction, show that Shakespeare was not only not unaware of the implication of his hero's colour, but was indeed intensely aware of it as one of the primary factors in his play.[1] I am therefore assuming in this lecture that the blackness of Othello has a theatrical purpose, and I intend to try to suggest what it was possible for that purpose to have been.

[Read as the British Academy Shakespeare Lecture, 19 April 1967. First published in *The Proceedings of the British Academy*, liii (1967).]

1. See R. B. Heilman, 'More Fair than Black; Light and Dark in *Othello*', *Essays in Criticism*, i (1951), 313–35.

Shakespeare intended his hero to be a black man—that much I take for granted;[2] what is unknown is what the idea of a black man suggested to Shakespeare, and what reaction the appearance of a black man on the stage was calculated to produce. It is fairly certain, however, that some modern reactions are not likely to have been shared by the Elizabethans. The modern theatre-going European intellectual, with a background of cultivated superiority to 'colour problems' in other continents, would often choose to regard Othello as a fellow man and to watch the story—which could so easily be reduced to its headline level: 'sheltered white girl errs: said, "Colour does not matter" '—with a sense of freedom from such prejudices. But this lofty fair-mindedness may be too lofty for Shakespeare's play, and not take the European any nearer the Othello of Shakespeare than the lady from Maryland quoted in the Furness New Variorum edition: 'In studying the play of *Othello*, I have always *imagined* its hero a white man.' Both views, that the colour of Othello does not matter, and that it matters too much to be tolerable, err, I suggest, by over-simplifying. Shakespeare was clearly deliberate in keeping Othello's colour; and it is obvious that he counted on some positive audience reaction to this colour; but it is equally obvious that he did not wish the audience to dismiss Othello as a stereotype nigger.

Modern rationalizations about 'colour' tend to be different from those of the Middle Ages and Renaissance. We are powerfully aware of the relativism of viewpoints; we distinguish easily between different racial cultures; and explicit arguments about the mingling of the races usually begin at the economic and social level and only move to questions of God's providence at the lunatic fringe.

The Elizabethans also had a powerful sense of the economic threat posed by the foreign groups they had daily contact with—Flemings or Frenchmen—but they had little or no continuous contact with 'Moors', and no sense of economic threat from them.[3] This did not mean, however, that they

2. I ignore the many treatises devoted to proving that he was of tawny or sunburnt colour. These are, however, very worthy of study, as documents of prejudice. For some historical comments see above, p. 29, n. 8.
3. See above, pp. 17, 21, 26.

had no racial or colour prejudice. They had, to start with, the basic common man's attitude that all foreigners are curious and inferior—the more foreign the more inferior, in the sense of the proverb quoted by Purchas: 'Three Moors to a Portuguese; three Portuguese to an Englishman.'[4] They had also the basic and ancient sense that black is the colour of sin and death, 'the badge of hell, the hue of dungeons, and the school of night' (as Shakespeare himself says).[5] This supposition is found all over the world (even in darkest Africa)[6] from the earliest to the latest times; which suggests a response to the basic antinomy of day and night. Certainly in the West there is a continuous and documented cultural tradition depending on it.[7] This is, however, surprisingly little discussed; and it may therefore be worthwhile giving some account of it. In Greece and Rome black was the colour of ill luck, death, condemnation, malevolence. The Roman feeling about the colour is well summed up in Horace's line:

hic niger est; hunc tu, Romane, caveto[8]

—on which the Delphin editor comments: 'Niger est] Homo pestilens, malus, perniciosus: contra est candidus, albus.' The soldiers of Brutus were dismayed to meet an Ethiop just before the battle of Philippi.[9] In Lucian's *Philopseudes* (§ 31) we hear of a ghost met in Corinth: 'when the Spirit appeared ... he was squalid and long-haired and blacker than the dark' (μελάντερος τοῦ ζόφου). Suetonius tells us of a play, being rehearsed at the time of Caligula's death, in which the infernal connotations of the colour were used with self-conscious art. In this play Egyptians and Ethiopians played the parts of the inhabitants of the underworld.[1]

4. See M. P. Tilley, *A Dictionary of Proverbs* (1950), M. 1132.
5. *Love's Labour's Lost*, IV. iii. 250 f.
6. See V. W. Turner, 'Colour classification in Ndembu ritual', *Anthropological Approaches to the Study of Religion*, ed. M. Banton (1966); Arthur Leib, 'The mystical significance of colours in ... Madagascar', *Folk-lore*, lvii (1946), 128–33; Joan Westcott, 'The sculpture and myths of Eshu-Elegba, the Yoruba trickster', *Africa*, xxxii (1962).
7. See Hoffmann–Krayer and Bächtold–Stäubli, *Handwörterbuch des deutschen Aberglaubens*, s.v. Schwartz.
8. Horace, *Satires*, I. iv. 85.
9. Plutarch, Brutus, xlviii.
1. Suetonius, Caligula, lvii.

The coming of Christianity made no break in the tradition.
Indeed, Christian eschatology seems to have taken over the
black man from the underworld with great speed and enthusiasm. In the dream of Marcellus in the *Acts of Peter*
(*c.* A.D. 200)[2] a demon appeared 'in sight like an Ethiopian
. . . altogether black and filthy'. In the third-century *Acta
Xanthippae* the devil manifested himself as the King of
Ethiopia.[3] In the so-called 'Epistle of Barnabas' the devil is
called ὁ μέλας.[4] In another early text the martyrdom of
Perpetua is represented as a battle between the saint and a
black-faced Egyptian—the devil, of course.[5] Among the
visitors to the much-tried St Anthony was the devil as
a μέλας παῖς,[6] in Cassian's *Collationes Patrum* the devil
appears several times *in figura Aethiopis taetri*.[7] And so on.
The same religious visions went on into Shakespeare's day.
St Birgitta (of the fourteenth century) tells us in her *Revela-
tions* that she saw the devil in the form of 'an Ethiope, ferefull
in syght and beryng'.[8] St Margaret had a similar experience.[9]
Even among those with a rationalist turn of mind, like
Reginald Scott, the assumption was hardly questioned. In
The Discovery of Witchcraft (1584) Scott tells us that 'A
damned soule may and dooth take the shape of a blacke
moore'[1] and that Bodin 'alloweth the divell the shape of a
blacke Moore, and as he saith he used to appear to Mawd
Cruse, Kate Darey, and Jone Harviller'.[2] Sara Williams,
another possessed woman, described in Samuel Harsnet's
Popish Impostures (well known as as a source of diabolical
names in *King Lear*), was said to have seen 'a blacke man
standing at the doore, and beckning at her to come away';[3]
this was a demon, of course. Later another black figure

2. M. R. James, *The Apocryphal New Testament* (1924), p. 323 (Acts of
Peter, § 22).

3. See M. R. James, *Apocrypha Anecdota* (*Texts and Studies*, ii. 3) (1893), 54.

4. Ed. Funk, *Patres Apostolici*, i. 48.

5. *Passio Perpetuae*, ed. J. A. Robinson, *Texts and Studies*, II. i (1891), 76 f.

6. See *Patrologia Graeca*, xxvi, col. 849 a.

7. See *Corpus Scriptorum Eccl. Latinorum*, xiii (1886), 32, 55.

8. E.E.T.S. O.S. 178 (1929), p. 43. I owe this reference to Mr B. F. Nellist.

9. See Reginald Scott, *The Discovery of Witchcraft* (1584) p. 456.

1. Ibid., p. 535.

2. Ibid., p. 89.

3. *A Declaration of Egregious Popish Impostures* (1603), p. 177.

1. Title-page of Samuel Purchas, *Purchas his Pilgrimes* (1625).

2. Crusader and Paynim (perhaps Richard I and Saladin). Luttrell Psalter (British Library MS. 42130), fol. 82.

3. The Agony in the Garden. Chichester Missal
(John Rylands Lat. MS. 24).

4. 'L.A. Senecae comoediae' (Vienna, Nationalbibliothek MS. 122):

(a) Fol. 44ᵛ: the Thyestean banquet (title-page for the play of *Thyestes*.)

(b) Fol. 96ʳ: Jocasta outside the walls of Thebes—*Thebais*, ll. 443 ff.

(c) Fol. 190ʳ: Andromache hides Astyana× in Hector's tomb when Ulysses enters—*Troades*, ll. 519 ff.

tempted her to break her neck down the stairs and (at another time) to cut her throat.[4] Samuel Butler, with characteristic acidity, summed up the whole tradition in a couple of lines:

> Some with the devil himself in league grow
> By's representative, a Negro.[5]

The linguistic change from Greek or Latin to English did not free the word *black* from the general associations that had formed round μέλας or *niger*. As *candidus* had combined the ideas of white skin and clear soul, so the word *fair* served to combine the ideas of beauty and whiteness. Black remains the adjective appropriate to the ugly and the frightening,[6] to the devil and his children, the wicked and the infidel. In the medieval romances, the enemies of the knights are usually Saracens, often misshapen and monstrous (eyes in forehead, mouth in breast, etc.) and commonly black.[7] This is a tradition that Shakespeare picks up in his description of Thomas Mowbray as a Crusader,

> Streaming the ensign of the Christian cross
> Against black pagans, Turks, and Saracens.[8]

There was then, it appears, a powerful, widespread, and ancient tradition associating black-faced men with wickedness, and this tradition came right up to Shakespeare's own day. The habit of representing evil men as black-faced or negroid had also established itself in a pictorial tradition that persists from the Middle Ages through and beyond the six-

4. Ibid., p. 178.
5. *Hudibras*, II. i. 399 f. Compare Heywood: '. . . a Moor / Of all that bears mans shape likest a divell' (*The Fair Maid of the West*, Part II (Pearson reprint, p. 350).
6. See Walter Clyde Curry, *The Middle English Ideal of Personal Beauty* (1916). I have not been able to see J. E. Willms, *Uber den Gebrauch der Farbenbezeichnungen in der Poesie Altenglands* (München, 1902). The kind of shock that could be produced by the association of blackness and beauty is illustrated by the Scottish tournament of 1505 in which James IV set up a negress as the Queen of Beauty, and himself as 'the wild knight' defended her honour. (See *Accounts of the Lord High Treasurer of Scotland*, III. xlviii ff., lii. 258 f.) The scandal that this caused can be discovered from Pitscottie.
7. See, for example, *Cursor Mundi*, 8077; *Sir Ferumbras*, 2785; *Alisaunder*, B. 6402.
8. *Richard II*, IV. i. 94 f. The blackness of Saladin and other infidels is illustrated in the Luttrell Psalter (f. 82). See Plate 2.

teenth century. This appears especially in works showing the
tormentors of Christ, in scenes of the Flagellation and the
Mocking, though the tormentors of other saints are liable to
have the same external characteristics used to show their evil
natures. Thus in the south porch of the Cathedral of Chartres,
the executioner of St Denis is shown as negroid.[9] The
alabaster tablets produced in England in the late Middle
Ages, and exported to the Continent in large numbers, frequently have enough pigment remaining to show some faces
coloured black. W. L. Hildburgh, writing in *Archaeologia*,
xciii (1949), assumes that there is a link between this characteristic and the medieval drama: 'the very dark colour of the
faces of the wicked persons [is] intended to indicate their
villainous natures; in some tables the faces of the torturers
and other iniquitous persons are black' (p. 76). E. S. Prior,
*Catalogue of the Exhibition of English Medieval Alabaster
Work* (1913), had made the same point: 'the blackening of
the faces of the ruffians and executioners and heretics as
seen in many of the tables was no doubt a stage trick' (p. 21,
n. 1). There is a good example in the Ashmolean Museum in
Oxford, a crucifixion which the 1836 catalogue describes
thus: 'the penitent thief looks towards Christ and the other
has his face averted and is painted as a negro' (p. 146). Again
A. Gardner, writing of English medieval sculpture, tells us
that 'In the martyrdom scenes the executioners are given
hideous faces which seem sometimes to have been painted
black', *English Medieval Sculpture* (1951), p. 310. He illus-
trates a good example showing the martyrdom of St
Catherine (fig. 609, p. 309). Further examples are described in
'Medieval English alabasters in American museums', *Speculum*, xxx (1955), where the Scourging and the Resurrection
are both marked by this feature. Wall-paintings in English
churches preserve evidence of the same usage. A Massacre of
the Innocents from Croughton (Northants.), illustrated in
Borenius and Tristram, *English Medieval Painting* (1927) as
plate 51, shows dark-faced soldiers. The Church of St Peter
and St Paul at Pickering (N. Yorks.) has splendid fifteenth-
century wall-paintings—not yet properly photographed—in
which both Herod and the scourgers are given dark faces.

9. See *Proceedings of the British Academy*, liii (1967), pl. xxia.

Herod is represented in the same way, it may be noticed, in an alabaster tablet reproduced in *The Archaeological Journal*, lxxiv (1917), pl. xiii.

Among the sixteenth-century painted windows of King's College Chapel, Cambridge, the Scourging itself does not have this feature, but the window above (window X), intended as a typological comment on it ('Shimei cursing David'), gives a dark face to Shimei, the *vir sanguinum et vir Belial* (2 Samuel 16: 7), as the legend tells us.

Among illuminated manuscripts, the Luttrell Psalter has a black scourger on fl. 92v,[1] and the Chichester Missal, now in the John Rylands Library, has several full-page pictures of the Passion, in which the tormentors are black with grossly distorted features (see Pl. 3). The *Très-Belles Heures de Notre Dame* du Duc Jean de Berry has a full-page Scourging, with two white tormentors and one black.[2] Bodleian MS. Douce 5—a Book of Hours of Flemish Provenance and four-teenth-century date—has a similar scene. The most celebrated picture in which this tradition appears is the Scourging by Giotto in the Arena Chapel in Padua. In this the negro scourger stands alone brandishing his rod above the head of Christ. Among the many monographs devoted to Giotto no one seems to have pointed to the tradition with which I am here concerned.

The latest picture which uses this tradition, so far as I know, is a martyrdom of St James, attributed to Van Dyck, sold by Weinmüller of Munich in 1958 (Catalogue 721, item 501).[3]

It is suggested by several of the authorities cited here that the pictorial tradition was associated with theatrical usage. Certainly the drama of the Middle Ages seems to have used black figures to represent the evil of this world and the next. Creizenach[4] describes the European diffusion of the black faces. The surviving accounts of the Coventry cycle (which

1. Ibid., pl. xxi*b*.
2. Ibid., pl. xxii*b*.
3. Ibid., pl. xxiii.
4. *Geschichte des neueren Dramas*, i (1911), 201. An interesting detail appears in footnote 3 on this page: 'Wie intensiv die Bemalung war, ergibt sich den Summen, die in Frankreich den Barbarien und Badestubenbesitzern für Reinigung der Teufel bezahlt wurden.' (See also E. J. Haslinghuis, *De Duivel in het drama der Middeleeuwen* [1912], p. 182.)

some think Shakespeare may have seen—and which he *could* have seen) retain the distinction between 'white (or saved) souls' and 'black (or damned) souls'[5] The English folk-play describes St George's enemy as (*inter alia*) 'Black Morocco Dog', 'Black Prince of Darkness', or even 'Black and American Dog'.[6] In Thomas Lupton's *All for Money* (1558⟨ ⟩77) 'Judas cometh in like a damned soul in black'.[7] Udall's *Ezechias*, acted in Cambridge in 1564 is stated to have represented the leader of the Assyrians as a giant and made his followers coal-black. As the reporter of the performance tells us:

> Dicta probat fuscis miles numerosus in armis
> Tam nullas tenebras dixeris esse nigras.[8]

In John Redford's *Wit and Science* (? 1530) we seem to have a moral transformation scene *coram populo*, expressed in terms of face colouring. Wit goes to sleep on Idleness's lap. Idleness then tells us:

> Well, whyle he sleepth in Idlenes lappe,
> Idleness marke on hym shall I clappe. (434 f.)[9]

When Wit awakens he is taken for Ignorance (child of Idleness); he looks in a glass and exclaims:

> hah, goges sowle,
> What have we here, a dyvyll?
> This glas I se well hath bene kept evyll
> . . .
> Other this glas is shamefully spotted,
> Or els am I to shamefully blotted.
> . . .
> And as for this face
> Is abhominable as black as the devyll.
> (826–40)

Even in a proverbial title like 'Like will to like quoth the Devil to the Collier' the widespread and universally accepted

5. See Thomas Sharp, *A Dissertation upon the Coventry Mysteries* (1825), pp. 66, 70.
6. E. K. Chambers, *The English Folk Play* (1933), p. 28.
7. Ed. E. Vogel, *Shakespeare Jahrbuch*, xl (1904), l. 1439.
8. See F. S. Boas, *University Drama in the Tudor Age* (1914), pp. 94 ff.
9. Malone Society Reprints (1951).

point is exposed as part of the air that Englishmen of Shakespeare's age breathed. Indeed, as late as Wycherley's *The Plain Dealer* (1676) stray reference to the Devil's theatrical appearance was supposed to be intelligible to a playhouse audience ('like a devil in a play . . . this darkness . . . conceals her angel's face').[1]

How mindlessly and how totally accepted in this period was the image of the black man as the devil may be seen from the use of 'Moors' or 'Morians' in civic pageants. 'Moors' were an accepted part of the world of pageantry.[2] There were Moors in London Lord Mayor's Pageants in 1519, 1521, 1524, 1536, 1541, 1551, 1589, 1609, 1611, 1624,[3] who seem to have acted as bogey-man figures to clear the way before the main procession. They were sometimes supplied with fireworks for this purpose, and in this function seem to have been fairly indifferent alternatives to green-men, wodewoses, devils. As Withington has remarked:

The relation between wild-men, green-men, foresters, Robin Hood, the Moors, and the devil is very difficult to clear up. A great many cross-influences must exist; and it seems obvious that all these figures are connected.[4]

They are connected as frightening marginal comments on the human state—as inhabitants of those peripheral regions in the *mappae mundi* where Moors, together with

> Anthropophagi and men whose heads
> Do grow beneath their shoulders,

rubbed shoulders (such as these were) with Satyrs, Hermaphrodites, savage men, and others of the species *semihomo*.[5]

1. *The Plain Dealer*, IV. ii.

2. Moors (like dwarfs and fools) were found also in the human menageries that the courts of the Renaissance liked to possess. The Moors at the court of James IV of Scotland appear often in the Treasurer's Accounts. One item there throws an interesting light on their status: 'The nuris that brocht the Moris barne to see (i.e. to be seen), be the Kingis command' (vol. iii, p. 182).

3. See Malone Society Collections, iii (1945).

4. R. Withington, *English Pageantry*, i (1918), 74.

5. The association of the negro with *semihomines* appears in a sixteenth-century sword-dance of 'Mores, Sauvages et Satyres', cited by Chambers (*Mediaeval Stage*, i. 199, n. 5), and in the decoration of the 'vasque de Saint Denis' (*c*. 1180) decorated with sculptures of 'Sylvanus, satyr and negro' (see

An extreme example of this status of the Moor appears in the
report of the pageant for the baptism of Prince Henry in 1594.
It had been arranged that a lion should pull the triumphal
car; but the lion could not be used, so a Moor was substituted.[6]

Renaissance scepticism and the voyages of discovery might
seem, at first sight, to have destroyed the ignorance on which
such thoughtless equations of black men and devils depended. But this does not prove to have been so. The voyagers
brought back some accurate reports of black and heathen;
but they often saw, or said they saw, what they expected to
see—the marvels of the East.[7] In any case the vocabulary at
their disposal frustrated any attempt at scientific discrimina-
tion. The world was still seen largely, in terms of vocabulary,
as a network of religious names. The word 'Moor' had no
clear racial status. Elizabethan authors describe 'Moors' as
existing all over the globe. We hear of 'Mores of Malabar'
from Spenser,[8] of Moors in Malacca from James Lancaster,[9]

H. W. Janson, *Apes and Ape-lore* [1952], p. 55). The *vasque* also uses a sculpture of an ape, and this may be associated with the others as a further illustration of the *semihomo*. The confusion of the ape and the negro has a considerable
history. The negress at the Court of James IV of Scotland who was set up as
'Queen of Beauty' (see above, p. 35, n. 6) was compared to an ape; Dunbar
tells us 'Quhou schou is tute mowitt lyk ane aep' ('of an blak-moir'). Joseph
Glanvill (*Scepsis Scientifica* [1665]) suggests that the apes (rather than the
negroes) are the descendants of Cham. The confusion was a useful one for the
defenders of negro slavery, and drew extra support from the often-repeated
stories that orang-utans frequently stole away and ravished black women.
Thus Edward Long in his *History of Jamaica* says that 'The equally hot
temperament of their women has given probability to the charge of their
admitting these animals [monkeys or baboons] to their embrace' (ii. 383).
Thomas Jefferson, in his *Notes on Virginia* (written in 1781), treats as an
acknowledged fact 'the preference of the Oranootan for black women' (Question XIV).

6. See *A True Reportary of the Baptisme of Frederik Henry, Prince of
Scotland* (1594) (S.T.C. 13163).
7. See R. Wittkower, 'Marvels of the East', *Journal of the Warburg and
Courtauld Institutes*, v (1942), 159–97. See also L. Oschki, *Storia letteraria delle
scoperte geografiche* (Firenze, 1939), and R. Romeo, *Le scoperte americane
nella coscienza Italiana* (1954), who puts the idea expressed here with great
clarity: 'Idee e valori preesistenti operano direttamente sui viaggiatori, spin-
gendo a intendere in conformità ad essi testimonianze dubbie, discorsi in
lingue sconosciute, fenomeni poco spiegabili' (p. 14).
8. *Faerie Queene*, VI. vii. 43.
9. Hakluyt (ed. cit.), vi. 399.

of Moors in Guinea from Eden, [1] of Moors in Ethiopia from Lodge,[2] of Moors in Fukien from Willes,[3] of Moors in America from Marlowe[4] and sundry others. There seem to be Moors everywhere; but only everywhere, we should note, in that outer circuit of non-Christian lands where the saving grace of Jerusalem is weakest in its whitening power. Throughout the Elizabethan period there seems to remain considerable confusion whether the Moor is a human being or a monster. In the 'plat' of the perished play of *Tamar Cam* (1592) we are told of an entry of 'Tartars, Geates, Amozins, Nagars, ollive cullord moores, Canniballs, Hermophrodites, Pigmies', etc.—a characteristic medley.[5] In *Volpone* we are given a list of the undesirables that Volpone has coupled with to produce his Fool, Dwarf, and Hermaphrodite. The supposed parents are described as

> beggars,
> Gipsies and Jews and black-moors.[6]

The geographical vagueness of these authors does not mean, however, that they are vague in their sense of an antithetical relationship between 'Moors' (wherever they live) and civilized white Christians. The first meaning given to the word 'Moor' in *O.E.D.* is 'Mahomedan' (with examples up to 1629); but in many of the examples this seems to mean no more than 'infidel', non-Christian. The pressure that defines the word is more negative than positive. Like *Barbarian* and *Gentile* (or *Wog*) it was a word for 'people not like us',[7] so signalled by colour. The word *Gentile* itself had still the religious sense of *Pagan*, and the combined phrase 'Moors and Gentiles' is used regularly to represent the

1. Peter Martyr Anglerius, tr. R. Eden, *The History of Travel* (1577), fl. 348v.
2. *Works* (Hunterian Society), ii. 52.
3. Hakluyt, vi. 321 (where it is quite clear that 'Moorish' means 'Mahomedan'.
4. *Doctor Faustus* (*Works*, ed. Tucker Brooke, p. 150). Compare the 'black Indians' in Brewer's *The Lovesick King* (Bang's Materialien [1907], 952 f.) and in Googe's *The Popish Kingdom* (translated from Kirchmeyer) (1570)—1880 edn, p. 39—and the 'African Indians' in *Sir Thomas Stukeley* (1596)—Tudor Facsimile Texts, 2169.
5. *Henslowe Papers*, ed. W. W. Greg (1907), p. 148. Compare the 'Negro-Tartars' in *Gesta Grayorum* (*M.S.R.* 46) and the 'Negarian Tartars' (ibid. 52).
6. Ben Jonson, *Volpone*, I. v. 44 f.
7. So that 'Wogs begin at Calais', etc.

religious gamut of non-Christian possibilities (see *O.E.D.* for examples). Similarly, *Barbary* was not simply a place in Africa, but also the unclearly located home of Barbarism, as in Chaucer (Franklin's Tale, 1451, Man of Law's Tale, 183).

I have suggested above that the discoveries of the voyagers contributed little to Renaissance scientific or non-theological explanations of the world.[8] And this was particularly true of the problems raised by the black-skinned races. No scientific explanation of black skins had ever been achieved, though doctors had long disputed it. Lodovicus Caelius Rhodiginus in his *Lectionum Antiquarum libri XXX* (1620) can cite column after column of authorities; but all without conclusive answers. We hear among the latest reports of Africa collected in T. Astley's *New General Collection of Voyages* (1745) that the blackness of the Negro is 'a Topic that has given Rise to numberless Conjectures and great Disputes among the Learned in Europe' (ii. 269). Sir Thomas Browne in three essays in his *Pseudodoxia Epidemica* (VI. x–xii) not only declared that the subject was 'amply and satisfactorily discussed as we know by no man' but proceeded to remedy this by way of amplitude rather than satisfactoriness. The theological explanation was left in possession of the field. Adam and Eve, it was assumed, were white; it follows that the creation of the black races can only be ascribed to some subsequent *fiat*. The two favourite possibilities were the cursing of Cain and the cursing of Ham or Cham and his posterity—and sometimes these two were assumed to be different expressions of the same event; at least one might allege, with Sir Walter Ralegh, that 'the sonnes of Cham did possesse the vices of the sonnes of Cain'.[9] The Cham explanation had the great advantage that 'the threefold world' of tradition could be described in terms of the three sons of Noah—Japhet having produced the Europeans, Shem the Asiatics, while the posterity of Ham occupied Africa, or, in a more sophisticated version, 'the Meridionall or southern partes of the world both in Asia and Africa'[1]—sophisticated, we should notice, without altering the basic theological

8. See pp. 3–10.
9. *The History of the World*, I. vi. 2.
1. A. Willet, *Hexapla in Genesin* (1605), p. 119.

assumption that Cham's posterity were banished to the most uncomfortable part of the globe, and a foretaste of the Hell to come. This geographical assumption fitted in with the wisdom that the etymological doctors had in the Middle Ages been able to glean from the name *Ham*—defined as '*Cham: calidus*, et ipse ex praesagio futuri cognominatus est. Posteritas enim eius eam terrae partem possedit quae vicino sole calentior est.'[2] When this is linked to the other point made in relation to the Cham story—that his posterity were cursed to be slaves[3]—one can see how conveniently and plausibly such a view fitted the facts and desires found in the early navigators. Azurara, the chronicler of Prince Henry the Navigator's voyages, tells us that it was natural to find blackamoors as the slaves of lighter skinned men:

these blacks were Moors (i.e. Mahomedans) like the others, though their slaves, in accordance with ancient custom which I believe to have been because of the curse which, after the Deluge, Noah laid upon his son Cain [*sic*], cursing him in this way: that his race should be subject to all the other races in the world. And from his race these blacks are descended.[4]

The qualities of the 'Moors' who appear on the Elizabethan stage are hardly at all affected by Elizabethan knowledge of real Moors from real geographical locations, and, given the literary modes available, this is hardly surprising. It is true that the first important Moor-role—that of Muly Hamet in Peele's *The Battle of Alcazar* (c. 1589)—tells the story of a real man (with whom Queen Elizabeth had a treaty) in a real historical situation. But the dramatic focus that Peele manages to give to his Moorish character is largely dependent on the devil and underworld associations he can suggest for him—making him call up 'Fiends, Fairies, hags that fight in beds of steel' and causing him to show more acquaintance with the geography of hell than with that of Africa. Aaron in *Titus Andronicus* is liberated from even such

2. Isidore of Seville, *Etymologiae*, VII. vi. 17. (*Patrologia Latina*, lxxxii, col. 276.)

3. See St Ambrose, *Comment. in epist. ad Philippenses* (P.L. xvii, col. 432): 'servi autem ex peccato fiunt, sicut Cham filius Noe, qui primus merito nomen servi accepit.'

4. *Discovery and Conquest of Guinea* (Hakluyt Society, XCV [1896], 54).

slender ties as associate Muly Hamet with geography. Aaron is in the play as the representative of a world of generalized barbarism, which is Gothic in Tamora and Moorish in Aaron, and unfocused in both. The purpose of the play is served by a general opposition between Roman order and Barbarian disorder. Shakespeare has the doubtful distinction of making explicit here (perhaps for the first time in English literature) the projection of black wickedness in terms of negro sexuality. The relationship between Tamora and Aaron is meant, clearly enough, to shock our normal sensibilities and their black baby is present as an emblem of disorder. In this respect, as in most others, Eleazer in *Lust's Dominion* (*c.* 1600)—the third pre-Othello stage-Moor—is copied from Aaron. The location of this play (Spain) gives a historically plausible excuse to present the devil in his favourite human form—'that of a Negro or Moor', but does not really use the locale to establish any racial points.

These characters provide the dominant images that must have been present in the minds of Shakespeare's original audience when they entered the Globe to see a play called *The Moor of Venice*—an expectation of pagan devilry set against white Christian civilization—excessive civilization perhaps in Venice, but civilization at least 'like us'. Even those who knew Cinthio's story of the Moor of Venice could not have had very different expectations, which may be summed up from the story told by Bandello (III. xxi) in which a master beats his Moorish servant, and the servant in revenge rapes and murders his wife and children.[5] Bandello draws an illuminating moral:

By this I intend it to appear that a man should not be served by this sort of slave; for they are seldom found faithful, and at best they are full of filth, unclean, and stink all the time like goats. But all this is as nothing put beside the savage cruelty that reigns in them.

5. Bandello, *Novelle*, Book III, novel xxi, derived from Pontanus (*Opera*, i. 25 b), and translated by Belleforest, *Histoires tragiques*. The story was apparently Englished in ballad form, in 1569, 1570, and again in 1624, 1675. See Hyder Rollins, 'Analytical Index' (*Studies in Philology*, xxi [1924]), item 2542: 'a strange petyful novell Dyscoursynge of a noble Lorde and his lady with thayre ij cheldren executed by a blacke morryon.'

It is in such terms that the play opens. We hear from men like us of a man not like us, of 'his Moorship', 'the Moor', 'the thick-lips', 'an old black ram', 'a Barbary horse', 'the devil', of 'the gross clasps of a lascivious Moor'. The sexual fear and disgust that lie behind so much racial prejudice are exposed for our derisive expectations to fasten upon them. And we are at this point bound to agree with these valuations, for no alternative view is revealed. There is, of course, a certain comic *brio* which helps to distance the whole situation, and neither Brabantio, nor Iago nor Roderigo can wholly command our identification. None the less we are drawn on to await the entry of a traditional Moor figure, the kind of person we came to the theatre expecting to find.

When the second scene begins, however, it is clear that Shakespeare is bent to ends other than the fulfilment of these expectations. The Iago/Roderigo relationship of I. i is repeated in the Iago/Othello relationship of the opening of I. ii; but Othello's response to the real-seeming circumstance with which Iago lards his discourse is very different from the hungrily self-absorbed questionings of Roderigo. Othello draws on an inward certainty about himself, a radiant clarity about his own well-founded moral position. This is no 'lascivious Moor', but a great Christian gentleman, against whom Iago's insinuations break like water against granite. Not only is Othello a Christian, moreover; he is the leader of Christendom in the last and highest sense in which Christendom existed as a viable entity, crusading against the 'black pagans'. He is to defend Cyprus against the Turk, 'hellish horseleaches of Christian blood'.[6] It was the fall of Cyprus which produced the alliance of Lepanto, and we should associate Othello with the emotion that Europe continued to feel—till well after the date of *Othello*—about that victory and about Don John of Austria.[7]

Shakespeare has presented to us a traditional view of what Moors are like, i.e. gross, disgusting, inferior, carrying the symbol of their damnation on their skin; and has caught our over-easy assent to such assumptions in the grip of a guilt which associates us and our assent with the white man

6. Hakluyt, *Principal Navigations* (1903–5 edn), v. 122.
7. See above, pp. 24–25.

representative of such views in the play—Iago. Othello acquires the glamour of an innocent man that *we* have wronged, and an admiration stronger than he could have achieved by virtue plainly represented:

> . . . as these black masks
> Proclaim an enshield beauty ten times louder
> Than beauty could, displayed.

(Is it an accident that Shakespeare wrote these lines from *Measure for Measure* in approximately the same year as he wrote *Othello*?) Iago is a 'civilized' man; but where, for the 'inferior' Othello, appearance and reality, statement and truth are linked indissolubly, civilization for Iago consists largely of a capacity to manipulate appearances and probabilities:

> For when my outward action doth demonstrate
> The native act and figure of my heart
> In compliment extern, 'tis not long after
> But I will wear my heart upon my sleeve
> For daws to peck at: I am not what I am.

Othello may be 'the devil' in appearance: but it is the 'fair' Iago who gives birth to the dark realities of sin and death in the play:

> It is engender'd. Hell and night
> Must bring this monstrous birth to the world's light

The relationship between these two is developed in terms of appearance and reality. Othello controls the reality of action; Iago the 'appearance' of talk about action; Iago the Italian is isolated (even from his wife), envious, enigmatic (even to himself), self-centred; Othello the 'extravagant and wheeling stranger' is surrounded and protected by a network of duties, obligations, esteems, pious to his father-in-law, deferential to his superiors, kind to his subordinates, loving to his wife. To sum up, assuming that *soul* is reality and *body* is appearance, we may say that Iago is the white man with the black soul while Othello is the black man with the white soul. Long before Blake's little black boy had said

> I am black, but oh my soul is white.
> White as an angel is the English child,
> But I am black as if bereaved of light.

and before Kipling's Gunga Din:

> An' for all 'is dirty 'ide
> 'E was white, clear white inside . . .
> You're a better man than I am, Gunga Din!

Othello had represented the guilty awareness of Europe that the 'foreigner type' is only the type we do not know, whose foreignness vanishes when we have better acquaintance; that the prejudicial foreign appearance may conceal a vision of truth, as Brabantio is told:

> If virtue no delighted beauty lack
> Your son-in-law is far more fair than black.

This reality of fairness in Othello provides a principal function for Desdemona in the play. Her love is of a spiritual intensity, of a strong simplicity equal to that of Othello himself, and pierces without effort beyond appearance, into reality:

> I saw Othello's visage in his mind.

Her love is a daring act of faith, beyond reason or social propriety. Like Beauty in the fairytale she denies the beastly (or devilish) appearance to proclaim her allegiance to the invisible reality. And she does so throughout the play, even when the case for the appearance seems most strong and when Iago's power over appearances rides highest. Even when on the point of death at Othello's hands, she gives testimony to her faith (martyr in the true sense of the word):

> Commend me to my *kind* lord.

Othello is then a play which manipulates our sympathies, supposing that we will have brought to the theatre a set of careless assumptions about 'Moors'. It assumes also that we will find it easy to abandon these as the play brings them into focus and identifies them with Iago, draws its elaborate distinction between the external appearance of devilishness and the inner reality.

Shakespeare's playcraft, however, would hardly have been able to superimpose these new valuations on his audience (unique as they were in this form) if it had not been for complicating factors which had begun to affect thought in this day.

The first counter-current I should mention is theological in origin and is found dispersed in several parts of the Bible. It was a fairly important doctrine of the Evangelists that faith could wash away the stains of sin, and the inheritance of mis-belief, that the breach between chosen and non-chosen peoples could be closed by faith. The apostle Philip baptised the Ethiopian eunuch and thereupon, says Bede, the Ethiop changed his skin.[8] The sons of darkness could be seen to become the sons of light, or as Ephesians 5: 8 puts it:

For ye were sometimes darkness, but now are ye light in the Lord: walk as the children of light.

Jerome remarks on this (in Epistle xxii, § 1):

He that committeth sin is of the devil (John, 3: 8). Born of such a parent first we are black by nature, and even after repentance, until we have climbed to Virtue's height we may say *Nigra sum sed speciosa, filiae Hierusalem.*

Only after conversion, he goes on, will the colour be changed, as by miracle, and then will the verse be fitting: *Quae est ista, quae ascendit dealbata?* (Cant. iii. 6 and viii. 5—Septuagint version).

Augustine hangs the same point on an interpretation of Psalm 73 (74 in the English Psalter), verse 14. The verse in the Authorized Version reads 'Thou brakest the heads of levia-than in pieces and gavest him to be meat to the people inhabiting the wilderness', but the Vulgate version has . . . *Dedisti eum in escam populis Ethiopibus.* Augustine[9] asks who are meant by the Ethiopians; and answers that all nations are Ethiopians, black in their natural sinfulness; but they may become white in the knowledge of the Lord. *Fuistis enim aliquando tenebrae; nunc autem lux in Domino* (Ephesians 5: 8). As late as Bishop Joseph Hall, writing one of his *Occasional Meditations* (1630) 'on the sight of a blacka-moor', we find the same use of *nigra sum sed speciosa*:

This is our colour spiritually; yet the eye of our gracious God and Saviour, can see that beauty in us wherewith he is delighted. The true Moses marries a Blackamoor; Christ, his church. It is not for us to regard the skin, but the soul. If that be innocent, pure, holy, the

8. Bede, *Super Acta Apostolorum Expositio* (P.L. xcii, col. 962).
9. St Augustine, *Enarrationes in Psalmos* (P.L. xxxvi, col. 938).

blots of an outside cannot set us off from the love of him who hath
said, *Behold, thou art fair, my Sister, my Spouse*: if that be foul
and black, it is not in the power of an angelical brightness of our
hide, to make us other than a loathsome eye-sore to the Almighty.

The relevance of this passage to Othello need not be stressed.

The grandest of all visual representations of this view that
all men are within the scope of the Christian ministry ('We,
being many, are one body in Christ', says St Paul in Romans
12. 5) is probably the portal of the narthex at Vézelay,[1] dis-
playing the relevance of the pentecostal spirit of evangelism
even to the monsters on the verge of humanity—Cynocephali
and long-eared Scythians, whose relation to the Christian
world had been debated by St Augustine and other Fathers.
But this monument has been treated with admirable fullness
by Emile Mâle,[2] and it is no part of my function either to
repeat or dispute what he has said.

Moreover, Vézelay does not touch on the colour question.
And visual images are obviously of crucial importance here
in establishing the idea of the black man as more than a
patristic metaphor, as a figure that might be met with in real
life. For the image of the black man, considered in relation to
the scheme of the Christian Evangel, we have to turn in the
main to representations of the three Magi. In early Christian
art there seems no evidence that the three kings were shown
different from one another. As early as the eighth century,[3]
however, the *Excerptiones Patrum*, attributed to Bede, had
described Balthazar, the third king, in the following terms:

Tertius, fuscus, integre barbatus, Balthazar nomine, habens
tunicam rubeam.[4]

I may quote Mâle on this description:

It should also be noted that ... the term *fuscus* applied to
Balthazar by the pseudo-Bede was never taken literally, and it was
only in the fourteenth and still more in the fifteenth centuries that
the king has the appearance of a Negro.[5]

1. See *Proc. B.A.* (1967), pl. xxiv.
2. Emile Mâle, *L'Art religieux du XIIe siècle en France* (1922), pp. 328 ff.
3. For the dating see P. Glorieux, *Pour revaloriser Migne* (1844), and J. F.
Kenney, *Sources for the Early History of Ireland* (1929).
4. Pseudo-Bede, *Excerptiones Patrum* (P.L. xciv, col. 541).
5. Emile Mâle, *The Gothic Image* (1958), pp. 214-15.

It would be interesting to know what factors impeded the development of the black Balthazar in iconography. For as early as 1180, in the great typological sequence at Klosterneuburg, Nicholas of Verdun had represented the Old Testament type of the Epiphany—the visit of the Queen of Sheba to Solomon—with a Negro Sheba[6]—a feature to be met with elsewhere.[7]

It was another typological parallel, however, that probably did most to establish the black Balthazar—that between the three kings and the three sons of Noah. The genuine Bede makes this point in his commentary on Matthew:

Mystice autem tres Magi tres partes mundi significant, Asiam, Africam, Europam, sive humanum genus, quod a tribus filiis Noe seminarium sumpsit.[8]

and this view was given general diffusion in the *Glossa Ordinaria*.[9] If we suppose that Cham became the father of the black races, it follows that one of the Magi must represent these races. Balthazar carries on his face the curse of Cham, but reveals the capacity for redemption through faith available to all races.[1]

Such was the strict theological position. But this is complicated in the Renaissance by the development of a more precisely focused and political primitivism spread apace as the voyagers gave their accounts, not of highly organized Mahomedan kingdoms set in opposition to Christ, but of simple quasi-pastoral innocents, timid, naked as their mothers brought them forth, without laws and without arms (as Columbus first saw them and first described them).[2] The old ideals and dreams of travellers, the terrestrial paradise—

6. See *Proc. B.A.* (1967), pl. xxv*a*.

7. Ibid., pl. xxv*b*.

8. Bede, *In Matthaei Evangelium Expositio* (P.L. xcii, col. 13).

9. Walafridus Strabus, *Glossa Ordinaria* (P.L. cxiv, col. 73).

1. An interesting comment on this point is supplied by a Portuguese picture of the Epiphany *c.* 1505 where a Brazilian chief in accurately feathered outfit replaces the black Balthazar (*Proc. B.A.* [1967], pl. xxvi). It has been suggested that, because of the early date, the Brazilian was in fact thought of as one of the Kings of the East. See Hugh Honour, *The European Vision of America* (1975), pl. 4 and commentary.

2. Quoted in R. Romeo, *Le scoperte americane nella coscienza italiana del Cinquecento*, p. 19; L. Olschki, *Storia letteraria delle scoperte geografiche*, pp. 11–22. See above, pp. 12–13.

which must be heresy if merely geographical—the fountain of youth, the kingdom of Prester John, acquired a new and sharper urgency. The pressure of these interests tended to suggest that such innocents as the Amerindians were already *per naturam* close to God.[3] The idea of salvation without sacraments, without baptism, and the casting out of the old black Adam, was of course heretical;[4] but it was a heretical tendency of long standing, for the quality of human mercy that it implies cannot be wholly removed from Christian thinking.

The opposition between the two views was nowhere more dramatically presented than in the famous Valladolid debate between Sepulveda and Las Casas.[5] Sepulveda asserted that the American Indians were 'slaves by nature', since their natural inferiority made it impossible for them to achieve the light of the gospel without enslavement.[6] Las Casas, on the other hand, dwelt on the innocence of the Indians, living *secundum naturam*, on their natural capacity

3. So Columbus in the journal of his first voyage (16 October 1492): 'They do not know any religion, and I believe they could easily be converted to Christianity, for they are very intelligent.' The Bull *Inter cetera* of 1493 (which divided the New World between Spain and Portugal) speaks of the Indians as *gentes pacifice viventes . . . nudi incedentes, nec carnibus vescentes . . . credunt unum Deum creatorem in celis esse, ac ad fidem catholicam amplexandam et bonis moribus imbuendum satis apti videntur.*

4. It is interesting that Hieronymus Bosch in his supposedly 'Adamite' altarpiece sometime called 'The garden of earthly delights' and now re-titled 'The Millennium' uses negro figures to represent the heretical Adamite assumption that salvation is available here and now in the flesh. Fränger, *The Millennium of Hieronymus Bosch* (1952), whose argument I am paraphrasing, notes (p. 108): 'This scene takes place in the presence of a Nubian girl, who is *nigra sed formosa* like the black bride of the Song of Songs (i. 5). We are doubtless justified in regarding these negresses, who appear so often in the picture, as embodiments of the innocence that had not yet vanished from the primal conditions of tropical nature.'

5. Described most fully in English in L. Hanke, *Aristotle and the American Indians* (1959).

6. See Eric Williams, *Documents of West Indian History* (1963), item 155, discussing the view that a 'negro cannot become a Christian without being a slave'. Cf. the summary of Sepulveda's position in Hanke, op. cit., pp. 44 f. The same views persist today, though with interesting modifications in the vocabulary: 'He (the Negro) requires the constant control of white people to keep him in check. Without the presence of the white police force negroes would turn upon themselves and destroy each other. The white man is the only authority he knows.' (Quoted in E. T. Thompson, *Race Relations* [1939], p. 174.)

for devotion, and on the appalling contrast between the mild
and timid Indians and the inhumanity of their 'civilized' or
'Christian' exploiters. Of these two it was of course Las
Casas who made the greatest impact in Europe. We should
not forget that the Valladolid debate was decided in his
favour; but it was not in Spain, but in France and England
that primitivism grew most rapidly. Spanish claims to the
New World and Spanish brutality in the New World combined the forces of jealousy, frustrated greed, and local self-
righteousness so as to create (even if with initially polemical
purpose) a whole new critique of European Christian pretensions. It could now be said that white European Christianity
had been put to the test in America (the test being the salvation of souls) and had been found wanting. 'Upon these
lambes', writes Richard Hakluyt (quoting Las Casas), 'so
meke, so qualified and endewed of their maker and creator as
hath bene saied, entred the spanishe, incontinent as they
knew them, as wolves, as lyons and as Tigres moste cruell of
long tyme famished.'[7]

The crown of all such Renaissance primitivism is Montaigne's *Essays*, and especially that on the Cannibals, where
the criticism of Spanish Christianity has become a *libertin*
critique of modern European civility. Shakespeare, in *The
Tempest*, seems to show a knowledge of this essay,[8] and
certainly *The Tempest* reveals a searching interest in the
status of Western civilization parallel to Montaigne's, and a
concern to understand the point of reconciliation between
innocence and sophistication, ignorance and knowledge.

Of course, we must not assume that Shakespeare, because
he had these concerns in *The Tempest*, must have had them
also in *Othello*; but *The Tempest* at one end of his career,
like *Titus Andronicus* at the other end, indicates that the
polarities of thought on which *Othello* moves (if I am correct)
were available to his mind.

I have spoken of 'polarities' in the plural because it is

7. *A Discourse on the Western Planting* (1584) printed in *The Writings of the
two Richard Hakluyts*, vol. ii (Hakluyt Society [second series], lxxvii [1935],
p. 258). Cf. above, pp. 12–13.

8. Disputed in M. T. Hodgen, 'Montaigne and Shakespeare', *Huntington
Library Quarterly*, xvi (1952), 23–42. Miss Hodgen finds a similarity of elements
used to praise primitive life in Louis le Roy, Boemus, Vespucci, Mexia, etc.

important to notice that Shakespeare does not present his *Othello* story in any simple primitivist terms. *Othello* is not adequately described as the exploitation of a noble savage by a corrupt European.[9] This is an element in the play, and it is the element that Henry James found so seminal for his own images of the relationship between American and European;[1] but it is not the whole play.

Othello has *something* of the structure of a morality play, with Othello caught between Desdemona and Iago, the good angel and the evil angel. Iago is the master of appearances, which he seeks to exploit as realities; Desdemona, on the other hand, cares nothing for appearances (as her 'downright violence and storm of fortunes | May trumpet to the world'), only for realities; Othello, seeing appearance and reality as indissoluble cues to action, stands between the two, the object of the attentions and the assumptions of both. The play has something of this morality structure; but by giving too much importance to this it would be easy to underplay the extent to which Othello becomes what Iago and the society to which *we* belong assumes him to be.

There is considerable strength in the anti-primitivist side of the great Renaissance debate (as that is represented in *Othello*) and this lies in the extent to which the whole social organism pictured is one we recognize as our own, and recognize as necessarily geared to reject 'extravagant and wheeling strangers'. I speak of the social organism here, not in terms of its official existence—its commands, duties, performances; for in these terms Othello's life is well meshed into the state machine:

> My services which I have done the Signiory
> Shall out-tongue his complaints.

I speak rather of the unspoken assumptions and careless prejudices by which we all conduct most of our lives. And it

9. But Iago's Spanish name (and his nautical imagery) may represent Shakespeare's awareness of this potentiality in his play at some level of his consciousness. The relevance of the figure of Sant' Iago Matamoros (Moor-slayer) has been suggested by G. N. Murphy, 'A note on Iago's name', *Literature and Society*, ed. B. Slote (1964).

1. See Agostino Lombardo, 'Henry James *The American* e il mito di Otello', *Friendship's Garland: Essays presented to Mario Praz*, ed. V. Gabrieli (1966), pp. 107–42.

is in these respects that Iago is the master of us all, the snapper-up of every psychological trifle, every unnoticed dropped handkerchief. It is by virtue of such a multitude of our tiny and unnoticed assents that Iago is able to force Othello into the actions he expects of him. Only the hermit can stand outside such social assumptions; but, by marrying, Othello has become part of society in this sense, the natural victim of the man-in-the-know, the man universally thought well of. And Iago's knowingness finds little or no resistance. We all believe the Iagos in our midst; they are, as our vocabulary interestingly insists, the 'realists'.

The dramatic function of Iago is to reduce the white 'reality' of Othello to the black 'appearance' of his face, indeed induce in him the belief that all reality is 'black', that Desdemona in particular, 'where I have garnered up my heart'

> . . . that was fresh
> As Dian's visage, is now begrimed and black
> As mine own face.

Thus in the bedroom scene (v. ii) Othello's view of Desdemona is one that contrasts

> that whiter skin of hers than snow
> And smooth as monumental alabaster

with the dark deeds her nature requires of her.

> Put out the light, and then put out the light,

he says; that is, 'let the face be as dark as the soul it covers'; and then murder will be justified.

This intention on Shakespeare's part is made very explicit at one point, where Othello tells Desdemona,

Come, swear it, damn thyself; lest, being like one of heaven, the devils themselves should fear to seize thee; therefore be double-damn'd—swear thou art honest.   (IV. ii. 36 ff.)

What Othello is asking here is that the white and so 'heavenly' Desdemona should damn herself black, as Esdras of Granada had done in Nashe's *The Unfortunate Traveller*, with the result that:

His body being dead lookt as blacke as a toad: the devill presently branded it for his own.[2]

It is, of course, to the same belief that Shakespeare alludes in Macbeth's 'The devil damn thee black, thou cream-faced loon'. The dark reality originating in Iago's soul spreads across the play, blackening whatever it overcomes and making the deeds of Othello at last fit in with the prejudice that his face at first excited. Sometimes it is supposed that this proves the prejudice to have been justified. There is a powerful line of criticism on *Othello*, going back at least as far as A. W. Schlegel,[3] that paints the Moor as a savage at heart, one whose veneer of Christianity and civilization cracks as the play proceeds, to reveal and liberate his basic savagery: Othello turns out to be in fact what barbarians *have* to be.

This view, however comforting to our sense of society and our prejudices, does not find much support in the play itself. The fact that the darkness of 'Hell and night' spreads from Iago and then takes over Othello—this fact at least should prevent us from supposing that the blackness is inherent in Othello's barbarian nature. Othello himself, it is true, loses faith not only in Desdemona but in that fair quality of himself which Desdemona saw and worshipped: ('for she had eyes and chose me'). Believing that she lied about the qualities she saw in him it is easy for him to believe that she lies elsewhere and everywhere. Once the visionary quality of *faith*, which made it possible to believe (what in common sense was unbelievable) that she *chose* him—once this is cancelled, knowingness acquires a claim to truth that only faith could dispossess; and so when Iago says

> I know our country disposition well:
> In Venice they do let God see the pranks
> They dare not show their husbands.

Othello can only answer 'Dost thou say so?' Once faith is gone, physical common sense becomes all too probable:

> Foh! one may smell in such a will most rank,
> Foul disproportion, thoughts unnatural.

2. Nashe, *Works*, ed. McKerrow, ii. 326.
3. August Wilhelm Schlegel, *Lectures on Dramatic Art* (1815), ii. 189.

The superficial 'disproportion' between black skin and white skin conquers the inward, unseen 'marriage of true minds'. Similarly with the disproportion between youth and age: 'She must change for youth'; being sated with his body she will find the error of her choice. The tragedy becomes, as Helen Gardner has described it, a tragedy of the loss of faith.[4] And, such is the nature of Othello's heroic temperament, the loss of faith means the loss of all meaning and all value, all sense of light:

> I have no wife.
> O insupportable! O heavy hour!
> Methinks it should be now a huge eclipse
> Of sun and moon, and that the affrighted globe
> Did yawn at alteration.

Universal darkness has buried all.

But the end of the play is not simply a collapse of civilization into barbarism, nor a destruction of meaning. Desdemona *was* true, faith *was* justified, the appearance was not the key to the truth. To complete the circle we must accept, finally and above all, that Othello was not the credulous and passionate savage that Iago has tried to make him, but that he was justified in his second, as in his first, self-defence:

> For nought I did in hate, but all in honour.

The imposition of Iago's vulgar prejudices on Othello ('These Moors are changeable in their wills', etc.) is so successful that it takes over not only Othello but almost all the critics. But Iago's suppression of Othello into the vulgar prejudice about him can only be sustained as the truth if we ignore the end of the play. The wonderful recovery here of the sense of ethical meaning in the world, even in the ashes of all that embodied meaning—this requires that we see the final speech of Othello as more than that of a repentant blackamoor 'cheering himself up', as Mr Eliot phrased it.[5] It is in fact a marvellous *stretto* of all the themes that have sounded throughout the play. I shall only dwell on Othello's self-judgement and self-execution, repeating and reversing the judgement and

4. Helen Gardner, 'The noble Moor', *Proc. B.A.* xli (1955).
5. T. S. Eliot, 'Shakespeare and the stoicism of Seneca', reprinted in *Selected Essays* (1932), p. 130.

execution on Desdemona and so, in a sense, cancelling them. Othello is the 'base Indian' who threw away the white pearl Desdemona, but he is also the state servant and Christian who, when the Infidel or 'black Pagan' within him seemed to triumph,

> Took by the throat the circumcised dog
> And smote him—thus.

With poetic justice, the Christian reality reasserts its superior position over the pagan appearance, not in terms that can be lived through, but at least in terms that can be understood. We may rejoice even as we sorrow, catharsis is achieved, for

> What may quiet us in a death so noble,

as this in the Aleppo of the mind?

It is often suggested that *Othello* is a play of claustrophobic intensity, painfully narrow in its range of vision. A. C. Bradley finds in it 'the darkness not of night, but of a close-shut murderous room'; he assumes that this is due to a limitation in its scope 'as if some power in his soul, at once the highest and the sweetest, were for a time in abeyance . . . that element . . . which unites him with the mystical poets and with the great musicians'. Elsewhere he refers to it as 'a play on a contemporary and wholly mundane subject'.[6] Many other notable critics have felt the same. Granville Barker believes that it is 'not a spiritual tragedy in the sense that the others may be called so . . . it is a tragedy without meaning, and that is the ultimate horror of it'.[7]

Given the approach to the play outlined in this essay I think it is possible to modify the view shared by these great critics. If we think of the action not simply in terms of the bad Iago's unresisted destruction of the good Othello, and of the bad Othello's unresisted destruction of Desdemona, but see these actions instead in terms of prejudice and vision, appearance and reality, indeed in terms of the whole question of civilization as canvassed, for example, in Montaigne's *Essays*—if we see these large questions as begged continuously by the action

6. A. C. Bradley, *Shakespearean Tragedy* (1904), pp. 177, 185, 186.
7. Harley Granville Barker, *Prefaces to Shakespeare* (fourth series [1945]), pp. 156, 175.

we may feel that some wider vision has been let into 'the close-shut murderous room'.

The domestic intensities of *King Lear* have been seen usefully and interestingly (by Theodore Spencer, for example) in relation to the intellectual history of the Renaissance.[8] The position of the king obviously calls on one set of traditional assumptions, while Edmund's doctrine of nature equally obviously draws on the views of the *libertins*, of Montaigne and Machiavelli. The pressure of these larger formulations may be seen to add to the largeness of scope in the play. *Othello*, on the other hand, is thought not to be a play of this kind. 'The play itself is primarily concerned with the effect of one human being on another',[9] says Spencer. It is true that Iago operates in a less conceptualized situation than Edmund; but the contrast between his world view and that of Othello is closely related to the contrast between Edmund and Lear. On the one side we have the chivalrous world of the Crusader, the effortless superiority of the 'great man', the orotund public voice of the leader, the magnetism of the famous lover. The values of the world of late medieval and Renaissance magnificence seem compressed in Othello—crusader, stoic, traveller, believer, orator, commander, lover—Chaucer's parfit knight, Spenser's Red Cross, the Ruggierio of Ariosto. In Iago we have the other face of the Renaissance (or Counter-Renaissance), rationalist, individual, empirical (or inductive), a master in the Machiavellian art of manipulating appearances, a Baconian or Hobbesian 'Realist'.

In the conflict of Othello and Iago we have, as in that setting Edmund, Goneril, and Regan against Lear and Gloucester, a collision of these two Renaissance views. Bradley points to a similarity between Lear and Othello, that they are both 'survivors of a heroic age living in a later and smaller world'. Both represent a golden age naivety which was disappearing then (as now, and always). Lear's survival is across a temporal gap; his long life has carried him out of one age and stranded him in another. But Othello's travel is geographical rather than temporal, from the heroic simplicities of

8. Theodore Spencer, *Shakespeare and the Nature of Man* (1943).
9. Spencer, op. cit. (1961 edn), p. 126.

> I fetch my life and being
> From men of royal siege

into the supersubtle world of Venice, the most sophisticated and 'modern' city on earth, as I have noted above (p. 24).

Here, if anywhere, was the scene-setting for no merely domestic intrigue, but for an exercise in the quality of civilization, a contest between the capacities and ideals claimed by Christendom, and those that Christians were actually employing in that context where (as Marlowe says)

> ... Indian Moors obey their Spanish lords.[1]

Othello's black skin makes the coexistence of his vulnerable romanticism and epic grandeur with the bleak or even pathological realism of Iago a believable fact. The lines that collide here started thousands of miles apart. But Shakespeare's choice of a black man for his Red Cross Knight, his Rinaldo, has a further advantage. *Our* involvement in prejudice gives us a double focus on his reality. We admire him—I fear that one has to be trained as a literary critic to find him unadmirable—but we are aware of the difficulty of sustaining that vision of the golden world of poetry; and this is so because *we* feel the disproportion and the difficulty of his social life and of his marriage (as a social act). We are aware of the easy responses that Iago can command, not only of people on the stage but also in the audience. The perilous and temporary achievements of heroism are achieved most sharply in this play, because they have to be achieved in *our* minds, through *our* self-awareness.

1. Marlowe, *Doctor Faustus*, I. i. 122

3

The theology of
Marlowe's *The Jew of Malta*[1]

That Marlowe was an intellectual has hardly ever been denied. Today, many critics would go further and admit that, in *Faustus* at least, he wrote, ideally, for an audience able to see intellectual ambiguities in his language, and able to bring an informed critical response to the images and half-quotations that are used in a self-consciously ironic way throughout.[2] The obvious and inescapable example is the *consummatum est* with which Faustus completes the sale of his soul to the Devil (506);[3] the ironic juxtaposition of the words in which Christ completed the ransom of mankind, and the act in which Faustus denied that mercy for himself, does more than characterize Faustus as a learned theologian; it sets the action in a framework of assumptions, so that we see *round* his self-assertion into the Order that it breaks, even at the moment when it breaks it; the audience which does not know the quotation misses the point. I think we might go further, and suggest that Marlowe assumes here that the audience[4] will not only know, but respect, the Order

[First published in *The Journal of the Warburg and Courtauld Institutes*, xxvii (1964).]

1. In the ten years or so in which I collected material for this essay I contracted many debts. Miss Grundy and Mrs Ewbank supplied me with useful examples, and Miss M. D. Anderson discussed cauldrons with me. But my greatest debt by far is to B. F. Nellist, whose expertise in the *Patrologia* saved me many a weary search and whose diligent eye improved every part of the work.

2. See especially the articles by Kirschbaum (*R.E.S.* xix [1943], 225–41) and by Greg (*M.L.R.* xli [1946], 97–107).

3. References are to *The Works of Christopher Marlowe*, ed. C. F. Tucker Brooke (1910). The typographical conventions are modernized.

4. Marlowe was a dramatist writing to earn a living as well as a poet expressing his ego. He had to provide plays that would pass the censorship and appeal to the orthodox and suspicious audiences. We cannot suppose that such an

implied by Christ's words, and judge Faustus accordingly.
This is perhaps even clearer in another of the ironies of this
play. When Faustus talks of Christ, contrary to his promise,
he is frightened into submission by a display of diabolical
force and then soothed by the variety show of the Seven
Deadly Sins; of this he remarks:

> That sight will be as pleasing unto me,
> As Paradise was to Adam, the first day
> Of his creation.   (716–18)

The ironic juxtaposition of the sight of Paradise and the vision
of Hell cannot be intended to persuade the audience that
Hell is preferable to Paradise; each term must retain its
traditional value; it is the attitude of Faustus, not the value of
Paradise that is being judged—a point that is thrust home by
Lucifer's reply to the speech:

> Talke not of Paradise, nor creation, but marke this shew:
> talke of the divel, and nothing else.   (719 f.)

But the passage in *Faustus* that seems to reveal, most con-
clusively, Marlowe's desire to be understood intellectually as
well as appreciated aesthetically is that in the opening speech
of the play, in which the hero quotes two passages from
Jerome's Bible. Out of these Faustus frames a syllogism
proving the necessity of damnation. In the first place we have,
'*Stipendium peccati mors est* ... The reward of sinne is
death'; and in the second, '*Si peccasse negamus, fallimur, et
nulla est in nobis veritas* ... If we say that we have no sinne,
we deceive ourselves, and there's no truth in us'; the conclusion is:

> Why, then, belike we must sinne, and so consequently die:
> [Ay], we must die an everlasting death.   (72 f.)

The fallacy of the argument here needs no subtle doctor to
expose it; I suspect that most Elizabethans would have
recognized it, and I am supported in this assumption by the
appearance of the same fallacy in the arguments of Despair

---

audience had the least natural sympathy with libertine views in religion. It was
certainly open to Marlowe to complicate their naïve assumptions, but not to
flout them.

in the First Book of *The Faerie Queene*. Despair tells Red Cross Knight:

> Is not his law, Let every sinner die:
> Die shall all flesh?

that is, 'The reward of sin is death'; and again (stressing the inevitability of sin),

> The lenger life, I wote the greater sin,
> The greater sin, the greater punishment;

as in, 'If we say that we have no sin, we deceive ourselves, and there's no truth in us.' The conclusion for Red Cross Knight is the physical expression of despair in suicide, not its intellectual expression in necromancy, but the steps taken are the same, and the words of Una, pointing out the fallacy, could equally well be applied to Faustus:

> Ne let vaine words bewitch thy manly hart
> Ne divelish thoughts dismay thy constant spright
> In heavenly mercies hast thou not a part?

Marlowe, however, makes the fallacy more precisely demonstrable than this by using as his texts two half-quotations; in each case the second half of the quotation denies explicitly the assumption that Faustus draws from the first half, introducing the concept of Grace which his syllogism bypasses: 'The wages of sinne is death' says Romans 6: 23 (in the Geneva Version),[5] 'But the gift of God is eternall life, through Jesus Christ our Lord.' And again, 'If we say that we have no sinne, wee deceive our selves and trueth is not in us; If we acknowledge our sinnes, hee is faithfull and just to forgive us our sinnes' (I John 1: 8 f.). The use of these texts in

5. Marlowe's Biblical quotations seem normally to be derived from the Geneva translation (which he quotes almost literatim in *The Jew of Malta* [429 ff.]), so it is from this version that I quote throughout the present article. But the reading, 'the reward of sin is death' is that of the Bishop's Bible which (like the Great Bible) has *reward* rather than the Geneva *wages* or Rheims *stipends*. Richmond Noble has shown how Shakespeare alternates between the Bishop's and Geneva versions, and suggested reasons why he should have done so (*Shakespeare's Biblical Knowledge* [1935]). The Spenser parallel has been cited by Virgil K. Whitaker, *Shakespeare's Use of Learning* (San Marino, 1953), p. 242, and a further parallel (with Thomas Becon's *Dialogue between the Christian Knight and Satan*) has been found by Paul Kocher (*Christopher Marlowe* [Chapel Hill, 1946], p. 106 f.).

this highly dramatic way not only reveals the skilled theological disputant in Marlowe himself; it implies an ideal audience that knows the suppressed halves of the quotations and can judge the hero by his understanding of the texts he uses. This judgement is supported by a tissue of ironies throughout the play, and attention to these is a key which unlocks its whole meaning and structure. The method is one that is more obvious to us in the work of Ben Jonson (for example, the opening speech of *Volpone*), but here (as elsewhere) surely T. S. Eliot is correct in finding Jonson to be Marlowe's dramatic 'heir'.[6]

But even if we allow that this method is one that is important in *Faustus*, it does not follow that Marlowe used it elsewhere. *Faustus*, it might well be pointed out, is uniquely intellectual in its method of presenting dramatic conflict (having an intellectual for its hero); and the ironic method of 'placing' the hero in relation to the text he uses might be linked to this rather than to the Marlovian drama as a whole. It is certainly true that the method is uniquely obvious in *Faustus*; but it seems improbable, *a priori*, that the technique could be switched on and off at will; and in fact, I find that even the images of *Tamburlaine* are less vapidly Swinburnian than Swinburnian critics supposed. But it is *The Jew of Malta* which seems to be, apart from *Faustus*, the greatest ironic structure in Marlowe's work. In the following pages I shall attempt to define a few key concepts in this structure, sketching in the theological background which seems to be here, as in *Faustus*, the clue to a correct focus on the central character.

If we grant that the Marlowe who wrote *The Jew of Malta*[7] was the skilled theologian[8] who composed *Faustus*, and that

6. 'Ben Jonson'; reprinted in *Selected Essays* (1934), p. 154.

7. I take it throughout this article that the whole of *The Jew of Malta* is by one author and that the text of the 1633 Quarto fairly represents the intentions of the author. See Kirschbaum in *M.L.Q.* vii (1946), and J. C. Maxwell, *M.L.R.* xlviii (1953).

8. Marlowe's Cambridge scholarship was 'tenable for three years, but if the candidates were disposed to enter into holy orders, they might be held for six ... As Marlowe held his scholarship for six years, he must have been at least ostensibly preparing for the Church'. (Bakeless, *Tragical History of Christopher Marlowe*, i [Cambridge, Mass., 1942], 49 f.) Cf. Boas, *Christopher Marlowe* (1949), p. 20 and Kocher, op. cit., p. 21.

he wrote part at least of *The Jew* 'with the Bible before him' (the words are H. S. Bennett's)[9] we may feel disposed to begin by asking why Marlowe gave to his hero the name of the 'thief and murderer' in Scripture, who was chosen for amnesty in place of Christ. To ask this simple-seeming question is in fact to get hold of the short exposed end of a long and tortuous tradition *adversus Judaeos*,[1] 'placing' the Jewish faith in relation to Christendom. Perhaps the simplest way to relate the major themes of this tradition to *The Jew of Malta* is to quote George Herbert's poem, 'Self-condemnation':

> Thou who condemnest Jewish hate,
> For choosing Barrabas a murderer
>   Before the Lord of glorie;
> Look back upon thine own estate,
> Call home thine eye (that busie wanderer):
>   That choice may be thy storie.
>
> He that doth love, and love amisse,
> This worlds delights before true Christian joy,
>   Hath made a Jewish choice:
> The world an ancient murderer is;
> Thousands of souls it hath and doth destroy
>   With her enchanting voice.
>
> He that hath made a sorrie wedding
> Between his soul and gold, and hath preferr'd
>   False gain before the true,
> Hath done what he condemns in reading:
> For he hath sold for money his deare Lord,
>   And is a Judas-Jew.
>
> Thus we prevent the last great day,
> And judge ourselves. That light, which sin & passion
>   Did before dimme and choke,
> When once those snuffes are ta'en away,
> Shines bright and clear, ev'n unto condemnation,
>   Without excuse or cloke.

Herbert is at one with a long patristic tradition in seeing Jewishness as a moral condition, the climactic 'Jewish choice'

9. *The Jew of Malta and The Massacre at Paris*, ed. H. S. Bennett (1931).

1. See A. Lukyn Williams, *Adversus Judaeos: a bird's eye view of Christian 'Apologiae' until the Renaissance* (Cambridge, 1935).

being that which rejected Christ and chose Barabbas, rejected
the Saviour and chose the robber, rejected the spirit and chose
the flesh, rejected the treasure that is in heaven and chose the
treasure that is on earth[2]—as the *Glossa Ordinaria* comments
on Matthew 27:21, 'Filium diaboli elegerunt pro filio dei . .
quae sua petitio hodie etiam haeret eis, amissa gente et loco et
libertate'.[3] The name Barabbas, says Ambrose (and other
Fathers repeat the information) means *filius patris*; but this
should be interpreted in the light of John 8:44, where Christ
says to the Jews, 'Ye are of your father the Devil',[4] and so
Barabbas is to be interpreted as *Antichristi typus.*[5]

The many people who have written about the image of the
Jew in Elizabethan literature[6] have concentrated, on the
whole, on social questions about real Jews, like 'what
knowledge could the Elizabethans have had of genuine
Jewish life?'; and, in respect of *The Jew of Malta*, have
looked for source materials or impulses among the exploits
of contemporary Jews like Juan Miques or David Passi. It is
understandable that most of those who have written on the
subject have had the modern 'Jewish question' in mind; but

2. The play of *The Jew* which Stephen Gosson refers to as having been
played at 'The Bull' (before 1579) must have turned on much the same moral
point, since Gosson speaks of it as 'representing the greedinesse of worldly
chusers, and bloody minds of usurers'. (See E. K. Chambers, *Elizabethan Stage*,
iv. 204.)

3. See also the gloss on the corresponding passage in Mark (15: 11): '*Data
enim optione sibi, pro Jesu latronem, pro Salvatore interfectorem elegerunt.*'
The choice of Barabbas is mentioned in the same anti-Jewish context in Acts
3: 14.

4. See Jerome: *Barrabbas latro . . . dismissus est populo Judaeorum, id est
diabolus qui hodie regnat in eis* (P.L. xxvi, col. 207). Cf. Augustine (P.L. xxxv,
col. 1941), Rupert of Deutz (P.L. clxvii, and 820), Hilarius (P.L. ix, col. 1073),
Isidore (P.L. lxxxiii, col. 129.)

5. On the effect of the idea of Antichrist as a Jew on the social attitudes to the
Jewish people see J. Trachtenberg, *The Devil and the Jews* (New Haven, 1943),
pp. 36 ff. Marlowe must have known about Kirchmeyer's Antichrist play, *Pammachius*, which was performed at Cambridge in 1545, and caused a famous
scandal in which the Chancellor, the Vice-Chancellor, and the whole University
was involved.

6. For example, J. L. Cardozo, *The Contemporary Jew in Elizabethan Drama*
(Amsterdam, 1925). H. Michelson, *The Jew in Early English Literature* (Amsterdam, 1926). M. J. Landa, *The Jew in Drama* (1926). H. Fisch, *The Dual Image*
(1959). C. Roth, *The Jews in the Renaissance* (Philadelphia, 1959). M. F.
Modder, *The Jew in English Literature* (New York, 1960). M. Hay, *Europe and
the Jews* (Boston, 1960).

this has had an unfortunate effect on scholarship, for it has
tended to push modern reactions to modern anti-Semitism
into a past where they do not apply. Dr Parkes has noted
that the anti-Semitism of the Christian tradition depended on
a different set of assumptions: 'Chrysostom's Jew was a
theological necessity rather than a living person' (*The
Conflict of the Church and Synagogue*, p. 166); and again,
'It is always the historical picture of the Jews in the Old
Testament which moves the eloquence of the [Patristic]
writers,[7] never the misdoings of their living, Jewish neigh-
bours' (ibid., p. 374). Guido Kisch, writing on the problem of
'Jews in medieval law' points out the ease with which we can
distort early anti-Semitism by imposing upon it a modern
racialist interpretation; he quotes from the *Schwabenspiegel*,
a law book of *c.* 1275, the penalty (death by fire) for sexual
relations between a Christian and a Jew. Is not this a concern
for racial purity? The author denies that it is so. The crime is
described as 'denial of Christian faith'. 'Considerations of a
religious nature alone are here at play. Of racial ideas not the
slightest trace is discoverable.'[8] Dr Cardozo in *The Contemporary Jew in Elizabethan Drama* (Amsterdam, 1925) makes
the further point that 'Marlowe's Barabas and Shakespeare's
Shylock are both replicas of the Jew as conceived by the
medieval imagination'. The Elizabethan word 'Jew', in fact,
like many other words which are nowadays taken in an exact
racialist sense ('Moor' and 'Turk' are the obvious other
examples), was a word of general abuse, whose sense, in so
far as it had one, was dependent on a theological rather than
an ethnographical framework. To make this point is the
specified aim of H. Michelson's book:

I intend to show that the New Testament and nothing but the
New Testament is to be blamed for the peculiar psychology of the
Jew in literature, that down to and inclusive of Shylock this psychology was never based on observation, but simply taken over
from the New Testament (pp. 4–5).

Dr Cardozo makes much the same point, supposing that the
explanation lies in the fact that England was still, in the

7. See F. Murawski, *Die Juden bei den Kirchenvätern und Scholastikern*
(1925), *passim*.
8. *Essays on Antisemitism* (New York, 1946 edn), p. 108.

Elizabethan period, 'a country bare of racial Jews'.[9] This must have been a factor but it does not seem to have been the central one. The whole Elizabethan frame of reference discouraged racial thinking. As late as 1582 we find the stage Jew swearing by Mahomet; in the Anglican service the Third Collect for Good Friday maintained the old attitude (and maintains it to this day) in praying for 'all Jews, Turks, Infidels and Heretics' as a group defined by faith (or lack of it) rather than race.[1]

The usual critical attitude to Marlowe's Jew is that the author (himself an 'outsider') has sympathetically identified himself with the powerful and magnetic alien figure in the opening scenes of the play, though, to be sure, he later loses interest and 'the Jew becomes the mere plaything of the popular imagination' (Bennett, p. 17). My aim in this article is to show that there is no reversal of general attitude; the Jew who descends to the cauldron in Act v has the same status as the Jew who counts his money in Act I, though, to be sure, there are plenty of ironic counter-currents throughout. Indeed if we allow that the structure of concepts in the play is theological and not racial, we must also allow that a bid for personal sympathy cannot *determine* our attitude; for the theological status of the Jew, typified by the name Barabas, was fixed and immutable until he ceased to be a Jew.[2]

One particular passage in the play defines this problem of status for us quite clearly; I refer to that speech in the opening scene, in which Barabas congratulates himself on his Jewish prosperity:

> Thus trowles our fortune in by land and Sea,
> And thus are wee on every side inrich'd:

9. On the evidence for Jewish colonies in London, see S. L. Lee, *Transactions of the New Shakspere Society 1887–92*, pp. 143 ff.; Bakeless, op cit. i. 363; C. J. Sisson, 'A colony of Jews in Shakespeare's London', *E.S.A.E.* xxiii (1937), 38–51.

1. Cf. Fynes Moryson: 'The Jewes are a nation incredibly dispised among all Christians, and of the Turkes also . . . They are a miserable nation and most miserable in that they cannot see the cause thereof, being the curse of the blood of their Messiah, which they tooke upon themselves and their children' (*Shakespeare's Europe*, ed. C. Hughes [1903], p. 487).

2. Michelson points out that in the *Cursor Mundi* 'the Jewish peculiarities disappear as if by magic by turning Christian' (op. cit., pp. 47 f.).

> These are the Blessings promised to the Jewes,
> And herein was old Abram's happinesse:
> What more may Heaven doe for earthly man
> Then thus to powre out plenty in their laps,
> Ripping the bowels of the earth for them,
> Making the Sea their servant, and the winds
> To drive their substance with successfull blasts? (141–9)

The natural modern tendency is to see this as a piece of proper racial piety, with Barabas as a sympathetic, though alien, figure honouring his own patriarch. From a Christian point of view, however, this relativism cannot be maintained; if Abraham and the other patriarchs of the Old Testament belong to the Christian tradition, they cannot belong to the Jewish one; and the Jewish invocation of them is not simply alien but actually subversive. This is the burden of the innumerable treatises *adversus Judaeos* which stretch through the Fathers, both Greek and Latin—to remove the Old Testament from the Jews and shackle its prophecies and promises to the New Testament. And Paul himself had given the lead in this matter. In Romans 9: 3–8 we may read:

For I would wish my selfe to bee separated from Christ, for my brethren that are my kinsemen according to the flesh:
Which are the Israelites, to whom pertaineth the adoption, and the glorie, and the Covenaunts, and the giving of the Lawe, and the service of God, and the promises;
Of whom are the fathers, and of whom concerning the flesh Christ came, who is God over all, blessed for ever, Amen.
Nothwithstanding it cannot bee that the Word of God should take none effect.
For all they are not Israel, which are of Israel.
Neither are they all children because they are the seede of Abraham: but in [Isaac] shall thy seede be called.
That is, They which are the children of the flesh, are not the children of God: but the children of the promise, are counted for the seede.

Again, in Galatians 3: 13–16, 29:

Christ hath redeemed us from the curse of the Law . . .
That the blessing of Abraham might come on the Gentiles through Christ Jesus, that we might receive the promise of the Spirit through faith.

Brethren, I speake as men do . . .
Now to Abraham and his seede were the promises made. He
saith not, And to the seeds, as speaking of many; but, And to thy
seed, as of one, which is Christ.

. . .

And if ye be Christs, then are yee Abrahams seed, and heires by
promise.

Luther, in his extended commentary on Galatians (published
in English in 1575) notes how the Jews use Abraham's
blessing 'applying it only to a carnal blessing, and do great
injury to Scripture' (1953 reprint, p. 237), for it was not what
Abraham *did* that made him blessed but what he believed
(p. 240). He cites the passage from Romans and notes, 'By
this argument he [Paul] mightily stoppeth the mouths of the
proud Jews, which gloried that they were the seed and children of Abraham' (p. 416). The Jews may be children 'after
the flesh', but 'we are the children of the promise, as Isaac
was; that is to say, of grace and faith, born only of the
promise' (pp. 345, 430).[3]

It is in the context of such views that we should look not
only at this passage, but also at Barabas's later self-con-
gratulation, while he is enticing Don Lodowick to his doom.
He walks *aside* to share his vicious thoughts with the
audience:

LODOWICK. Whither walk'st thou, Barabas?
BARABAS. No further: 'tis a custome held with us

3. Luther uses the patristic notion that the Jews were represented in the
Abraham story by the figure of Ishmael, and the Christians by Isaac. Isidore has
this to say on Genesis 17–21:

'Hic iam declaratur promissio de vocatione gentium in Isaac filio promis-
sionis, quo significatur gratia, non natura, quia de sene patre et sterili matre.
Et quia hoc non per generationem, quae est in Ismaele, sed per regenerationem
futurum erat, ideo imperata est circumcisio, quod de Sara promittitur filius in
typo Ecclesiae, non quando Ismael, qui typum gerit Judaeorum.'

And again later,

'Sara vero libera populum genuit qui non est secundum carnem, sed in
libertatem vocatus est, qua libertate liberavit Christus . . . quid ergo significat
quod exiens Agar infantem in humeros suos imposuit? nisi quod peccator
populus et insipiens cervicem matris suae Synagogae gravavit, dum dixit:
Sanguis eius super nos et super filios nostros.'

(Quaestiones in Vet. Test., *P.L.* lxxxiii, cols 242, 248.) Cf. *P.L.* lxxxiii. 270,
xcii. 1007.

That when we speake with Gentiles like to you,
We turne into the Ayre to purge our selves:
For unto us the Promise doth belong.   (804–8)

Barabas speaks the last line with the self-confidence or
'security' that the Jew (theologically conceived) was supposed to feel; but a Christian audience could hardly be
expected to endorse the anti-Christian sentiments it contains;
for the 'promise' was the very thing that the Gentiles were
believed to have been given. We may quote one last Pauline
text to this effect:

For the promise that he should be the heire of the world, was not
given to Abraham, or to his seed, through the Law, but through
the righteousnes of faith.   (Romans 4: 13)

In the context of such statements, Barabas's self-congratu-
lation in the first passage quoted may seem to be a clear
expression of that preference for the flesh rather than the
spirit, which the original 'Jewish choice' of Barabbas rather
than Christ was taken to imply. Barabas's joy in what he
calls, with complete orthodoxy, 'the blessings promised to
the Jews' (money, or The Flesh) may seem to be rather like
Faustus's joy in the 'paradise' of the seven deadly sins. Indeed,
even without the theological framework one might suspect
that statements like

What more may Heaven doe for earthly man
Then thus to powre out plenty in their laps,
Ripping the bowels of the earth for them?
                              (145–7)

were loaded against the speaker; the method is more like
that of the opening scene in *Volpone* than has been generally
admitted, if we will allow that the contrasting spiritual ideal,
there explicit ('Open the shrine that I may see my saint'), is
here implicit in orthodox theology.

A far more important sequence of ironic contrasts in the
play is concerned with the figure of Job. The biblically
minded would be quick to notice the reference in the opening
lines of the play:

So that of thus much that returne was made:
And of the third part of the Persian ships,

There was the venture summ'd and satisfied.
As for those [Samnites], and the men of Uzz, etc.
                                                    (36–39)

'Uzz' is, of course, a country only known from the opening
verse of Job:

There was a man in the land of Uz, called Job, etc.

The echo is not allowed to lie fallow very long; about 130
lines later, '*Enter three Jews*', one of whom bears the sugges-
tive name of Temainte (215); this is usually supposed to be
some perversion of the name of one of Job's three friends,
Eliphaz the *Temanite*. In the next scene the three friends
appear as comforters, in what is clearly a parody of Job's
afflictions. Marlowe here cites the actual book of Job, following the Geneva version with literal fidelity:

. . . to inherit here
The months of vanity, and losse of time,
And painefull nights have bin appointed me.
                                                    (429–31)

. . . had as an inheritance the moneths of vanity,
and painefull nights have bene appointed unto me.
                                                    (vii. 3)

The reference to Job here is not incidental 'Jewish' colouring,
but is indeed central to the whole conception of Barabas.

Yet, brother Barabas, remember Job
                    (143)

says the First Comforter. The parallel is cited in order to
present Barabas as the opposite, as an Anti-Job, characterized
by his *impatience* (l. 497), and choosing the road, not of
Christian patience, but of its opposite, revenge.[4] The Fathers
had referred to Barabbas as the type of Antichrist; in presenting Barabas as Anti-Job, Marlowe is not departing very far
from this, for Job was one of the greatest of the 'types' of
Christ found in the Old Testament, his descent into poverty
mirroring Christ's into the flesh, and his patient triumph over
Satan foretelling Christ's final triumph.[5]

4. For Revenge as the opposite of Patience see the *Magna Moralia* of Gregory
the Great (*P.L.* lxxv, lxxvi), comment on Job 4: 2 ff.
5. The parallel had its most famous exposition in Gregory's *Magna Moralia*,
reflected in Odo of Cluny (*P.L.* cxxxiii) and Bruno of Asti (*P.L.* clxiv).

Indeed the whole course of Barabas's career can be seen as
a parody of Job's; both men begin in great prosperity, and
then, for what appears to be no good reason, lose their
possessions; both are restored to prosperity before the end of
the action; both are accused of justifying themselves in the
face of their adversity. But there the parallel ends; the frame
of mind in which these events are lived through is precisely
opposite. Barabas's self-justification and self-will proceeds
from a monstrous egotism, which is the basis of his character.[6]

> How ere the world goe, I'le make sure for one . . .
> *Ego mihimet sum semper proximus.*   (225 ff.)

Job's justification, however one takes the difficult point,
must be seen to spring from an anguished awareness that
God is unanswerably just. Barabas recalls Job's curse on
himself (iii. 3):

> So that not he, but I may curse the day,
> Thy fatall birth-day, forlorne Barabas;
> And henceforth wish for an eternall night,
> That clouds of darknesse may inclose my flesh,
> And hide these extreme sorrowes from mine eyes.
> (424–8)

But Job's words acquire in the mouth of a revenger a meaning which they could not have from the 'pattern of all
patience'. Gregory the Great points out that just men (such
as Job) do not curse for vengeance, 'non . . . ex voto ultionis,
sed ex iustitiae examine erumpunt . . . non est eius maledictio
ex malitia delinquentis, sed ex rectitudine judicis' (*P.L.*
lxxv. 639); and the whole effort of the Christian appropria-
tion of Job was to distinguish between the action of a man
whose vision of this world was coloured by an awareness
'that my Redeemer liveth', and the superficially similar action
of the man whose vision is limited to this world. 'Ye judge
after the flesh', said Christ to the Pharisees (John 8: 15); and
Isaac Barrow is carrying on a long tradition when he remarks that Jewish observances are 'justifications of the mere

6. Cf. Gower, *Confessio Amantis* (ed. Macaulay, iii. 321):

> I am a Jew, and be mi lawe
> I schal to noman be felawe

flesh' . . . 'for their Religion in its surface (deeper than which their gross fancy could not penetrate) did represent earthly wealth, dignity and prosperity as things highly valuable; did propound them as very proper (if not as the sole) rewards of piety and obedience; did imply consequently the possession of them to be certain arguments of the Divine good-will and regard.'[7] Barabas is a 'Jewish' Job, in this theological (non-racial) sense of the word 'Jew'; hence an anti-Christian Job, who sees the loss of his wealth as a physical disaster, as a matter for despair (l. 496), and not at all as a spiritual trial, who supposes that recovery of prosperity is simply a matter of buying and selling (men or towns) at a sufficiently advantageous rate.

This parody of Job's spiritual Odyssey in terms of Barabas's fleshly one is, of course, conducted chiefly in terms of his wealth or treasure. Indeed the whole play can be seen in Empsonian terms as an extended pun on the word 'treasure'. Barabas's attitude to treasure is clearly different from that recommended to Christians:

Lay not up treasures for your selves upon the earth . . .
But lay up treasures for your selves in heaven . . .
For where your treasure is, there will your heart be also.
. . .
No man can serve two masters: for either he shall hate the one, and love the other; or else he shall lean to the one, and despise the other. Ye cannot serve God and riches.   (Matthew 6: 19–24)

An extended passage in the book of Job (25: 12 ff.) lists the precious objects that are valueless when compared to the wisdom which is in 'the fear of the Lord'—gold, onyx, sapphire, crystal, coral, pearls, rubies, 'the topaz of Ethiopia'; the list sounds like an enumeration of Barabas's 'infinite riches'; but to Barabas these represent the sum of human felicity, the ultimate treasure, whereas Job, a little later, puts them into their true relative position:

If I restrained the poore of their desire, or have caused the eyes of the widow to faile, . . .

7. *The Theological Works of Isaac Barrow*, ed. A. Napier (Cambridge, 1859), v. 435, vi. 33. As early as Augustine Christian writers were accusing the Jewish religion of being one that supposed 'God . . . to be worshipped for earthly benefits' (*City of God*, v. xviii).

If I made gold mine hope, or have said, to the wedge of gold,
Thou art my confidence,
If I rejoyced because my substance was great, or because mine
hand had gotten much, . . .
If I rejoyced at his destruction that hated me, or was mooved
to joy when evill came upon him,
Neither have I suffered my mouth to sinne, by wishing a curse
unto his soule, . . .
Let thistles grow in stead of wheate, and cockle in the stead of
barley.   (xxxi. 16–40)

The actions that Job is denying are precisely those that
Barabas rejoices in, and again he appears as an anti-Job.

We may look back to Herbert's poem quoted at the beginning of this paper and note how quickly 'this world's delights'
are particularized in the 'false gain' of gold, as its most telling
example. In Herbert's poem it is Judas,[8] not Barabbas, who
represents this aspect of the 'Jewish choice', but the theological view of Jewish usury is not to be explained by any one
figure; Judas's choice, preferring thirty pieces of silver to the
life of his Lord, is easy to conflate with the general Jewish
choice of Barabbas rather than Christ. The Fathers collected
types to explain the theological status of the Jews, though
they seldom bothered to relate them to one another; but
everywhere they looked they found avarice, whether in Cain
(whose 'mark' was said to be *signum avaritiae*)[9] or in the
brethren of Joseph; for their sale of their brother was read as
an anticipation of the Jewish 'sale' of Christ.[1] The Jewish
usurer was no doubt a known contemporary figure in Marlowe's day, even if absent from England; but Marlowe's
Barabas is not presented primarily in terms of economic

8. The idea that *Judas* was the eponym of the *Judaei* was particularly attractive to the etymologically minded Fathers. See Leo the Great (sermon 29),
P.L. li, cols 313–15, cxvii, col. 775, lxxxiii, col. 479.
9. Bonaventura, *Opera Omnia*, xiii (ed. Peltier, Paris, 1864–71), 293. Cain, in
the Towneley Plays, is characterized by his desire to cheat God over the number
of sheaves in the sacrifice (cf. Chester Plays [E.E.T.S.], p. 41) just as Judas is, in
the haggling over thirty pieces of silver. In some legends about Judas he is
branded in a manner reminiscent of Cain (see W. D. Hand, 'A dictionary of
words and idioms associated with Judas Iscariot', *University of California
Publications in Modern Philology*, xxiv [1942], s.v. *Judasmärket*).
1. See Bonaventura, xi. 136b, and Glossa Ordinaria on Genesis 37 et seq.
Cf. the *Mystère du Viel Testament*, ll. 16760 ff., 16936 ff.

reality.[2] Marlowe's interest seems to be rather in the contrast between a fabulous degree of wealth, and a spiritual sterility which, throughout the play, cries out for fruition and is not answered, just as in *Volpone*. If this is true, then the standard critical view that Barabas's wealth represents a kind of spiritual hunger for the infinite, is ludicrously inappropriate.[3]

The most famous line in the play is presumably that with which Barabas sums up his vision of desirable riches:

Infinite riches in a little roome. (72)

This line is usually taken to express a transfiguration of avarice into poetic rapture, as the Helen speech in *Faustus* is supposed to transfigure lust into idealism. It has been pointed out several times in recent years, however, that the Helen speech contains a great deal that is other than poetic rapture, and much indeed that implies detachment of the author from the action that is depicted, and criticism of it. I suggest that the 'Infinite riches' line is also less simple than has been implied, and contains in itself the material by which we 'distance' and judge Barabas's passion for treasure.

An external witness that the line involves echoes, which would have been more audible to Renaissance readers than to modern ones, can be found in a note by Professor Helen Gardner, to a line of Donne's 'Annunciation' sonnet:

... shutst in little roome
Immensity cloystered in thy deare wombe.

'Donne rarely appears to borrow from another English poet', writes Miss Gardner, 'but cf. "Infinite riches in a little room".' At the same time Miss Gardner quotes the Matins Hymn in the feasts of the Virgin, 'The cloistre of Marie

2. David Strumpf notes that even in France, where the economic and social reality of the Jewish usurer was not in doubt, 'Die Anfänge der Figur des judischen Wucherers in der französichen Literatur finden sich schon in den "Mystères de la Passion", nämlich dort, wo Judas Christum um dreissig silberlinge an die Juden verkauft' (*Die Juden in der mittelalterichen Mysterien, Mirakel und Moralitaten Dichtung Frankreichs*, p. 30).

3. F. S. Boas, *Shakspere and his Predecessors* (1896), says 'avarice becomes transfigured. It ceases to be a sordid vice and swells to the proportions of a passion for the infinite' (p. 50). Bennett cites this and adds, 'We have thus in Marlowe's Jew a vein of idealism'.

berith him whom the erthe, watris and hevenes worshipen'. Miss Gardner would seem to be correct in finding a similarity between the Marlowe line and the Donne one, but it seems doubtful if Donne here made an exception and went to a profane poet for an image which lay everywhere around him in the poetry and liturgy of the medieval church. The similarity of the two lines would seem to derive from a tradition[4] which gives resonance and meaning to Marlowe's image, and sets Barabas's treasure against the spiritual treasure represented by Christ.

The Marlowe line actually draws on two persistent images of Christ *in utero Virginis*. One tradition contrasts the 'little room' of the Virgin's womb with the infinitude of Christ's power:[5]

> Quem totus orbis non capit
> Portant puellae viscera

says the hymn *Agnoscat omne saeculum* of Venantius Fortunatus.[6] We may quote the same author a second time:

> Beata mater munere
> Cuius supernus artifex
> Mundum pugillo continens
> Ventris sub arca clausus est.
> ('*Quem terra . . .*')[7]

St Ambrose in his hymn *A solis ortus* says

> Creator cuncti generis
> Orbis quem totus non capit
> In tua, sancta genetrix
> Sese reclusit viscera.[8]

St Damasus in *Christe potens rerum* (Carmen II) has

4. The fullest documentation of this tradition is in Yrjö Hirn, *The Sacred Shrine* (1912), pp. 451 ff., where the European diffusion of the commonplace is well illustrated.

5. J. W. Parkes notes that the Jews, when they denied the divinity of Christ, pointed out that if the heavens were not able to hold the glory of God he could not be contained in the womb of a woman. (*The Conflict of the Church and Synagogue* [1934], p. 114.)

6. H. A. Daniel, *Thesaurus Hymnorum*, i (Leipzig, 1855), 159.

7. Ibid. i. 172.

8. Ibid. i. 21. The editor compares Luther, 'Den aller Weltkreis nie beschloss / Der liegt in Mariens Schooss.'

... sub imo
Pectore, quo totum late complectitur Orbem.
Et qui non spatiis terrae non aequoris undis
Nec capitur caelo, parvos confluxit in artus.[9]

The responsary to the sixth lesson of the second nocturn of the Office *In nativitate Domini* says:

quem coeli capere non poterant, tuo gremio contulisti.[1]

Peter Damian speaks of

maiestatem illius virginalis ventris brevitate conclusam. O venter diffusior coelis terris amplior ... qui totum claudit omnia concludentem in quo Deus gloriae reclinatur.[2]

Hugh of St Victor,

quod non capit mundus, totum se intra viscera virginis collocavit.[3]

and Bonaventura,

quem totus non capit orbis, in tua se clausit viscera factus homo.[4]

It will be noticed that not only the image but even the wording is repeated from writer to writer. From Latin devotional prose or verse to the Middle English counterparts is a very small step indeed, but one may quote the Middle English poem 'There is no rose of swich vertu' (an expansion of the *Laetabundus* of St Bernard):

> For in this rose conteined was
> Hevene and erthe in litel space,
> *Res miranda.*[5]

In Renaissance Latin we have Giles Fletcher,

> Quem nec mare, aether, terra, non coelum capit,
> Utero puellae totus angusto latens.[6]

And Crashawe,

> Pellibus exiguis arctatur Filius ingens,
> Quem tu non totum (crede) nec ipsa capis.

9. *P.L.* xiii, col. 376.
1. *Breviarium Romanum.*
2. *P.L.* cxliv, col. 558.   3. *P.L.* clxxv, col. 415.
4. *Opera Omnia*, xiv. 245a.
5. Sidgwick and Chambers, *Early English Lyrics* (1907), no. lii.
6. *Christ's Victory and Triumph* (ed. Grosart, 1876, p. 244).

> Quanta uteri, Regina, tui reverentia tecum est,
> Dum jacet hic, caelo sub breviore, Deus.[7]

The same authors make similar points in English; Fletcher speaks of the Virgin's *arms*:

> See how small roome my infant Lord doth take,
> Whom all the world is not enough to hold.[8]

And Crashawe describes the situation as

> Æternity shutt in a span[9]

It is clear then that one tradition of images expresses the paradox of infinitude in little space, and that this tradition stretches before and after Marlowe, so that we may suppose it accessible to him and to his audience. A second tradition stressed not so much the infinite extent of Christ's power as its infinite richness. The Virgin's womb was not only 'litel space' but also infinitely rich in a monetary sense. The comparison of Christ to jewels, gold, silver, coinage, is too obvious to require illustration, and I shall limit my examples to contexts where this idea is associated with the Virgin's womb. I have already mentioned the passage in Job where Wisdom is preferred to precious stones. A similar sentiment appears in Proverbs (8: 19):

> My fruit is better than gold, yea, than fine gold; and my revenue than choice silver.

By a natural transition from Wisdom to the Virgin, we find this verse being applied to her in the second lectio in the first nocturn of the Feasts of the Blessed Virgin.[1] In possessing Christ the Virgin is infinitely rich;[2] her womb, in consequence, is seen as a treasury, a purse, an alms-box or a mint. As George Herbert says of her:

---

7. 'Deus sub utero virginis', in *Poems*, ed. L. C. Martin (Oxford, 1927), p. 23.
8. *Christ's Victory and Triumph*, i. 79 (Grosart, p. 157).
9. 'In the holy Nativity', *Poems*, ed. Martin, p. 250.
1. *Breviarium Romanum*, 'In Festis Beatae Mariae Virginis'.
2. See, for example, the comment of Rupert of Deutz on Canticles 5: 2: 'Quid tam pretiosum, ut hoc verbum? Ego dilecta pondus auri huius ineffabiliter in memetipsa persenis, quando de caeol in uterum meum descendit ... verum etiam delectaretur pondere eius parvitas uteri mei, cum sit ipse quem tremunt angeli, quem totus non capit orbis.' (*P.L.* clxviii, col. 1922.)

Thou art the holy mime, whence came the gold . . .
Thou art the cabinet where the jewel lay
             ('To all angels and saints')

Donne has a typically extended conceit on the idea of the womb as mint:

for this work [*the Atonement*], to make Christ able to pay this debt, there was something to be added to him. First, he must pay it in such money as was lent; in the nature and flesh of man; for man had sinned, and man must pay. And then it was lent in such money as was coyned even with the Image of God; man was made according to his Image: That Image being defaced, in a new Mint, in the wombe of the Blessed Virgin, there was new money coyned: The Image of the invisible God, the second person in the Trinity, was imprinted into the humane nature. And then, that there might bee *omnis plenitudo*, all fulnesse, as God, for the paiment of this debt, sent downe the Bullion, and the stamp, that is, God to be conceived in man, and as he provided the Mint, the womb of the Blessed Virgin, so hath he provided an Exchequer, where this mony is issued; that is his Church . . .³

The image in 2 Corinthians 4: 7, 'habemus thesaurum in vasis fictilibus—we have this treasure in earthen vessels', is a natural place to notice the collocation of the infinite richness of the treasure (Christ) and the humility of the vessel. *Vas*⁴ is one of the recurring images of the Virgin, both small and humble. St Bernard refers to the Virgin as *vasculum Dei capax*⁵—the idea of immensity in a little room⁶ again.

    Thus the double paradox of Marlowe's line, infinite extent in little space and infinite wealth in humble surroundings is already present in a religious tradition which sets the

    3. *Sermons*, iv, ed. Potter and Simpson, p. 288.
    4. See the thirteen columns of *vas* titles in J. J. Bourassé, *Summa aurea de laudibus B.V.M.* (Paris, 1862–6, 13 vols), x. 450–62.
    5. So quoted in Migne's 'Index Marianus', but I have not been able to verify the reference. Yrjö Hirn (op. cit., p. 452) quotes Lionardo Giustiniani to the same effect:
                O vaso picciolino, in cui si posa
                Colui, che il Ciel non piglia.
    6. The 'little room' was itself an image of the Virgin's womb. Bourassé cites innumerable examples of *camera, domus, casa, domicilium, cella, cellula, tabernaculum, habitaculum* used in this way. In Middle English poetry we find 'chamber of the Trinity' (Brown and Robbins, *Index of Middle English Poetry*, 2107), 'Christes bur' (*Index* 2988), 'bygly bowre . . . chief chambre . . . conclave and clostre clene' (*Index* 3297), 'closet' in Dunbar's 'Haile stern superne'

thesaurus of Christianity against the treasure of those who judge by the flesh. St Bernard of Clairvaux, who most elaborately celebrated the Virgin as *thesaurus Dei*, puts them together with great brevity:

In te sola Rex ille dives et praedives exinanitus; excelsus, humiliatus; immensus, abbreviatus . . .[7]

Bonaventura, preaching *in nativitate domini*, draws on a phrase of Wisdom which is close to Marlowe, *infinitus thesaurus est hominibus* (Wisdom 7: 14), and applies this to the nativity in terms of the parable of the treasure that was hidden in a field (Matthew 13: 44); Christ is the true treasure though hidden in human nature. The moral he draws is one which might well serve as a gloss on Barabas's line: 'O avare, hunc thesaurum quaere, qui finiri non potest'[8]—seek infinite riches in the only place where infinity can exist. The treasure that is Christ exists for the use of others ('hominibus'—later he calls Him *thesaurus mendicis*) and here again the contrast between the sterile treasure that is hoarded by man and the liberal treasure that is disbursed by God is obvious: 'fructus ventris Mariae est liberalium contra avaritiam.'[9] Barabas remarks of his jewels that

> . . . one of them indifferently rated,
> And of a Carrect of this quantity,
> May serve in perill of calamity
> To ransome great kings from captivity.
>
> (64–67)

But we know that the only king that Barabas will rescue is himself; the magnificence of his imagery is shown up by the framework of belief to be base at heart.

There is one other passage in the play where the pun on the word *treasure* seems to be central. Barabas's house is seized and converted into a nunnery; but, not to be outdone in policy, he persuades his daughter Abigail[1] to enter the house

7. *P.L.* clxxxiii, col. 396.
8. *Opera Omnia*, xiii. 49b.
9. Ibid. xiv. 287a.
1. Abigail, the wife of Nabal (1 Samuel 25) is seen by some commentators as a type of the Jews who were converted to Christianity. See *P.L.* cix, col. 64.

as a novice so that she may dig up the treasure that he has
hidden there. This gives Marlowe a splendid opportunity to
play off his contrasting values, the fruits of the spirit and the
fruits of commerce, one against the other, with the full
brilliance of savage farce. Abigail, prompted by her father,
requests of the Abbess that she may

> . . . lodge where I was wont to lye.
> I doe not doubt by your divine precepts
> And mine owne industry, but to profit much.
>
> (574–6)

Marlowe cannot resist the pun on *profit*, and Barabas in an
Aside interprets for our benefit, what he supposes the line to
mean:

> As much, I hope, as all I hid is worth. (577)

We find the same play on these ideas in a later scene where
Barabas is teasing the Governor's son towards his destruction:

> Your father . . .
> Seiz'd all I had, and thrust me out a doores,
> And made my house a place for nuns most chast.
> LODOWICK. No doubt your soule shall reape the fruit of it.
> BARABAS. [Ay], but my lord, the harvest is farre off:
> And yet I know the prayers of those Nuns
> And holy Fryers, having money for their paines,
> Are wondrous *and indeed doe no man good*:   *Aside.*
> And seeing they are not idle, but still doing,
> 'Tis likely they in time may reape some fruit,
> I meane in fulnesse of perfection.   (833–48)

There is a variety of innuendos here; the nuns and friars are
lecherous ('still doing') and in the perfection[2] (of their
womanhood) the nuns may produce the fruit (of bastardy);
again, they are greedy ('having money for their pains'); but

2. Cf. Marston's *Antonio's Revenge*, III. ii. 11: 'woman receiveth perfection
by the man.' In *Hero and Leander*, I. 266 ff., Marlowe speaks of

> . . . men's impression . . .
> By which alone, our reverend fathers say,
> Woman receave perfection everie way

The refrain of Donne's 'Epithalamium made at Lincoln's Inn' runs,

> To-day put on perfection and a womans name.

behind this, as behind the earlier passage is a deeper play on the idea of profit, spiritual or financial.

The austere life which Abigail promises to engage in, when she is accepted into the nunnery, will lead to *profit*, by repaying the debt owed to God for her sinful past. Behind this lies the whole theory of monastic deprivation. The *Catholic Encyclopaedia* tells us that 'by penance they [the contemplatives] strive to atone for the offences of sinful humanity, to appease God's wrath and ward off its direful effects by giving vicarious satisfaction to the demands of his justice'. The nunnery which has been set up in Barabas's house is thus, in a new sense, still a place of profit.[3] Marlowe's pun on *thesaurus* here would seem to be justified by the monetary and financial imagery in which this aspect of the church's power was often expressed. The later scholastics spoke of a *thesaurus Ecclesiae* or *thesaurus meritorum* to which the church, like a banker, had *keys*. This 'treasury of merits' had accumulated a massive credit balance because of works done in excess of those required *ad mensuram debitorum suorum* (as the *Summa Theologica* puts it [III. Q. 25, A. 1]). The vows of poverty, chastity, and obedience which the nuns have taken are such 'works of supererogation', and the profit that they produce is part of

3. One of the images of a cloister was a *gazophylacium* or alms-box. The explanation of this in Peter Cellensis' *Tractatus de Disciplina Claustrali* is worth quoting:

'Est et gazophylacium claustrum, ubi aurum, argentum et lapides pretiosi reconduntur; et ubi thesaurum nostrum in vasis fictilibus, id est conscientiam bonam in observantiis regularibus habemus. In claustro thesauri sunt sibi vitam aeternam negotiantes religiosi, quibus homo nobilis peregre proficiscens tradidt bona sua; singuli psalmi, singulae orationes, singulae confessiones, singulae lacrymae, singula jejunia, singulae eleemosynae, singulae immemorabilium laborum afflictiones, nonne acervum faciunt gratiarum, quae est thesaurus desiderabilis in congregatione claustrali? Super gazas istas eunuchus Candacis reginae constituitur. Cando ille qui se castravit propter regna caelorum, in officio praelationis praeficitur; siquidem pudicitiae et castitatis titulo insignitus, tanquam renibus accinctus custos sponsae Christi non immerito constituitur...
(*P.L.* ccii, col. 1118)

Cf. *The Rewle of Sustris Menouresses enclosid* [E.E.T.S. o.s. 148 (1914)]:

'For as moche we purchasin þe more willi[nglye] þe encrese of religioun, as bi þat þe continementis of owre lorde been encresid, and þe helþe of sowles þereof comiþ to profite... Eche womman... for to dwelle alle dayes of her life enclosid as a tresoure kepte to þe sovereyne kynge.   (p. 81 f.)

what Marlowe's age called a 'treasure', though it is not the kind of treasure that Barabas is interested in.

Lest the doctrine of supererogatory works and the *thesaurus meritorum* seem too remote from life to be known by a mere playwright, we ought to observe that this was one of the dogmas which it was difficult for anyone with the slightest acquaintance with the reformers to avoid. For the doctrine of a surplusage of merits is what lies behind the practice of selling Indulgences, and is indeed one of the doctrines which is specifically named in the thirty-nine articles as abhorrent to the Anglican Church (Article 14). Nearly all the reformers, Luther,[4] Calvin,[5] and the Anglican divines[6] through to Andrewes[7] and Barrow,[8] mention it as one of the most noxious of Roman beliefs. We may assume that Marlowe knew about it.

The final twist of the ironic screw in the episode of the nunnery appears in Barabas's instructions to his daughter:

BARABAS. Child of perdition,[9] and thy fathers shame,
    What wilt thou doe among these hatefull fiends?
    I charge thee on my blessing that thou leave
    These divels and their damned heresie.
ABIGAIL. Father, give me—
BARABAS.   Nay backe, Abigall.
    And thinke upon the jewels and the gold,   ⎰ *Whispers*
    The boord is marked thus that covers it.   ⎱ *to her*
    Away, accursed, from thy fathers sight.

4. Luther, 'Explanation of the 95 theses' (*Luther's Works*, xxxi [Philadelphia, 1957], 244 f.).
   5. Calvin, *On the necessity of reforming the church* (*Theological Treatises*, ed. J. K. S. Reid [Library of Christian Classics] [1954], p. 200).
   6. See, for example, Becon, *Acts of Christ and of Antichrist* (Parker Soc. iii. 527 f.) and *A comfortable epistle* (iii. 200), and Hooker, *Laws*, VI. v. 9.
   7. *Responsio ad Apologiam Cardinalis Bellarmini*, ed. Bliss (Oxford, 1851), p. 267 f.
   8. *A Treatise of the Pope's Supremacy*, *Works*, viii. 320.
   9. This phrase must be allowed to have ironic overtones. 'Child of perdition' is the Geneva translation of John 17: 12 ('son of perdition' in the A.V.), in a context where it is usually allowed to have particular reference to Judas (see, for example, Augustine, *Ennaratio in Psalmum CVIII* [*P.L.* xxxvii, cols 1431 ff.]). The parallel usage in 2 Thess. 2: 3 ('son of perdition' in all English versions) where Antichrist seems to be intended, may also have influenced Marlowe's mind. In any case there is a fairly obvious irony in the application of the phrase to the most Christian (and least Judas-like) character in the play, and in the grammatical equation of Barabas himself with 'perdition'.

FRIAR JACOMO. Barabas, although thou art in mis-beleefe,
  And wilt not see thine owne afflictions,
  Yet let thy daughter be no longer blinde.
BARABAS. Blind, Fryer, I wrecke not thy perswasions.
  The boord is marked thus † that covers it   (585–98)

The resurrection that Barabas expects from under the sign of
the cross on his upper-chamber floor is not spiritual one; the
profit he hopes to extract from the nunnery is judged 'after
the flesh'; his 'soul's sole hope', like his ship the *Speranza*, is
freighted only for the earthliest kind of voyage:

> Now I remember those old womens words,
> Who in my wealth wud tell me winters tales,
> And speake of spirits and ghosts that glide by night
> About the place where treasure hath bin hid:
> And now me thinkes that I am one of those:
> For whilst I live, here lives my soules sole hope,
> And when I dye, here shall my spirit walke. (663–9)

The multiple ironies of the savage farce in these nunnery
scenes may indicate to us the dramatic flexibility of Marlowe's handling of his theological knowledge; there is no
suggestion of the *drame à thèse*, no wooden enactment of
predetermined attitudes. The framework of belief in the play
is, I have suggested, quite rigid, but there is a continuous
fluctuation of sympathy backwards and forwards round the
figure of Barabas himself. In this the play is extraordinarily
like *Doctor Faustus*: the religious status of the hero is never in
doubt; he has fatally mistaken the nature of value; the Hell
he lives in does not permit escapes; but like those earlier
denizens of 'the old English humour',[1] the emissaries of Hell
in the medieval Moralities—Iniquity, Ill-Report, Ambidexter,
Titivillus, etc.—Barabas takes us a good deal of the way with
him in his scorn of the other characters in the play. *Faustus*
reveals the poetry that is latent in the self-deceptions of a
damned soul; we cannot quarrel with the justice of his
damnation, but Marlowe keeps our response in motion by a
counter-balance of admiration for Faustus's powers and
sympathies. In *The Jew of Malta* the same balance is

---

1. T. S. Eliot, *Selected Essays* (1934), p. 123.

achieved, though by different methods. The theological status of the Jew is not in doubt; but he is placed among Christians whose 'profession' is the merest policy, among nuns of dubious virtue and friars whose timid carnality makes them easy and proper meat for Barabas. In such company it is easy to rejoice with the Jew at the destruction of 'Christians'; but here (as in the Moralities) we need not suppose that Christianity itself is being attacked, or that Jewishness is being approved.

We should notice first the setting which Marlowe has given his play. In placing his Jew in Malta, at the time when Malta was menaced by Turkish attacks, Marlowe is not choosing place and time at random. For here was one of the decisive struggles of Marlowe's age—a struggle not simply between nations (operating by 'policy') but between faiths, between virtue and iniquity, God and the devil. Such at least was the common European attitude; to see it one need go no further than the prayers appointed to be read throughout England 'every Wednesday and Friday' at the time of the Turkish attack on the island in 1565, 'to excite all godly people to pray unto God for the delivery of those Christians that are now invaded by the Turk':

Forasmuch as the Isle of Malta . . . is presently [*at the moment*] invaded with a great Army and navy of Turks, infidels and sworn enemies of christian religion . . . it is our parts, which for distance of place cannot succour them with temporal relief, to assist them with spiritual aid . . . desiring [Almighty God] . . . to repress the rage and violence of Infidels, who by all tyranny and cruelty labour utterly to root out not only true Religion, but also the very name and memory of Christ our only Saviour, and all christianity. (*Liturgical Services of Queen Elizabeth* [Parker Soc.], p. 519)

Choosing Malta, Marlowe might seem to be selecting one of the few historical scenes where the moral issues were completely cut-and-dried. And I think this potentiality is always in his mind. The 'Knights of Malta' who provide the defence, were no ordinary soldiers, but the celebrated Knights Hospitaler of St John of Jerusalem, monastic soldiers vowed to poverty, chastity, obedience, and (as William Segar points out in his *Honor, Military and Civil* [1602]):

every Knight of this order was sworne to fight for the Christian faith, doe Justice, defend the oppressed, relieve the poore, persecute the Mahomedans, use vertue and protect Widowes and Orphanes.   (sig. I. 1ᵛ)

Marlowe seems to have chosen his world of men, as he chose his place, to raise highest expectations of rectitude. But he did so only to reveal the more effectively his view of man's (even monastic man's) essentially fallen condition. The vision of Malta as a Christian bulwark serves merely as a bass line in his play; and over this he works a variety of cynical variations and inversions. In the actual life of the play the heroic conflict of the Crescent and the Cross, with its idealistic rhetoric of honour and piety, is only a window-dressing, behind which, on both sides, lies the reality of greed—what the warriors themselves accept as 'the wind that bloweth all the world besides, / Desire of gold' (1422 f.)—and this is an estimate of the fallen or actual world depicted in the play from which we can hardly dissent. The international relationships shown are either based on money or on illusion. Malta *buys* its peace from the Turk:

> This truce we have is but in hope of gold, (731)

and it is only in accord with the prevailing morality that Barabas should decide to *buy* back the Christians' freedom at the end of the play. The representative of honour, Martin del Bosco, Vice-admiral to the King of Spain, persuades the Knights of St John to refuse their tribute, and does so with a rousing speech:

> Will Knights of Malta be in league with Turkes,
> And buy it basely too for summes of gold?
> My lord, remember that to Europ's shame,
> The Christian Ile of Rhodes, from whence you came,
> Was lately lost, and you were stated here
> To be at deadly enmity with Turkes.   (733-7)

But the occasion of his arrival on the island is to *sell* the 'Grecians, Turks and Africk Moores' whom he has captured. The one tangible element in the course of honour which del Bosco proposes:

> I'le write unto his Majesty for ayd, (745)

never materializes, so that Calymath can scoff at the end:

> Now where's the hope you had of haughty Spaine? (2103)

This is a world where everything has its price, where Barabas can properly presume that it is

> A kingly kinde of trade to purchase townes
> By treachery, and sell 'em by deceit (2330 f.)

—assuming that the difference between a monarch and a thief is only a matter of degree—and find no contradiction from the Christians.

It is then in a world as entirely devoted to greed as the Venice of Jonson's *Volpone*, but with theological expectations, that Marlowe has chosen to set down his theologically conceived Jew. Barabas, like Volpone, is a specimen perfectly adapted to his environment. Self-interest is his only motive. He stands aside from the contestants,

> Damn'd Christians, dogges, and Turkish infidels, (2370)

seeing their conflict as concerned about nothing, and certainly as a tiresome interruption in the real life of profit-making:

> Why, let 'em [*the Turks*] come, so they come not to warre;
> Or let 'em warre, so we be conquerors:
> Nay, let 'em combat, conquer, and kill all,
> So they spare me, my daughter, and my wealth.   (189–92)

At the personal level, Barabas's conflict happens to be with the Christians, and at this personal level he is prepared to make common cause with Ithamore, as an individual Turk:

> make account of me
> As of thy fellow; we are villaines both:
> Both circumcized, we hate Christians both.
> (977–80)

But his hatred for the Christians is no mere reduplication of the Turkish hostility which expresses itself in the major political action of the play; in Act v he finds it more profitable to sell Turks than Christians and does so without a qualm:

> For he that liveth in Authority,
> And neither gets him friends, nor fils his bags,
> Lives like the Asse that Aesope speaketh of.
> (2139–41)

The Turks, like the Christians, are inconsistent in their pursuit of financial self-interest; they pursue riches, but they also hanker after honour, knowing that

> Honor is bought with bloud and not with gold. (761)

Barabas, however, is the thing itself, allowing neither race, faith, blood, service, nor even the illusion of grandeur, to stand in the way of his splendidly consistent monomania. And in so far as he is free from the cant of idealism (as it appears in this play) or the timidity of personal dependence on others, we are prepared to admire him, to allow that (in his own terms),

> Barabas is borne to better chance,
> And fram'd of finer mold then common men.
> (452 f.)

This degree of sympathy and admiration that Barabas is capable of exciting I have referred to as a counterpoint over a secure bass line of theological condemnation. The terms in which Barabas is admirable, the terms in which the fate of Malta is a mere financial transaction, may reflect things as they are (and so the view of Machiavelli, who introduces Barabas to us as his protégé) but this does not obliterate the importance and even the ultimate truth of the orthodox view that self-interest is self-destroying. And this is what the progression of the plot would seem to indicate as Marlowe's view. The lines I have quoted above (189–92) indicate a rhetorical progression of ever-narrowing range:

> Why, let 'em come, so they come not to warre;
> Or let 'em warre, so we be conquerors:
> Nay, let 'em combat, conquer, and kill all,
> So they spare me, my daughter, and my wealth.

We could regard this, by itself, as simply a preference for private security, a preference natural enough in a Jewish alien. What cannot be seen in these terms is the subsequent progression of the whole play, in which the 'daughter' of the last line is first assimilated to the gold, and then destroyed. Indeed we may even suspect that the first word we hear of Abigail is fraught with ironic overtones:

> I have no charge, nor many children,
> But one sole daughter, whom I hold as deare
> As Agamemnon did his Iphigen.   (174–6)

This sounds rather like the Semele image in the Helen speech in *Faustus*, and perhaps we ought to weigh it as more than merely decorative mythology; certainly we ought to remember that Agamemnon's one notable act as a father was to preside over the sacrifice of Iphigeneia. However this be, the middle of the play shows us a comic but also significant confusion between the girl and the gold; it is difficult to tell which is being referred to in the following speech:

> O my girle
> My gold, my fortune, my felicity;
> Strength to my soule, death to mine enemy;
> Welcome the first beginner of my blisse:
> Oh Abigal, Abigal, that I had thee here too,
> Then my desires were fully satisfied,
> But I will practise thy enlargement thence:
> Oh girle, oh gold, oh beauty, oh my blisse!
> [*Hugs his bags*]   (688–95)

Certainly it is in terms of his gold rather than his daughter that Barabas looks to the future; and it is the 'barren breed of metal' that he broods over like a fond father:

> Now Phoebus ope the eye-lids of the day,
> And for the raven wake the morning Larke,
> That I may hover with her in the Ayre,
> Singing ore these [*the money-bags*] as she does ore her young.
>   (701–4)

The following scenes show a further progression in this relationship: the purchase of Ithamore in the slave-market is set against the sale of the 'diamond' Abigail to Lodowick:

> [*To Ithamore*]   Come Sirra you are mine.
> [*To Lodowick*]   As for the Diamond it shall be yours.
>   (899 f.)

and the actual selling of the 'diamond' is threaded through with cross-talk about real finance:

LODOWICK. Oh Barabas well met;
   Where is the Diamond you told me of?

BARABAS. I have it for you, Sir; please you walk in with me;
    What ho, Abigall; open the doore I say.
                [Enter Abigail]
ABIGAIL. In good time, father, here are letters come
    From Ormus, and the post stayes here within.
BARABAS. Give me the letters, daughter, do you heare?
    Entertaine Lodowicke the Governors sonne . . .
    I am a little busie, Sir, pray pardon me.
    Abigall, bid him welcome for my sake . . .
ABIGAIL. Oh father, Don Mathias is my love.
BARABAS. I know it: yet I say make love to him;
    Doe, it is requisite it should be so.
    Nay on my life it is my Factors hand,
    But goe you in, I'le thinke upon the account:—
    The account is made, for Lodowicke dyes.
    My Factor sends me word a merchant's fled
    That owes me for a hundred Tun of Wine:
    I weigh it thus much; *[snapping his fingers]* I have wealth
    enough.
    For now by this has he kist Abigall.   (983–1011)

Abigail is seen not only as good as gold, but as acting like a
human investment; and when she refuses to act in this way
she is withdrawn from circulation, and Barabas's other investment, Ithamore, is issued in her place:

> For she that varies from me in beleefe
> Gives great presumption that she loves me not;
> . . .
> Oh trusty Ithimore; no servant, but my friend;
> I here adopt thee for mine onely heire.
>   (1312 f., 1344 f.)

The original trinity of 'me, my daughter, and my wealth' has
shrunk to 'me and my wealth', which in this case is only a
double view of a single entity. There is never any suggestion
that Ithamore is more than a tool; and the descent from
Abigail to Ithamore is one which carries Barabas, logically
and inexorably, through ever-diminishing circles of personal
freedom into depths of ever pettier criminality, into spheres
where the cut-purse (Pilia-Borza) and courtesan are natural
inhabitants.

In this structure of decline, *The Jew of Malta* is (once
again) extraordinarily similar to *Doctor Faustus*. To argue

this in detail would require a separate article,[2] but it can be easily seen, I think, how the general outlines conform. Both heroes begin with a splendid assertion of the individual will (even if it is only the will to self-frustration). Acts III and IV, however, carry them into the shallows of low-life clowning, and here the frustrations of the original false choice begin to show. In *Faustus* it might be pointed out, of course, that this aesthetic decline in the middle of the play is redeemed, if not cancelled, by the magnificent final scenes, whereas, in *The Jew of Malta*, farce is not redeemed by a denouement wholly given over to melodrama. It is true that the inner landscape of terror and despair which appears so powerfully at the end of *Doctor Faustus*, is not duplicated in *The Jew of Malta*, where the psychological condition of the Jew is not discussed. But the final scenes are not so emptily melodramatic as is sometimes supposed. There is a return to the model of Antichrist. Like Antichrist in the one surviving English play on this topic,[3] Barabas temporarily defeats his enemies by pretending to die; the defenders of Malta think his menace is removed, and dispose of him by throwing him over the walls of the city:

> For the Jewes body, throw that o're the wals,
> To be a prey for Vultures and wild beasts.
> So now away and fortifie the Towne. (2060–2)

But Antichrist is not so easily excluded. With magnificent carelessness about means, Marlowe recovers Barabas from his 'death':

> I dranke of Poppy and cold mandrake juyce;
> And being asleepe, belike they thought me dead,
> And threw me o're the wals: so, or how else,
> The Jew is here, and rests at your command.
> (2083–6)

The defenders may hurl Barabas over the walls; he returns with the enemy through the town sewers; once again, 'so, or how else, the Jew is here'.

The final episode, where Barabas seeks to blow up the Turks in return for Christian gold, and is caught in his own

2. Compare below, pp. 335–49.
3. *The Chester play of Antichrist*, ed. W. W. Greg (Oxford, 1935).

trap, is usually seen simply as a *coup de théâtre*. But the Elizabethan stage inherited from the medieval pageant-wagon a moral as well as a physical structure, with Heaven above and Hell beneath; and we should see that the scenic enactment of Barabas's descent into the pit or cauldron[4] has moral meaning as well as stage excitement. Here we have the proper consummation of Barabas as Antichrist, for he 'praecipitabit in infernum in manibus patris eius diaboli'.[5] Indeed there is a surviving precedent for the stage use of an infernal cauldron. In the fifteenth-century French Miracle Play 'Le Martyre de S. Pierre et S. Paul' (Jubinal, *Mystères Inédits* [Paris, 1837]), after the martyrdoms are completed, devils enter and seize Nero (who has presided over the occasion):

LES DYABLES. Ha! ha! ha! ha! Néron, Néron,
Ou puis d'enfer te porteron.
Lors l'emportent et puis le jetent en une chaudière assise un
pou haut enmy le champ.
[the devils then recite the sins of Nero]
Lors souffle ly uns soubz la chaudière et face .i. pou de fumée,
et l'autre face semblant de ly faire boire or guele baée, et
bientôt cessent.
[they taunt him]
Cy le portent hors du champ.
AGRIPPE. Néron est mort; par son défault
.i. autre emperiere nous fault.
Regardez qui bon y sera.

It is clear that on such an occasion the cauldron was more than a simple piece of stage horror. A cauldron was, in fact,

---

4. The text of the play only says the victim of the trap will

sinke
Into a deepe pit past recovery
(2318 f.)

but the Stage Direction 'A Caldron discovered' (2346) and the item 'j cauderm for the Jewe' among Henslowe's accounts (*Henslowe Papers*, p. 118) both point to the existence of a real cauldron on the stage. The contradiction between *pit* and *cauldron* may be reduced if we remember that the bottom or pit of Hell was sometimes thought of as cauldron-shaped. Lydgate says 'This is cleped the Cauldron and the pytte of helle' (*Pilgrimage of the Soul* [1483], III. x. 56). The cauldron on the stage may therefore be considered as symbolic of the *pit*. In Dekker's *News from Hell* it is said that the River Acheron 'vehemently boyles at the bottome (like a Caldron of molten leade')'.

5. *P.L.* clxvii, col. 820. For an illustration of Antichrist's fall into no less than three cauldrons see pl. 28a in the original printing of this article.

a traditional image of hell. The standard iconography of Hell in the Middle Ages was derived from the final chapters of Job, where Behemoth and Leviathan (images of the devil) are described in graphic detail. From these, of course, was derived the image of hell-mouth as the mouth of a fearful monster, familiar to many moderns from the revived Mystery Plays. But among the descriptions of Leviathan are features that are not so familiar:

Out of his nostrils commeth out smoke, as out of a boyling pot or cauldron.
He maketh the depth to boyle like a pot   (xli. 11, 22)

Emile Mâle has remarked the effect of these verses on the iconography of hell:

The thirteenth-century artist put a literal construction on these passages, and carried his scruples so far as to represent a boiling cauldron in the open jaws of the monster.[6]

Sometimes hell itself is seen as a cauldron, and sometimes the cauldron is only one item of the furnishings of hell.[7] In the latter case, the sins that are punished in the cauldron seem to vary from text to text; avarice, however, appears often enough to make Barabas's end seem appropriate enough to those whose visual education had come to them from block-books, stained glass, and wall-paintings (which usually included a 'Doom' or Last Judgement,[8] showing the torments of the damned). In the Croxton play of the Sacrament (ed. Adams, ll. 405 ff.) the wicked Jews try to throw the bleeding Host into a cauldron of oil, to boil for three hours

6. *The Gothic Image* [= *L'Art religieux du XIIIe siècle*] (New York, 1958), p. 380.
7. In the *Mystère d'Adam*, after the Fall (l. 590) the devils emerge from Hell, 'et eos [Adam and Eve] suspicient et in infernum mittent; et in eo facient fumum magnum ex[s]urgere, et vociferabuntur inter se in inferno gaudentes, et collident caldaria et lebetes suos ut exterius audiantur.' In this case the cauldrons and kettles ('caldaria et lebetes') were, presumably, smaller than those used for boiling the Jew. D. C. Stuart, in 'The stage setting of hell and the iconography of the middle ages' (*Romanic Review*, iv [1913], 330–42) points out that 'the Hell scene of *Bien avisé et mal avisé* is set to resemble the kitchen in the house of a great lord' (p. 337). This would seem to imply a development of the *Mystère d'Adam* presentation.
8. The 'Doom' paintings surviving in the Guild Chapel, Stratford-on-Avon, and at Chaldon, Surrey, are good examples.

(symbolizing the three days Christ spent among the dead). Among the plates in the popular *Kalender of Shepherdes* is one which shows the covetous being boiled in cauldrons of lead and oil.⁹ In the vision of hell contained in Bosch's table-top *Seven deadly sins* there is a cauldron marked AVARITIA within which several heads can be seen. In *The Revenger's Tragedy* we hear of 'A usuring father to be boiling in hell'.¹

All this would seem to imply that to the original audience Barabas's end was more than a piece of empty melodrama. Though there is no hint of psychology in it, it has a moral inevitability which makes it fitting to the largest concerns of the play. This does not mean, however, that the final victory of the Christians in Malta is to be an occasion for uncritical rejoicing. Antichrist may have exploited the rottenness of the world into which he is sent, but Marlowe studiously avoids any hint of the collateral Second Coming of Christ. Though the end of Barabas is proper, the survival of the Christians has no moral justification. Indeed throughout the play Marlowe has missed no opportunity to use his damned Jew as a means of tormenting and exposing those who pride themselves on their Christianity, but give little evidence of charity. The most extraordinary example of the ironic method by which Marlowe sets the malevolence of Barabas against the hypocrisy of the Christians, occurs in the early scene where his wealth is seized to pay the Turkish tribute. The arguments of the Governor here are extraordinarily like those used by Peter the Venerable (in a letter to Louis VII) urging that the Jews be forced to contribute to the cost of the Second Crusade:

9. See plate 28b in the original printing of this article.

1. *Works*, ed. Allardyce Nicoll, IV. ii. 90 f. In York Minster there is 'a carved stone, now in the crypt, showing a cauldron, and in it two souls with great purses round their necks. It is possibly a work of Archbishop Roger's time (1154–81)' (*York Minster*, by Gordon Home [1947], p. 82). Mr Nellist points out that there is a second line of association between avarice and the cauldron. Foxe tells us that in 1388 Thomas Wimbledon preached at Paul's Cross, citing the text of Zechariah 5: 5–11 (the woman sitting on the ephah). The woman is Impiety; the 'pot' into which she is thrown is 'covetise': 'for right as a pot hath a wide open mouth, so covetise gapeth after worldlie good'. Cf. the cauldron on the innermost column of figures on the right-hand of the main door of Notre Dame de Paris.

Let their [the Jews'] lives be spared, but their money taken away, in order that, through Christian hands helped by the money of blaspheming Jews, the boldness of unbelieving Saracens may be vanquished . . . it were foolish and displeasing, I believe, to God, if so holy an expedition . . . were not assisted much more amply [than by Christian money] by the money of the ungodly.[2]

The parallel with our play is of course all the stronger if we remember the extent to which all wars against the Turkish infidels were seen as Crusades, so that the situation in Malta is simply an extension of the one that Peter the Venerable is writing about.

The tone of this scene does not suggest, however, that Marlowe is entirely sympathetic to these arguments, however venerable. By a daring reversal of the standard irony of the play, he seems to imply that, though Barabas is the opposite of Christ, his trial is conducted by figures who approximate to Pilate and Chief Priest. Caiaphas had remarked,

it is expedient for us, that one man die for the people, and that the whole nation perish not.   (John 11: 50)

The Governor of Malta repeats the sentiment, without any suggestion that he is more sincere:

> And better one want for a common good,
> Then many perish for a private man. (331 f.)

Likewise, as Pilate

tooke water and washed his hands before the multitude, saying, I am innocent of the blood of this just man.   (Matthew 27: 24)

So the Governor tells Barabas,

> to staine our hands with blood
> Is farre from us and our profession. (377 f.)

'Profession' here (as normally in the play) means 'religious faith', and throughout the scene the gap between Christian doctrine and Christian behaviour is emphasized. In terms of the latter we are required to reject the Governor, but in terms of the former, Barabas rejects himself; it is failure to modify

---

2. *P.L.* clxxxix, col. 368, cited from S. W. Baron, *A Social History of the Jews*, iv (1957), p. 122.

the former (emotional) response in the light of the latter (learned) one that is responsible for the usual attitude, that the play is disordered and so a failure.[3]

The Christians are able to point to the basic text for the damnation of the Jews—Matthew 27: 25: 'his blood be on us, and on our children'—as justification for their treatment of Barabas:

> If your first curse fall heavy on thy head,
> And make thee poore and scornd of all the world,
> 'Tis not our fault, but thy inherent sinne.   (340–2)

In reply, Barabas makes the Christian point that righteousness is not a tribal or racial possession, but an individual covenant:

> But say the Tribe that I descended of
> Were all in generall cast away for sinne,
> Shall I be tryed by their transgression?
> The man that dealeth righteously shall live:
> And which of you can charge me otherwise?
> (346–70)

This is very like the Gloss which the Geneva version of the Bible supplied to the eleventh chapter of Romans:

. . . the Jewes in particular are not cast away, and therefore wee ought not to pronounce rashly of private persons, whether they bee of the number of the elect, or not.

2. The first proofe: I [Paul] am a Jew, and yet elected, therefore we may & ought fully resolve upon our election, as hath been before sayd: but of another mans we cannot be so certainly resolved, and yet ours may cause us to hope well of others.

3. The second proofe: Before that God is faithfull in his league or covenant, although men be unfaithfull: so then, seeing that God hath said, that he will be the God of his unto a thousand generations, we must take heede, that we thinke not that the whole race and offspring is cast off, by reason of the unbeleefe of a few, but rather that we hope well of every member of the Church, because of God's league and covenant.

---

3. See Kocher, for example: 'The *Jew of Malta* as a whole is far more shapeless in construction and confused in meaning than even the *Tamburlaine* plays, and provides a notable contrast with *Faustus*. Not only is it an unreasoned mass of melodramatic incident, but it bulges grotesquely under the pressure of Marlowe's satirical impulses' (op. cit., p 288).

4. The third proofe taken from the answere that was made to Elias: even then also, when there appeared openly to the face of the world no elect, yet God knew his elect and chosen, and of them also great store and number. Whereupon this also is concluded, that wee ought not rashly to pronounce of any man as of a reprobate, seeing that the Church is often times brought to that state, that even the most watchfull and sharpe sighted pastors, thinke it to be cleane extinct and put out.

Barabas's argument reminds us of this Gloss, but I think that Marlowe (once again) intended us to see the fallacy in the handling of the argument. In particular it seems probable that we are intended to catch the double sense of *righteously* and *live* in l. 349.[4] Barabas argues that he has kept to the law, that he has not dealt illegally, and that therefore he has the right to *live*, or prosper in this world. In terms of Old Testament theology he might seem to be justified. Bennett remarks on l. 349 that this is 'an idea that is continuously expressed in the Old Testament', and we might quote from Tobit: 'Do righteousness all the days of thy life . . . For if thou doest the truth, thy doings shall prosperously succeed to thee, and to all them that do righteousness' (4: 6), or Ezekiel: 'But if a man be just, and doe that which is lawfull, and right . . . he is just, and shall surely live, saith the Lord God' (18:5-9). Barabas's extension of his legal status in Malta to a religious legality under the terms of the Jewish *Law* does not fit in, however, with his claim to a personal covenant. The Pauline assumption that even a Jew may be elected depends on a freedom from the Law, so that he may 'imbrace the Gospel'. The Geneva Gloss should be read in conjunction with the denial of the efficacy of works in Romans 11: 6, and with the condemnation of Jewish righteousness in chapter 10:

For they, being ignorant of the righteousnes of God, and going about to establish their owne righteousnes, have not submitted themselves to the righteousnes of God.

For Christ is the end of the Lawe for righteousnesse unto every one that beleeveth.   (Romans 10: 3-4)

---

4. Landa takes 'The man that dealeth righteously' couplet as 'evidence of a first intention on the part of Marlowe to depict a figure of fine tragedy.' He then goes on, 'The conception of Barabas as a wholesale assassin appears to have been an afterthought' (*The Jew in Drama*, p. 67).

The Geneva Gloss on this runs:

The first entrance into the vocation unto salvation, is to renounce our owne righteousnesse: the next is to imbrace that righteousnesse by faith, which God freely offereth us in the Gospel.

It must be obvious that *righteousness* as it appears in the speech of Barabas is a distinct and antithetical concept to the righteousness of the New Testament, and that a Christian audience might be expected to reject Barabas's defence as a patent piece of self-justification. This is the point that the Governor makes in his reply:

> Out, wretched Barabas,
> Sham'st thou not thus to justifie thy selfe,
> As if we knew not thy profession?
> If thou rely upon thy righteousnesse,
> Be patient and thy riches will increase.
>
> (351-5)

'Profession' here means 'Jewish faith'. For the Jew to claim an individual covenant, that is, for the Jew to claim true faith, is a contradiction in terms. Paul explicitly denies the possibility in Romans 10: 5-6:

For Moses thus describeth the righteousnesse which is of the Law,
That the man which doeth these things shall live thereby,
But the righteousnesse which is of faith . . .

Once again Barabas is referred to the figure of Job, whose attempts at self-justification were futile, but who in the end was justified by his patience and his faith, not by his righteousness. The comparison shows up Barabas again as an Anti-Job figure, whose one alternative to *despair* ('to make me desperate in my poverty') is Machiavellian cunning:

> for in extremitie
> We ought to make barre of no policie.
>
> (507 f.)

To this extent we must accept the arguments against Barabas in this scene of the confiscation of his money. Doctrinally they seem to be sound. But the last two lines of the Governor's speech show that more than doctrinal correctness is involved:

> Excesse of wealth is cause of covetousnesse:
> And covetousnesse, oh, 'tis a monstrous sinne.
>
> (356 f.)

This comes to us with a strong tone of hypocrisy; our sympathy swings into line with the persecuted (however in the wrong), and we reject, on one level, what on another we are required to endorse.

Among the blasphemies which Richard Baines attributed to Marlowe was one 'That Christ deserved better to dy than Barabbas, and that the Jewes made a good choise, although Barabbas were both a theif and a murtherer'. One can see in *The Jew of Malta* a mode of thinking which could explain the genesis of such a statement, one which, if it holds, throws some light on the vexed question of Marlowe's 'atheism'. I take it, in general, that Marlowe's purpose in the statements cited by Richard Baines's deposition ('concernynge his damnable opinions and judgement of Religion & scorne of Gods worde') was to shock rather than persuade; certainly that seems to have been the effect on Baines. Professor Kocher, however, believes that he can reconstruct from the Baines statements the outlines of the 'atheist lecture' with which Marlowe is said to have made converts to anti-theism. But who would be converted by a statement like 'all they that love not Tobacco and Boies were fooles'? And to what? Such a statement is effective because of its power to upset our preconceptions, but it does not lead anywhere. If we are to use the Baines document as a touchstone of Marlowe's temperament (Kocher calls it our 'Rosetta stone') we can only deduce from it that he was violently hostile to conventional ideas and orthodox codes of behaviour.

That to some extent Marlowe identified himself with the rebels at the centres of his plays—Tamburlaine, Barabas, Faustus, Edward II—is inherently probable. But that this indulgence of one part of his temperament blinded him to the immutable laws of God, society, and man is very improbable. The statement that 'all they that love not ... Boies were fooles' does not lead him to present the homosexual infatuation of Edward and Gaveston as other than corrupt and destructive. His Cambridge background and his social contacts (for example, with the Walsinghams) suggest that his

closest contracts with an orthodoxy were with Calvinism.
The iconoclastic fervour of a Tamburlaine or a Barabas
would not contradict this; the strongest emotional effect in
the writings of the reformers often comes from their sense of
God's infinite transcendence, and man's infinite debasement.
And this is precisely the emotional effect made in *Tamburlaine*:

> Can there be such deceit in Christians,
> Or treason in the fleshly heart of man,
> Whose shape is figure of the highest God?
> . . .
> That he that sits on high and never sleeps,
> Nor in one place is circumscriptible,
> But every where fils euery Continent,
> With strange infusion of his sacred vigor,
> May in his endlesse power and puritie
> Behold and venge this Traitors perjury.
>
> (2893–911)

The ring of the verse here suggests the passionate involvement of the speaker, a passionate involvement with the idea
of God's purity and transcendence, on the one hand, and with
the betrayal of that purity in human nature, on the other
hand. This is not a passion particularly relevant to Orcanes,
the dramatic mouthpiece, and I suspect we ought to involve
Marlowe himself in the sentiments. At the very least he *knew*
what it was like to worship transcendence, to take the Cal-
vinist view of a fallen world for ever tragically defacing a
power and a beauty beyond its comprehension.

Marlowe was called an atheist in his own day; the word
served then to describe any unorthodoxy. But the combined
evidence of the plays and the Baines note suggest that if he
was an atheist in the modern sense at all, he was a God-
haunted atheist, involved simultaneously in revolt and the
sense of the necessity for punishment against such a revolt,
simultaneously fascinated and horrified by the apparent self-
sufficiency of the fallen world. Characters like Faustus and
Barabas are at once Marlowe's representatives and his scape-
goats; and the multiple ironies of the plays serve to make this
double focus effective.

The Baines note tells us that Marlowe thought that 'the

Jews made a good choice'; and he has created a situation in the Malta of the play which seems to justify the 'Jewish choice':

> This is the life we Jewes are us'd to lead;
> And reason too, for Christians doe the like.
> (2217 f.)

That is, 'Jewish' behaviour is justified, since the same Machiavellian tactics appear in Christian lives:

> [Ay], policie! that's their profession,
> And not simplicity, as they suggest.
> (393 f.)

The area of the whole play's range of possible activity is defined by the Prologue of Machiavelli which establishes the alternatives of strong (and successful) villainy, or weak (and soon crushed) villainy. In such a context we must prefer the 'Jewish' profession of Barabas to the hypocrisy of the Christians; the Jews 'made a good choice'. But, of course, Marlowe's primary purpose is not to justify the Jew, but to belabour the Christian. The belabouring, is, however, here as in the *Tamburlaine* quotation above, concentrated on Christendom's betrayal of Christ, rather than on doctrine itself. Christianity's pretensions cannot be justified by the behaviour of its adherents; but this is not to say that they cannot be justified at all. The position is only an extreme version of the standard Protestant view that man could not be justified by anything that belonged to him. The world of Marlowe is a completely fallen world; but so is the world of Calvin. *The Jew of Malta* is strongly built upon a stratum of orthodox theological attitudes; its heterodoxies and per-versities take a savage delight to show how inapplicable these attitudes are to the political or commercial ambitions of most men; but the satire is as strong against 'most men' as against Christianity. Marlowe's irony, like that of other men (Swift, for example) points with equal force in opposite direc-tions, and requires a knowledge of his presuppositions before we can plot its true course. It has been usual to interpret the plays in the light of the Baines note, taken as autobiographi-cal and 'straight'; I suggest that it is as least as plausible to see the Baines note (and the contemporary reputation) as rather the simple-minded, univocal version of the richly complex and ambivalent attitude to Christianity which we may see in a play like *The Jew of Malta*.

4

English folly and Italian vice

The moral landscape of John Marston

The year 1599 is generally supposed to have seen the first productions of two very different plays, by authors whose attitudes and controversies were to keep the next decade entertained, and to provide between them much of the impetus for its dramatic development—the two plays were Jonson's *Every Man Out of His Humour* and Marston's *Antonio and Mellida* (Parts One and Two). The power and the newness of Jonson's play do not require any laborious exposition: here is a comic logic coupled to an unsparing social realism, and an insistence on judgement, which is completely new in Elizabethan comedy. Marston's play, on the other hand, is seldom seen as more than a sophisticated variant of the old 'Tragedy of Blood'; and it is certainly not an obvious example of what, in normal language, we would call 'realism'. Yet if we listen to what Marston says about his own play in the Prologue to Part Two (*Antonio's Revenge*), we find that it is in such terms that he speaks about its horrors:

> Therefore we proclaim
> If any spirit breathes within this round
> Uncapable of weighty passion
> (As from his birth being hugged in the arms
> And nuzzled twixt the breasts of happiness)
> Who winks and shuts his apprehension up
> From common sense of what men were, and are,
> Who would not know what men must be—let such
> Hurry amain from our black-visaged shows;
> We shall affright their eyes.

[First published in *Jacobean Theatre*, ed. J. R. Brown and B. Harris (Stratford-upon-Avon Studies, 1) (1960).]

How are we to treat this curious appeal from the abattoir to the Stoa? Does it in any way explain the Italianate horrors of the play, and does it justify any association of Marston with Jonson as a pioneer of Jacobean 'realism'?

We should begin by noting that the central idea found in the Prologue to *Antonio's Revenge*, the idea of 'what men were, and are . . . what men must be' is not mere window-dressing; it is found in the play itself. At the end of the revenge, when the tyrant Piero Sforza has been disposed of, a grateful senate offers the revengers 'what satisfaction outward pomp can yield':

I. SENATOR. You are well seasoned props,
  And will not warp or lean to either part.
  Calamity gives a man steady heart.
ANTONIO. We are amazed at your benignity;
  But other vows constrain another course.
PANDULPHO. We know the world, and did we know no more
  We would not live to know; but since constraint
  Of holy bands forceth us keep this lodge
  Of dirt's corruption till dread power calls
  Our souls' appearance, we will live enclosed
  In holy verge of some religious order
  Most constant votaries.   (v. ii. 141)

The first lines of Pandulpho's speech here are very close to Fulke Greville's 'I know the world and believe in God',[1] and in that light we may see our quotation from the Prologue as another statement of the Christian-Stoic position so characteristic of the Jacobean outlook. We know (says Pandulpho) the nature of 'dirt's corruption' in the world; and if we did not acknowledge truths beyond the world we would be obliged to commit suicide; but under Christianity this is not possible, and monastic retreat until death is the only alternative way of dissociating the soul from the world.

The image here of the real nature of the world—'what men were, and are . . . what men must be'—is not a sunny one, but it provides a natural tragic counterpart to the equally unrelenting language of the Induction to *Every Man Out of His Humour*:

1. Quoted by G. Bullough, *Poems and Dramas of Fulke Greville* (1939), I. i.

Who can behold such prodigies as these
And have his lips sealed up? . . .
I fear no mood stamped in a private brow
When I am pleased t'unmask a public vice
I fear no strumpet's drugs, nor ruffian's stab,
Should I detect their hateful luxuries;
No broker's, usurer's, or lawyer's gripe,
Were I disposed to say, they are all corrupt.
I fear no courtier's frown, should I applaud
The easy flexure of his supple hams.

And indeed it should be related to a whole group of Jacobean statements preferring the downward (realist) estimate of man's potentialities to the upward (romantic) vision of many Humanists. As Bacon remarks,

we are much beholden to Machiavel and others, that write what men do and not what they ought to do.[2]

Plainly, Marston and Jonson were as 'beholden' as Bacon himself. In *Every Man Out*, however, Jonson is not 'disposed to say' the worst that can be said about such a world: the play is to be a *comicall* satyre and the gripe of the satirist will content itself with squeezing out 'the humour of such spongy souls As lick up every idle vanity'. It is the function of such a play 'to sport with human follies not with crimes'; but tragedy is, by definition, concerned with crimes, and with the magnified world in which crime may be expected and analysed. The most obvious of such worlds is the world of power.

If we transfer the judgements of *Every Man Out* to the world of courtly power we arrive at attitudes very close to those of *Antonio and Mellida*. The private and privileged vantage-points of Jonson's commentators—Asper or Macilente—cannot be preserved in the more violent world of tragedy, and the evils of court life have to be focused from the viewpoints of those who endure them (Antonio, Andrugio, Pandulpho); but what they see is the same 'monster bred in a man by self love and affectation',[3] which is 'humour' in a person without power, and political crime in a sovereign.

2. *Advancement of Learning*, ed. J. M. Robertson (1905), p. 140.
3. *Every Man in His Humour* (quarto version), III. i. 157 f.

Both dramatists assume that this is the reality of human nature, which romantic or sentimental outlook may keep concealed, but whose truth must become apparent to any unprejudiced and experienced spectator. In one case the care for reality produces an anatomy of

> deeds and language such as men do use,

since the reality of folly is most easily seen in the petty everyday pretensions of our contemporaries. In the other case, however, the reality of man's criminal corruption demands both 'the rarity of Art' in language and a dramatic scene remote enough from the pettiness of everyday life to allow those simplifications and exaggerations that tragedy requires.

It is then as an image of the 'realities' of power (i.e. *Realpolitik*) that Marston defends his *Antonio and Mellida*, and it is in this respect that we ought to see the newness of his play. This is not the same thing, of course, as propounding its aesthetic success. Compared with the maturer version of the same outlook which we find in Jonson's *Sejanus*, Marston's play only weakly realizes the potentialities of political tragedy. It lacks both the unity of tone which Jonson preserves and the historical 'truth of argument' which Jonson attests by his continuous reference to Tacitus, Suetonius, Dio, etc. Yet the decisive advance or distinction that is achieved in *Antonio and Mellida* cannot be ignored if we set it against its predecessors (in many cases its sources).

The play has often been viewed in relation to earlier 'tragedies of blood', but always (I think) in terms of the mechanics of the revenge plot—how the delay is motivated and drawn out—and in the shadow of its potent relative, *Hamlet*. This I take not to represent the central interest of Marston himself (the Marston who wrote *Certain Satires*), nor the resting-place of his excellences, and certainly it is not the gift he bequeathed to his successors. I shall, in consequence, ignore it.

Antonio and Mellida is based almost everywhere on the tried favourites of the earlier Elizabethan period—Sidney's *Arcadia*, Kyd's *Spanish Tragedy*, Lyly's pageboy comedies, and (in its two-part structure) Marlowe's *Tamburlaine*. It was natural for a young dramatist to play safe by imitating proved successes; but it was also natural for a self-conscious graduate into the new age to see what he imitated with new eyes, and this is just what we find in this transitional and unsatisfactory play—a tension between the interests of the writer and the natural tendency of the plot-material he has selected. Andrugio, the deprived father of the play, is obviously modelled on Kyd's Hieronimo, but the effect of his tirades is quite different. The role of Hieronimo, like that of Titus Andronicus, is a martyr role: we see human suffering pushed up to (and beyond) the extreme edge of endurance. The structure of the play lines up trial after trial and the force of the speeches depends on the passionate eloquence with which they reveal the depths of human love and suffering:

> Where shall I run to breathe abroad my woes,
> My woes, whose weight have wearied the earth?
> Or mine exclaims, that have surcharged the air
> With ceaseless plaints for my deceased son?
> The blust'ring winds, conspiring with my words,
> At my lament have mov'd the leafless trees,
> Disrobed the meadows of their flowered green
> Made mountains marsh with spring-tides of my tears
> And broken through the brazen gates of hell
>
> (III. vii. 1)

The rhetoric of *pathos* here, the repetitions, exaggerations, and pathetic fallacy, serves to concentrate our interest on the woes of Hieronimo himself, freed from any background of people or ideas. Hieronimo is placed in a court which is fixed geographically, and one which will not hear his appeals:

> Go back, my son, complain to Aeacus,
> For here's no justice; gentle boy, be gone,
> For justice is exiled from the earth.
>
> (III. xiii. 137)

But no political image of the court is presented to us, no image of how courtly intrigue really works. In Marston's play, on the other hand, most of the energy of the dramatist goes into a vivid and detailed picture of life in a court from which justice has been exiled. The underlying thematic structure of the play is a series of contrasting philosophic

and political poses: flattery at court is set against the honesty
of exile; the unhappiness of the Stoic at court against the
fulfilment of the Stoic in penury, the kingdom of the self-
sufficient man against the kingdom of the successful politi-
cian. Inside such a framework the tirades of the deprived
father, Andrugio, take their place less as exposures of human
nature in extremity and more as demonstrations of an attitude to courtly corruption:

> Come soul, resume the valour of thy birth;
> Myself, myself, will dare all opposites;
> I'll muster forces, an unvanquished power;
> Cornets of horse shall press th'ungrateful earth;
> This hollow-wombed mass shall inly groan
> And murmur to sustain the weight of arms;
> Ghastly amazement with upstarted hair
> Shall hurry on before, and usher us
> While trumpets clamour with a sound of death.
> LUCIO. Peace, good my lord! Your speech is all too light.
> Alas! survey your fortunes, look what's left
> Of all your forces and your utmost hopes!
> A weak old man, a page, and your poor self.
> ANDRUGIO. Andrugio lives, and a fair cause of arms.
> Why, that's an army all invincible!
> He who hath that hath a battalion royal,
> Armour of proof, huge troops of barbed steeds,
> Main squares of pikes, millions of harquebus.
> O, a fair cause stand firm and will abide.
> Legions of Angels fight upon her side.   (III.i. 72)

This is at once more personal and more political than the
corresponding passages in *The Spanish Tragedy*. Andrugio
is meaningful to us less as a representative of human misery
and more as a philosophic stance, in a world which can be
commented on and exposed from this point of view—
though the point of view will hardly serve as a basis for action
or 'improvement'.

Here is another essential difference between the world of
The Spanish Tragedy and that of *Antonio and Mellida*:
Hieronimo's bewilderment is not one that we share—not, at
least, outside the individual speeches in which it is so powerfully expressed—for we know (through the Induction

figures of Andrea and Revenge) that a whole supernatural machinery is directing and guaranteeing the revenge. When Hieronimo calls

> O sacred heavens, may it come to pass
> That such a monstrous and detested deed
> So closely smothered and so long concealed
> Shall thus by this be venged or revealed?
>
> (III. vii. 45)

there is no real surprise that the sword so long suspended over the heads of the evil-doers should begin to fall. In *Antonio and Mellida*, however, there is no external reason why (in the world of the play) one political attitude should conquer another, and this is perhaps the central weakness of the development. The story is a violent one, and to motivate its violence we feel the need for passionate involvement; but the interest of the author is in the cold realities of power, revealed in detached satiric portraiture, and in philosophic stances which comment on one another, but never really engage with or necessarily issue into action. Given this lack of momentum, all the events in the play are equally surprising; the central actions seem as accidental as the others (Mellida's death is a case in point), and the conclusion completes nothing but the thematic picture of a world of Hobbesian individualism. Clearly, this is what Marston cared about, and it is certainly what his successors borrowed from him. As an author he is notoriously careless and perhaps contemptuous of his means of expression. His satires rejoice in a barbarity of diction and discontinuity of structure. The theory of the genre no doubt encouraged this, but Marston took to the genre like a duck to its dirty water, and shows no great willingness to abandon its methods even when he writes for the stage. Given all this, the plot and counter-plot intrigue of the revenge play can be seen to be ludicrously unapt to his genius, though one can see why he was attracted to the Hamlet-like problems of philosophic minds required to engage in the corrupted world of political action.

What are apt to his genius are the scenes of satiric social observation which spread the action of *Antonio and Mellida* across ten acts. From the point of view of revenge-plotting these are tedious irrelevancies, but in terms of the leading ideas, they supply a complementary social image to the political one of sovereign corruption and tyranny. The frivolous courtiers, denied responsibility, punished for truth and advanced for flattery, present a coherent image, no less moral for being comic, of what indeed 'men were, and are . . . what men must be'. If we regard simply as sensationalism the horrific elements in the intrigue of *Antonio and Mellida*, we can only support Fredson Bowers's temperate remark, 'Marston was no artist in comic relief' (*Elizabethan Revenge Tragedy*, p. 120); but if we see the play in terms of the ideas he himself presents in his Prologues, we may allow the social satire as an integral part of a new vision, though a vision only imperfectly realized in this play.

Perhaps the most obvious aspect of Marston's innovation in tragedy is his discovery of a suitable background for his vision of reality. Critics who handle the 'Italianate' element in English drama usually speak as if attitudes to Italy were simple, and equally diffused throughout the whole period; but early tragedies like *The Spanish Tragedy* and *Titus Andronicus* have 'Italianate' subject-matter (as the most distinguished exponent of literary relations between the two countries has recently called it[4]) only in a very special sense. Villainy of an individualistic, self-justifying kind was often called Machi-villainy by the Elizabethans themselves, but the relation of this attitude to any image of Italy as a whole was very tenuous, especially in the drama before *Antonio and Mellida*. Marlowe brings Machiavelli himself on to the stage, but he is a spirit, and he is not confined to Italy: he ranges through France and appears in England itself. In fact, the atheism, political opportunism, and libertine views about love and family, supposed to be characteristic of the Machiavellian villain on the Elizabethan stage, are all natural enough as extensions of the Medieval 'Vice', given the substitution of political and social manners for the direct moral presentation of the later Middle Ages—and this substitution

4. Praz, p. 96. More tenable is his statement in 'L'Italia di Ben Jonson' (*Machiavelli in Inghilterra ed altri saggi* [1943], p. 173) that *The Spanish Tragedy* is set in 'un generico Mezzogiorno'; but even this is to avoid the stated fact that the scene is Spain.

is already a cliché of literary history. Marlowe's Lightborne (in *Edward II*)

> Learned in Naples how to poison flowers,
> To strangle with a lawn thrust through the throat,
> To pierce the windpipe with a needle's point,
> . . . Or open his mouth, and pour quicksilver down,
>
> (2362–9)

but his name is that of a devil in the Chester Cycle, presumably equivalent to Lucifer.

The earliest Italians on the English stage[5] appear as comic foreigners, comic because foreign; and there is nothing particularly sinister about them. Concurrently, we find the traditional romantic image of Italy, as 'the country which to Shakespeare's fellows was the hallowed land of romance',[6] a land of rich and elegant young students whiling away the golden time of youth in

> fruitful Lombardy,
> The pleasant garden of great Italy.[7]

This is the Italy of the *Cortegiano*, of courtship in both senses of the term, and of Euphues' proverb, 'If I be in Crete I can lie, in Greece I can shift, if in Italy I can court it'.[8]

There is little enough in all this to make Italy appear a natural home for sin. Indeed, when heinous deeds appear on the stage before 1599, or characters of monstrous wickedness, the background of the Vice is made obvious by the choice of specifically anti-Christian nationalities—Turkish in *Selimus* and *Alaham*, Moorish in *Titus Andronicus*, *Lust's Dominion*, and *The Battle of Alcazar*, Jewish in *The Jew of Malta*. It was only when the dramatists became politically minded[9] and saw tragedy as concerned (in Greville's phrase)

5. For example, in *The Rare Triumphs of Love and Fortune* (1582), *Three Ladies of London* (1582), Haughton's *Englishmen for my Money* (1598).

6. H. B. Charlton, *Shakespearian Comedy* (1938), p. 33.

7. *Taming of the Shrew*, I. i. 3.

8. J. Lyly, *Euphues* (edn 1916), p. 13.

9. By 'politically minded' here I mean, 'concerned with politics as the art of exploiting human weakness, and with history as a chart of political success or failure'. Political problems had been presented on the stage before this time (as in Shakespeare's histories) and had bulked large in books like the *Mirror for Magistrates*. But political action is seen in the chronicles and the *Mirror* largely in the light of what men ought to do, and essentially as the fruit of God's will;

'to trace out the high ways of ambitious governors, and to
show in the practice that the more audacity, advantage and
good success such sovereignties have, the more they hasten
to their own desolation and ruin',[1] to analyse the human
motives in power pollitics, that the Italian court became the
natural *venue* for lurid criminal behaviour. The applicability
of Greville's idea of tragedy to the Italian background is
obvious in the dedication of Robert Gomersall's Italianate
Tragedy of Lodovic Sforza (1628), which is designed (he
claims), to 'make the ambitious see that he climbs but to a
fall, the usurper to acknowledge that blood is but a slippery
foundation of power, all men in general to confess that the
most glorious is not the most safe place'.

Of course, Marston's use of Italian courts as a setting for
the personal abuse of power drew on expectations which
were fixed before his day. Protestant polemic had kept up a
running fire at Papistry and Epicurism (not always clearly
distinguishable) which must have had an influence, but the
effect in terms of art is neither obvious nor simple. A certain
continuity in the English idea of Italy may be seen if we consider the spectrum of words associated with 'wit'—cleverness, cunning, artfulness, artistic power, originality, individualism, etc.—but there is no evidence that any Elizabethan
saw these different aspects, some admirable, some the opposite, in this organized way. We can see that Spenser is naïve
(or virile) where Tasso is sophisticated to an almost pathological degree, or that Byrd is fresh where Marenzio (not to
mention Gesualdo) is on the edge of decadence; but we
should beware of importing this perception into the period:
Spenser and Byrd themselves seem to have felt only admiration and kinship with these contemporary Italian masters.[2]

so that 'all men seeing the course of God's doings may learn to dread his judgement and love his providence' (Preface to Grafton's *Chronicle*, 1569). Shakespeare's politics are not as blatantly moralized as this, but he does not seek to
make a scientific separation of political from moral activity. This was the
avowed aim of the new historiographers—like Sir John Hayward and Sir Francis
Bacon—and it is to this I am referring when I speak of 'politically minded'.

---

1. *Life of Sidney*, ed. N. Smith (1907), p. 221.
2. On Marenzio see T. Watson's Latin sonnet, set before his *Italian Madrigals
Englished* (1590)—a volume with which Byrd seems to have been closely connected.

The dangers affecting 'le jeune Anglais brusquement jeté dans ce milieu corrompu'[3] seem to have been much simplified and therefore much exaggerated. Euphues, like other Elizabethans, sees Italy as a land of opportunity open to conquest by wit, where the rooted pieties of a traditional way of life are broken up. But this does not argue 'Italofobia';[4] the 'Naples' of Euphues is London to the same extent as its 'Athens' is Oxford; 'Italian' vices are metropolitan vices and in fact duplicate those in the home life of their own dear Queen. We seriously distort relations between the two countries in this period if we ignore the fact that Italian culture was at least fifty years ahead of English in urban sophistication, in political and capitalistic theory, in philosophy, in moral casuistry, and in social relations, and that much of the English reaction is rustic distrust of urban manners.

In Jacobean comedy the breakdown of traditional values in the face of the new sophistications has been seen as a central issue, with the dramatists asserting the old pieties against the new opportunism of knights and merchants.[5] Likewise it was only in the Jacobean period that the background of ultra-modern opportunist Italy (familiar from the *novelle*) acquired sinister connections with tragedy; Italy was an awful warning about the state of Hobbesian individualism into which England seemed to be moving. Comedy satirized knights and city ladies for their failure to keep their appointed places; tragedy and tragicomedy revealed the new Hell around the corner, when the alternatives of eat or be eaten were all that remained to man. Italy became important to the English dramatists only when 'Italy' was revealed as an aspect of England.

Fredson Bowers has remarked that 'it is curious that Marston who with Webster and Tourneur was one of the most Italianate of Elizabethan dramatists in the sense that he more correctly portrayed the Italian scene and character as the Italians themselves would have recognized it, was at the same time one of the most Senecan' (p. 124). The dilemma that is proposed here, between real-life Italy and an ethical

3. A. Feuillerat, *John Lyly* (1910), p. 51.
4. I take the word from L. Torretta, 'L'Italofobia di John Lyly', *Giornale Storico della Letteratura Italiana* (1934), but the idea is fully developed in Feuillerat, op. cit.
5. See L. C. Knights, *Drama and Society in the Age of Jonson* (1937).

code remote from it, is one which we may now see as not
strictly applicable. The real Italy of the turn of the seventeenth century is not one that appears in the plays. The Italy
of the Counter-Reformation, of Spanish hegemony and of
Baroque art is not one that we hear mentioned. The Italy of
Marston and his successors is, in fact, chosen out of Italian
history with as much deliberation and artifice as Jonson used
when he came to choose the reign of Tiberius out of Tacitus.
The world of competing petty princelings, bearing names
like Sforza, Gonzaga, d'Este, and Medici, belongs to the
period portrayed in Guicciardini's *Storia d'Italia* (1492–
1534). It was a world long vanished when Marston wrote:
the Sforza line was extinct by 1535 and the others seem to
have become submerged in the responsibilities rather than
the excitements of their roles. In his choice of the period of
Guicciardini Marston is in fact very close to Jonson in the
latter's choice of Tacitus as a principal source, for the two
historians were favourites at the same time, of the same men,
and for the same reasons. Overbury's 'Mere Fellow of an
House' (a kind of Oxford Politic-Would-Be) feeds his self-
regard on 'state-policy' out of 'Tacitus, Guicciardine or
Gallo-Belgicus'. Justus Lipsius, the great editor and inter-
preter of Tacitus for this age, himself one of its prime
formative influences,[6] calls Guicciardini 'inter nos summus
historicus', and again, 'prudens peritusque scriptor et qui
tales lectores suos facit'.[7] Both writers may be called Jacobeans before the letter; both see clearly the incapacity of
individual virtue to outmanœuvre tyranny, or succeed in
politics, lost as it is bound to be in the bewildering variety of
causes and contingencies that rule the world. Both seem to
belong by nature to that 'Counter-Renaissance' movement
which denied the interpenetration of Divine and Natural
Law, and both saw the world of power as a jungle of *homo
homini lupus*. In the tract of history he covered Guicciardini
showed to the world 'la grande tragedia di una nazione che
rovina per l'egoismo dei propri governanti',[8] and pointed to

6. See L. Zanta, *La Renaissance du Stoïcisme au XVIᵉ Siècle* (1914).

7. *Politicorum libri sex* (1589), annotations on Bk I, cap. ix. Dallington's
Aphorisms (see below) quotes the former on its title-page.

8. N. Orsini, *Studii sul Rinascimento Italiano in Inghilterra* (1937), see p. 77.
Also H. Haydn, *The Counter-Renaissance* (1950).

the key figure of Lodovico Sforza (Il Moro) whose egotism destroyed the whole Italian nation when he called in the French to assist his own private usurpation. The figure of Lodovico clearly fascinated the English dramatists: Marston's 'swart' Piero Sforza must be meant to recall Lodovico, and two other plays (Gomersall's *Sforza* and Massinger's *The Great Duke of Milan*) use him as the central character.

Both Tacitus and Guicciardini were closely associated with the spread across Europe of ideas about *ragione di stato*: while the name of Machiavelli himself was being vilified, his political philosophy was purveyed under their names; and this is the philosophy we find in Marston and Jonson, derived, it would seem, not from the sensational Machiavelli of the earlier English stage, but from the real Machiavelli, mediated by historians and scholars. The spread of *Tacitismo* (this political use of Tacitus) at the end of the sixteenth century, and the relationship with Machiavelli has been amply described by G. Toffanin,[9] but since Toffanin does not mention England we ought to point to Jonson's apparent knowledge of the tradition—where he speaks of

> a chrysolite, a gem, a very agate
> Of State and Policy, cut from the quar
> Of Machiavel; a true Cornelian
> As Tacitus himself.
> (*Magnetic Lady*, I. vii. 29)

It is presumably no accident that Tiberius, who stands at the centre of Jonson's tragedy, is called by Toffanin 'questo capolavoro di "ragione di stato" lavorato da Tacito' (p. 51) and was selected by the Tacitisti as one who used the techniques of Machiavelli's prince in their full perfection. The political conclusion that one must draw from *Sejanus* is very close to that which Toffanin describes as derived from Tacitus' Tiberius by the Tacitisti: 'in spite of Tacitus' antipathy to Tiberius the logic of his history is that Tiberius' iniquity *worked*, and this logic is undoubtedly one of the motives inspiring the *Principe*' (p. 52 f.).

9. *Machiavelli e il Tacitismo* (1921). That Jonson got his Machiavellism from the classics was long ago recognized by E. Meyer in *Machiavelli and the Elizabethan Drama* (1897), p. 101; but the method by which it reached him has not, I think, been noticed.

The case of Guicciardini is more problematical. It may be approached, however, by considering the evidence of the English 'discourses'—historical essays in the empirical and disenchanted manner of Machiavelli. Machiavelli's *Discorsi* were not printed in English till 1636, but by then the *Discorso* approach to history was well attested in England. In 1600 Sir Clement Edmondes published his *Observations on the first five books of Caesar's Commentaries*, with a clear reference to Machiavelli as one of the 'pregnant wits who have presented decades of History to these later ages' (p. 3). Edmondes's book claims to be a discourse on war, 'for the better direction of our modern wars', but an approach to war implies an attitude to politics, and this we find Edmondes to handle in a strictly empirical and coldly scientific manner extraordinarily like that later recommended by Bacon:

for, unless the understanding be in this sort qualified and able by logistical discourse to ascend, by way of composition, from singularity to catholic conceptions [i.e. from particular to general]; and return again the same way to the lowest order of his partitions, the mind cannot be said to have the perfection of that art, nor instructed in the true use of the knowledge. (p. 2)

Edmondes's words did not fall on stony soil: the book came bearing commendations from Camden, Daniel, Sylvester, and Ben Jonson: it was enlarged by command of Prince Henry, and went through four editions in the next ten years.

There are no less than two of these English discourses to show the convenience of Guicciardini's material for this kind of treatment. In 1601 Remigio Nannini's book of discourses (Bacon possessed a copy of the original) was Englished as *Civil considerations upon many and sundry histories as well ancient as modern, and principally upon those of Guicciardine*. In 1613 Sir Richard Dallington published his *Aphorisms civil and military . . . out of the first quaterne of Fr. Guicciardine*. Both of these approach the *Storia d'Italia* as a natural landscape for political observation. Commonplace books of the time tell the same story. N. Orsini has pointed to the dozen or so manuscript commonplace books in the British Museum and Bodleian Libraries which contain extracts from the *Storia d'Italia*; indeed Guicciardini himself had pointed to this use of his material in his own *Ricordi* or *Precetti*, which appear in both Nannini and Dallington, and had appeared earlier still in Hitchcock's translation, *The Quintessence of Wit* (1590).[1] Indeed, the large number of derivatives from Guicciardini, all over Europe, show the extent to which he had made Italian history what one of these compilations uses as its title—a *speculum aulicorum*, a mirror for courtiers, wherein they might see (as in Jacobean tragedy) the methods of political action, and its fruits. It need not surprise us that the political interests of Jacobean tragedy turn it naturally towards material that had been, as it were, predigested.

The evidence would suggest then that the Guicciardini period of Italian history was well known to the Jacobeans as a *corpus vile* for political dissection by the new scientific methods. I suggest further that it was this rather than any general reputation of Italy for immoral behaviour or any heritage of the popular Machiavel that drove Marston to choose it as a background for a tragedy of the individual under tyranny.

The image of warring states selfishly absorbed in the effort to betray one another, together with a variety of philosophic and satirical poses is not, however, enough to convey any idea of the political seriousness needed to relate Stoicism to a tyrant's court. When Marston shows us

1. The transmission of the material in this book is quite complex. Its full title runs as follows: *The quintessence of wit, being a corrant comfort of conceites, Maximies and politicke devices, selected and gathered together by Francisco Sansovino. Wherin is set foorth sundrye excellent and wise sentences, worthie to be regarded and followed.* Translated out of the Italian tung, and put into English for the benefit fo all those that please to read and understand the works and worth of a worthy writer. 1590. The book is dedicated to Robert Cecil. The Italian original from which the translation is taken is *Propositioni overo consideratione in materia di cose di stato sotto titolo di Avvertimenti, Avvedimenti Civili et Concetti Politici di M. F. Guicciardini, G. F. Lottini, F. Sansovino.* (Vinegia, 1583). This is in its turn a combination of existing anthologies: (1) Francesco Guicciardini, *Avvertimenti politici: piu consigli et avvertimenti di MFG in materia di republica et di privata* (edited with annotations by J. Corbinelli), Parigi, 1576; (2) G. F. Lottini, *Avvedimenti civili . . . ne' quali si contegnono molti ammaestramenti utili per la vita politica.* Vinegia, 1575; (3) Francicso Sansovino, *Concetti politici, raccolti dagli scritti di diversi auttori Greci, Latini et volgari.* Venezia, 1578.

> Young Galeatzo? Ay, a proper man,
> Florence, a goodly city: it shall be so.
> I'll marry her to him instantly.
> Then Genoa mine by my Maria's match,
> Which I'll solemnize ere next setting sun.
> Thus Venice, Florence, Genoa, strongly leagued.
> Excellent, excellent! I'll conquer Rome,
> Pop out the light of bright religion;
> And then, helter skelter, all cocksure!
>   (*Antonio's Revenge*, IV. i. 260)

he gives us *material* which might have come out of the *Storia d'Italia*, but the jauntiness of the manner blurs any sense of the cold and unpredictable web of politics which we find in Guicciardini himself. If Marston is to express throughout this material 'what men were, and are ... what men must be', and achieve a standpoint as expressive as that of the Jacobean essayists, or writers of Characters, clearly he must acquire a voice which can sound both knowing about the situation and yet detached from it, an individual and personal point of view which can focus both the attraction and corruption of the world of power. The fairy-tale figure of the disguised prince has obvious potentialities in this direction, and Marston utilizes some of these in *Antonio and Mellida*, though in a typically incoherent way. Antonio, the disinherited heir, stays at court disguised as a fool in order to observe the reports of his own death:

> ANTONIO. Antonio's dead, the fool will follow too; he, he, he.
>   Now works the scene; quick observation scud
>   To quote the plot, or else the path is lost.   (IV. i. 224)

But this stance can provide no more than one element in the complicated plotting of the revenge, though it is an effective element in itself:

> I never saw a fool lean: the chub-faced fop
> Shines sleek with full-crammed fat of happiness;
> Whilst studious contemplation sucks the juice
> From wizards' cheeks; who making curious search
> For Nature's secrets, the first innating cause
> Laughs them to scorn, as man doth busy apes
> When they will zany men. Had Heaven been kind,

Creating me an honest senseless dolt,
A good poor fool, I should want sense to feel
The stings of anguish shoot through every vein.
I should not know what 'twere to lose a father,
I should be dead of sense to view defame
Blur my bright love, I could not thus run mad
As one confounded in a maze of mischief,
Staggered, stark felled, with bruising stroke of chance.

                                                      (IV. i. 42)

The status of the fool is an obvious vantage-point for moral
comment, but commentary on government is hardly within its
scope, as the source (Erasmus's *Praise of Folly*) might indicate.

When Antonio puts on his fool's coat, however, his confidant, Alberto, suggests another disguise:

Rather put on some trans-shaped cavalier,
Some habit of a spitting critic, whose mouth
Voids nothing but gentile and unvulgar
Rheum of censure.   (IV. i. 3)

This reads like a first idea for the plot of Marston's best play,
The Malcontent (1604), where the disguised prince (Altofront) does in fact assume the guise of a 'spitting critic' or
Malcontent in order to observe and describe (with loathing
and relish) and decadent court of the usurper. In this play
Marston has avoided the difficulties of his revenge plot in
Antonio and Mellida, yielding to his natural bent for satiric
observation. The plot is one which keeps passion, by constantly satirizing it, at the reduced level of a somewhat
ridiculous distance. The aims of the wretched eminent beings,
whose lives we observe, are all frustrated, but frustrated
without bloodshed and almost without violence. The function of the Malcontent, Malevole, is to expose (and if possible
convert) rather than punish, and the play concludes naturally
with a judgement rather than a bloodbath. The satiric (or,
rather, *satyric*) violence of language, which made farce out of
many of the strained revenge poses in *Antonio and Mellida* is
here harnessed to a coherent though violently disillusioned
outlook:

Now good Elysium, what a delicious heaven it is for a man to be
in a prince's favour! O sweet God! O pleasure! O Fortune! O all

thou best of life! what should I think? what say? what do? to be a
favourite! a minion! to have a general timorous respect observe a
man, a stateful silence in his presence, solitariness in his absence,
a confused hum and busy murmur of obsequious suitors training
him; the cloth held up and way proclaimed before him; petition-
ary vassals licking the pavement with their slavish knees, whilst
some odd palace lampreys that engender with snakes and are full
of eyes on both sides, with a kind of insinuated humbleness fix
all their delights upon his brow. O blessed state! what a ravishing
prospect doth the Olympus of favour yield!   (I. i. 325)

In *Antonio and Mellida*, exuberant satire of the courtlings
had made it difficult to refocus on the solitary Stoics who
provide the only possible alternative to the world of flattery,
corruption, and power. The Stoicism of Pandulpho and
Feliche was so pure that it was difficult to see what they were
doing at the court of the tyrant Piero. But in *The Malcontent*
the materials are more genuinely mixed into a tragicomic
compound—and much borrowing from Guarini's *Pastor
Fido* may indicate that Marston had been reading up this
prototype of tragicomedy while preparing his own *aspera
Thalia*.[2] Malevole, as his name suggests, is eaten into by the
evil he beholds. He is the cynical *observer* (the word is a
favourite of the period), disillusioned almost beyond sanity
and scornful of remedies or ameliorations. It is his voice we
hear behind the exchange.

BILIOSO. Marry, I remember one Seneca, Lucius Annaeus Seneca.
PIETRO. Out upon him! He writ of Temperance and Fortitude, yet
    lived like a voluptuous epicure and died like an effeminate
    coward.   (III. i. 24)

Sic transit philosophia! The Malcontent is sufficiently close to
the empirical scientist to know (and demonstrate) that there
is no substitute for experience, and that experience is only
available to those who are, in some sense, part of the world
they observe. Hence, of course, the tension between the
different desires of the disguised prince figure who is so
common in the first decade of the seventeenth century[3]—
between the desire to participate in the life of power, and the

2. See below, pp. 133–56, and my edition of *The Malcontent* (1975).
3. See Shakespeare's *Measure for Measure*, Marston's *Malcontent and
Fawn*, Sharpham's *Fleer*, Day's *Law Tricks*, Middleton's *Phoenix*.

desire to condemn and withdraw. It is this that makes Malevole their prototype, rather than Jonson's Macilente who had preceded him by several years. Macilente is the envious man of *Every Man Out of His Humour*: he is both contemptuous of the fools and envious of their success, and so anticipates the complex of attitudes in Malevole. But Macilente is presented as unmenaced by the follies he observes. He is detached from the main current of the action; the well-weighed quality of his vocabulary and the rounded organization of his speeches give his attitudes an angry superiority very different from the half-crazed involvement of Malevole inside affairs he is helpless to control. Macilente is quite clear about what he believes; the Malcontent is only really clear about what he disbelieves. The anticlericalism of *The Malcontent* presents this position with a directness rarely attempted in Elizabethan drama; here Protestant individualism has reinforced Stoicism in its rejection of corporate values. The hero is left alone with what Tourneur calls

> that Eternal Eye
> That sees through flesh and all[4]

—and this means the hero's flesh no less than that of the others.

In creating the type and the tone of the Malcontent (or deriving these from *Hamlet*[5]) Marston has created an instrument which can expose and anatomize the pettiness of individual effort in a world of chance, emptied of effective moral norms and governed by competing power-politicians. 'Let's mutiny and die', says Celso (Malevole's confidant). Malevole replies

> O no! climb not a falling tower, Celso;
> 'Tis well held desperation, no zeal,
> Hopeless to strive with fate. Peace! Temporize.
> (I. i. 238)

The patience of Malevole here is very different from the patience of Hieronimo or Titus: it is the patience of the

4. The *Revenger's Tragedy*, I. iii. 74.
5. H. R. Walley and E. E. Stoll discuss the relative dates of *Hamlet* and *The Malcontent* in *The Review of English Studies* (1933 and 1935).

poker-playing individualist who knows that his turn will
come when the others (inevitably) make their mistakes.:

MALEVOLE. Discord to malcontents is very manna; when the ranks
are burst, then scuffle Altofront.
CELSO. Ay, but durst?
MALEVOLE. . . . Phewt! I'll not shrink
He's resolute who can no lower sink   (I. i. 250)

The Malcontent is a philosopher who knows the ineffectiveness of philosophy, and the brutality of action; yet still seeks
for power. Hence his vocabulary is deprived of ideals, and
even of self-regard, as appears in Tourneur's Vindice's

I'll . . . be a right man then, a man o' the time;
For to be honest is not to be i' the world.[6]

The most Malevole can be is an 'honest villain' (I. i. 130).

In fixing this figure, and handing him on as an effective
presenter of the individual's fate in a world of power politics,
Marston gave a clear indication of how the problem of
'what men were, and are . . . what men must be' could be
treated on the public stage. It is hardly to be doubted that the
Italianate tragedies of Tourneur, Webster, and Middleton
owe much of their tone and their technique to the example
set by Marston. It was he who discovered in the world of
Guicciardini's Italy a natural background for the self-
torturing individualism of the Malcontent observer, who saw
that the atmosphere of corrupted power could be crystallized
by setting a solitary, cynical 'observer' against a procession
of sophisticated and self-confident vice. The opening
pageant of *The Revenger's Tragedy* (1606?) shows what
poetic power the method can achieve. As a mere location for
sin other places were as effective as Italy, and went on being
used; but for the background for political plotting and
counterplotting Italy remained, from the time of Marston,
the favourite location.

This does not mean, of course, that Marston or his successors had any desire to complicate the 'realism' of political
outlook with the *reality* of Italian life. How much Marston
and Tourneur are concerned with ideas, and how little with

6. *The Revenger's Tragedy*, I. i. 101–3.

places, is indicated by a brief glance at their *dramatis personae*. Florio's Italian dictionary gives us the key to what is, in the main, a Morality company. Thus in *The Revenger's Tragedy* we have *Supervacuo*, 'too much, superfluous, overmuch, vain, not necessary, unprofitable, to no use'; *Spurio*, 'a bastard, a base born. Also adulterate or counterfeit', etc., etc. In Marston's *Fawn* we find *Nymphadoro*, 'an effeminate fellow, a spruce ladies' courting fellow'; and *Frappatore*, 'a bragger, a boaster, a vaunter, a craker. Also a crafty prattler, a coney catcher, a cheater.' These occur in a play where the Duke of Ferrara is called Hercules (no doubt intended to recall the real Ercole d'Este) and the Duke of Urbino is named Gonzago (*sic*). To see any contradiction here is to forget the tradition which set historical plays on the Elizabethan stage, where *Stephen Langton* and *Sedition* can be alternative names for one character, with *Usurped Power* and *The Pope* as another interchangeable pair. For Bale (from whose *King John* these names are taken), as for Spenser, there is here no contradiction; the importance of history was just this, that it made actual the preordained patterns of vice and virtue: if the Pope is the living embodiment or incarnation of Usurped Power, one must expect to find in his court characters like Treason, Private Wealth, or Dissimulation, wearing the flesh and individuality of named men. The pattern of historical thinking in Marston and Tourneur is different from this, but if we substitute social observation for the intense moral scrutiny of Bale or Spenser we find that the corrupt court of a Renaissance prince is in fact no less a Morality masque of skulls beneath the skin, no less a parade of Lussurioso and Spurio and Sordido and Bilioso and Maquerelle.

This treatment of Italy, as a mode of human experience rather than as a country, may seem to apply less to Webster than to Marston and Tourneur; since Webster's two Italian tragedies are probably the greatest plays in the tradition, the exception would have some importance. F. L. Lucas has remarked: 'Again and again critics have cried out at characters like Flamineo or Francisco or Ferdinand with the refrain of Judge Brack—"But people do not do such things". And to that the only answer is, "They did"; and the only remedy is

to read the history of the time' (i. 92). This may be true, but
it has little relevance to the art-form that Webster was working in, which can only seem incredibly ramshackle if judged
by the standards of any school of historical realism. It is true
that Morality structure is not obvious in Webster: his
characters do not generally have significant names (though
Zanche, Cariola, and Doctor Julio seem to be exceptions[7]).
It is only possible to regard the plays in a realistic way, moreover, if we disregard the explicit gnomic statements which
stud every scene. This is, of course, regularly done; I. Jack
tells us that the moral statement 'has nothing to do with the
action of the plays',[8] and Una Ellis-Fermor has elaborated this
attitude quite fully. If we approach Webster's plays via
Marston's it is possible, however, to see within his dramatic
actions a structure and an attitude which may be able to
reconcile their sententiousness and their liveliness. In Webster, as in Marston, we have the political conditions of Guicciardini's Italy, the mazes of Princes and Cardinals with their
plots and counterplots, their dynastic ambitions and their
ruthlessness, to provide a natural milieu for the discontented
scholar or 'spitting critic' who stands at the centre and
mediates all the action. Flamineo and Bosola, like Malevole
(and Vindice), are also the centre of the plays' gnomic
activity; they keep before us an idea of virtue which may be
helpless in the world and therefore rejected, but which continues to exercise its appeal

> to scorn that world which life of means deprives.

They, like Malevole, are the individualists who know all the
rules for individualists, know the meaninglessness of success,
yet carry on, as if hypnotized by their own expertise. They
indeed of all characters in the plays are least able to achieve
any of their desired ends. As tool-villains they have to obey
the rules of those who have hired them, and lack even the
satisfaction of a Lodovico in 'limning' the night-piece of *The
White Devil* (1612)—a satisfaction which seems to survive
even when the artist himself is about to be 'dis-limbed'. They
end their lives where the plays started them—intelligent,
self-aware, disenchanted, poor, envious, and damned.

7. See *Notes and Queries* (1957), p. 55.   8. *Scrutiny* (1949), pp. 38–43

Webster's Malcontents, like Marston's, hold together inside their minds a world which involves obvious logical contradictions and which (in another presentation) might fall apart—a world of greed, cunning, madness, ambition, melancholy and contempt for the world, priggishness, and cynicism —but since the play *is* what they see (and since the dramatist has found a compelling language for their vision of it) the play does not fall apart. Indeed we can see the dramatist altering his Italian narrative so that the pressure of real life will not obscure his obsessive rephrasing of it into Morality terms, so that it will fulfil what the Malcontents tell us:

> This busy trade of life appears most vain
> Since rest breeds rest, where all seek pain by pain.
> (*White Devil*, v. vi. 273)

The choice allowed here is so narrow as to be inadmissible in any but Morality terms, but it supplies the framework for Webster's Italy, where the only rest is the rest of innocuousness, unimportance, and death (the rest that Spenser's Despair offers Red Cross Knight), and where the only activity that is effective is what leads through 'policy' to wickedness and punishment.

The intense gnomic activity of the plays is not irrelevant to their action; for the action is organized on principles that depend on such gnomic understanding. Webster is obsessively concerned with certain patterns of action which show man to be lost, isolated, or in a state of servile subjection; but these patterns are only important if the author can convey some sense of the values they exclude, the sense of loss in the world of power, the tension between Virtue and Fortune, or (as the Humanists would have put it) between *vita contemplativa* and *vita activa*.[9] Webster carries to its logical extreme the concern with 'what men were, and are', assuming that it is only in action that men are truly themselves, and that contemplation of pure knowledge is beautiful but (in terms of the world) unreal. This was the basic assumption that the Humanists handed on to these dramatists and to the modern world. The line of tragic drama from Marston to Webster explores the assumption in terrifying

9. See especially the *Dialogue between Pole and Lupset* by T. Starkey.

detail, facing the Italianate or modern world of success-at-all-costs with scorn and horror. The scorn and horror remain relevant to us in the modern world of today.

The vision of Italian vice that descends through *Antonio and Mellida* and *The Malcontent* to Tourneur and Webster may seem at a great remove from London citizen comedy as written (for example) by Middleton. The fact that Middleton also wrote *Women Beware Women* ought, perhaps, to make us pause; but a clearer demonstration of the relationship may be given if we consider the comic descent from Marston parallel to that which we have already traced for tragedy.

In *Antonio and Mellida* the corrupt Italian court is set against a variety of Stoic poseurs and disguised persons who comment on the scene, but do not dominate or distance its horrifying and extraordinary activities. In *The Malcontent* the commentator stands fairly and squarely between us and the life of the court; the detachment with which we view this world is consequently greater and its comic potentialities increased. In Marston's later comedy, *Parasitaster, or The Fawn* (1604–6), we meet once again a disguised Duke commenting cynically, and even encouraging malevolently, the excesses of court folly and vice. But here the detachment of the audience from the scene is still greater: the court observed is not the commentator's own court; there is an absence of the intense involvement which marks Malevole; and the end in view is not power, but love:

> Let it be lawful to make use, ye powers,
> Of human weakness . . .
> So may we learn that nicer love's a shade—
> It follows, fled; pursued, flies as afraid—
> And in the end close all the various errors
> Of passages most truly comical
> In moral learning; with like confidence
> Of him who vowed good fortune of the scene
> Should neither make him fat, or bad make lean.
>   (v. i. 17)

The intrigue, in short, has become more important in its own right, as a maze traced through courtly follies, than the emotions of those trapped inside it. 'Moral learning' remains important, but largely as a means of controlling and winding up the 'passages most truly comical'.

The course of comic development from *The Fawn* may be conveniently indicated by jumping a few stages and looking now at a little-known and hideously disorganized, but (for that reason) historically revealing play—Edward Sharpham's *The Fleer* (1606). *The Fleer* is disorganized just because it tries to move from Italian melodrama to citizen comedy inside the action of one play, and without any subtlety of modulation. The central character is a dispossessed Italian duke (called Antifront, in obvious imitation of Marston's Malcontent duke, Altofront), whose disguise as an old serving man, Fleer, allows him to spy on his two daughters, who have (of all things!) moved from Florence to London and set up a bawdy-house. Once the disguised duke reaches London, the play turns into pure citizen intrigue of weak knights and cheeky servants, improbably dragged back by a restitution of the forgotten dukedom in the last few lines. The play contains evil—an attempt to poison (frustrated by the usual benevolent apothecary); the one thing it does not contain is Marston's 'moral learning', a coherent response to vice or folly, which does not allow intrigue simply to carry away what is repugnant. Sharpham seems to have taken Hamlet's 'poison in jest; no offence i' the world' as a motto for his action, and to suppose that deeds done among citizens need no such integrity of judgement as is required when the actors are great men.

The same weakness of response might be thought to be present in other plays that Sharpham brings into relation with his own:

FLEER. And will you to the Southward i' faith? will you to the confines of Italy, my gallants? take heed how ye go Northwards; 'tis a dangerous coast; jest not with 't in winter; therefore go Southwards my gallants; Southwards ho! (II. 397)

Dekker and Webster's *Northward-Ho* (1605), to which this seems to refer, has only a tenuous relation to the tradition we are describing, but the first play of the series, *Westward-Ho* (1604), is clearly related to it as a further variant on the

Marston situation of the disguised Italian. The Italian is now
only an Italian merchant, resident in London, who disguises
himself as a writing-master to watch the supposed infidelities
of his wife; and who, in this disguise, malevolently enjoys and
encourages the adulterous plottings of other citizens' wives:

> if . . . all wives love clipping, there's no fault in mine. (II. i. 232 f.)

The disguised husband is here principally an intriguer and
hardly at all a commentator; and our sense of vice and
corruption is further softened or sentimentalized into a view
that it is all a harmless if spicy frolic. The denouement is
achieved without moral judgement, but simply by showing
that the husbands are as bad as the wives they accuse, and by
arranging the reconciliation on this *quid pro quo* basis. There
is, of course, in *Westward-Ho*, the highly rhetorical episode
of the Italian's wife and her would-be seducer, the Earl, with
its blank-verse orations, pseudo-corpse, husband disguised
as his own wife, etc. It is true that this presents an image of
virtue; but it is of virtue so melodramatic that it does not
modify our judgement of the realistic main intrigue. The
impression we get is that virtue is a matter of theatrical
extremes, while casual vice is the real substance of living.

That such attitudes did not satisfy Marston seems to be
clear enough from the 'reply' concocted with Jonson and
Chapman under the title of *Eastward-Ho* (1605). There is
good ground for supposing that Marston was the leading
spirit behind this venture, and that he constructed the general
outlines of the play. In *Eastward-Ho* it is made clear that a
background of citizen life need not infringe the strictest
moral judgement; the methods of the Morality play are used,
without reducing the social documentation or the precise
local allusions. The story of the good apprentice and the
wicked apprentice is as authentic and as diagrammatically
moral as the images it so strangely resembles in Hogarth's
Idle Apprentice and Industrious Apprentice series of en-
gravings:

> As I have two prentices, the one of a boundless prodigality, the
> other of a most hopeful industry; so have I only two daughters,
> the eldest of a proud ambition and nice wantonness, the other of a
> modest humility and comely soberness. (I. i. 83)

In this play Security, the usurer, encourages his own wife (supposing her to be the wife of his colleague and neighbour) to liberal infidelity. The contrast with the Italian merchant of *Westward-Ho* is that we are never in any doubt about the moral status of Security; and his end (shipwrecked at Cuckoldshaven, and then put in prison) is entirely appropriate to the strictest canons of justice:

> Alas I am a cuckold,
> And why should it be so?
> Because I was a usurer
> And bawd, as you all know.
>   (V. V. 147)

There is more than a hint here (as throughout the denouement) of a self-consciously simpliste handling of the pattern. But there is no evidence that we are being invited to extend our superior laughter at the mode of expression into a rejection of the morality it expresses. Simple citizens may be laughable and yet their simple assumptions preferred to the worse alternative of having no ethical assumptions at all.

It is in the context of this conflict of dramatic ideals that we should look at Marston's one independent London comedy, *The Dutch Courtesan* (1603–4). This play has sometimes been supposed to bear some relation to Dekker's *The Honest Whore* (Part One) (1604). Whether or not one play was written in answer to the other is not certain, but the two plays have enough points of similarity to make the contrast between them a profitable mode of exposition. The two titles sound as if they had been designed in competition with one another, and this sense is strengthened by the note that Marston appends to his Prologue: 'The difference betwixt the love of a courtesan and a wife is the full scope of the play.' It is just this difference that *The Honest Whore* is concerned to smooth away. Bellafront, Dekker's honest whore, is a sinner who is brought to repentance, and so (the play assumes) to virtue, by a fine poetic speech and a handsome face in the speaker. She is made an attractive figure, even in the days of her sin; but the play concentrates, in any case, on her subsequent, Magdalene-like state. There is much talk about sin, but the play (it might be said) is not prepared to show the nastiness that dwells in real-life sin: certainly the dramatic emphasis falls on the graces of repentance.

Marston could never be accused of wishing to avoid the nastiness of real-life sin. But his play is not simply a slice of nasty life. Like *Eastward-Ho* and unlike Dekker's play it is braced by a rigid Morality framework, which shows itself most clearly in the names and the strict *decorum* of his persons—however their careers may be illustrated by real-life vignettes. It is one of the oldest dramatic rules that courtesans should always behave like courtesans, and this Dekker's Bellafront does not do. Franceschina, Marston's Dutch courtesan, bears a famous Venetian prostitute's name, which was also the type-name of the *Commedia dell' Arte* servant-girl; in its English equivalents, often used in the play— Frances or Frank—the name implies one who is frank or free with her favours. Nothing complicates the simple moral discriminations on which the play is founded. But though the structure of the play is as simple as that of a Morality, the Everyman (or Prodigal Son) who stands at its centre is no simple moralist's conception. Here the average self-centred man of Machiavelli and Bacon can be seen in the process of becoming the *gallant* of Caroline or Restoration Comedy, the man whose virtue (if that is the correct word) comes to him by his experience of vice and not at all by precept. In *The Honest Whore* virtue triumphs because it is shown as more eloquent than vice in appealing to the softer emotions; in *The Dutch Courtesan* it triumphs because one character (Freevil) steps aside to direct the plot and interpret it; the method does not presuppose any natural bias towards virtue in the life depicted: The centre of *The Dutch Courtesan* lies in the soliloquies with which Freevil explains his move into disguise and into control of a medicinal or purgative plot— that is, one which will end with punishment for the vicious Franceschina, and self-knowledge for the rigid Malheureux, who has succumbed to her influence. Freevil himself is actuated by no romantically simplified emotions, but is obliged to rest on what is useful:

> But is this virtue in me? No, not pure;
> Nothing extremely best with us endures,
> No use in simple purities; the elements

> Are mixed for use; silver without alloy
> Is all too eager to be wrought for use;
> Nor precise virtues ever, purely good,
> Holds useful size with temper of weak blood.
>
> (IV. ii. 40)

By this rough ethic the gallant is able to justify his manipulation of other people's weaknesses, but this is not the whole ethic of the play. Freevil can justify his earlier resort to Francischina by the argument that he (unlike Malheureux) was never besotted, could handle pitch without being defiled; but the 'full scope' of the play is that there is no compromise between love and lust, and we judge Freevil accordingly. *The Dutch Courtesan*, no less than Marston's tragedies, is concerned with 'what men must be'. Though here it is sex and not power that is the motive force in the play, the position of Freevil, as one who has to be part of the depraved world before he can accurately describe it, or effectively manipulate it, makes him obviously parallel to Malevole. Though never encouraging a tragic response, *The Dutch Courtesan* moves throughout in a world of fallen creatures, where depravity may be checked but cannot be forgotten. It is this that explains Freevil's desire to test and retest virtue, his unwillingness to trust its existence, till he has proved it against his pulse; the speech in which he expresses this aim may serve indeed as a comment on the whole Jacobean movement to overload human virtue till it breaks under the rigour of mad inquisition (as, in a sense, the inquisitors must wish it to):

FREEVIL. I will go and reveal myself; stay! no, no;
  Grief endears love. Heaven! to have such a wife
  Is happiness to breed pale envy in the saints.
  Thou worthy dove-like virgin without gall,
  Cannot that woman's evil, jealousy,
  Despite disgrace, nay (which is worst) contempt,
  Once stir thy faith? O Truth, how few sisters hast thou!
  Dear memory! With what a suff'ring sweetness, quiet modesty,
  Yet deep affection, she received my death!
  And then with what a patient yet oppressed kindness
  She took my lewdly intimated wrongs.
  O' the dearest of Heaven! Were there but three

Such women in the world, two might be saved.
Well, I am great with expectation to what devilish end
This woman of foul soul will drive her plots.
But Providence all wicked art o'er-tops.
'And Impudence must know (though stiff as ice)
'That Fortune doth not alway dote on vice.'   (IV. iv. 85)

The victory of Providence is scored throughout in this minor
key; the comedy avoids the obvious trap of a falsely romantic
ending only by conveying this sense of restriction in the victory. Indeed this local victory even gives us a renewed sense
of the prevalence of tragic disorder in ordinary human life;
its integrity may serve to remind us that English folly and
Italian vice are in this period only complementary images to
express a single vision of the human state.

5

Italian tragicomedy
on the English stage

That Shakespeare was unlike Jonson is well known and
widely believed. That Shakespeare was *like* anyone else
(Heywood and Dekker are the names Webster suggests[1]) is
found less plausible. We tend to suppose that he worked by
the light of his own genius—usually called the light of nature
('Shakespeare and Nature were, he found, the same'). Yet
this dramatist, like the others, spent his creative life in the
literary–theatrical milieu of a town the size of a modern
provincial centre. Are we to suppose that the fashions, the
enthusiasms, the feuds, inevitable in such an environment,
left him totally unmoved? Were the forms of his works never
affected by rivalry, a new literary model suddenly discovered,
a new generic possibility opening up? Our prejudgements
lead us to believe not. When we notice that his vision expresses itself inside traditional genres, our first effort is to
seek explanation in his personal psychology, or, if that is too
obviously crude, in the subject requirements of the particular
play. We do not normally attribute to Shakespeare any
desire to fulfill external expectations based on genre. Rather,
we describe (for example) the set of tragedies he wrote after
1600 as reflections of a 'tragic vision' particular and personal
to Shakespeare; and though the final 'romances' are sometimes explained by the new Blackfriars theatre or by the
influence of the court masque or some other external aspect
of the age, our deepest sense of these plays still arises from our
response to Shakespeare the individual.

[First published in *Renaissance Drama*, N.S. vi (1973).]
1. John Webster, Preface to *The White Devil* (1612), speaks of '. . . the right
happy and copious industry of Master Shakespeare, Master Dekker and Master
Heywood'.

The group of 'problem plays' or 'dark comedies' written 1601–4 faces us with the same situation in a slightly different form. Can this group of plays be defined as belonging to an aesthetically distinct genre or broadly shared fashion? The fact that the genre was defined as separate only as late as F. S. Boas's *Shakspere and His Predecessors* of 1896 must make us pause. The obvious alternative explanation would attribute any repetitiveness of form or content among the 'problem plays' to the pressure of Shakespeare's individual vision. One time-honoured explanation sees these plays as the fairly helpless personal response of an artist caught in the grip of a tragic view of the world, but committed to the comic forms in which he had generally expressed himself, and which his audience expected from him.

The suggestion I wish to offer here is that much in *All's Well that Ends Well* and *Measure for Measure* can be seen as response to the stimulus of a new genre absorbed by a number of dramatists at approximately the same time. I believe it can be shown that Shakespeare is drawing in these plays on a sense of genre which he, along with hwis fello playwrights, perceived through 'the spectacles of books'. If am I right, he shows himself an artist very much aware of the European avant-garde and quick to respond to the latest seductions of cinquecento taste.

It confirms our standard expectations about the Renaissancc to hear that it was Italy that provided Shakespeare and his fellows with critical stimulation. That there was an 'Italian influence' on Elizabethan drama has been asserted for so long that we tend to assume it must exist, for this reason if for no other. And of course it is true that many plays of the Elizabethan popular theatre are set in a so-called 'Italy', or refer to things or habits as 'Italian'.[2] But if we define influence with any degree of literary severity, restricting it to the area implied by the question, 'What Elizabethan plays are direct imitations of Italian plays?', then we are given an interestingly muted answer.[3] The one section of

2. For the distinction between the true Italy and the dramatized Italy, see above, pp. 110–26.

3. See David Orr, *Italian Renaissance Drama in England before 1625* (Chapel Hill, N.C., 1970) for a refreshingly objective look at the actual evidence.

Elizabethan drama which shows a direct and significant debt to Italian drama is occupied by that sterile and unrepresentative group of plays written by gentlemen amateurs for their privileged peers. This situation is not altogether surprising; for these plays are the only English ones that reproduce, even approximately, the social conditions of the serious Italian drama. The fact that influence can be detected here gives us good reason why we do not find it elsewhere. The Elizabethan professional theatre, the context of all the worthwhile drama of the period, had, if it were to succeed commercially, to satisfy audience requirements far outside the scope of amateur or Italian drama.

The situation is certainly curious. The professional drama was the peculiar glory of the English Renaissance. But in one respect it seems to be quite distinct from other aspects of the English literary Renaissance. Italian works such as Ariosto's or Tasso's epics were not only talked about, translated, and reprinted in England; they provided the necessary precondition for England's attempts to achieve its own monuments. In music, in art, in love lyric, civil treatise, and short story, the Italian example fired the English imagination. But the Italian play seems not at all necessary to explain the nature or the growth of the English play.

There is, however, one exception to this general truth. When we consider the reception and translation of Italian plays in England, we notice first of all the poverty of the connections. But two or possibly three Italian plays must be allowed to be exceptional; and all these plays belong, significantly enough, to the same new genre, and are in fact its first mature expressions[4] as well as its most celebrated exemplars. The two plays I refer to are Tasso's *Aminta* and Guarini's *Il Pastor Fido*, and the third is Bonarelli's *Filli di Sciro*; the new genre is, of course, pastoral tragicomedy. The *Aminta* stimulated at least five separate English translators in the first hundred years or so of its existence.[5] *Il Pastor*

4. In saying this I am treating previous pastoral plays, such as Giraldi's *Egle* (1545), Beccari's *Il Sacrificio* (1554), and Argenti's *Lo sfortunato* (1567) as experimental rather than mature examples.

5. The *Aminta* was first translated by Abraham Fraunce in 1591, and later by Henry Reynolds in 1628, (in part at least) by Kenelm Digby in 1635, by John Dancer in 1660, and by John Oldmixon in 1698.

Fido was translated by five seventeenth-century Englishmen, and nine editions of English versions were published in the same century.[6] *Filli di Sciro* enjoyed two English and one Latin translation in the first half of the century.[7] And all this is, we should remember, in the context of a situation where no other Italian play had more than a single translation and where the vast majority had none.

The response to the new genre was continuous throughout the seventeenth century. But this might be taken to reflect Caroline rather than Elizabethan or Jacobean taste. More important for our purposes is to note how early the English response appears. *Aminta* was first published in 1580; *Il Pastor Fido*, first published in 1590, did not reach its final revision till 1602, in the twentieth edition. But as early as 1591 Italian texts of both plays were published in London, from the press of John Wolfe. Wolfe had published a number of Italian texts in the 1580s, but these can be explained by impeccably commercial motives; no question of taste arises.[8]

6. *Il Pastor Fido* was translated by 'Dymock' (first published in 1602; rpt 1633), translated into Latin for a Cambridge performance by ?W. Quarles about 1604, retranslated by Jonathan Sidnam (1630), by Sir Richard Fanshawe (1647; rpt 1664, 1676, etc.), and adapted from Fanshawe by Settle (1676; rpt 1689, 1694).

7. *Filli di Sciro* was first published in 1607. It was translated into Latin by Samuel Brooke in 1613, into English by Jonathan Sidnam in 1630 (published in 1655), and translated again by Gilbert Talbot in 1657 (while the author was in exile in Paris and hoping for a providential intervention to turn the Stuart tragedy into a tragicomedy). *Filli di Sciro* is not only the third most translated play; it is also the third play in the sequence of Italian pastoral tragicomedies, derivative from *Il Pastor Fido* as *Il Pastor Fido* is from *Aminta*.

8. The works that might seem most directly comparable with the 1591 volume are Wolfe's editions of two Machiavelli comedies (1588) and of four Aretino comedies (1588). The commercial justification for these volumes is, however, very clear. They belong to a large-scale plan to publish the complete works of the two most scandalous Italian authors, Machiavelli and Aretino, which Wolfe worked on between 1584 and 1589. The Machiavelli is slightly more complete. In 1584 Wolfe published the *Principe* and the *Discorsi*. In 1587 appeared the *Historie fiorentino* and the *Arte della guerra*. *L'Asino doro* and the comedies were published in 1588. The set of volumes is bound together by the prefaces to the early ones, which promise the later publications. The order of publication shows the nature of the market at which they were aimed: the most scandalous works appear first and secure public interest, and the more insipid works follow in their wake. The same pattern appears with the Aretino. The first and second parts of the *Ragionamenti* appear in 1584. The preface to the first part promises later publication of the letters, the religious works, the comedies. The comedies appeared in 1588; the letters were licensed to Wolfe in

The edition of the two pastoral plays seems, however, not to have been a commercial venture. It was printed, the title-page tells us, *a spese di Giacopo Castelvetri*. Giacopo (or Giacomo) Castelvetro[9] seems to have had considerable acquaintance among the educated nobility of Britain, to many of whom he acted as tutor in Italian; his pupils included King James of Scotland, the ninth Earl of Northumberland, Lord North, and Sir Charles Blount. As Miss Rosenberg has remarked, it was part of his role as cultural middleman to 'offer himself as a purveyor of fashionable masterpieces *e transmarinis partibus*' (p. 126). What is interesting, from the point of view of this article, is that *Il Pastor Fido* should have occupied this category as early as 1591. Castelvetro's dedication of the volume to Sir Charles Blount (the successful lover of Sidney's Stella, we may remember) dilates in a very interesting way on the reasons which prompted him to procure the publication.[1] It appears from what he says that literary relations between London and Italy were closer than is usually supposed. In mid 1591 he seems to regard it as remarkable that a book published in Ferrara in 1590 is difficult to find in London. He seems also to be saying that the *Aminta* is now getting harder to find (presumably again in London); and this I take to imply that it was once quite easy. We have not normally thought

---

1588, but never published. In 1589 Wolfe published the third part of the *Ragionamenti*, and that (so far as we know) was the end of his adventure to exploit English fascination with Italian wickedness and the desire to read, even if in a half-understood language, works never likely to be available in English.

---

9. For comment on the life of Castelvetro and his literary work, see Sheila A. Dimsey, 'Giacopo Castelvetro', *M.L.R.* xxiii (1928), 424–31, and Eleanor Rosenberg, 'Giacomo Castelvetro, Italian publisher in Elizabethan London and his patrons', *H.L.Q.* vi (1943), 119–48.

1. He tells us that the fame of *Il Pastor Fido* had quickly travelled from Italy to England and that thus there was caused, among the English *singulari spiriti*, a great desire to see it. Castelvetro had tried to use his connections in Italy to raise a copy, but found this very difficult; eventually, however, he received one exemplar. On reading it he realized what a treasure it was, and how difficult it would be for others to share the pleasure. So he resolved to have the work reprinted. Other gentlemen *fornite di maggior letteratura & di maggiore agutezza d'ingegno* agreed as soon as they read the work that it must not be lost sight of. Castelvetro resolved to reprint *Il Pastor Fido* in a double volume, together with *Aminta*, since *chi legge il Pastor Fido divenghi volonteroso di veder l'Aminta, & poi anchora perche di lei si ritrovano hoggi pochissimi essempti da vendere.*

that the latest Italian literature was looked for in London. Castelvetro's words imply that there is an audience in London, small perhaps but important, of persons who have an immediate response to the Italian graces of *Il Pastor Fido* and (he assumes without question) to 'l'Aminta del gran TASSO'. But English taste for these early portents of *seicentismo* is less surprising if we remember how well known in the nineties were the swooning madrigal verses of the Italians.[2] The long Italian dialogue between Antonio and Mellida, in Marston's play of that name (1599), is very much in the manner of the lyric verses of Tasso and Guarini. As early as 1605 Ben Jonson is rounding on the imitators of Guarini, who are thought to have already weakened the moral fibre of English poetry. In *Volpone* Jonson puts into the mouth (or rather parrot beak) of the literary Lady Would-Be an ironic praise of Italian authors, including Guarini:

> Here's PASTOR FIDO. . . . All our *English* writers,
> I mean such, as are happy in th'*Italian*,
> Will deigne to steale out of this author . . .
> He has so moderne, and facile a veine,
> Fitting the time, and catching the court-eare.
>   (III. iv. 86–92)[3]

Jonson clearly regards Guarini as the kind of effeminate and relaxing author whose chief appeal will be to women.[4]

In accepting the predictive value of the 1591 volume, one should not lose sight of the differences between the two plays it contains and the different kinds of success they were to enjoy in England. The *Aminta* is a short and simple work; its charms are those of a gentle and polished eroticism, of psychology, of style, and of sentiment. It has little direct to offer to the sophisticated technical demands of the theatres

2. The relationship between *Il Pastor Fido* and current madrigal verse was much noted by Italian critics of the play. G. P. Malacreta calls it *una dissipata raccolta di madrigali*; Udeno Nisiely speaks of *filza di madrigali amorosi*; N. Villani says that Guarini *potrai coglier da questa favola una sessantina di madrigadetti*. (All quoted in N. J. Perella, *The Critical Fortune of Battista Guarini's 'Il Pastor Fido'* [Florence, 1973], pp. 21, 35; cf. p. 50.)

3. Ben Jonson, *Works*, ed. C. H. Herford and P. and E. Simpson, xi vols (Oxford, 1925–52), v. 73–74 (hereafter cited as 'Herford and Simpson').

4. The condemnation of *Il Pastor Fido* as a dangerously relaxing, sentimental, and effeminate work is also found among the Continental critics. See Perella, *The Critical Fortune of 'Il Pastor Fido'*, pp. 50 ff.

of the English metropolis. The response to it is, in consequence, primarily a literary response, deriving from an established taste for pastoral poetry. Thomas Watson's *Amyntas* of 1585 has been hailed as the first English acknowledgement of its existence, and if any connection between the two works could be established, Watson's poem would mark an extraordinarily early assimilation into England. Alas, the point cannot be made in these terms. Watson's volume (a set of eleven, hundred-line, Latin lamentations, in which Amyntas mourns for the death of Phyllis, at the rate of a hundred lines a day) exhibits no connection whatsoever with Tasso's play.

Abraham Fraunce, who translated Watson's eclogues into English in 1587, seems in fact to be the first who conceived of them as *parerga* to Tasso. In 1591 he added to his Watson translation a translation of Tasso's *Aminta* (newly available in Wolfe's edition) in the same metre, English hexameters. Further, he doctored Watson's text so that the eclogues would seem to follow naturally from the play. He sees good generic reasons for linking them:

> But Tassoes is Comicall, therefore this verse [hexameter] unusual: yet it is also pastoral, and in effect nothing els but a continuation of aeglogues, therefore no verse fitter than this.   (sig. A2)

In its rather pedantic terms this is an interesting early expression of the idea of a mixed genre, which was later to be a central concern of tragicomedy. The *Aminta* is a comedy (it ends happily), it deals with the private emotions of humble persons, but it is seriously poetic as well, and so justifies hexameters. The theatrical problems of tragicomedy do not arise here, of course; the play being 'nothing els but a continuation of aeglogues', the context is poetic rather than dramatic. There is no evidence indeed of any of the translations of the *Aminta*, before Oldmixon's of 1698, being designed for the stage.

Il Pastor Fido shares with *Aminta* (and derives from it) many of the basic features of pastoral tragicomedy; but it pushes these in a direction which, while it may be destructive of the poetic charm of pure pastoral, none the less makes possible a tenuous but effective relationship with the pratical English theatre. The elaboration and complexity of Guarini's play, its careful imitations of the *Andria* and the *Oedipus Rex*, ensured that it should be of technical interest to English playwrights in a way that the poetically charming but dramatically slight *Aminta* could hardly be. Moreover, though the *Compendio della poesia tragicomica* attached to the 1602 edition of *Il Pastor Fido* does not seem to have been translated into English in the seventeenth century, it does seem to have been known. There can be little doubt that Fletcher's preface to *The Faithful Shepherdess* (1610) indicates some knowledge of it (or of the *Verrati* which preceded it, in 1588 and 1591). It seems likely that Fletcher knew the *Compendio* before he wrote the play—about 1608. Any knowledge of the *Compendio* must, of course, have sharpened the focus of dramatists' technical interest in the new genre.

Il Pastor Fido can be seen as pushing toward the test of actual performance the claim of pastoral tragicomedy to represent a significant imitation of reality. This is a test that Italian tragedy had signally failed to pass; and the possible reasons why are not irrelevant to thoughts about the cultural transmission of the tragicomic form. The lack of contact between Italian tragedy and English public performance must be due, in large part, to the different views of reality found in the two theatrical traditions. Italian tragedy is, by and large, centred on the figure of the tyrant, seen together with his (often female) victims. A tyrant is by definition one who has subjugated social responsibility to personal passion. The royal power of Dolce's Herod or Giraldi's Sulmone is shown mainly in the freedom with which he can indulge in himself and promote in others the personal violences of jealousy, suspicion, anger, and revenge. But the Elizabethan tragic sense seems to have demanded more explicitly political conflicts. The tyrant, when we meet him in Elizabethan public tragedy, is part of a fully represented political scene. So it is (for example) with Macbeth, with Piero (in Marston's *Antonio's Revenge*), or with the Duke in *The Revenger's Tragedy*. In such plays the passions of the individual tyrant are always judged in terms of social and political responsibility.

It is hard to resist the assumption that these opposed forms of tragedy reflect the day-to-day political experience that author and audience brought to the composition and reception of tragedies, rather than any simply aesthetic tastes. If this is a fair assumption, we find in it a clue to the theatrical as well as poetical claims of pastoral tragicomedy in England. The material of Italian tragedies encroached on the English tragic vision, but the terms of its development prevented it from expressing a full political meaning, and therefore it seemed to the English to be stunted and incomplete. Pastoral tragicomedy was, on the other hand, quite without political pretension. The social structure of Guarini's Arcadia is more defined than that of the *Aminta*, but its utmost definition is only vaguely theocratic. Montano, the chief priest, exercises the only visible authority, but his function does not fully emerge till the end of the play, when he conducts the sacrifice to Diana. No hierarchy or system of government is declared. One can say that society here is represented (and even more obviously in the *Aminta*) by loving (or about-to-be-loving) couples, acknowledging only the authority of their parents and the gods. The great affairs of oracles, plagues, sacrifices, etc., impinge directly on private individuals and their families, without the intervention of any state apparatus.

The generic 'openness' of tragicomedy—the quality so often cited against it in the critical controversy around *Il Pastor Fido*—can be paralleled by a blankness in its political dimension. Having nothing at all to say about political life, it could pass into the English theatre through the barrier of different audience assumptions about power and its distribution; in this area it offered nothing for rejection. But the political blankness or blandness of the genre may be seen not as an advantage but rather as a deprivation. This seems to have been a natural early response in England. Ben Jonson's comment on Guarini's 'moderne and facile . . . veine' (cited above) makes this point with characteristic directness. Guarini's ability to give meltingly smooth expression to tremulous love-emotions and feminine reticences seems to Jonson to be both trivial ('moderne') and facile. *Il Pastor Fido* reads to Jonson like a confession of poetic irresponsibility, an abandonment of the traditional Humanist position:

that poets gave advice to princes, so that even the public stage
had a moral role.

The English public-theatre audience might be thought to
have made the same point in their rejection of Fletcher's
attempt to infuse Guarini neat on to the London stage in *The
Faithful Shepherdess* of *c.* 1608. Fletcher, in his supercilious
epistle 'To the Reader', represents this as only an ignorantly
conservative reaction to the new mode, a reaction in which
the public took tragicomedy to be Sidney's 'mongrel' genre,
combining mirth and killing as well as clowns and kings, and
also supposed (sympathetically) that pastoral meant 'lower
class'. They were, therefore, on both counts, unadjusted to
the blending of gods and economically independent shepherds that Fletcher intended. In this case Jonson's difficulty,
caught between Humanist political seriousness and upper-
class loyalty, is nicely exposed. In his sonnet to Fletcher,
Jonson condemned the audience who

> had, before
> They saw it halfe, damd thy whole play, and more.

The moral Jonson makes of the occasion is interestingly
different from Fletcher's:

> Their motiues were, since it had not to do
> With vices, which they look'd for, and came to.
> . . . thy Innocence was thy guilt.
>   (Herford and Simpson, viii. 370)

The moral blankness or evasiveness of the Guarinian play,
its lack of interest in the social dimension of crime and violence, is now alleged to be a sign of innocence rather than
triviality. Here friendship with Fletcher and hatred for the
mob seem to have betrayed Jonson into a position very close
to that of his much-despised colleague, Samuel Daniel. It is
often supposed that Jonson had Daniel in mind when he
made Lady Would-Be tell Volpone that English authors steal
out of Guarini. The two men, however, seem to be at one
in describing the relationship of Guarini to the English stage,
though Jonson's valuation differs sharply, outside the poem
to Fletcher. *Il Pastor Fido* provides the obvious model for
Daniel's *The Queen's Arcadia* (1605), described on the title-

page as 'a pastoral tragicomedy presented to her majesty and
her ladies by the University of Oxford'. In the prologue
Daniel speaks of his properly humble and apolitical mode of
writing as entirely appropriate for students, who share with
shepherds the innocency of a secluded existence:

> And though it be in th'humblest ranke of words,
> And in the lowest region of our speach,
> Yet is it in that kinde, as best accords
> With rurall passions; which vse not to reach
> Beyond the groues and woods, where they were bred:
> And best becomes a claustrall exercise,
> Where men shut out retyr'd, and sequestred
> From publike fashion, seeme to sympathize
> With innocent, and plaine simplicity:
> And liuing here under the awfull hand
> Of discipline, and strict obseruancy
> Learne but our weakenesses to understand. (ll. 9–20)[5]

For Daniel, this scholarly quasi-pastoral seclusion allows the
student actors to avoid the vices of the public stage, for such
actors

>   dare not enterprize to show
> In lowder stile the hidden mysteries,
> And arts of Thrones; which none that are below
> The Sphere of action, and the exercise
> Of power can truely shew: though men may straine . . .
> Whereby the populasse (in whom such skill
> Is needlesse) may be brought to apprehend
> Notions, that may turne all to a tast of ill . . .
> . . .
> Yet the eye of practise, looking downe from hie
> Vpon such ouer-reaching vanity,
> Sees how from error t'error it doth flote,
> As from an unknowne Ocean into a Gulfe:
> And how though th'Woolfe, would counterfeit the Goate
> Yet euery chinke bewrayes him for a Woolfe.
> And therefore in the view of state t'haue show'd
> A counterfeit of state, had beene to light
> A candle to the Sunne.   (ll. 21–45)

5. *The Complete Works in Verse and Prose of Samuel Daniel*, ed. Alexander
E. Grosart (1885; rpt New York, 1963), iii. 213–14.

In Daniel's view the sovereign would be most improperly served by the political and social commentary that was the staple of the public stage. And the public stage itself is censured for meddling in mysteries above the capacities of the 'populace'. It is clear that Guarini provides a model of how the stage can avoid these strong and dangerous excitements. It is equally clear that the English populace had no intention of doing without them.

The Malcontent of John Marston is the play that shows most brilliantly how pastoral tragicomedy and the English stage could be brought into a relationship more fruitful than that envisaged by Daniel, or achieved by Fletcher. As I have pointed out above,[6] *The Malcontent* has many quotations from *Il Pastor Fido*, which seem to be taken literatim from the 1602 'Dymock' translation. Borrowing from *Il Pastor Fido* proves, of course, that Marston had been reading *Il Pastor Fido* but does not prove that the shape and nature of Marston's play is affected by Guarini's. There is some evidence, however, of this further and larger connection. Marston's play was entered in the Stationers' Register as 'An Enterlude called the Malecontent Tragicomedia'. Such entries often reflect something written on the manuscript; internal as well as external evidence suggests that Marston was deliberately experimenting with a new genre for which Guarini's play provided the most celebrated and most embattled example. *The Malconent* is not, need I say, a simple reproduction of the mode of *Il Pastor Fido;* the surface appearances of the two plays could hardly be more distinct. The one is as much a critique of the other as an imitation. Perhaps it should be seen as a critical return to the roots of the genre. The pastoral tragicomedy form had grown out of attempts to reinvent the Greek satyr play.[7] The satyr and the shepherd are presented by the theorists as its alternate protagonists. The English awareness of this notion is nicely illustrated by the engraved title-page to Ben Jonson's *Workes* (1616 and 1640). In this design *Tragicomoedia* appears aloft, supported on one side by *Pastor* and on the other by *Satyr*.

6. P. 120.
7. See, for example, Giraldi's *Egle*, and the theoretical gloss supplied in his *Discorso sulle satire atti alle scene*.

In the *Compendio della Poesia Tragicomica* Guarini traced back the origins of the new form to the *tertium quid* (between Tragedy and Comedy) that the satyr play provided:

> Ma niuno meglio d'Orazio nella sua poetica *Pistola a' Pisoni* ci ha descritta la tragicommedia con questi versi:
> mox etiam agrestes satyros nudavit et asper
> incolumi gravitate iocum tentavit eo quod
> illecibris erat et grata novitate morandus
> spectator, functusque sacris et potus et exlex.
> Verum ita risores, ita commendare dicaces
> conveniet Satyros, ita vertere seria ludo . . .[8]

In such a passage the satyr ceases to be simply the wild man of the pastoral scene and becomes the urban expression of irreverence and license, the presiding genius of sophisticated satire. Marston has reworked Guarini's idyllic pastoral in terms of the tragicomic urban satyr rather than the shepherd, so that the surface appearances are bound to be wholly different. The non-political world of Arcadia becomes the charged political confine of an Italian palace (as imagined by Englishmen); the intervention of the gods to fulfill the promise of the oracle becomes a political revolution to overthrow the usurpers and re-establish the legitimate duke.

But these political happenings in *The Malcontent* are tragicomic rather than tragic because Marston has taken from Guarini a primary concern with love, faithful and unfaithful, reworking it in urban terms and in the context of

---

8. P. 247 in the Laterza edition (1914) in the 'Scrittori d'Italia' series. The quotation is from Horace's *Ars Poetica*, ll. 221–6. The passage reads in English: But no one has done better than Horace, who in his poem *Epistle to the Pisos* has described tragicomedy in these verses:

> Hee . . . soone after, forth did send
> The rough rude Satyres naked; and would try,
> Though sower with safetie of his gravitie,
> How he could jest; because he mark'd and saw,
> The free spectators, subject to no Law,
> Having well eat, and drunke (the rites being done)
> Were to be staid with softnesses, and wonne
> With something that was acceptably new.
> Yet so the scoffing Satyres to mens view,
> And so their prating to present was best,
> And so to turne all earnest into jest.

The translation of the Horace is Ben Jonson's (Herford and Simpson, viii. 319–21.

court intrigue. The danger of death is omnipresent but no one dies; revenge is limited to satiric ends—the public exposure of the wicked, assisted self-discovery for those who have lost their moral bearings, and expulsion for the incorrigible. And this limitation is possible because erotic corruption provides the primary terms for the social viciousness that issues also in usurpation, atheism, Machiavellian plottings, and intended murder. Mendoza's claim to the throne of Genoa derives from his exploits in the Medici Duchess's bedchamber; and it was she who engineered the earlier coup when her husband Piero replaced Altofront, the virtuous and legitimate ruler. The pattern of loves that Guarini establishes in his play, with the separated ideal pair, Mirtillo and Amarilli, flanked on one side by the less perfect Silvio and Dorinda, and on the other by the largely corrupt and opportunist Satyr and Corisca, is repeated in *The Malcontent*, Altofront and Maria representing the ideal, Pietro and Aurelia the imperfect, Mendoza and Maquerelle the corrupt. The pattern repeats, but of course the tone and range of reference is entirely different. The love attitudes of *The Malcontent* may provide the basic analysis of the material, but every love attitude turns out to have a train of political consequences. The ideal love of Altofront and Maria establishes not only an emotional relationship between individuals but also a model of the political fidelity of self-consciously righteous sovereigns. The infidelity of Aurelia has its most poignant treatment as personal loss but its most elaborate development in terms of political betrayal. And it is in the public sphere that these relationships are finally fixed —as versions of the political responsibility that arises from personal integrity.

Marston's satyric bias also leads him to give greater emphasis to the bottom end of this scale of love than Guarini does. The passages of *Il Pastor Fido* that attract Marston's direct imitation (or rather transcription) belong predominantly to the satyr and to Corisca the libertine nymph. Corisca's *carpe diem* advice is transferred to Maquerelle, the court bawd, while the satyr provides rhetoric for the cuckoldmaker and usurper, Mendoza. These attitudes toward love thus become political forces. Both Tasso and Guarini give emphasis to nostalgia for a *bella etá de l'oro*, when tyrant honor did not frustrate natural love-making. In *The Malcontent* the nostalgia is rather for the old simplicities of patriarchal rule and family fidelities, before sophisticated female rulers turned political action into sexual intrigue.

The Malcontent is not a freak play standing alone in the dramatic world of its time. It is one of a series of plays that reflect, in the period 1602–4, a movement away from the grand confrontation with corruption that *Hamlet* had implied and toward the compromises by which justice and forgiveness could be embodied in the action. *Hamlet* had dealt with the overthrow of order when the sovereign mind was dispossessed of command both of the state and of itself. The hero's 'disguise' in madness, designed to give him room to manoeuvre for the cure of corruption, operates in the manner of *The Malcontent* only in that small part of the action dealing with Gertrude. Elsewhere, Hamlet's estrangement from the corrupt court lies under the pressure of the Ghost's morality. The answer to corruption implied by Hamlet's verbal control and his conceptual transformation of its images is not allowed to be an adequate response. In the world of Fortinbras and the elder Hamlet only active physical opposition is 'real'; the stains of corruption can only be washed out by decimation and a tide of blood. But in the group of later plays with which I am concerned—Shakespeare's *All's Well* and *Measure for Measure*, Marston's *The Malcontent* and *The Fawn*, Middleton's *The Phoenix*—the sovereign mind, though eclipsed and dispossessed of its effortless superiority, is able, in the midst of corruption, to retain an adequate control through disguise and cunning and verbal superiority.

The reason why these plays appear at this time has been discussed at what might seem inordinate length, given the inconclusiveness of the results, especially, of course, Shakespeare's so-called 'dark comedies' or 'problem plays', which have been seen as resulting from 'mythical sorrows' (dark ladies, etc.) or from the new political tone of James's reign. If Guarini's *Il Pastor Fido* is a factor in this change of direction in the Elizabethan public repertory, then the whole movement begins to look more technical, more deliberate than has been supposed. This does not mean, of course, that

the vogue of these plays has no connection with the intellectual temper of England in the years 1602–4. The fact that *Il
Pastor Fido* exercised an influence I am prepared to call
decisive is in itself a measure of the responsiveness of the time
to this exotic model.

The early and seminal influence of *Il Pastor Fido* is
focused for critics of Shakespeare by a number of parallels
between that play and Shakespeare's *All's Well that Ends
Well.*[9] My sense of the relationship was first stimulated by
reading the speech in Act III, scene v, in which the lecherous
nymph Corisca advises Amarilli that love is more natural
than chastity:

> Qual è tra noi piú antica,
> la legge di Diana o pur d'Amore?
> Questa ne' nostri petti
> nasce, Amarilli, e con l'etá s'avanza;
> né s'apprende o s'insegna,
> ma negli umani cuori,
> senza maestro, la natura stessa
> di propria man l'imprime.[1]

9. A connection between the two plays was long ago noticed in passing by
J. L. Klein, *Geschichte des Dramas* (Leipzig, 1867), p. 198. Klein, in the course
of an extended treatment of *Kusswissenschaft*, mentions the similarity between
Dorinda's reluctance to ask openly for the kiss she desires:

> Vorrei senza parlar esser intesa (II. ii. 61),

and Helena's similar reluctance:

> I would not tell you what I would, my lord (II. v. 83).

The absence of verbal connection weakens the case here if taken as basic; but
given the other examples cited in this article it may be thought to lend confirma-
tory strength.

1. Pp. 98–99 in the Laterza edition. The 1602 translation is here, as elsewhere,
rather curt, and appears to be, if anything, more remote from Shakespeare than
the original:

> ... which is more auncient among us,
> *Dianaes* lawes or loues? this in our breasts
> Is bred and growes with vs, *Nature* her selfe
> With her owne hands imprints in our hearts breasts.
> (sig. H4)

I am not anxious to use anything in this article as a basis for an assertion that
Shakespeare must have known Italian. The evidence suggests that Shakespeare
read the original rather than the 1602 translation of *Il Pastor Fido* but is not
substantial. It is commonly supposed, of course, that Shakespeare in the years
about 1603 read the *Othello* story in Italian (it was not translated into English).
A detailed response to the stylistic qualities of *Il Pastor Fido* implies a better
reading ability than any made necessary by a capacity to get the gist of Cinthio's

We should compare with this the Countess's speech in Act I, scene iii, of *All's Well*, where she comments on the discovery that Helena loves her son:

> If ever we are nature's, these are ours; this thorn
> Doth to our rose of youth rightly belong;
> Our blood to us, this to our blood is born.
> It is the show and seal of nature's truth,
> Where love's strong passion is impress'd in youth.
>
> (ll. 120–4)

The general argument that love is natural is, of course, too commonplace to justify any claims of relationship. But it is remarkable that in both authors the theme is particularized by the image of Nature stamping itself (*imprime / impress'd*), as in a seal or a signature, directly on to the physical constitution of the person (*umani cuori / our blood*) and justifying its authenticity by the legal evidence of *propria man* or *show and seal*.[2] Secondary evidence of Shakespeare's knowledge of this passage may be found slightly later in the same scene of *All's Well*. Helena tells the Countess that she will know how to pity her predicament if she herself did ever

> Wish chastely and love dearly that your Dian
> Was both herself and love.   (ll. 203–4)

The antithesis of *Dian* and *love* here is perfectly intelligible. The editors usually tell us that we should substitute *Venus* for *love*. But the English idiom is somewhat strained, since *love* cannot normally mean 'the goddess of love'. The same idiom is, however, much more acceptable in Italian. If Shakespeare had in his mind here Guarini's *la legge di Diana*

story of the Moor of Venice, but this is where the existence of the 1602 translation may be important. It is certainly an interesting coincidence that Shakespeare was writing *All's Well* in the year of the translation or the year after. The existence of the crib may have made it possible for him to work fruitfully with the Italian as well as the English, deploying the two in a manner familiar to most students of the foreign classics.

2. My colleague, Miss Jennifer Lorch, whose help I sought to uncover the range of meaning in *propria man* writes to me as follows:
'Professor Domenico De Robertis of the Accademia della Crusca confirmed that "di propria man l'imprime" can be understood in a regal/legal sense with implicit reference to *sigillo*. But he stressed that this was only one of a number of possible meanings and that there was nothing in the text to support that interpretation rather than another.'

o pur d'Amore, we would have an explanation of the appearance of the un-English idiom at this point. Exactly the same English wording (*Diana . . . love*) appears, we may note, in the 1602 translation.

A more important connection between the two plays appears to be established in the denouements. Act v, scene iii, of *All's Well* is the first example in Shakespeare and (so far as I know) in Elizabethan drama of a resolution of a dramatic tangle by bittersweet, self-consciously legal, and sophistic juggling, where the anagnorisis is achieved by the unwilling testimony of morally dubious characters, dragged out of them in paradoxes by a half-comic, half-punitive method. In *All's Well* this process is presented twice, first with the evidence of Parolles and then with that of Diana. The whole passage is therefore rather long, but I hope it may be represented fairly by the following:

KING. Tell me, sirrah—but tell me true I charge you,
 . . .
 By him and by this woman here what know you?
PAROLLES. So please your Majesty, my master hath been an honourable gentleman; tricks he hath had in him, which gentlemen have.
KING. Come, come, to th' purpose. Did he love this woman?
PAROLLES. Faith, sir, he did love her; but how?
KING. How, I pray you?
PAROLLES. He did love her, sir, as a gentleman loves a woman.
KING. How is that?
PAROLLES. He lov'd her, sir, and lov'd her not.
KING. As thou art a knave and no knave.
 . . .
KING [to Diana]. This ring, you say was yours?
DIANA. Ay, my good lord.
KING. Where did you buy it? Or who gave it you?
DIANA. It was not given me, nor I did not buy it.
KING. Who lent it you?
DIANA. It was not lent me neither.
KING. Where did you find it then?
DIANA.   I found it not.
KING. If it were yours by none of all these ways,
 How could you give it him?
DIANA.   I never gave it him.
             (V. iii. 232 ff.)

In Act v, scene v, of *Il Pastor Fido,* Carino, the supposed father of Mirtillo, uncovers to Montano (the true father— about to sacrifice his son on the altar of Diana) the complex circumstances of Mirtillo's early life, a process that will lead in the end to the discovery of true paternity. The machinery of this anagnorisis is derived from the *Oedipus Rex,* but the tone and detail of the discovery is quite un-Sophoclean:

CARINO. Perché nol generai, straniero il chiamo.
MONTANO. Dunque è tuo figlio, e tu nol generasti?
CARINO. E, se nol generai, non è mio figlio.
MONTANO. Non mi dicesti tu ch'è di te nato?
CARINO. Dissi ch'è figlio mio, non di me nato.
CARINO. Come puo star in un figlio e non figlio . . .
MONTANO. Chi è dunque suo padre,
   se non è figlio tuo?
CARINO. Non tel so dire;
   so ben che non son io.
MONTANO. Vedi come vacilli?
   E egli del tuo sangue?
CARINO. Né questo ancora.
MONTANO. E perché figlio il chiami?
   . . .
MONTANO. Il comprasti? il rapisti? onde l'avesti?
CARINO. In Elide l'ebb'io, cortese dono
   d'uomo straniero.
MONTANO. E quell' uomo straniero
   donde l'ebb'egli?
CARINO. A lui l'avea dat'io.
MONTANO. Sdegno tu movi in un sol punto e riso.[3]

3. Pp. 186–7 in the Laterza edition. The 1602 translation reads:
CARINO. I call him Stranger, for I got him not.
MONTANO. Is he thy sonne, and thou begots him not?
CARINO. He is my sonne, though I begot him not.
MONTANO. Didst thou not say that he was borne of thee?
CARINO. I sayd he was my sonne, not borne of mee.
   . . .
MONTANO. How can it be sonne, and not sonne at once?
   . . .
MONTANO. Who is his father since hee's not your sonne?
CARINO. I cannot tell you, I am sure not I.
MONTANO. See how he wauers, is he not of your bloud?
CARINO. Oh no.
MONTANO. Why do you call him sonne?
   . . .

The obvious verbal connections here are between the 'He
lov'd her and lov'd her not ... knave and no knave' and the
Italian paradox of 'figlio e non figlio,'⁴ together with the
contradictions about possession: 'Where did you buy it ...
who gave it you ... lent it ... find it ... give it?' and 'It was
not given ... I did not buy it ... was not lent ... I found it
not ... I never gave it', set against the Italian 'Il comprasti?
Il rapisti? onde l'avesti? ... donde l'ebb'egli?' (with the implied contradiction of the first two and the absurd answer to
the last: '[l'ebb'egli] a lui l'avea dat'io'). Shakespeare turns
this final paradox into its negative form: Carino claims he
does not own the child because he received him from a
stranger to whom he had already given him; while Diana
denies having given her ring to Bertram, because she never
possessed it in such a way as to be able to give it; but the
common play on possession and giving links the two, to my
mind, in undeniable fashion.

It is worthwhile trying to establish verbal correspondence,
for without this it is difficult to argue for a necessary relationship. But much more interesting, from a critical point of view,
are the more vague and general points that may be made
about the tone of these passages taken as wholes. The final
line of the quotation from Guarini makes an important point
about this tone:

> Sdegno tu movi in un sol punto e riso

The questioner is seen, in terms of the play, as moving,
though slowly and circuitously, nearer to the truth; but to
himself he seems only to be sinking deeper into paradox and
absurdity. The clash of tragic urgency on one side with
cumbrous levity on the other establishes a tone important to
the tragicomic effect. The tragic potential of the situation is

MONTANO. Bought you him? stole you him? where had you him?
CARINO. A courteous straunger in *Elidis* gaue me him
MONTANO. And that same straunger, where had he the childe?
CARINO. I gaue him.
MONTANO. Thou mou'st at once disdain and laughter.
(Sig. O4v–P1)

---

4. Compare the later 'guilty and not guilty' paradox (l. 283) and the having
a husband but not married situation in *Measure for Measure* (v. i. 170–8).

not simply contradicted by the happy ending. Eventually, the collision of two opposed attitudes, *sdegno* and *riso* on one side, and the passionate gravity of the situation on the other, resolves into a sense of the divine dispensation by which the flaunted impossibilities surrounding Carino's son or Diana's ring are shown to belong to a higher simplicity. But before the sudden and unexpected unknotting of the paradoxes an atmosphere of social insolence and moral rejection is powerfully established. From the point of view of Providence, *sdegno* and *riso* may be seen as complementary parts of human response to its processes, but we are not allowed to forget that in the human terms that provide the substance of the play there is a painful and unbridged gap. The route to the genuine comedy of a providential re-establishment of social cohesion involves a seeming dissolution of order, more alarming than comic. Montano's loss of authority and understanding can only provide, in the asocial world of *Il Pastor Fido*, a muted paradigm. But one can see why the politically self-conscious world of Jacobean drama should seize upon it to express a radical unease. We can think of the uncharacteristic effrontery of Diana to the King at the end of *All's Well*:

> Great King, I am no strumpet, by my life;
> I am either maid, or else this old man's wife.
>
> (v. iii. 286–7)

The same uneasy atmophere pervades what may well have been Shakespeare's next play—*Measure for Measure*—which appears to be, whatever the chronological detail, a second attempt to achieve Guarinian tragicomic effects within an English theatrical context. There are this time, so far as I know, no verbal parallels with *Il Pastor Fido*. Perhaps one should not expect them. The English tragicomic convention of the duke who observes his subjects' licence while moving among them in disguise has here almost completely absorbed the Guarinian basis of oracular confusion and discovery. *Measure for Measure* resembles *The Malcontent* (it seems impossible to say which way the debt—if there is any—is owed) not only in its use of this convention, but in its whole approach to political corruption through sexual licence. In an even more skeletal form than in Marston's play, it offers the structure of a range of couples who show kinds of loving relationships, extending from perfect through imperfect to corrupt. Clearly, Duke-Isabella achieve the ideal politico-moral position. Claudio-Juliet and Angelo-Mariana may be seen as alternative versions of morally damaged but recover able relationships (comparable to Marston's Pietro and Aurelia), while Lucio and Kate Keepdown (the eventual representative of the brothel world of Mistress Overdone) mark the nadir of presumably irrecoverable corruption. Shakespeare's characteristic concern for the individual psychology of his characters weakens, however, the exemplary force of the relationships, so that the structural point is hardly evident.

But the most interesting element in relationship to Guarini remains, in *Measure for Measure* as in *All's Well that Ends Well*, the final unknotting. Here again we face the painful process of sifting through absurdities and social solecisms to reach a truth which seems to claim validity almost because of the bizarre processes and paradoxes that its discovery has involved. The role of Lucio in the final scene of *Measure for Measure* has puzzled many critics. His comments seem designed to bring into ridicule the processes of a justice that elsewhere claims a quasi-divine sanction.

Take, for example, Mariana's paradox-laden entry in Act V:

[*Enter Mariana veiled*]
DUKE.   Is this the witness friar?
First let her show her face, and after speak.
MARIANA. Pardon, my lord; I will not show my face
Until my husband bid me.
DUKE. What, are you married?
MARIANA. No, my lord.
DUKE. Are you a maid?
MARIANA. No, my lord.
DUKE. A widow, then?
MARIANA. Neither, my lord.
DUKE. Why, you are nothing then; neither maid, widow, nor wife.
LUCIO. My lord, she may be a punk; for many of them are neither maid, widow, nor wife.
DUKE. Silence that fellow. I would he had some cause
To prattle for himself.

LUCIO. Well, my lord.
MARIANA. My lord, I do confess I ne'er was married,
    And I confess, besides, I am no maid.
    I have known my husband; yet my husband
    Knows not that ever he knew me.
LUCIO. He was drunk, then, my lord; it can be no better.
DUKE. For the benefit of silence, would thou wert so too!
LUCIO. Well, my lord.   (v. i. 167–90)

What is the dramatic point of Lucio's interruptions here?
How are they related to the context into which they obtrude?
Are we meant to laugh at him or to sigh with the Duke at his
ineptitude, feel *riso* or *sdegno*? Given the connection suggested above, we may guess that Shakespeare is here com-
pacting with even greater boldness than in *All's Well* the
sdegno e riso of Guarini's denouement, together with the
providential movement toward understanding and forgiveness. Mariana's paradoxes here resemble those of Carino and
of Diana Capilet. But here they are subject not only to the
contemptuous disbelief of her questioner but also to the
further debasement of Lucio's interpretations. To the world
as it really exists, Shakespeare seems to be saying, such high-
strained paradoxes of salvation are only dirty jokes. With
Donnean brilliance he impacts against the providential figure
of the Duke the *contempt* which is shown here as a fully
realized figure. What in Guarini is only a fleeting impression
of *sdegno*, in *All's Well* only a psychological response,
becomes in *Measure for Measure* a man of flesh and blood
with a whole social milieu to support him and give him depth
of reality. When Lucio pulls the hood from the supposed friar
and reveals the duke beneath the cowl, two totally disparate
views of what the scene is about are pushed together. For
Lucio, slander, evasion, and disguise are the natural processes
of society. He knows himself and assumes that the rest of the
world shares with him the desire to wriggle out of every
responsibility as it arises, without a thought beyond the
immediate advantages that are opened up. And, in truth, the
uncovering of the situation in *Measure for Measure* cannot
be wholly divorced from some such sense of shuffling subter-
fuge. If we are to see in perspective the quasi-providential and
self-denying responses of the Duke and Isabella, we cannot

afford to forget the world of Vienna, where the very flesh, through which they too operate, is subject to *sdegno e riso*.

It is a long time since *Il Pastor Fido* read like a crucial text; it is hard for us even to imagine what shock of novelty it could ever have imposed upon its readers. We therefore find ourselves unwilling to allow that it could ever have had a crucial effect on a mind as original and actively creative as Shakespeare's. On the other hand it becomes increasingly clear that Shakespeare's originality operated inside formal and generic assumptions which he shared with his fellow dramatists and which can eventually be fitted into the larger European context. In particular, it begins to appear that his 'discovery' of tragicomedy was, in part at least, like that of his fellow dramatists, a discovery of Guarini. Only in his case, however, was the discovery so handled that it gave every appearance of spontaneous personal creation.

TRADITIONS

6

Seneca and the Elizabethans: a case-study in 'influence'

Once-upon-a-simple-time, while the modern languages were seeking to make their way as serious studies, the subject of 'The influence of Seneca on Elizabethan tragedy' was quite self-evidently an example of what serious study in modern literature could provide. The scholar who set out to study an author ('B') learned that the scientific way of doing this was to discover, embedded in B, the echoes or reminiscences of an earlier author or work (which we may call 'A'). It was the business of the Ph.D. student, charged with the investigation of B, to discover his 'A'; then he could list the echoes and reminiscences, enlarge these into a discussion of 'influence'—and his dissertation was made. Of such a kind, in the field under discussion here, the most notable example is John W. Cunliffe's 1893 D.Litt. dissertation 'The influence of Seneca on Elizabethan tragedy'—a book which has occupied its field with apparent adequacy since 1893, and which was reissued as recently as 1965. Professor Peter Ure could remark (in his *Durham University Journal* article of 1948, 'On some differences between Senecan and Elizabethan tragedy') that the day of Cunliffe 'is now apparently past'; but this cannot be allowed to be entirely true in 1966. The central attack on Cunliffe, in Howard Baker's *Induction to Tragedy* (1939), seems to have disappeared into the sands of time, and Cunliffe's assumptions remain the common assumptions. I notice a bland restatement of them, as if of undisputed truth, in the preface to the excellent Penguin translation of five Senecan plays (1966).

Cunliffe's book is, at its kernel, a list of parallel passages, and it takes the influence of Seneca on Elizabethan tragedy

[First published in *Shakespeare Survey* 20 (1967).]

to be 'proved', or demonstrated in detail, by the existence of
these parallel passages; but it is not clear that the conclusion
follows from the premiss. Certainly we must ask what are the
Elizabethan tragedies involved in Cunliffe's book, and to
what extent his parallels are continuously persuasive. The
central play for the thesis is, obviously, Thomas Hughes's
The Misfortunes of Arthur (1587), whose 'imitations of
Seneca' occupy twenty-five pages—the whole of 'Appendix
II' in this book. The case that *The Misfortunes of Arthur* is a
cento of Senecan imitations is a brilliant example of what this
kind of study can do: it is proved beyond doubt.[1] If Thomas
Hughes had been the central figure of English Renaissance
tragedy, or if *The Misfortunes of Arthur* were the great
seminal play of the period, then 'the influence of Seneca on
Elizabethan tragedy' would be as categorical as Cunliffe and
other early investigators[2] supposed it to be. Fair-minded
literary history cannot, however, make either of these
assumptions.

Not only is Cunliffe's book centred on a minor play; but
the thesis becomes less convincing as the works he treats
become aesthetically more important. It works very well for
The Misfortunes of Arthur, well for *Gismond of Salerne* (and
not badly for Dr Legge's *Richardus Tertius*) but it is on very
shaky ground with *The Spanish Tragedy* (where Baker's
strictures are especially important) and works not at all for
Marlowe's plays or for Shakespeare's. Even more telling is the
objection that it fails to take account of an alternative line of
serious writing, running through *Damon and Pithias*, *Horestes*,
and *Cambyses*. This would seem to show, at the very least,
that something else was going on around English tragedy of
the period beside the influence of Seneca. Nor would I regard
this progressive thinning-out of Cunliffe's thesis as an
accident; indeed I suggest that it points to something basic in
Quellenforschung. The process involved in this type of study

1. I do not wish to be taken to mean that Cunliffe says all that can be said
about *The Misfortunes of Arthur*. See W. A. Armstrong, 'Elizabethan themes
in *The Misfortunes of Arthur*', *R.E.S.* vii (1956), 238–49.
2. For example, J. A. Symonds, *Shakespeare's Predecessors in the English
Drama* (1884); A. H. Thorndike, *Tragedy* (Boston, 1908); H. E. Fansler,
The Evolution of Technic in Elizabethan Tragedy (Chicago, 1914); F. E.
Schelling, *Elizbethan Drama*, 2 vols (Boston, 1908).

is, as I have said, that the scholar looks at work B for evidence that it derived elements from work A, which then may be elevated to the status of '*an influence*'. But if work B is more than a passive and parasitic object—that is, if it is any good—it will make new whatever it borrows, it will render what it treats into organic substance, into substance whose principal relationship is to context, not to source. The danger of *Quellenforschung* is that it tends to treat as *passive* a situation in which good work is essentially active, creative, and to this extent unique. And this is why a book like Thorndike's *Influence of Beaumont and Fletcher on Shakspere* can never command simple assent; for the Last Plays of Shakespeare (the 'B' of Thorndike's thesis) are too rich, various, and difficult to place to be put under the influence. They refuse to stay etherized upon the table.

It is interesting and important, of course, to know where plots come from, and I do not seek to deny this. But 'the influence of Painter (or Brooke or Sidney) on Shakespeare' obviously fails to emerge as a possible thesis subject, even though plots are taken from these authors; unless, that is, we are content to derive 'influence' from the most flaccid of linkages. John Webster's tragedies raise this problem in an acute form. We know that Webster's plays are mosaics of borrowings. Should we therefore discuss 'the influence of Sir William Alexander, Sidney, Montaigne, Guazzo, Guevara, Matthieu, etc., on Webster'? Surely not, unless we have evidence of a more general relationship than is provided by the lists of parallels. One must return here to the important point already made (*vis-à-vis* Seneca and Renaissance tragedy) by Professor Jacquot: 'Un dénombrement des emprunts directs ne suffit donc pas à rendre compte de l'influence du poète latin' (*Sénèque et le Théatre de la Renaissance* [1964], p. 307).

But if the 'scientific' definiteness provided by parallel passages disappears from literary theses dealing with 'influence', what then is left? It might seem that the concept of influence then becomes too vague to be tenable. But we should take comfort by remembering that the etymology of *influence* suggests no single link, but rather a stream of tendency raining down upon its object. The complexity of the situation in which any really independent B is subject to the influence of A need not prevent us from trying to describe it. Certainly the point must be made that we cannot talk effectively about the influence of A on B unless we are prepared to see A (as B saw him) as part of an whole intellectual climate. We should not discuss 'the influence of Seneca on Elizabethan tragedy' except in the context of the other competing influences that were raining down at the same time. Ideally, indeed, we should know the whole nature of the air breathed by English writers between the 1560s and the 1590s, the literary, historical, artistic scenery of these years, before we discuss 'the development of English tragedy'. Such knowledge would, inevitably, produce complex views; but it does not follow that it would rule out of court the present vulgate supposition that classical literature played a vital part in the development of English tragedy; indeed I do not suppose it. I do not suggest that such knowledge would cause the name of Seneca to die away from Shakespeare conferences. But I do assume that the limpid simplicities of the person-to-person type of influence-study would have to be broken up by the cross-currents and complexities of a larger view. And it is to these complicating factors that I wish to devote the rest of this study.

I have used Cunliffe's 1893 thesis as my paradigm of a scientific study of 'influence'. The thesis itself contains no direct statement of its simplest assumptions, no plan of the intellectual model that is being used; but an admirably economical statement of this kind occurs in the opening paragraph of Cunliffe's *Cambridge History of English Literature* article on 'Early tragedy' (vol. v, p. 61), published in 1910, some seventeen years after the thesis, but sharing with it, I think, the same basic attitudes:

The history of renascence tragedy may be divided into three stages, not definitely limited, and not following in strict chronological succession, but distinct in the main: the study, imitation and production of Senecan tragedy; translation; the imitation of Greek and Latin tragedy in the vernacular.

I am not concerned to dispute how far this is, or is not, true of continental tragedy; but as far as English tragedy is concerned the lucidity of the pattern of development described depends on a rejection of competing relevant factors. Two simplifying assumptions may be noted in particular: first, that the vernacular tradition need not be mentioned, because it had nothing positive to offer; and that, in the main, the Renaissance served up classical tragedy on a *tabula rasa*. This might *resist* influence, it is allowed, but it could hardly exercise it. The second assumption is that one can talk about tragedy as a simple watertight genre, open to influence by other tragedy in the first place, and only secondarily and subordinately influenced by other genres.

I wish to discuss the second of these assumptions first. Most of us nowadays have learned to go behind the Chinese wall of the theory of genres and to apply in detail our general knowledge that the Renaissance was an age of syncretism and eclecticism. Farnham[3] and Baker[4] have laid great stress on the continuity of tragic narrative and what we tend to call 'tragedy proper'; and there is no need to reiterate the point that Seneca's 'non-theatrical' or narrative qualities helped to make him assimilable; but at the same time as we say this we should see that his assimilability helped to submerge *his* qualities among the apparently similar qualities of the Gothic tradition,[5] his ghosts melting away into the throng of their ghosts, his horrors rendered barely visible against the background of their horrors.[6]

The Gothic willingness to juxtapose things historically distinct, preferring flat anachronism to the perspective of

3. Willard Farnham, *The Medieval Heritage of Elizabethan Tragedy* (Berkeley, Cal., 1936).
4. Howard Baker, *Induction to Tragedy* (Louisiana S.U.P., 1939).
5. The use of the word 'Gothic' in such a context may seem barbarous. I use it deliberately in order to suggest that pre-classical literary practice in the Tudor period is not to be explained by ignorance, is not necessarily haphazard, but may often belong to a recognizable *system* of art.
6. The horrors of the 'Senecan' plays of the Elizabethan period are often very close to those in the medieval plays concerned with the lives (and deaths) of the saints. Long before Hieronimo bit out his tongue to defy his interrogators, St Catherine did the same. St James the dismembered, moralizing each limb as it is severed, reminds us of the horrific grotesquerie of Theseus (at the end of the *Phaedra*) reassembling the jig-saw portions of Hippolytus. Indeed, even the most horrific of the 'tragedies of blood' have nothing to rival the disembowelling of St Erasmus, to take only one example in the catalogue of horrors that the *Golden Legend* bequeathed to the medieval imagination.

history, made such assimilations both inevitable and easy. If we wish to see how visual anachronism can alter the whole tone of a work impeccably classical in origin, we may look at the plates drawn from the only illuminated manuscript of Seneca known to me[7] (Pl. 4 *a*, *b*, *c*). We may see the same principle operating in the 1581 translation where Studley translates

sed quale soles leviora lyra / flectere carmen / simplex
(*Agamemnon*, 334–6)

as

But on thy treble Lute (according to thy use)
Stryke up a playnsong note

What we cannot know for certain is how far this anachronistic principle operated in the Elizabethan reading of the Latin text. But it would surely be wrong, in the light of what we know about Elizabethan anachronism, to suppose that stories from the classics were received in a distinctly 'classical' frame of mind, which caused them to appear potentially classical in manner. This is the assumption of H. B. Charlton, who tells us that plays like *Cambyses*, *Horestes*, and *Apius and Virginia* were, because 'classical in story, . . . potentially classical in dramatic motive and incident, and thus competent to create in due season a taste for certain elements of classical tragedy'.[8] The assimilative powers of the Renaissance would in fact have been impossible if separate contributions to the age had remained as distinct as this implies; it is only in the compost-heap of history that new literatures breed. Panofsky's *Renaissance and Renascences in Western Art* (1960) is, indeed, devoted to just this discontinuity between subject matter of the classical past (seen clearly but in terms of a modern—usually Christian—meaning) and a feeling for classical form (applied to a close imitation of contemporary

7. The manuscript ('L. A. Senecae comoediae') is of North French or Flemish provenance, and is probably to be dated in the first quarter of the fifteenth century. It may have been made for Charles VII of France. It is described in the *Bulletin de la Société française de reproduction des MSS*, xxi (1938) and (more fully) in H. J. Herrmann, *Verzeichnis der Illuminierten Handschriften in Österreich*, Band vii. 3 (1938), 86–100.

8. H. B. Charlton, Introduction to the *Works of Sir William Alexander*, ed. Kastner and Charlton, i (S.T.S. N.S. xi. 1921), p. cxlii.

reality). The discontinuity is one that does not seem to be resolved at any point in Elizabethan literature.

Moreover, the lack of a clear practical division between tragedy and other genres meant that a greater proportion of the classical inheritance was relevant to Elizabethan tragedy than Cunliffe seemed to allow. The great importance of Ovid in this respect should never be underestimated. Scaliger's typical tragedy (Book III, chap. xcvii of the *Poetices libri septem*) came from Ovid's story of Ceyx and Alcyone, at the end of Book XI of the *Metaphorphoses*—the same tragedy as Chaucer had used in *The Book of the Duchess*, and which W. Hubbard, the 1569 translator, called 'the tragicall and lamentable historie of Ceyx, Kynge of Trachine and Alcione his wife'—and a glance at this will show the extent to which the ingredients of 'Senecan' tragedy were present in Ovid. I would point to the brilliantly horrific description of the storm in which Ceyx died (a description imitated, I believe, in the *Antonio and Mellida* of Marston), the effective scene where the ghost of Ceyx comes to Alcyone to announce his own death, the tragic irony of Alcyone's weaving a garment for the husband who is already dead, the supernatural brilliance of the descent of Iris to the Underworld and to the Cave of Morpheus (imitated by Spenser), the effective rhetoric of the divided mind in the scene with Alcyone at the seashore, torn between despair of the future and memories of the past; finally the horrific climax of the recovery of Ceyx's body and the strange metamorphosis of the lovers into birds. All that is lacking is moralization, and this Scaliger finds easy enough to supply in the Choruses he invents:

1. 'detestans navigationes';
2. 'vota approbans';
3. 'exempla adducens naufragiorum';
4. '[naufragium] deplorans'.

The cardinal tragedies of the popular tradition—Kyd's *Spanish Tragedy* and Shakespeare's *Titus Andronicus*—draw heavily on Ovid for both matter and manner. *Titus Andronicus* (like *Lucrece* and *Venus and Adonis*) is a mainly Ovidian piece; as Baker has pointed out, only a determination to find Seneca in every woodpile could have suppressed the Philomela story in order to reveal *Thyestes* as the source. Tenderness in the midst of horror is a characteristic of both *Spanish Tragedy* and *Titus*; it is a characteristic of Ovid; it is not a characteristic of Seneca. In fact, take down the artificial barriers between tragedy and narrative, and Seneca all but disappears into the engulfing sea of Ovidian and quasi-Ovidian imitation. Modes of rhetoric and subject matter are often so similar in the two poets that it is difficult to separate them as models; but there can be no doubt where we must place the preference if a single name has to be adduced. For Ovid is everywhere in Elizabethan England, in schooling, in art and in endless quotations, translations, paraphrases, imitations. But Seneca (in spite of Cunliffe's confident assertion) seems to have played little or no part in the Tudor scheme of grammar school education;[9] we should also notice that there was only one translation of each tragedy in the period 1540–1640, and that the one complete edition of 1581 enjoyed only one printing. Where Seneca *does* differ from Ovid—as in his gloomy devotion to horror as the only real truth about humanity—the Elizabethans seem to have avoided noticing the fact. As Christians they could hardly endorse his resolute sense of divine malevolence, and in their adherence to the idea of 'the Christian Ethnicke Seneca' as Studley, the first translator of the *Medea*, learned from Erasmus to call him, they probably did not observe it. Studley's well-known mistranslation of the last line of the *Medea*

> testare nullos esse, qua veheris, deos

into

> Bear witness, grace of God is none in place of thy repayre

may serve as a paradigm of this easy distortion.[1]

Even the formal aspects of tragedy, such as its five-act structure, once confidently attributed to Seneca, the massive researches of T. W. Baldwin have shown as more likely to

9. See T. W. Baldwin, *William Shakspere's Five-Act Structure* (Urbana, 1947), p. 741.

1. I should perhaps enter a caveat here, and make the point that I am not seeking to deny the influence of Seneca in order to sell the influence of Ovid. I wish rather to suggest the danger of extracting any *one* name from the generalized mass of classical example, splayed out by the methods of imitation in terms of topics rather than authors.

derive from Terence. Terence, not Seneca, was at the centre of school instruction in drama, and therefore of formal adult practice. The chorus, which Seneca has and Terence lacks, is a dead letter. We are left with a few well-worn anthology passages and a few isolated tricks like stichomythia (and even that occurs outside tragedy)[2] as relics of the once extensive empire of Seneca's undisputed influence.

2. If by stichomythia we mean 'dialogue in alternate lines, employed in sharp disputation' (as *O.E.D.* seems to imply) there seems to be a largely comic tradition of this in English drama, quite independent of classical models. The earliest English example known to me (missed by J. L. Hancock, *Studies in Stichomythia* [Chicago, 1917]) occurs in the *Mactatio Abel* of the Wakefield Cycle (first half of the fifteenth century) in the concluding dialogue (though here the antitheses are formally public, not private):

CAYM: I commaund you in the kyngys nayme,
GARCIO: And in my masteres, fals Cayme,
CAYM: That no man at thame fynd fawt ne blame,
GARCIO: Yey, cold rost is at my masteres hame.
CAYM: Nowther with hym nor with his knafe,
GARCIO: What! I hope my master rafe.
CAYM: For thay ar trew full manyfold.
GARCIO: My master suppys no coyle bot cold.
CAYM: The kyng wrytys you vntill.
GARCIO: Yit ete I neuer half my fill.
CAYM: The kyng will that thay be safe.
GARCIO: Yey, a draght of drynke fayne wold I hayfe.
CAYM: At thare awne will let tham wafe.
GARCIO: My stomak is redy to receyfe.
CAYM: Loke no man say to theym, on nor other—
GARCIO: This same is he that slo his brother.
CAYM: Byd euery man thaym luf and lowt.
GARCIO: Yey, il-spon weft ay comes foule out.
CAYM: Long or thou get thi hoyse, and thou go thus aboute!

Similar passages occur among early Tudor plays, and, again, Classical influence seems not to be the determining factor. Indeed, in plays written in couplets, the witty division of the couplet between two speakers is so obvious a device that it needs no messenger from Argos to make the point. In Bale's *King Johan* (1534) the stichomythia of divided couplets fits in well enough with the dialectical purpose of the play. The anonymous *Jacob and Esau* (1554) uses quite an amount of comic stichomythia—as between Esau and his servant Ragau (*M.S.R.* 105–18) and between Isaac and Rebecca, husband and wife (381–413). *July and Julian* (1570) shows it between the two servants Fenell and Wilkin. In *The Marriage of Wit and Science* (?1567), Wit and his servant Will have many short dialogues in line-by-line exchange.

On the other hand, plays as 'Senecan' as *Gorboduc* and *Cambyses* show no traces of stichomythia. *Damon and Pithias* has one passage (861–91) clearly modelled on that between Seneca and Nero in the *Octavia*; but this is the only one, out of the many passages of stichomythia in the play, that has a clearly classical origin.

Mention of these formal characteristics brings me back to the first part of Cunliffe's simplified diagram of English tragic origins. He took it for granted that the vernacular tradition was a passive or dying body waiting for replacement, ripe only for modernization. Memory of the process by which classical influence affected other arts in the period, and the extent to which a broad survey like Panofsky's *Renaissance and Renascences* is able to find similarities of process, should, however, make us pause. In general it would seem that the Gothic style only gradually admitted modifications, and those superficial ones. It continued to exercise its powers with ease and authority, not as a senile creature waiting for the end and the take-over-bid of the new generation, but as a master well able to command such newfangled servants as it chose to employ. Hampton Court (1515–36), Henry VII's chapel at Westminster (1502–12), Christ Church, Oxford (1525 et seq.) are not obviously the products of decay or degeneracy. Wolsey might place medallions with the heads of the Roman Emperors on the gateways of Hampton Court, but this is as far as his interest in classical models seems to take him. As Sir John Summerson has remarked:

. . . although foreign fashions in ornament, and sometimes in plan, were excitedly adopted, they were adopted for the intrinsic pleasure they gave rather than from any sense of apprenticeship to foreign achievements greater than [Tudor Englishmen's] own. If ancient Rome and modern Italy received their homage, it was homage to a legend . . . it is only by insisting falsely on the importance of accurate grammatical interpretation of classical elements that we are tempted to see them as groping preliminaries to the Italian classicism of Inigo Jones . . . Classical architecture made its way in England not as a method of building but as a mode of decorative design . . . of columns and entablatures, pediments and consoles.[3]

The Latin quotations which abound in Elizabethan drama

3. *Architecture in Britain 1530–1830* (Pelican History of Art) (1953), p. 20. The process here described may remind some of the transformations that appear in Lebègue's account of *La Tragédie religieuse en France . . . 1514–1573* (Paris, 1929); as, for example, the process which turns the scene of Judas's repentance, in Nicholas Barthelemy's classical passion-play, *Christus Xylonicus* (1529), into a dialogue (in good hexameters) with *Alecto* rather than with *Desespoir*. The substance remains but a classical 'finish' has been applied to it.

form an obvious example in literature, parallel to Wolsey's medallions. As found in florilegia, polyanthea, thesauruses, books of quotations and commonplaces these sententiae bear an obvious relation to the 'classical' designs found in pattern-books. The Senecan quotations which appear in Elizabethan plays, even when the quantity is as great as that which decorates Marston's *Antonio and Mellida,* bear little or no relation to the contexts of the plays in which they originally appeared. This was indeed one of the rules of imitation, as Ralph Johnson noted in his *Scholars Guide from the Accidence to the University* (1665), under the heading 'Rules of Allusion':

We may allude to Sentences of Authors, applying them to another matter . . . We may say of drunkenness as the Poet did of love, *raptam tollit de cardine mentem.*   (p. 9)

Seneca's name appears frequently in such florilegia as list authors, but the quotations often do not come from Seneca at all (the whole set of Publilius Syrus' *Sententiae* gets attached to Seneca's name)[4] Seneca as a name for a collection of grave

4. For the so-called 'Collectanea Senecae' MSS. of Publilius Syrus see J. Wight Duff, *Minor Latin Poets* (Loeb Classical Library) (1934), pp. 6–12. The general role played by Seneca in the florilegia of the Renaissance can only be sketched here in respect of a few of the most popular books. The *Fiori di Virtu,* which had a European circulation under sundry titles—*Le Livre des Vices & des Vertus, La Fleur de Vertu* (Brunet ii. 1286), *Le Livre de Saigesse* (Brunet iii. 1123), *Armonia coi Soavi accenti, The Book of Virtues and Vices* (?1485) (E.E.T.S. o.s. 217), *The Boke of Wisdome* (?1575)—devotes some of its space to Seneca (as well as to Boethius, Solomon, David, Socrates, Tully, etc.), usually through the medium of the *Compendium moralium notabilium* of Geremia da Montagnone; but of the 38 'Seneca dice . . .' paragraphs noted by Carlo Frati (*Richerche sul 'Fiore di Virtu',* Studii di filologia romanza, vi. 1893) only three seem to derive from authentic works of Seneca, and these are prose works. As Frati remarks: 'per Seneca in fine, delle cui sentenze troviamo riscontro, sia in opere autentiche di Seneca . . . sia nel *De forma honestae vitae* . . . o nel *De moribus* . . . o in alcuni *Proverbi volgari di Seneca* . . . che ci attestano quanto consentita fosse nei tempi, in che fu scritto il *Fior di Virtu* l'attribuzione di essi a Seneca' (p. 272).

The *Manipulus Florum* or *Flores omnium pene doctorum* of Thomas Hibernicus—often reprinted, and much used by such a popular Elizabethan writer as Dekker—draws on Seneca as the most notable pagan author in a company of scholastics, saints, and fathers—Augustine, Bernard, Bede, Jerome, Cassiodorus, Alanus, Innocent, etc.—but, again, the references are largely to the supposititious works, the *proverbia* and the *de moribus,* though the *epistulae* and *de remediis fortuitorum* are also heavily drawn on. The tragedies do not seem to be mentioned. Of the English florilegia of the Elizabethan period the *Treatise*

moral and near-Christian sentiments is one thing; Seneca as
an instructor in tragedy is quite another; and we should
beware of turning the first into the second. We should not
forget that the first works of Seneca to make their way into
English in the Tudor period are the *De Quattuor Virtutibus*
and the *De Moribus*, not by Seneca at all, but most probably by St Martin of Braga, writing in the sixth century.
Indeed, throughout the Renaissance, Seneca the moral sage is
much more widely acclaimed than Seneca the tragic exemplar.
The name of Seneca gave a classical gloss to moral collections; it did not give either a classical form or a classical
substance. Indeed, even where the tragedies were read, the
practice of digesting reading-matter into private commonplace books placed an effective barrier between the original
(as a literary structure) and the 'imitation'. I would direct
attention back again to the interesting case of John Webster.[5]

The tendency to pile up examples, to enrich by amassing
materials from a wide variety of sources, to treasure the
curious detail—these are, from a formal point of view, signs
of the Gothic rather than the classic, even when the materials
so collected have classical origins. The idea that tragedy as a
classical structure would be 'spoiled' by over-repetition, by
addition of side-chapels, secondary plots, new episodes
(especially if these had Greco-Roman origins), would not I

of *Moral Philosophy* by William Baldwin (1547 and numerous later editions) is
probably the most popular early example. It is in the same tradition as the two
works already mentioned, of heavily moral paragraphs conveying at undue
length the tritest of sentiments. To Seneca are attributed such statements as
'Marry a young maid that thou mayest teach her good manners', 'order thy
wife as thou wouldest thy kinsfolk', etc., etc. If any of the sharp sayings of the
tragedies lie buried in Baldwin's massy prose, it is difficult to disinter them.

The *Politeuphuia* or *Wits Commonwealth* (which S.T.C. lists under Nicholas
Ling) had numerous editions from 1597 onwards and was obviously much used.
L. B. Wright has said that 'of all the handbooks of wisdom, the one having the
greatest popular acceptance was *Politeuphuia*' and the Jacobean schoolmaster,
Hoole, tells us that 'it is generally imposed upon young scholars to translate out
of English into Latin'. *Politeuphuia* did not list authors in the early editions, but
later included Seneca's name with those of Guevara, Socrates, Gregory, Olaus
Magnus, Augustine, Aristotle, Solon, Hermes, etc., etc. But no image of Seneca
as different from these almost professional purveyors of wisdom emerges.
Seneca Moralis emerges only as a mouthpiece for standard wisdom.

5. It is Seneca in this anthology sense, I suspect, that Nashe is referring to in
the famous passage of the preface to *Menaphon* where 'English Seneca read by
Candlelight yields many good sentences, as *Bloud is a begger* and so forth',

suspect, have made a great deal of sense in the period; for the equation of 'classicism' with 'purity' had not yet been made. The Gothic minds of the Elizabethan audience exercised a natural sovereignty over the classical past. They looked at the classics out of their own eyes, seeing as most central those Greco-Roman authors whose styles were close enough to their own preferences to be intelligible. And the landscape of classical literature that their minds allowed them to see was different in many respects from that which has prevailed in Western Europe since Winckelmann. Not Sophocles or Horace,[6] but Ovid and Plutarch were at the centre of their vision of classicism. We should remember that English Greek studies begin with a translation not of Homer or Plato, but of Synesius on baldness,[7] that More and Erasmus concentrated their literary attention on Lucian and the Anthology, and that Lucretius had to wait until 1682 before his work was translated into English.

Tragedy, though seen as a classical genre, was not exempted from this general sense that the road to intensity lay through the multiplication of instances. We may find this equation of intensity with horrific repetitiveness in as popular an area as the Induction to *A Warning for Fair Women* (before 1599), where the materials of popular tragedy are thus described:

> How some damn'd tyrant to obtain a crown
> Stabs, hangs, impoisons, smothers, cutteth throats;
> And then a Chorus too comes howling in
> And tells us of the worrying of a cat:
> Then [too] a filthy whining ghost
> Lapt in some foul sheet, or a leather pilch
> Comes screaming like a pig half-stick'd,
> And cries Vindicta!—Revenge, Revenge!
> With that a little rosin flasheth forth
> Like smoke out of a tobacco pipe, or a boy's squib.
> Then comes in two or three like to drovers,
> With tailors' bodkins stabbing one another—

6. I mean 'not the Horace of the *Odes*'. *Orazio Satiro* was, of course, well known, and had been translated by several hands.

7. The translation, made before 1461, was by John Free. See Roberto Weiss, *Humanism in England during the Fifteenth Century* (1941).

We find the same enumeration in no less a classicist than
Julius Caesar Scaliger; he defines the materials of tragedy
as follows:

Res tragicae grandes, atroces, jussa Regum, caedes, desperationes,
suspendia, exilia, orbitates, parricidia, incestus, incendia, pugnae,
occaecationes, fletus, ululatus, conquestiones, funera, epitaphia,
epicedia.

The searcher for classical purity would find little comfort
here: he might, indeed, seem to be little beyond the definition
in Dante's letter to Can Grande:

dicitur propter hoc a *tragos*, quod est *hircus*, et oda, quasi *cantus
hircinus*, id est foetidus ad modum hirci, ut patet per Senecam in
suis tragoediis.

A strange confirmation of Scaliger's 'Gothic' presentation of
tragedy as an accumulation of its horrors appears in an
English work very remote from Scaliger, in John Greene's
perfervid diatribe against acting, called *A Refutation of the
Apology for Actors* (1615). Greene is concerned to make the
point that tragedy is concerned exclusively with wicked-
nesses, and that therefore it corrupts its spectators. The
resultant description reads almost like a translation of Scaliger. To the seventeenth-century Puritan (writing, we should
note, at the end of Shakespeare's career), as to the neo-classical
critic, tragedy is characterized by its trail of horrors:

The matter of tragedies is haughtinesse, arrogancy, ambition,
pride, iniury, anger, wrath, envy, hatred, contention, warre,
murther, cruelty, rapine, incest, rovings, depradations, piracyes,
spoyles, roberies, rebellions, treasons, killing, hewing, stabbing,
dagger-drawing, fighting, butchery, trechery, villany, etc. and all
kind of heroyick evils whatsoever.   (p. 56)

While we are thinking of tragedy in these terms, we ought
to remember that a vernacular acting tradition already
existed, to encourage a repetitive, aggregative dramatic
structure. The tradition of the vernacular drama, unlike that
of the neo-classical drama, was already a theatrical tradition.
It sometimes seems to be assumed that, because the Middle
Ages defined Tragedy in terms of literary rather than a
theatrical experience, the Renaissance drama had to await the

recovery of the classics before it could recover the art of acting. But this, of course, must be nonsense. Bevington[8] has shown very clearly how the exigencies of acting in late medieval England shaped the kinds of plays that were produced, and how this repetitive structure was carried forward by the acting profession into the art of Marlowe. The arts of spectacle, of emblematic presentation, of dumb show, of multi-level statement, of pictorial metaphor—these go forward from the miracle plays and the interludes as a continuous tradition, and something like a guild structure of actors exists to preserve them and keep innovation at bay. The texts of Seneca, especially given their avoidance of stage-direction, could contribute nothing more than occasional *sententiae* to this stage-tradition; and we should remember that it was in this tradition that all the major plays of the Elizabethan age were produced. It is not classical tragedy, but *The Famous Victories of Henry V, The Chronicle History of King Leir, The Troublesome Raigne of King John,* that Shakespeare can use for his foundations. The diagram of development that sees Elizabethan tragedy beginning from the Senecan translations of the 1560s, going on to Academic drama in the late sixties or seventies (*Misfortunes of Arthur, Gismond of Salerne, Richardus Tertius*), and so, without a glance left or right, to similar and therefore 'Senecan' plays like *The Spanish Tragedy, Locrine,* and *Selimus,* omits too much to be convincing.

If we look more closely at the tradition of repertory drama, of *Apius and Virginia, Horestes, Damon and Pithias, Cambyses,* and *Patient Grissil,* I think we can see, inside a single acting tradition, a gradual but continuous adaptation of the discursive and moralizing drama of the later Middle Ages into the multi-dimensional story-drama of mature theatre. This is a movement that could not have taken the course it did without the criticism of vernacular methods that the classics imply. But the exact composition of that classical front does not seem to be so vital. If Seneca's tragedies had not survived, some details would have had to be changed—but the over-all picture would not have been altered.

8. D. M. Bevington, *From 'Mankind' to Marlowe* (Cambridge, Mass., 1962).

7

Seneca and English tragedy

The *Literaturwissenschaft* within which the origins or causes of Renaissance (or more usually 'modern') tragedy have been sought was bound by its method to give importance to the tragedies of Seneca. The seminal surveys of Cloetta, Fischer, and Creizenach[1] adopted, inevitably enough, a chronological view of the development of a separate genre 'tragedy', at the head of which, as the *fons et origo* of everything that followed, stood the tragedies of Seneca. Progression inside the genre was thus seen in relation to a simple defining norm, and growth was charted in terms of the use made of materials shared with the source. Variation between one 'tragedy' and another could then be expressed by comparisons of nearness to or distance from the original, and a simple chronological pattern emerged in which the vernacular exemplars were explained by being placed at an appropriate point along a scale of increasing diffusion and increasing attenuation of classical models.

The declared sequence of events, reading or performance of the originals, then translations, then free imitations, then independent works imbued with the spirit of the source,[2] leaves out too much, I have noted, to be wholly convincing; yet it has a neatness which is very attractive, especially when one adds to the basic pattern a geographical diagram of the diffusion, beginning in Italy and then moving to France and then to England. In this pattern we see each country in turn pick up not only the original model, Seneca, but also the

[First published in *Seneca*, ed. C. D. N. Costa (1974).]

1. See R. Fischer, *Die Kunstentwicklung der englischen Tragödie* (Strasbourg, 1898); W. Cloetta, *Beiträge zu Literaturgeschichte des Mittelalters und der Renaissance*, 2 vols (Halle, 1890, 1892); W. Creizenach, *Geschichte des neueren Dramas*, 4 vols (Halle, 1909).
2. See the sentence from Cunliffe's C.H.E.L. article, cited above, p. 162.

sub-Senecan developments that had happened on the way. Thus M. T. Herrick tells us that Seneca's 'vivid depiction of horrible deeds and black thoughts . . . fascinated the Italians, just as much as the sixteenth-century Italian tragedies of blood and lust and revenge fascinated French and English playwrights' (*Italian Tragedy in the Renaissance* [Urbana, 1965], pp. 2–3).

H. B. Charlton's elaborate and deeply researched essay on 'The Senecan tradition in Renaissance tragedy' (first published as the Introduction to vol. 1 of the Scottish Text Society edition of Sir William Alexander's *Poetical Works* [Edinburgh, 1921]) is probably the prime example in English of the charting of these routes, and I shall use this as a model presentation of received attitudes. Charlton sees a powerful Italian influence on Elizabethan tragedy as well as a general Senecan influence. He also sees that the Italian imitators of Seneca made him more horrific and 'romantic' by combining his form with material from the *novelle*, and therefore brought him closer to Elizabethan taste. This means that, in Charlton's view, something called 'the Italian Seneca' is present in Elizabethan borrowings of horrific *novelle* materials. The logical flaw in the argument is perhaps too obvious to require much elaboration. The danger of charting the changes in 'Seneca' as he passes through Dolce or Corraro or Garnier and so reaches England is that elements genuinely Senecan (i.e. characteristically if not uniquely present in Seneca's plays) may cease to be present at all, while elements generally characteristic of later medieval and Renaissance taste (sententiousness, a gloomy sense of overpowering rule by fortune or fate in human affairs, a morbid interest in the limits of human suffering), or indeed characteristic of tragedy as a genre (horror, blood, desolation)[3] come to be labelled 'Senecan' because Seneca also displays them and is therefore thought responsible for the tradition (late medieval tragedy) in which they appear. The Senecan example may have provided

3. The late Victorians, who invented that tautologous genre 'the tragedy of blood', showed their incapacity for tragedy by imagining that blood, cruelty, and spectacular horror are optional extras in the tragic experience, only to be explained by Seneca's decadence on the one hand and Elizabethan primitiveness on the other. We should remember that the balanced Horace chose *cena Thyestae* as his type of the tragic episode (*A.P.* 91).

the earliest formal model for European tragedy, but it could quickly become (in spite of this status) totally irrelevant to the day-by-day imagination of tragic playwrights.

The same flaw is manifestly present in the use of the chronological sequence: reading and producing Seneca, translation of Seneca, 'Senecan' plays in the vernacular. That these three things happened is abundantly clear, and undoubtedly examples can be cited to make the sequential point; but the third element in the sequence can only be said to be logically dependent on either the first or the second if the features called 'Senecan' are necessarily derived from the preceding stages of the reception of Seneca and from no other source. The *post hoc ergo propter hoc* argument, which has supported much chronological study and 'explanation' of European or English tragedy, is clearly not enough by itself to establish a detailed and inescapable proof that similar features appearing in some Elizabethan tragedies and some Senecan tragedies are in the former only because they are in the latter.[4] And this is particularly the case when the features in question are available in other (and in some cases more immediate) sources.

I have argued in the preceding essay[5] that stichomythia, ghosts, five-act structure, rhetorical speeches, a devotion to horror, a stress on the ineluctable quality of fate—features traditionally thought to derive from Seneca—were equally available in Renaissance England from more immediate sources. The emphasis of the present essay is, however, rather on the quality of what Seneca actually had on offer to later tragedy rather than on the particular limiting conditions of Elizabethan and Tudor England.

It is therefore proper to note here that 'Seneca' himself

---

4. Cf. Jean Jaquot, writing on 'Sénèque, la Renaissance et nous': Si on appelle 'sénéquienne' tout pièce qui a pour ressort la tyrannie ou la vengeance, où les atrocités et les lieux communs abondent, où il y a des rêves prémonitoires, des apparitions, des scènes de magie, on emploie l'épithète dans un sens assez vague, qui n'est pas faux, mais qui ne nous assure nullement d'une familiarité de l'auteur avec le tragique latin. Tout ceci est vite devenu monnaie courante au théâtre et, nous l'avons vu, le sujet des pièces de Sénèque, loin d'être exceptionnel, est dans la bonne moyenne des histoires tragiques susceptibles d'être portées à la scène. (*Les Tragédies de Sénèque, et le théâtre de la Renaissance* [Paris, 1964], p. 282.)

5. See above, pp. 159–73.

never offered anything like a simple or homogeneous set of characteristics. Critics have tended to speak of 'Senecan influence' as if a single and homogeneous quality was being transmitted. I will not return here to the problem of excluding from our sense of 'Seneca' the moral treatises that were (in Renaissance England at any rate) his primary source of fame. Even if we suppose that the plays were read in isolation from the treatises and the letters, we are still far from homogeneity. Out of the ten (or nine, or eight) plays in the canon, which are the central texts? When we speak of 'Seneca', do we refer to the doom-laden family histories of the Pelopidae (the *Thyestes* and the *Agamemnon*), or do we refer to the tales of passionate and sorrowful womanhood (*Phaedra* and *Medea*), or are we thinking of the comparatively open atmosphere of the *Hercules Furens*, in which paternal and wifely loyalties are not destroyed and where the father and the friend (Theseus) survive to comfort the hero? The *Troades* offers yet another model: of passive and undeserved suffering caught in the impersonal toils of war, while the *Oedipus* describes the inevitable defilement of even the hero in flight from defilement.

If we are to take as 'Senecan' only what is common to the whole body of plays we are left with a residue of pretty obvious features. There is a continuity of style of course, though what I. Scott-Kilvert has recently called 'Seneca's sharply distinct varieties of speech'[6] is often overlooked; and to this I shall return. In formal terms there is the classically simple linear or progressive construction ('arguments . . . naked and casual', as Fulke Greville calls them in *Life of Sidney*, ed. Nowell Smith [Oxford], p. 222), usually centred on the woes of the protagonist, showing an attempt to avoid fate or alleviate suffering, with the consequence that misery is only hastened and suffering deepened.

In these formal elements, Elizabethan publicly performed tragedy shows absolutely no interest at all. However, in a rigorously progressivist theory the lack of interest may be explained as showing, not the presence of an alternative (Gothic) concept of unity, but the slowness of the Elizabethans to learn the one lesson that is possible. In Brander

6. Ian Scott-Kilvert, 'Seneca or scenario', *Arion*, vii (1968), 511.

Matthews's *A Study of the Drama* (1910) we hear (p. 102) that:

The development of English tragedy ... out of the lax chronicle play, which was only a straggling panorama of the events of a reign, was due largely to the influence exerted by Seneca's tragedies, poor enough as plays, but vigorous in the stoical assertion of man's power over himself and of his right to control his own destiny.

It is difficult to see just what this is saying, but it may be thought to be trying to describe a relationship between individual self-assertion and unity of action. If Shakespeare's *King John* is better than Bale's *King Johan* or the anonymous *Troublesome Reign of King John*, it may be implied that this is because Seneca had taught Elizabethan drama to centre action on a single dominant individual.

The trouble with such a theory is that Elizabethan drama shows a total reluctance to unify by other than the thematic interests which had appeared in *Damon and Pithias* (1564), *Cambyses* (?1561), and other pre-Senecan examples of the 'lax chronicle play'. The advance from these plays to the drama of Marlowe, Shakespeare, and Webster is not an advance along a line of increasing 'unity of motive', but an advance to an increasingly subtle and brilliantly focused organization of thematic interests. The route to the drama of Scribe and Ibsen could have been shortened by an appropriate attention to the tragedies of Seneca, but in fact quite another route was being followed by the major tragedies of the English Renaissance. Their aim is to crowd the stage and create complex and ironic evaluations. Person is set against person and group against group, so that the validity of alternative positions is allowed to appear. And in this respect (as in others) one must make the point that the formal differences which separate Elizabethan tragedies from Seneca's mark ethical distinctions. All Seneca's plays stress the malevolent power of fate to bring men beyond what they had thought of as the final limits of cruelty and injustice. In all (except the Hercules plays) the ending is shown without any alleviation of misery: either cruel tyranny is triumphant, or the martyr sinks into further degradation, or both happen together.

Elizabethan tragedy's complex structure reflects a different attitude to fate. While allowing the cruelty of tragic destiny, it is also strongly assertive of the redeeming features of a tragic existence: the gratuitous loyalties, the constancy under pressure, the renewed faith. Its variety of moods allows such tragedy to be placed in a context of different and less shadowed lives.

T. S. Eliot has presented Othello,[7] especially at the end of the play when he looks back over his life (*O sors dura!*), as Senecan, but in fact Othello's position is totally unlike anything existing or possible in any of Seneca's plays. Othello does in a sense 'dramatize himself' (and so does the Medea of *Medea superest*), but vivid self-description seems to be an inescapable dramatist's device (surely Sophocles's Oedipus 'dramatizes himself', not to mention Ibsen's Hedda). The quality of Othello's end is derived from the awareness of a normal world existing in his own past and in other people's future, for whom he will be only a name (if that). The perspectives of the ordinary world are essential to Shakespearian tragedy; but they are quite absent from Seneca.

The difference I have suggested here may be subsumed under the general rubric that Shakespeare's ethic is Christian, and Seneca's is not. But this distinction has not always been allowed the central importance it undoubtedly has to explain both the attraction of Seneca for the Elizabethans and the inevitability of their failure to be like him. It was often suggested in the late nineteenth and early twentieth centuries that, given the immeasurable superiority of Aeschylus and Sophocles to subsequent tragedies (according to the taste of the nineteenth and twentieth centuries), the Elizabethan drama would have been immeasurably benefited by imitating Sophocles instead of Seneca. The wish that the Elizabethans could have shared modern preferences shows a lack of historical perspective and an unpreparedness for the different (and shocking) revaluation that the past exacts from those attentive enough to it. The Greek drama (except for Euripides in some of his aspects) was necessarily inaccessible to the Elizabethans, not only because the possession of

7. T. S. Eliot, 'Shakespeare and the stoicism of Seneca', *Selected Essays* (London, 1948).

enough Greek to read it properly was rare (after all there were
Latin translations), but principally because the Greek drama
was embedded in a socio-religious matrix that a Christian
writer could not afford not to despise.

It was Seneca's freedom from any real response to the
numinous that made him particularly repellent to the
nineteenth- and twentieth-century Romantics, for whom his
bleak moralism seemed denatured and pedantic. It was this
same merely intellectual relationship to the 'leaden gods' (as
Stephen Bateman called the Roman deities in 1577) that
allowed the Renaissance to regard him as a proto-Christian,
and enabled them to accept his views without changing their
own. In a more credulous age this quality had been expressed
by the forged correspondence between Seneca and St Paul,
and also by the forged treatises then read as Seneca's, but
now attributed to St Martin.

Erasmus was, of course, free of these pious frauds, but he
reflects their legacy. As he says in his prefatory letter to his
edition of Seneca, sent to the Bishop of Durham (*Opus
Epistolarum*, ed. Allen [Oxford], ii. 51 ff.) (p. 53):

Et Senecam tanti fecit divus Hieronymus, ut hunc unum ex
omnibus ethnicis in Catalogo scriptorum illustrium recensuerit,
non tam ob epistolas illas Pauli ad Senecam et Senecae ad Paulum
(quas nec a Paulo nec a Seneca scriptas probe noverat . . .) quam
quod hunc unum dignum iudicarit qui non Christianus a Christia-
nis legeretur.

(Indeed St Jerome made so much of Seneca that he included him
as the only pagan in his Catalogue of famous authors, not so
much on account of those letters of St Paul to Seneca and Seneca
to St Paul (which he knew perfectly well to be by neither Seneca
nor St Paul) but rather because he judged that he alone among
non-Christians was fit to be read by Christians.)

In the new prefatory letter he addresses to the Bishop of
Cracow in 1529 (Allen, viii. 25 ff.), he repeats these senti-
ments and adds a rather crisp and memorable statement of
Seneca's ambiguous position (p. 31):

Etenim si legas illum ut paganum, scripsit Christiane; si ut
Christianum, scripsit paganice.

(For if you read him thinking of him as a pagan, then he appears to have written like a Christian; but if you read him as a Christian then he appears to have written like a pagan.)

He also, in this later letter, explains why Jerome included Seneca in his *Catalogus sanctorum* (p. 29): *non admodum probatae sanctitatis* ... *[sed] ob religionis amorem* (not because of proven sanctity ... [but] on account of his love for religion). In the *Institutio Principis Christiani* he praises Seneca as the most suitable to be read (*Opera Omnia* [Leiden, 1703–6], vol. iv, p. 587):

Qui scriptis suis mire exstimulat et inflammat ad honesti studium, lectoris animum a sordidis curis in sublime subvehit, peculiariter ubique dedocens Tyrannidem.

(Who in his writings marvellously incites us and stirs us up to a zeal for honest action, carrying the mind of the reader into the heights, far above the base concerns of men, especially where he is warning against tyranny.)

It was thus possible in the Renaissance to think of Seneca as a man wholly acceptable in his moral outlook, and to view the fables of his plays therefore as wholly defensible didactic structures. Dean Nowell defended the *Phaedra* because of its similarity to the story of Potiphar's wife in the Holy Scripture.[8] Indeed the primitive and horrific moral compulsions of the Old Testament provided a natural field for 'Christian Seneca'. Buchanan's *Jephthes* and Jean de la Taille's *Saul le Furieux*, Velo's *Tamar* and Bishop Watson's *Absalom*[9] all reduce Biblical history to quasi-Senecan fable. But the fables

8. Nowell's draft preface to a performance of the *Phaedra*, presumably at Westminster School and probably in 1546, is preserved in Brasenose College MS. 31, fols 25 ff.:

Senecae tragici poetae hypolitum, spectatores candidissimi, apud vos acturi, non formidamus haec praefari, ut inter tragicos omnes latinos non tantum primus, sed propemodum etiam solus—vel fabii iudicio—dignus [est] quod legatur est hic Seneca; ita inter omnes huius tragedias longe primas obtinet, haec quam sumus representaturi hyppolitus fabula. ad eius, tum apud alios omnes, tum apud vos praecippue, utpote sacrarum literarum Audiosos, commendationem etiam hoc accedit, quod a iosephi et pitipharis uxoris historia in sacris genesios libris prodita haec hypoliti fabula non procul alludit: et quod illic citra omnem controversiam revera gestum legitur.

9. See John Hazel Smith, ed., *A Humanist's 'Trew Imitation': Thomas Watson's 'Absalom'* (Urbana, 1964).

of Seneca's plays could be defended at a rather simpler moral level. Philip Melanchthon (*Corpus Reformatorum* [Halle], vol. xix, p. 787) took out of the *Thyestes*: 'O how much evil does ambition breed':

> Proinde spectaculum exemplum damus utile;
> Nam cernere licebit hac in tragoedia
> Nil esse peius ambitione, quae omnia
> Divina humana, iusque et fas vertere solet.

(We present this to the spectators therefore as a useful model; for you will be justified in finding from this tragedy that there is nothing worse than ambition, which commonly overturns all things human and divine, both human law and divine law.)

Below this rather superficial level, at which Seneca could be thought of as quasi-Christian, the problems of true imitation are (and were) more difficult to solve. The ethic of Seneca was, as a unifying factor in his plays, quite hostile to the ethic that is tolerable to a Christian community. The most memorable statement of this incompatibility comes, fortunately enough, from the period of our principal concern and from a 'Senecan' dramatist, Fulke Greville. Greville in his life of Sir Philip Sidney describes his own tragedies and makes in the course of his description a distinction which is curiously overlooked when Elizabethan Senecan imitation is discussed, for it should be central to any such discussion. He speaks first of ancient tragedies which 'exemplify the disastrous miseries of man's life, where Order, Laws, Doctrine and Authority are unable to protect Innocency from the exorbitant wickedness of power, and so out of that melancholic vision stir horror, or murmur against Divine Providence' (p. 221). On the other hand, modern tragedies 'point out God's revenging aspect upon every particular sin, to the despair or confusion of mortality' (ibid.). The central distinction is, as Greville sees it, that the ancient (and he means Senecan) world was, because its gods were unjust, a world of total injustice. On the other hand, the Christian world shows man unable to face up to the justice of God, but hunted down in terms of particular sins, not over-all corruption. The point is not that the innocent do not perish in modern tragedy: Lavinia, Cordelia, and young Macduff perish just as surely as Hippolytus and the children of Thyestes and Medea. But the massacre of those innocents is part of a larger catastrophic movement which is eventually moral: the universe in casting out the particular evil also casts out the good. In Seneca's tragedies the evil are regularly left in manic possession of what their wickedness has achieved: Atreus with his brother (who now incorporates his nephews) in his gloating power, Nero disposing of his relatives, Medea carried off in her magic car, Aegisthus and Clytemnestra in possession of Argos. The impotent chorus can only generalize from these instances that man's lot is indeed hard and (as Greville says) 'murmur against Divine Providence'.

Even a play as concerned to avoid explicit Christianity as Shakespeare's *Titus Andronicus* suggests in the end that justice can return to the world with comfort to the good as well as punishment to the wicked, and decent behaviour all round:[1]

> Some loving friends convey the emperor hence
> And give him burial in his father's grave
> My father and Lavinia shall forthwith
> Be closed in our household's monument.
> As for that ravenous tiger, Tamora
> . . .
> [Then afterwards, to order well the state,
> That like events may ne'er it ruinate.]

Greville's distinction is one that is particularly important when we deal with that strain of Elizabethan tragedy concerned with revenge—a strain often thought to be particularly dependent on Seneca—though often this means no more than that there is horror in both. Shakespeare and other revenge dramatists do, of course, show deeds of horror and violent states of criminal irresponsibility, and in this are like Seneca (and Ovid and the martyrologies). But there is an essential difference. Reuben Brower speaks well of 'the amorality of Seneca's *Agamemnon*, where the heroine joyously gives way to crime and where—for all the detachment and highmindedness of the choral odes—there is no

---

1. The last two lines quoted are not found in Q1. They were doubtless added to the later texts to make Shakespeare's rather abrupt ending more 'normal'.

assurance of a mind or a society outside the criminal mind'
(*Hero and Saint* [Oxford, 1971], p. 200). But when Brower
speaks of Titus Andronicus joining 'the happy criminal
society of Seneca's Clytemnestra or Medea or Aaron, Tamora
and her sons' (p. 199), one must regretfully part company
from him.

When Seneca's slaves of passion are taken over by inhuman
or anti-human emotions they are released from human
responsibility, and in this sense 'happy' has its own ghastly
appropriateness; they become the vessels or instruments of
the *furor* which is personified by the *Furiae* we meet in the
infernal prologues. When Medea, contemplating her final
crime, begins to relent, the *Antiqua Erynis* snatches her unwilling hand, and forces her into the scream: *Ira, qua ducis,
sequor* (Where wrath leads I follow) (953). She is sucked into
an infernal and maddening vision (958–68):

> Quonam ista tendit turba Furiarum impotens?
> . . .   quem trabe infesta petit
> Megaera? cuius umbra dispersis venit
> incerta membris? frater est, poenas petit.
> dabimus, sed omnes fige luminibus faces,
> lania, perure, pectus en Furiis patet.
> Discedere a me, frater, ultrices deas
> manesque ad imos ire securas iube.

(Whither goes that mob of Furies, powerless to restrain itself?
. . . Who does Megeara search for, waving her torch?
What dubious ghost, limbs torn apart, comes forth?
It is my brother; he seeks revenge. He will have it.
But first set all your torches in my eye-sockets
Tear in pieces, set on fire. Lo, my heart receives the Furies.
Now, brother, you may order the revenging goddesses to leave me
and return satisfied to the deep-buried dead.)

What we seem to be given here is a passage of infernal possession, such as Lady Macbeth talks about, but does not
display.[2] It is impossible to know just how subjective or how
objective Seneca intended *Erynis* or *Megaera* to be, but
clearly we are not dealing only with a fluctuation of inner
mood. A more objective description of human processes

2. Cf. I.-S. Ewbank, 'The fiend-like queen', *Shakespeare Survey*, xix (1966),
82–94.

seems to be involved: reason has struggled with *furor* and lost, and thereafter the inner resource of the individual is empty and the infernal passions take its place; as Phaedra remarks (184–5):

> Quid ratio possit? vicit ac regnat furor
> potensque tota mente dominatur deus.

(What can reason do? *Furor* has conquered and reigns over me. The powerful god controls the whole of my mind.)

The Elizabethan model of the human state is more complex than this, and the more complex form of the Elizabethan play reflects it. Revenge as a passion, perhaps as *the* passion, stalks the Elizabethan stage; but in the form of what Greville calls a 'particular sin', as an isolated madness, not as the objective and possessive power of the *ultrices deae*. The *Ultrix Deus* of the Elizabethan world ('Vengeance is mine, saith the Lord, I will repay') is, of course, quite different: not the abrogator of rational order, but its guarantor. Providence, even if only in the form of 'God's revenging aspect', is never wholly withdrawn from the Elizabethan scene, where potential grace is a condition of being alive. Revengers are absorbed into the horror of their own obsessed imaginings, but they continue to exist inside a world where justice is remembered as a value.[3] Indeed a central point about revenge on the Elizabethan stage is that it is a perverted form of justice.

Of course, the most famous Elizabethan remark about revenge has always told us so: 'Revenge is a kind of wild Justice', says Bacon, where 'wild' (as the imagery following seems to show) means 'fit for the wilderness, run to seed, like

3. It is interesting that even the translators of Seneca transform this central point so far as they can. Thomas Nuce in his poem before Studley's translation of the *Agamemnon* changes Seneca's meaningless victory of passion over reason to a demonstration about justice:

> This deed was done by Talion law,
> here blood did blood require,
> And now Thyest hath that revenge
> that he did long desire.
> Whereby thou chiefly mayst be taught
> the providence of god
> That so long after Atreus' fact
> Thyest's revenge abode.

a briar'. The madness of Titus Andronicus is a withdrawal into the dream of perfect justice, over which Astraea and not the *ultrices deae* presides as deity. He is the martyr of a world from which the true strain of justice has vanished, in which only the briar is left. Much of his madness turns on the search for justice (IV. iii. 4 f.):

> *Terras Astraea reliquit.*
> Be you remembered, Marcus: she's gone, she's fled.

He sends his family to spread nets, to dig into the earth for justice, but he is told that only her 'wild' brother is available (IV. iii. 37–39):

> Pluto sends you word,
> If you will have Revenge from hell, you shall.
> Marry, for Justice, she is so employed . . .

And in the end his sanity snaps and he grasps at the perverted justice of the 'wilderness of tigers' where he lives. If Seneca is present in the Terean banquet of the final act it is as a kind of antimasque to the central ethic of the play. Tamora and her sons come to Titus's house to play-act for his madness the simplifying possession of Revenge, the 'dread Fury' of Seneca's plays. But Titus and the play accept these simplifications only at a level of make-believe beyond that of the actual play-world (V. ii. 142 f.):

> I knew them all . . .
> And will o'er-reach them in their own devices.

He is content (like Hieronimo in *The Spanish Tragedy*) to join their play of revenge, but outside that play he knows well enough what justice is, what its cruxes and problems are (V. iii. 35–37):

> My lord the Emperor, resolve me this:
> Was it well done of rash Virginius
> To slay his daughter?

The play ends, not with the 'happy' murderer enjoying his infernal reward and proving that *nullos esse, qua veheris, deos* (wherever you go [Medea] there will be no gods), but with the brief madness of revenge atoned for in the formal terms of established precedent and true justice.

The revenge play of the Elizabethans would have been wholly unacceptable if Titus, or Hieronimo, or Hoffman, or Hamlet had been rewarded for their revenges, as Atreus or Clytemnestra or Medea are. Even if we take an extreme case —that most gloatingly horrific and smugly immoral of scenes, in which Antonio murders the little Julio (Marston, *Antonio's Revenge*, III. i)—we are still in a moral world directly opposite to that of Seneca. The difficulties of taste here are often attributed to a surfeit of Seneca, and the quotation from *Thyestes*, 151 f. (Atreus rejoices in his capture of Thyestes and his children) shows that the corresponding episode was in Marston's mind. In fact, however, the tastelessness of the scene belongs to a quite un-Senecan branch of tastelessness. It sentimentalizes the child in a way that is foreign to the Roman. Julio says (III. i. 142–6):

> Brother Antonio are you here, i' faith?
> Why do you frown? Indeed my sister said
> That I should call you brother, that she did,
> When you were married to her. Buss me; good truth,
> I love you better than my father.

Antonio welcomes Julio into his embrace with ironies which recall Atreus, but his motivations are quite distinct (it is indeed difficult to speak at all of Atreus's motivations). He apostrophizes heaven and justice, and declares his devotion to a mad purism of justice which will unambiguously separate guilt and innocence (III. i. 161–4):

> O that I knew which joint, which side, which limb,
> Were father all and had no mother in't.
> That I might rip it, vein by vein,
> In bleeding rases.

Once again revenge is presented as a monstrous mutation of justice, isolating and maddening, in a world still ruled by 'God's revenging aspect upon every particular sin'.

The Senecan ethic was, by a curious paradox, most tolerable when the subject-matter was not the intrigues and passions of individuals but the dynastic quarrels of the modern political world. Greville speaks of these as if somewhere between ancient and modern tragic practices, and reflecting his own interest to 'trace out the high ways of ambitious governors, and to show in the practice that the more audacity, advantage and good success such sovereignties have, the more they hasten to their own desolation and ruin' (loc. cit.). Of course the Elizabethan audience did not suppose politics was eventually free of the revenging hand of God, but knowledge of recent history (e.g. the Wars of the Roses) and the Chronicles of those events, showed men that a time-scale longer than any single life was likely to operate before divine justice was seen to be fulfilled. And there was also the awareness that Machiavelli and others had suggested that the political world operated apart from God's providence, and was therefore open to Seneca's interpretation.[4] Shakespeare's *Richard III* deals with a doomed dynasty like those of Argos or Thebes, where the pressure of the past justifies the abrogation of normal standards in the present; but the play is eventually a complex image of a whole world under moral siege, not a linear development of crime and possession. Richard has specific political aims, and a specific social context within which these aims have to be achieved; Atreus has neither.

The wailing queens in Act IV, scene iv, of *Richard III* have often been thought to derive from the wailing ladies of the *Troades*; and so they may, as Clarence's dream seems to derive from Virgil. In both cases a hint of classical material may have triggered off the development of a highly stylized exercise in rhetoric, meant no doubt in its solemn and witty formalism to recall a classical mode (Ovid in particular), but reflecting little or nothing of the meaning of any original. The queens create a joint interpretation of what history means: their repetitive stanzas reflect their repetitive destinies, and the extent to which history can be reduced to royal fate, and fate distilled into formal rhetoric. They create a patch of sombre

4. Mario Praz in his 1928 British Academy lecture, 'Machiavelli and the Elizabethans', suggested a notable simplification of the map of 'influence'. He argues (cf. Charlton, cited above, p. 175) that the 'Italian Seneca' which reached England had already (mainly through Cinthio) combined the Senecan tyrant with the Machiavellian *principe*. But the 'Machiavel' in English drama is seldom a tyrant: he is an intriguer aiming at power, and enjoying the complexities of intrigue in quite un-Senecan fashion. The maxims of amorality are similar in Seneca and Machiavelli, but 'Machiavellian' amoralism does not carry anything else plausibly 'Senecan' into Elizabethan drama. Cf. W. A. Armstrong, 'Seneca, Machiavelli and the Elizabethan tyrant', *R.E.S.* (1948), pp. 19–35.

colour, set against other patches, other interpretations; and beyond all interpretations lies the quite un-Senecan truth of Richmond's virtue and divine right to found the Tudor line. The ghosts who throng to Richard's or Richmond's tents in Act v of *Richard III* indicate the supernatural world as the guarantor of justice, not its opposite; and in this they are typical of the Elizabethan supernatural. The ghosts who appear in Elizabethan plays may come from heaven or hell, but their interest is not (like Seneca's) in degrading and destroying humanity, but in achieving the satisfaction of justice seen to be done. It is the hunger for justice that drives them to appear and to demand action, whether to Baldwin, the author of the *Mirror for Magistrates*, who gives them satisfaction by telling their sad stories, or later to sons who will destroy their fathers' murderers. The ghosts in the *Mirror for Magistrates* offer a clear link between the dream-visions of hell that medieval literature shows and the 'filthy whining ghost / Lapt in some foul sheet or a leather pilch / . . . screaming like a pig half-stick'd / . . . Vindicta! Revenge, Revenge!'[5] who provides a stock image of Elizabethan revenge tragedy. The prose links of the *Mirror* carry the burden of evoking the supernatural occasion, and relating the 'history' told in the monodrama to the moral pressures that force the individual to reveal all and ask for judgement:

I waxed drowsy and began indeed to slumber. But my imagination still prosecuting this tragical matter brought me such a fantasy: methought there stood before us a tall man's body full of fresh wounds, but lacking a head . . . And when through the ghastfulness of this piteous spectacle I waxed afeared and turned away my face methought there came a shrieking voice out of the wesand pipe of the headless body, saying as followeth . . . (Prose 12)

And therefore imagine, Baldwin, that you see him all to be mangled, with blue wounds, lying pale and wan all naked upon the cold stones in Paul's Church . . . (Prose 4)

I will take upon me the personage of the last who, full of wounds, miserably mangled, with a pale countenance and grisly look, may make his moan to Baldwin as followeth . . . (Prose 1)

5. Anon., *A Warning for Fair Women*, Induction. See above, p. 171.

The quality of the ghost is thus evoked in terms of description
rather than narrative or drama (and I shall return to this
point later); the narrator himself is made the principal agent
of the pattern which leads from these violent disruptions of
silence to the final silence of the conclusion, when all that is
required for resolution has been said. The process is strongly
reminiscent of a confession and absolution. The ghost is
finally satisfied (or exorcized) by having his personal history
fitted into an exemplary framework. As James I of Scotland
remarks when he begins his tale:

> If for examples' sake thou write thy book,
> I charge thee, Baldwin, thou forget me not.

The fully dramatized ghosts of later drama live, of course,
in a world of multiple personal relations, but their motivation
is like that of the *Mirror* ghosts and unlike that of Seneca, in
that they seek (and achieve) a personal and fully human
satisfaction: seeing the criminal destroyed, the usurper
brought low. The *furor* which rages unchecked through
Seneca's world, the boundless horror and destruction that
Umbra Tantali is forced to promote: these are held in
Elizabethan tragedy within the dimension of a personal or
political displacement of the natural equilibrium which justice
holds. The Elizabethan playhouse ghosts may begin their reaction to this displacement with screams of 'Revenge, revenge'
or '*Vindicta*' (phrases not in the vocabulary of Seneca's
ghosts) but end with expressions of family or social stability.
Thus Old Andrugio in *Antonio's Revenge* watches the final
action from 'betwixt the music houses' and departs saying:

> 'Tis done; and now my soul shall sleep in rest.
> Sons that revenge their father's blood are blest.
> (v. ii. 114–15)

At the end of *Locrine* the ghost of Corineus takes his stand to
'stay and see revenge'. This is satisfied, and then Até (the
chorus) can pronounce an absolution on the turmoil:

> Lo, here the end of lawless treachery,
> Of usurpation and ambitious pride,
> And they that for their private amours dare
> Turmoil our land, and set their broils abroach
> Let them be warned by these premises.

At the end of Kyd's *The Spanish Tragedy* the ghost of Andrea seems to praise murder with equal enthusiasm whether the victims be innocent or guilty. But justice is assured for the afterlife, where

> . . . will I beg at lovely Proserpine
> That by the virtue of her princely doom
> I may consort my friends in pleasing sort
> And on my foes work just and sharp revenge.
>
> (IV. V. 13–16)

And this is the note on which the whole play ends, with Revenge promising a final absolute of punishment:

> For here though death hath end their misery,
> I'll there begin their endless tragedy.

In its distribution of the cast into eternally separated sheep and goats this conclusion is more reminiscent of the Last Judgement sequence in the Mystery Cycles than of Seneca.[6]

The chronological basis of literary history has, in the view propounded here, led scholars to overestimate the force of transmission into an alien culture. The superficial quasi-Christianity of Seneca's morals should not blind us to the real hostility of received English dramatic patterns to the nature of his plays. This is especially important if we concentrate on the popular and public drama of the Elizabethans, putting to one side the plays written for readers or for one specific performance before a noble patron. The force of this distinction is often overlooked.

The Senecan tragedies of the Italian cinquecento all seem to be designed for specific or private production. In this they

---

6. See the 'Last Judgment' play (xxiv) in the Chester cycle (E.E.T.S. edn, 655–60):

DEMON PRIMUS. Goe we forth to hell in hye;
  Without ende ther shall you lye;
  For you have lost, right as dyd I,
  The Blisse that lasteth ever.

  Judged you be to my Belly
  Ther endlesse Sorrow is and nye;
  One thinge I tell you truly:
  Deliverd bene you never.

are like tragedies in England before the opening of the public
theatres in 1576, like *Gorboduc* of 1561, or Gascoigne's
Jocasta of 1566 (from Dolce), like *Gismond of Salerne* of
1567–8, or the Latin tragedies of the universities, such as
Legge's *Richardus Tertius* (1573) or Alabaster's *Roxana* of
1592 (from Groto's *La Dalida*), or the later 'closet' (unacted)
plays of aristocratic amateurs, the Countess of Pembroke's
Antonius, Sir William Alexander's *Darius*, Fulke Greville's
Alaham, etc., written in this way, no doubt, in reaction to the
'vulgar' form of the acted drama. As Greville says: 'be it
known it was no part of my purpose to write for them against
whom so many good and great spirits have already written'
(p. 224).

This whole strain of English tragedy is manifestly close to
its Italian and French counterparts, and nearer to Seneca than
the popular form. The chronological model would however
go further and suggest that the aristocratic plays of the 1560s
should be regarded not only as precursors but also as pro-
genitors of the popular tragedies of the 1580s and 1590s, so
that Seneca operates on the popular drama at two removes, as
well as directly, but with crucial effectiveness. From this point
of view there is a continuum of tragedy in England, running
unbroken from 1561—from *Gorboduc*, *Jocasta*, Hughes's
The Misfortunes of Arthur, through *The Spanish Tragedy*,
Locrine, *Hamlet*, *The Revenger's Tragedy*, and so to Shirley's
The Cardinal—to 1641. Fansler has put this view succinctly: 'One thing that bound all Elizabethan tragedies
together, from *Gorboduc* to *The Traitor* and *The Cardinal*,
was the influence of Seneca.'[7] It seems doubtful, however, if
the Inns-of-Court private tragedies in fact led directly to or
provided the primary stimulus for the public tragedies.
University men writing for professional actors and a paying
public had to take note of the popular interest in a crowded
stage, a wide variety of passions, a Christian ethic, a patriotic
enthusiasm, a joking immediacy of theatrical contact.[8]
Seneca, Groto, Thomas Hughes, and the Countess of Pembroke could provide little guidance to deal with such

7. H. E. Fansler, *The Evolution of Technic in Elizabethan Tragedy* (Chicago,
1914).
   8. See above, p. 140–4, 172–3.

demands, less indeed than the popular strolling theatricals of the English countryside. If Seneca were to be a powerful influence on the tragedy of the public theatre he would have, it seems, to make a fresh impact. His forms and his outlook could not be carried over, passively, from the private tragedies of the preceding decades.

H. B. Charlton, with his sights fixed eventually on Sir William Alexander, takes the Senecanism of the popular drama to be already proven by others, but the very brevity of his reference to its Senecan inheritance is convenient. He takes Nashe's famous attack on a dramatist (who may be Kyd) as representative of the methods of a school of popular tragedians, who[9]

busy themselves with the endeavours of art, that could scarcely Latinize their neck-verse if they should have need; yet English Seneca read by candle-light yields many good sentences, as *Blood is a beggar* and so forth; and if you entreat him fair in a frosty morning he will afford you whole Hamlets, I should say handfuls, of tragical speeches, But O grief! *Tempus edax rerum.* What's that will last always? The sea exhaled by drops will in continuance be dry, and Seneca, let blood line by line and page by page, at length must needs die to our stage; which makes his famished followers . . . to intermeddle with Italian translations. Wherein how poorly they have plodded . . . let all indifferent gentlemen that have travelled in that tongue discern by their twopenny pamphlets.

Charlton takes Nashe's description of popular tragedians' methods quite literally: 'Seneca . . . was their great storehouse of tragic material' (clxix). However, a quite literal reading of the passage seems impossible: Nashe's contempt is more clear than his argument. The opening gibe (in the section I have quoted) is aimed at those who cannot read Latin and have to read bloodthirsty Senecan *sententiae* in translation. Unfortunately for literalism, no English line 'blood is a beggar' is known, neither from the 1581 nor other translation of Seneca, nor does the line appear in any extant English play. It may be answered that Nashe is talking in particular about a perished play, the so-called *Ur-Hamlet*, and that this play must have

9. Nashe, Preface to Greene's *Menaphon* (McKerrow ed., *Works*, London, iii. 315–16).

had all the characteristics he lists. But it is obviously dangerous to explain a whole movement in terms of a perished and
indeed hypothetical play.

What other plays of the supposed movement show these
characteristics? The usual answer is, 'Kyd's *The Spanish
Tragedy*'. If *The Spanish Tragedy* fitted Nashe's description,
then much of the case would be proved, since it was the most
popular tragedy of the early period and exercised a profound
influence on subsequent plays like *Titus Andronicus,
Antonio's Revenge, Hamlet*, Chettle's *Hoffman*, and others.
However, *The Spanish Tragedy* seems to contain not a single
line derived from the 1581 translation of Seneca. It has
some Senecan lines in Latin and some original lines in Latin,
which implies (I take it) some knowledge of that language.
And there are no 'tragical speeches' taken out of Seneca in
this play. We may wish to continue to believe, however, that
Nashe's points, though not true literally, have a general
truth, in that Kyd's play is Senecan in its general cast. The
evidence for this is hard to find unless we take 'Senecan' to
mean things not found in Seneca, or found in many places as
well as Seneca.[1] In this context 'Senecan' is sometimes, of
course, taken to mean 'having a unified structure',[2] the
assumption being that *The Spanish Tragedy* is more unified
than its predecessors (*Cambyses, Horestes, Apius and
Virginia*) and that this improvement must be due to Seneca.
In fact, *The Spanish Tragedy* is far from having what has
been ascribed to it: 'unity of action, and . . . also unity of
motive, for it all centres round revenge'.[3] Revenge as a
motive, or a psychological propellant to action, only appears
halfway through the play. *The Spanish Tragedy* is unified,
far more effectively than the preceding plays, it is true; but
not by motive; rather by the impersonal but pervasive idea of
justice, which appears not only in the Hieronimo story, but
also in the ghostly chorus, in the Portuguese episode, and the

1. I trust there is no need to argue with absurdities like G. B. Harrison's
'from Seneca Kyd had drawn the notion that Tragedy was to be measured by
the number of the corpses' (*The Story of Elizabethan Drama*, Cambridge,
1924, p. 23).
2. See above, p. 178.
3. Legouis and Cazamian, *History of English Literature* (London, 1937 edn),
pp. 398 f.

episodes of Pedringano and Bazulto.[4] And in this mode of organization there is no influence of Seneca.

It is also true that *The Spanish Tragedy* has, in its interludes, a ghost (together with a Morality Personification); but this ghost has the usual non-Senecan characteristics I have described above. It may be said, on the other hand, that the ghost here is a *protatica persona* like the ghosts of Tantalus and Thyestes. And this is true. But the purpose of his eruption from hell and the atmosphere he brings into the play are quite distinct from anything in Seneca. Kyd's hell is a place of love and justice (I. i. 78–80):

> Proserpine began to smile
> And begged that only she might give my doom.
> Pluto was pleased, and sealed it with a kiss.

Seneca's ghosts are given a causal relationship to all that follows: they cause the mortal characters to act as they do. The ghost of Andrea in *The Spanish Tragedy* is, however, only a spectator and commentator. It might be thought that his companion Revenge is more like a Senecan *Furia* 'causing' revenge to triumph in the play. In fact, however, the revenge that takes place is wholly determined by the natural emotions of the characters: Revenge is given no direct relationship to Hieronimo, the hero and revenger. The revenge that Andrea returns to see and that Revenge is sent to show him, in the manner of a dream, 'through the gates of horn' (I. i. 82), is in fact quite peripheral to the main dramatic action. The ghost of Andrea is puzzled by what is going on (II. vi. 2–3):

> I looked that Balthazar should have been slain
> But 'tis my friend Horatio that is slain

And the ghost's puzzlement is meant to represent, I take it, a natural if simple-minded reaction. Kyd creates, in short, a gap between the supernatural concern in the play, and the more central matter, the individual lives, which exhibit that unexplained capacity to make free valid choices which is essential to a Christian view of the world and to modern drama. It is not any Senecan machinery, but this power to show emotion turning into action by the mysterious alchemy

4. See below, pp. 214–29.

of free personal choice that gives *The Spanish Tragedy* and *Hamlet* and *Titus Andronicus* their grip on the audience. The tension between an external set of expectations and an internal set of compulsions ('God's revenging aspect' and 'particular sin') throws the weight of the play on the character of the protagonist in a manner wholly unclassical. Far from being the channel of Senecan influence into Elizabethan popular drama, *The Spanish Tragedy*, in this view of it, forged, in parallel to Marlowe, a dramatic vision of humanity to which Seneca's plays could offer only peripheral decoration.

It may be thought that a description of Seneca's relationship to English drama in terms of his dramatic structures and effects on the one hand and his ethical positions on the other, is too limited. It may be felt, in particular, that more important than any of these is his literary style. The recent Penguin translation of five plays[5] tells us that 'the effectiveness of the spoken word was all that mattered in Seneca's conception of drama' (p. 25). Certainly the style of Seneca's plays was a point that few English critics of the Renaissance failed to mention:

the stately style of Senec sage ('H. C. to the Reader' before Studley's *Agamemnon*, 1566)

... grace and majesty of style (Preface to Heywood's *Thyestes*, 1560)

... endight/with wondrous wit and regal style (Preface to Heywood's *Thyestes*)

... penned with a peerless sublimity and loftiness of style (Newton's Preface to *Seneca his Ten Tragedies*, 1581)

... stately speeches and well-sounding phrases, climbing to the height of Seneca his style (Sidney, *Apology for Poetry*, 1595)

Seneca's tragedies, Plautus' comedies, Virgil's Georgics and Warrior, of the Latins, for the stateliness of the matter and style are most honoured (L. Humphrey, *The Nobles*, 1563)

5. Translated E. F. Watling (Harmondsworth, 1966).

Albeit he borrowed the argument of his tragedies from the Grecians, yet the spirit, loftiness of sound and majesty of style is merely his own (H. Peacham, *The Complete Gentleman*, 1622).[6]

The terms in which the style is praised remain remarkably constant: high, majestic, regal, lofty, stately,; all these seem to be pointing to a single aesthetic category, the sublime.

This categorization tells us about the critics' admiration; it is less helpful in giving us a comparative description of the mode of Seneca's poetry. Seneca's prose style has been described with great exactitude (e.g. succinctly and conveniently in W. C. Summers's edition of *Select Letters*), but it is not clear if his verse belongs to the same class. Certainly some of the features of 'Senecan' prose rhetoric appear also in the poetry. The taste for sharp, compressed, and weighty utterance is important here also, especially of course in stichomythia. But we should not forget that Quintilian speaks of Seneca's *ingenium facile et copiosum* (X. i. 128). The style of the plays can veer quickly from sharp desiccated 'points' (*harena sine calce*)[7] to flowing and hyperbolic eloquence, as in the following reply of the blinded Oedipus to Jocasta's attempted comfort (*Oed.* 1012–18):

> Quis frui tenebris vetat?
> quis reddit oculos? matris, en matris sonus!
> perdidimus operam. Congredi fas amplius
> haut est. nefandos dividat vastum mare
> dirimatque tellus abdita et quisquis sub hoc
> in alia versus sidera ac solem avium
> dependet orbis alterum ex nobis ferat.

(Who forbids me to enjoy the darkness? Who returns me my eyes? Look, my mother, the voice of my mother! The good work is thrown away! It is God's law that we should meet no more. Let the vast ocean divide the guilty, let the spaces of the earth yawn between us, bearing away one of us to whatever world hangs beneath this one, looking only at other stars and at a truant sun.)

6. Derived from J. C. Scaliger, *Poetices*, lib. VI. cap. vi: *Inventiones sane illorum sunt: at maiestas carminis, sonus, spiritus ipsius.*

7. The description of Seneca's style by the Emperor Caligula: see Suetonius, *Caligula*, 53.

We do not know how the Elizabethans responded to these polarities of style or how their conception of the sublime depended on one or another pole. We do know, however, that they had a sustained taste for tricksy and conceited writers—Ovid and Lucan as well as Seneca—and that 'height of style' was closely associated in their minds with daring conceits and sustained rhetorical structures. The natures of the Latin and the English languages hardly permit any carry-over of actual details of style, but the Neo-Latin plays of the period show their authors as happy to reproduce Seneca's range of rhetorical effects. Indeed even so considerable a Grecian as George Buchanan[8] shows the extent to which Greek drama was seen through the rhetorical lenses of Seneca's style: translating *Alcestis* 488: κτανὼν ἄρ' ἥξεις ἢ θανὼν αὐτοῦ μενεῖς, he sharpens its rhetoric into a typically Senecan glitter: *Caeso redibis rege, vel caesus cades.*[9]

The 1560–81 translators into English, however, have command of a rhetorical mode which would seem to be directly opposite to Seneca's. They are totally incapable of sharpness or compression; the hobnailed violence of their vocabulary is without self-conscious capacity for variation. To the modern ear, long inured to standards of the 'natural', the 'elegant', the 'easy', the 'conversational', in its excess and obviousness Seneca's rhetoric may seem like that of his translators. But the sophistication (even decadence) of his repetitive cleverness seems outside the range of their language.

There is one modern frame of reference, however, which may be responsible for creating a greater disparity between Seneca's rhetoric and that of his 1560–81 translators than was seen to be the case in Elizabethan times, and it may be that in this case the modern frame distorts the picture.

Reading Seneca's plays as plays, and thinking of plays as immediate experiences, sharply focused, tensely direct in their confrontations and in the close-up attention they demand, we inevitably find their style grotesquely unreal in its simplified exaggeration and stridency, like posters seen at very short

8. On Buchanan's 'completely Senecanized' style, see the comments of Charlton, op. cit., pp. xlix ff., and Boas, *University Drama* (Oxford, 1914), pp. 60–61, together with the evidence collected by John Hazel Smith, op. cit.

9. When Roger Ascham translated Sophocles' *Philoctetes*, he did it *ad imitationem quantum potui Senecae* (*Letters*, ed. Giles, Letter XVI, i. 32).

range. In the sixteenth century it was possible to think of a 'tragedy' anywhere along a range of considerable amplitude, stretching from the immediacy of theatrical tragedy to the dreamy and distancing vagueness of late medieval narrative tragedy. We have already noticed the descriptive bias of the *Mirror for Magistrates*. The Elizabethan translators of Seneca (belonging to the same intellectual group as Baldwin) impose a similar bias towards centralizing the narrator and distancing the action behind narrative and description. Jasper Heywood's preface to his translation of the *Troades* sets that work inside the framework of medieval and chivalric narrative of the 'matter of Troy':

> The ruins twain of Troy, the cause of each,
> The glittering helms, in field the banners spread,
> Achilles' ires and Hector's fights they[1] teach,
> There may the gests of many a knight be read:
> Patroclus, Pyrrhus, Ajax, Diomed.

Heywood's versified Preface to *Thyestes* turns this work into the dream-vision of a request to write, in parallel fashion, to the *Mirror for Magistrates*:

> Then dreamed I thus, that by my side
>   methought I saw one stand
> That down to ground in scarlet gown
>   was dight, and in his hand
> A book he bare: and on his head
>   of bayes a garland green.
> Full grave he was, well stepped in years
>   and comly to be seen.
> . . .
> Good sir (quod I) I you beseech
>   (since that ye seem to me
> By your attire some worthy wight)
>   it may your pleasure be
> To tell me what and whence you are.
> . . .
> Spain was (quod he) my native soil:
>   a man of worthy fame
> Sometime I was in former age,
>   and Seneca my name.

1. Dares, Dictys, Homer, Maro, mentioned in the preceding stanza.

Heywood's addition of a final scene at the end of the *Thyestes* has a similar function. It gives narrative expansion to the pressures of the play, takes away the stark finality of the confrontation between Atreus and Thyestes with which Seneca ends. In this added scene Thyestes exclaims against his fate, forecasts his exile (in lines imitated from the end of the *Oedipus*) and suggests the eventual operation of justice:

> Ye scape not fro me so, ye gods,
>   still after you I go,
> And vengeance ask on wicked wight
>   your thunderbolt to throw.

The 'now-read-on' extension of the *Agamemnon* in Studley's translation has a similar effect. The particularity of the single play is absorbed into, and softened by, the longer perspectives of destiny.

The supply of a context or framework of this kind has the effect of making Seneca much closer to Ovid than he seems to be in our modern response to the tragedies. *The Metamorphoses* exhibits the same combination of smug horror and epigrammatic passion that revolts us in Seneca. But those characteristics do not seem to dominate Ovid's telling of his stories. In the tale of Tereus and Procne in Book VI of *The Metamorphoses* (very close in matter to the *Thyestes*) the tragic speeches of the principals are held within a mediating framework of author's narrative and description, and (even more) in the larger perspective of things remote, legendary, and exemplary. Seneca's plays may be more like this than their genre suggests; for they are not in any real sense 'imitations of action'. They are comments on the mental states which would be appropriate to action; the interaction they contain is wholly static and sets static positions against one another. At the end of a typical Senecan exchange between *tyrannus* and *satelles*, or *regina* and *nutrix*, the dialogue is not led to a conclusion. A decision is simply taken to move to the next stage of the fable, a decision that could have been taken at any point in the dialogue.

In these terms Seneca's plays are unlike the modern conception of drama, and the style of the Elizabethan translations may be more appropriate than appears at first sight. Moreover, the assumption that Seneca's plays were like narrative tragedies is not one that is confined to the early translators who wrote before the English theatre existed. As late as 1599 Thomas Storer in his *Life and Death of Thomas Wolsey* invokes Seneca as the patron of this *Mirror for Magistrates* image of a tragic fall:

> Now write, Melpomene, my tragic moan,
> Call Nero's learned master, he will aid
> Thy failing quill with what himself once said:
> Never did Fortune greater instance give
> In what frail state proud magistrates do live.

Samuel Daniel's *Complaint of Rosamond* (1592) shows how the rhetoric of these *Mirror*-type ghosts has advanced towards dramatic sharpness:[2]

> Out of the horror of infernal deeps
> My poor afflicted ghost comes here to plain it.

But though this is sharper than the 1560–81 translators of Seneca, the basis of the rhetoric is still narrative, as is the relationship of the author to his material (64–67):

> Then write (quoth she) the ruin of my youth,
> Report the downfall of my slippery state,
> Of all my life reveal the simple truth
> To teach to others what I learnt too late.

Seneca is not himself, of course, a figure in his own plays (though he quickly figures in his disciple's *Octavia*), but the mode of his rhetoric seems designed to remind us that this is a particular way of telling facts widely known, where the mode of narration or description is at the centre of interest rather than the facts narrated.[3] When Hecuba tells us at the beginning of the *Troades* of the murder of Priam she says that when Pyrrhus drew out his sword, *ensis senili siccus e iugulo redit* (the sword comes out of the old man's throat still dry).

2. A rhetoric copied, it seems, in the academic play, *Caesar's Revenge*: 'Enter *Caesar's Ghost*: Out of the horror of those shady vaults / . . . My restless soul comes here to tell his wrongs.' (Malone Society Reprint, Oxford, 1972 ff.)

3. See Friedrich Leo, *L. A. Senecae Tragoediae* (Berlin, 1878), p. 148: *novum autem genus, tragoedia rhetorica, inventa est, cuius indoles breviter sic describi potest, ut* ἦθος *in ea nullum,* πάθος *omnia esse dicatur.* Cf. H. V. Canter, *Rhetorical Elements in the Tragedies of Seneca* (Urbana, 1925), pp. 18–22.

A little later she remarks that: *Priamus et flamma indiget /
ardente Troia* (Though Troy is burning Priam lacks a funeral
pyre). We seem to be asked to applaud the teller rather than
wonder at the tale.

When we turn to the rhetoric of the popular Elizabethan
drama, the 'real' drama, we find a very different deployment
of rhetoric, for which Seneca can be little except a source of
occasional *sententiae*. Kyd's *The Spanish Tragedy* is again a
useful text to display the actual differences between Seneca
and the so-called Senecan drama. The most famous of the
many passionately rhetorical arias in *The Spanish Tragedy* is
the speech of Hieronimo when he discovers his son hanging
in his orchard (II. v. 1–33):

> What outcries pluck me from my naked bed
> And chill my throbbing heart with trembling fear,
> Which never danger yet could daunt before?
> Who calls Hieronimo? speak, here I am.
> I did not slumber, therefore 'twas no dream.
> No, no, it was some woman cried for help,
> And here within this garden did she cry,
> And in this garden must I rescue her.
> But stay, what murd'rous spectacle is this?
> A man hanged up, and all the murderers gone,
> And in my bower, to lay the guilt on me.
> This place was made for pleasure, not for death.

> *He cuts him down.*

> These garments that he wears I oft have seen –
> Alas, it is Horatio my sweet son,
> O, no, but he that whilom was my son.
> O was it thou that call'dst me from my bed?
> O speak, if any spark of life remain.
> I am thy father. Who hath slain my son?
> What savage monster, not of human kind,
> Hath here been glutted with thy harmless blood,
> And left thy bloody corpse dishonoured here
> For me amidst these dark and deathful shades
> To drown thee with an ocean of my tears?
> O heavens, why made you night to cover sin?
> By day this deed of darkness had not been.
> O earth, why didst thou not in time devour
> The vild profaner of this sacred bower?

O poor Horatio, what hadst thou misdone
To lose thy life ere life was new begun?
O wicked butcher, whatsoe'er thou wert,
How could thou strangle virtue and desert?
Ay me, most wretched, that have lost my joy
In losing my Horatio my sweet boy.

These lines are specifically designed to make vivid and moving a spectacle visually presented (or imagined) on the stage. A man enters before us; he tells us where he has been and what his state of mind is. He makes a direct appeal to identification. We too have been wakened by night-noises and felt our scalps tingle. Here is no Senecan *nuntius* informing us that his veins freeze to remember a mythological horror for which he is a witness; but instead we have the principal person of the play asking us to participate in his mimesis. Seneca's rhetoric is used to distance from us the highly charged events described, and continuously resolves them into wit and abstraction. Hieronimo's soliloquy, on the other hand, keeps him close beside us as step-by-step we proceed through the process of discovery, even though by tragic irony we already know what it is he is going to find. He addresses us directly, not simply as an audience, but as if he might expect an answer. To whom is the opening question proposed? Is he addressing himself or us? Are we involved or not? The theatrical situation feeds on these tensions: we are caught in a guilty complicity with the action.

The movement of Hieronimo's speech mimics the movement of circling round and identifying not only the situation but the subject of the situation. Is the call real or imaginary? 'I must find out, I am not a coward, I will name myself. It was not imaginary, it must have been real. It was here and it was to me the call came. I must act.' At the moment of resolve the image of horror is revealed, though still not understood. Kyd skilfully allows a momentary pause on the agonizing brink of recognition, a technique more regular in comedy. Here a powerful effect of pathos is built up by the contrast between what Hieronimo still thinks and what we know, reinforced by the contrast between the bower (and the love-scene we have seen in it) and the present horror. The actual recognition has been delayed till line 14, and a series of relationships have been established between us and Hieronimo, and with the place and the object, the body of Horatio. The triple anaphora on 'O' marks the climax of the speech and a return to the opening question, addressed now to a specific answerer, with specific self-definition, 'I am thy father', and a specifically appropriate context, 'these dark and deathful shades'. The remainder of the speech is a circuit of anguished rhetorical questions based on the male *pieta* pose of father and son, aimed (as it were) at the world of values standing behind the audience: 'O heavens ... O earth ... O poor Horatio ... O wicked butcher', and so returning to himself, the only answerer as the only speaker.

The situation of this speech (the discovery of a horror) is paralleled in Seneca, but the mode of its rhetoric is wholly unlike Seneca's. A line like 'O heavens, why made you night to cover sin?' could well have come from Seneca, but the method by which it makes its effect here is un-Senecan. In the *Thyestes*, after the death of Thyestes's children, an unnatural darkness settles over the earth. But this darkness is not conveyed to us as anyone's idea of darkness. The fourth chorus asks: *cur, Phoebe, tuos rapis aspectus?* (Why, O sun, do you hide your face from us?) But the idea of darkness is immediately developed as a general theme. The questions or answers proposed do not reflect on the minds of those speaking. The darkness of Hieronimo's garden acquires importance because we see Hieronimo coming to feel it is important: it is part of the world he creates for us out of the experience he undergoes.

Seneca's characters often describe their own feelings, or their position between alternative feelings. Medea describes the alternation in her mind between guilt and love, her rage for revenge and her desire for peace. But none of this is presented as feeling whose growth we have shared with the character, so that the more extreme moments of rhetoric are backed by a shared humanity. The classical technique of Seneca's plots means that the roots of character are in the distant past, in the habits of ancestors or the crimes of history. Medea presents her emotions as if she were the *nuntius* of her own situation. When we hear (943–4) *ira pietatem fugat / iramque pietas* (wrath chases away affection and affection, wrath), we seem to be hearing about the general qualities *ira* and *pietas* rather than participating in the psychological battle between them. In so far as they have a personal context it is one which requires us to enlarge *ira* to include all the acts of violence that Medea's history has encompassed, and *pietas* to stretch from her own family *pietas* in Colchis to that involving her children by Jason. The individual moment strains always to a generalization that (unlike the generalizations of Elizabethan dramatic rhetoric) lacks any personal, here-and-now dimension in the emotions we see and share with the common humanity of the presented character.

I have suggested that, below the level of cultural generality, the points of contact between Seneca and the public drama of the English Renaissance were small in number, distorted by great (though sometimes obscured) differences of outlook and expectation, and seldom wholly separable from other exemplars of similar taste. But Seneca remained, in spite of all this, an ancient, and praise of his morals and his style could not easily be evaded in an age hungry both for opportunities to reconcile the morality of Christian art with that of classical antiquity, and for models of power and sophistication in language. And this is as true in the England of the seventeenth century as in that of the sixteenth. In some senses the seventeenth century may be said to have increased Seneca's reputation, not only in the neo-Stoic movement associated with the names of Lipsius and Du Vair, Bacon and Feltham, but (in English at any rate) in an increasing sophistication and concision in the use of the language. When Drayton (in his epistle to Reynolds) speaks of 'strong Seneca'[4] he is making the appropriate stylistic connection between Seneca's mode and the 'strong lines' of the Metaphysical poets and the sinewy prose of the early seventeenth century, which we know to exist in terms of the mode of thought and general moral outlook of the period.

It would seem to be no accident that the best English translation of the most translated passage of Seneca (the end of the second chorus of the *Thyestes*) should be the work of Andrew

4. See J. E. Spingarn, *Critical Essays of the Seventeenth Century* (Oxford), i. 138.

Marvell.[5] The middle of the seventeenth century saw a second
wave of English translations of the plays, the first since the
sixties of the preceding century. Three of the plays (*Medea*,
Phaedra, and *Troades*, the three tragedies centred on female
figures) were translated by Sir Edward Sherburn; the *Medea*
being printed separately in 1648, the *Troades* in 1679, and all
three issued together in 1701. It is a pity that the supposed
historical significance of the 1581 volume has caused it to be
twice reissued, when Sherburn's much more competent and
readable work remains unknown. In addition, Edmund
Prestwich translated the *Phaedra* in 1651. The *Troades*,
translated by Samuel Pordage, was printed in 1660; and in
1674 came *Thyestes*, translated by John Wright. These
remained the last translations of Seneca's plays till the
historical interests of this century caused scholars to turn to
them again.

   With the fading of the Baroque the last connection between
the taste of Seneca and that of any possible modern literature was broken. For, though the seventeenth century offered
a more sophisticated response to Seneca's style and to the
quality of his moral sensibility, the mode of his plays grew
less and less acceptable, even to critics. Increasingly the
English drama came to judge dramatic rhetoric by standards
appropriate to real speech, and think of construction in
terms of a fluent *liaison des scènes*.

   It is predictable perhaps that Thomas Rymer, as an avowed
enemy to non-realistic drama, should despise Seneca:[6]

It was then a strange imagination in . . . Seneca, to think his dry
Morals and a tedious strain of sentences might do feats or have
any wonderful operation in the drama.

Dryden says in the *Essay of Dramatic Poesy* that Seneca had
the gift to make vulgar things sound lofty (ed. Ker, i. 105):

One would think, *unlock the door*, was a thing as vulgar as could
be spoken; and yet Seneca could make it sound high and lofty
in his Latin: *Reserate clausos regii postes laris*.

In the context of the defence of rhyme in the Essay, this is

5. See Appendix.
6. See Spingarn, op. cit. ii. 211–12.

clearly an admired gift, but the occasions when it needs to be exercised are allowed to be very few.

And Dryden's defence of rhyme and other 'heroick' appurtenances of tragedy is in any case clearly something of a paradox in the drama of his times. Even in the preface to his own and Lee's furibund *Oedipus* he says much the same thing as Rymer:

> Seneca on the other side, as if there were no such thing as nature to be minded in a play, is always running after pompous expressions, pointed sentences and philosophical notions, more proper for the study than the stage.

The pomposity of Seneca's style offended the canons of naturalness and ease which were to become increasingly the overriding requirements of both stage and study. Theobald in his *Double Falsehood* (1727), alleged to be based on an old play, was still Baroque enough to enjoy (presumably) and paraphrase a typical Senecan conceit (*H.F.* 84): *Quaeris Alcidae parem? / Nemo est nisi ipse* (You are looking for the equal of Hercules? He has no equal except himself) as 'None but thyself can be thy parallel'. Pope seized on the conceit as typical of Theobald's bad taste and inserted the 'marvellous line' into *The Dunciad* (three-book version), iii. 271.

The final appearance of Seneca in *The Dunciad* marks very well what happened to his plays in the period of the Enlightenment. After this it clearly needed a complete shift of priorities to bring Seneca's plays back into anything like favour. Today we may be on the edge of some such shift. In 1968 London had what is probably its first ever public presentation of a Seneca play: *Oedipus*, in a translation or rather adaptation by Ted Hughes, produced by Peter Brook with Sir John Gielgud in the title role. Hughes writes (perhaps with memories of Camus's *La Peste*) of a world disintegrated by the Theban plague into separate moments of pain and incomprehension. His style is without sentence-structure, a series of vividly particular phrases expressing separate emotional and sensory responses, the connections unstated, and perhaps unimagined. By this technique the desperateness of man's state is brilliantly exposed; but it is a long way from the dignity and lucidity of Seneca's *senarii*. The 'Senecan

style' is certainly one which reduces the power of connectives
—'shattered eloquence' is Dryden's fine phrase for it (in his
Life of Plutarch)—but his contraction of meaning from large
gestures of interpretation, to the privacy and limitation of
individual integrity is not a retreat into incoherence and
meaninglessness. The taste that lay behind this production
goes back to the crazy theatrical theorist Antonin Artaud,
who in 1932 was praising Seneca as a model for what he
called 'The Theatre of Cruelty'. Writing to Jean Paulhan on
16 December 1932, he says: (*Œuvres Complètes* [Paris],
iii. 303):

Je suis en train de lire Sénèque . . . Quoi qu'il en soit celui-ci me
paraît le plus grand auteur tragique de l'histoire, un initié aux
Secrets et qui mieux qu' Eschyle a su les faire passer dans les mots.
Je pleure en lisant son théâtre d'inspiré, j'y sens sous le verbe des
syllabes crépiter de la plus atroce manière le bouillonnement
transparent des forces du chaos . . . une fois guéri j'ai l'intention
d'organiser des . . . lectures publiques ou je lirai des Tragédies de
Sénèque, et tous les commanditaires possibles du Théâtre de la
Cruauté seront convoqués. On ne peut mieux trouver d'example
écrit de ce qu'on peut entendre par cruauté au théâtre que dans
toutes les Tragédies de Sénèque, mais surtout dans Atrée et
Thyeste. . . . Dans Sénèque les forces primordiales font entendre
leur écho dans la vibration spasmodique des mots.

In these terms Seneca is treasured largely because his plays
are an affront to the bourgeois sensibilities of traditional
theatregoers. The violence, the *bouillonnement transparent
des forces du chaos*, assault and disturb, force the spectators
to admit the power of the frightening, the unknown, the
disgusting. Artaud planned a version of *Thyestes* (*Le Supplice
de Tantale*), but this seems not to have survived. The Ted
Hughes version of *Oedipus*, however, shows the same ideals,
in its intensification and increased particularity of horror
and its avoidance or reduction of both morality and wit, the
qualities which were earlier thought of central importance to
an appreciation of Seneca the dramatist.

APPENDIX
English translations and imitations of *Thyestes*, 391–403

> Stet quicumque volet potens
> aulae culmine lubrico;
> me dulcis saturet quies;
> obscuro positus loco
> leni perfruar otio,
> nullis nota Quiritibus
> aetas per tacitum fluat.
> sic cum transierint mei
> nullo cum strepitu dies,
> plebeius moriar senex.
> illi mors gravis incubat
> qui, notus nimis omnibus,
> ignotus moritur sibi.

1. First published 1557; written before 1542.

Of the same meane and sure estate

> Stond who so list vpon the slipper whele,
> Of hye astate and let me here reioyce,
> And vse my life in quietnesse eche dele,
> Vnknowen in court that hath the wanton toyes.
> In hidden place my time shall slowly passe
> And when my yeres be past withouten noyce
> Let me dye olde after the common trace
> For gripes of death doth he to hardly passe
> That knowen is to all: but to him selfe alas,
> He dyeth vnknowen, dased with dreadfull face.
> (*Sir Thomas Wyatt*)

2. First published 1560.

> Let who so lyst with mighty mace to raygne,
> In tyckle toppe of court delight to stand
> Let mee the sweete and quiet rest obtayne.
> So set in place obscure and lowe degree,
> Of pleasaunt rest I shall the sweetnesse knoe.
> My lyfe unknowne to them that noble bee,
> Shall in the steppe of secret sylence goe.
> Thus when my dayes at length are over past,
> And tyme without all troublous tumult spent,

An aged man I shall depart at last,
In meane estate, to dye full well content.
But greevuous is to him the death, that when
So farre abroade the bruite of him is blowne,
That knowne hee is to much to other men:
Departeth yet unto him selfe unknowne.

(Jasper Heywood)

3. First published 1681; probably written before 1660.

Climb at *Court* for me that will
Tottering favor's Pinacle;
All I seek is to lye still.
Settled in some secret Nest
In calm leisure let me rest;
And far of the publick Stage
Pass away my silent Age.
Thus when without noise, unknown,
I have liv'd out all my span,
I shall dye, without a groan,
An old honest Country man.
Who expos'd to others Ey's,
Into his own Heart ne'r pry's,
Death to him 's a Strange surprise.

(Andrew Marvell)

4. First published 1668.

Upon the slippery tops of humane State,
    The guilded Pinnacles of Fate,
Let others proudly stand, and for a while
    The giddy danger to beguile,
With Joy, and with disdain look down on all,
    Till their Heads turn, and down they fall.
Me, O ye Gods, on Earth, or else so near
    That I no fall to Earth may fear,
And, O ye Gods, at a good distance seat
    From the long Ruines of the Great.
Here wrapt in th' Arms of Quiet let me ly;
Quiet, Companion of Obscurity.
Here let my Life, with as much silence slide,
    As Time that measures it doth glide.
Nor let the Breath of Infamy or Fame,
From town to town Eccho about my Name.
Nor let my homely Death embroidered be

With Scutcheon or with Elegie.
An old *Plebean* let me Dy,
Alas, all then are such as well as I.
    To him, alas, to him, I fear,
The face of Death will terrible appear:
Who in his life flattering his senceless pride
By being known to all the world beside,
Does not himself, when he is Dying know
Nor what he is, nor Whither hee's to go.
                    (*Abraham Cowley*)

5. First published 1676.

Let him that will, ascend the tottering Seat
Of Courtly Grandeur, and become as great
As are his mountain wishes; as for me,
Let sweet Repose, and Rest my portion be;
Give me some mean obscure Recess, a Sphere
Out of the road of Business, or the fear
Of falling lower, where I sweetly may
My self, and dear Retirement still enjoy.
Let not my Life, or Name, be known unto
The Grandees of the Times, tost to and fro
By Censures or Applause; but let my Age
Slide gently by, not overthwart the Stage
Of publick Interest; unheard, unseen,
And unconcern'd, as if I ne'er had been.
And thus while I shall pass my silent days
In shady Privacy, free from the Noise
And busles of the World, then shall I
A good old Innocent Plebeian dy.
Death is a mere Surprize, a very Snare,
To him that makes it his lifes greatest care
To be a publick Pageant, Known to All,
But unacquainted with Himself, doth fall.
                    (*Sir Matthew Hale*)

6. First published 1674.

While he that loves Ambition's pains
On the Court's slippery top remains;
Let me sweet peace enjoy; content
I am to live where none frequent;
There shall I fill my longing breast
With the still blessings of soft rest,

Free from their knowledge great who are,
Free from the noise of business, there
I'll cast my life, and thus shall I
Rich in an humble fortune die.
But heavy doth that death befall
To him who too much known to all
By fame of his great honours past
Dies to himself unknown at last.

(John Wright)

7. Bodleian MS. Rawlinson 76, second half of the seventeenth century.

Let him who likes it be stiled great
Upon the slippery tops of state.
Give me, O Gods, a quiet life,
Nor let debate, nor law nor strife
E'er haunt my cottage, where I find
All joys can bless a mortal's mind.
Let time as smooth as swiftly run
And all the craggy roads quite shun
Which lead to honour, which at last
Is lost, and life, in seeking past.
A life I wish wherein I may
Live old, and silent pass away.
Unhappy he who dies, well known
To all but to himself alone,
A man of outside who lives high
Is called a Wit, a Debauchee,
But knows not, vain fool, how to die

(Anon.)

8. First published 1732.

An imitation of the 2nd chorus, in the second act of
Seneca's Thyestes
Whom worldly luxury and pomps allure,
They tread on ice and find no footing sure;
Place me, ye powers! in some obscure retreat,
O! keep me innocent, make others great;
In quiet shades, content with rural sports,
Give me a life remote from guilty courts,
Where, free from hopes or fears, in humble ease,
Unheard of I may live and die in peace.

Happy the man, who, thus retir'd from sight,
Studies himself, and seeks no other light:
But most unhappy he, who sits on high,
Exposed to every tongue and every eye;
Whose follies blaz'd about to all are known,
But are a secret to himself alone:
Worse is an evil fame, much worse than none.

(George Granville, Lord Lansdowne)

8

Ironies of justice in
The Spanish Tragedy

The assumption that *The Spanish Tragedy* is usefully cate-
gorized as a 'revenge play' and that this categorization gives
us a means of differentiating what is essential in the text from
what is peripheral—this has governed most that has been said
about Kyd's play. And this is a pity, because the play when
looked at in these terms shows up as rather a botched piece
of work.

It is no doubt an inevitable part of the tendency of literary
historians that they should look everywhere for indications
of historical progress. Certainly this has caused them to
search among the 'amorphous' (i.e., non-modern) dramatic
forms of the Elizabethans for signs and portents of the
coming of Scribe and the 'well-made' play. The revenge
motif, in particular, has been seen as important because
(to quote Moody Prior) it

had the advantage of imposing a fairly strict pattern on the play.
It thus assisted in discouraging multiple narratives and irrelevant
episodes, and, in general, acted as a check on the tendency toward
diffuseness and digression which was a common defect of popular
Elizabethan drama.[1]

Percy Simpson, in the same general terms, sees the revenge
motif as imposing on Elizabethan dramaturgy the Aristo-
telian virtues of beginning, middle, and end: 'The beginning is
effectively supplied by the murder; the end should be effectively
supplied by the vengeance. The problem for the working
dramatist was skilfully to bridge the gap between the two.'[2]

[First published in *Renaissance Drama*, viii (1965).]
1. Moody E. Prior, *The Language of Tragedy* (New York, 1947), p. 47.
2. Percy Simpson, 'The theme of revenge in Elizabethan tragedy', British
Academy Shakespeare Lecture for 1935, p. 9.

Unfortunately this pattern of progress shows the actual products it seeks to explain as rather unsatisfactory parts of the very progression which is adduced to explain them. Prior finds *The Spanish Tragedy* to be ensnared in the very 'multiple narratives and irrelevant episodes' that the revenge motif was supposed to discourage. He speaks of 'the disproportionate amount of preliminary preparation necessary before Hieronimo is introduced as the avenging agent',[3] and also of 'the introduction of the story of the treacherous noble in the Portuguese Court, which has no bearing on the main action'.[4] Fredson Bowers tells us that 'the ghost has no real concern with the play' and that 'the fundamental motive for the tragic action . . . is not conceived until midway in the play'.[5] Simpson has much the same attitude. After the passage quoted above, he goes on to apply it to Kyd:

Now Kyd, who had a keen eye for dramatic situation and, in his happy moments, a powerful style, does at critical points fumble the action. His main theme, as the early title-page announces, is 'the lamentable end of Don Horatio,' avenged at the cost of his own life by his aged father Hieronimo. But the induction brings in the ghost of Horatio's friend, Don Andrea, and the personified figure of Revenge.[6]

Later Simpson speaks more unequivocally of

the disconnectedness, the waste of opportunity, and the dramatic unevenness of much of the writing.[7]

This attitude toward the revenge play in general and *The Spanish Tragedy* in particular has persisted in criticism. Philip Edwards's recent and excellent edition of the play (1959) speaks of the 'prolix early scenes' and tells us that 'it is very hard to justify the sub-plot . . . the relevance of theme is very slight' (p. liii). But at the same time as these attitudes persist, their historical foundations are disappearing. The assumption that the Elizabethan play inherited from the Tudor interlude a diffuse form which reflects mere incompetence—this becomes increasingly difficult to sustain in the

3. Prior, pp. 46 f.   4. Ibid., p. 46.
5. F. T. Bowers, *Elizabethan Revenge Tragedy* (Princeton, 1940), p. 71.
6. Simpson, pp. 9 ff.   7. Ibid., p. 14.

light of recent studies of the interlude by Craik,[8] Spivack,[9] Bevington,[1] and Habicht.[2] These, in their different ways, present the interlude as a serious form, in which flat characterization, repetitiveness, and dependence on a multiplicity of short episodes are not defects, but rather means perfectly adapted to express that age's moral and religious (rather than psychological or social) view of human destiny. Persons are seen to be less important than theme; they exist to illustrate rather than represent; and narrative line gives way to the illustration of doctrine. I may quote Bevington's remarks on the late morality, Lupton's *All for Money* (*c.* 1577):

The unity of *All for Money*, as in so many popular 'episodic' plays, is the singleness of theme (man's greed) manifested in a variety of episodes. This theme becomes more important than the fate of individuals. Characters are drawn to illustrate a single motif of human behavior, and are given no more depth than is necessary to make a point. The full course of their lives has no relevance here. It is the course of the moral formula that is all-important: the genealogy of sin, the analysis of its origins, motivations, and processes, the depiction of its wordly success and ultimate downfall—all seen in the perspective of moral uprightness, the beginning and end of virtuous living. The parts succeed each other as *exempla* to a homily, written for an audience that perceived a rich totality in matters of faith. The success of the play lies in varied illustration, in 'multiple unity' and gathering of impact, not in the crisis of the individual moment.[3]

If *The Spanish Tragedy* is seen not so much as the harbinger of *Hamlet* (not to mention Scribe), but more as the inheritor of a complex and rich tradition of moralizing dramaturgy, the actual structure of the play begins to make more sense, and the traditional strictures that Prior and Simpson re-echo lose much of their relevance. The text of the play does not appear to give its complete attention to the enactment of revenge. True. But this may be because the

8. T. W. Craik, *The Tudor Interlude* (Leicester, 1958).

9. Bernard Spivack, *Shakespeare and the Allegory of Evil* (New York, 1958).

1. D. M. Bevington, *From Mankind to Marlowe* (Cambridge, Mass., 1962).

2. Werner Habicht, 'Sénèque et le théâtre pré-Shakespearien', in *Sénèque et le théâtre de la Renaissance*, ed. Jacquot (Paris, 1964). Dr Habicht's book *Studien zur Dramenform vor Shakespeare* (Winter Verlag, Heidelberg, 1968) is a full-scale survey of early dramatic forms.

3. Bevington, p. 166.

play is not centrally concerned with the enactment of revenge. Much more obsessive is the question of justice. Indeed we may hazard an initial statement that if revenge provides the plot line of the play (i.e., play structure as seen from Scribe's point of view), justice provides the thematic centre of the play (i.e., play structure as seen from the point of view of the Tudor interlude).

The centrality of the concept of justice serves to explain much of the so-called 'preliminary preparation' of the first two acts. The play opens with Don Andrea, who has been slain in the late war between Spain and Portugal. Don Andrea's journey after death is through an infernal landscape devoted to working out justice. He is set before Minos, Rhadamanthus, and Aeacus, the judges of the classical afterlife; they are unable to resolve his legal status and refer him to a higher authority—to the monarchs of the under-world, Pluto and Proserpine. On his way to their court he passes through the enactments of Hell's precisely organized justice—horribly poetic justice indeed:

> Where bloudie furies shakes their whips of steele,
> And poore *Ixion* turnes an endles wheele;
> Where vsurers are choakt with melting golde,
> And wantons are imbraste with ouglie Snakes,
> And murderers grone with neuer killing wounds,
> And periurde wightes scalded in boyling lead,
> And all foule sinnes with torments ouerwhelmd
> (I. i. 65–71)[4]

But Don Andrea is not allowed to complete his search for justice amid the palpable abstractions of Hell. What the higher court orders is that he should be sent back to earth to observe how the gods operate *there*, and for this purpose is he given Revenge as his companion and guide:

> Forthwith, *Revenge*, she rounded thee in th' eare,
> And bad thee lead me through the gates of Horn,
> Where dreames haue passage in the silent night.
> No sooner had she spoke, but we were heere,
> I wot not how, in twinkling of an eye.

4. The text of quotations from *The Spanish Tragedy* is that of F. S. Boas (Oxford, 1901, 1955).

REVENGE. Then know, *Andrea*, that thou art ariu'd
Where thou shalt see the author of thy death,
. . .
Depriu'd of life by *Bel-imperia*.   (I. i. 81–87, 89)

Revenge here seems to bear the same relation to justice as
Talus (in Book v of *The Faerie Queene*) does to Artegall—
that is, he is the emotionless and terrifyingly non-human
executive arm of the legality that is being demonstrated. But
Revenge, unlike Talus, does not act in his own person; his
presence guarantees that the human action will work out
justly, but he is not seen to make it do so. The departure of
Andrea and Revenge through the gates of horn, Virgil's
porta—

Cornea, qua veris facilis datur exitus umbris—

and their arrival at the Spanish court, can indeed be seen as
dramatic equivalents to the introductory sequences of
medieval dream allegory. The play may be viewed in this
sense as what Andrea dreams, as an allegory of perfect
justice: 'The gods are indeed just; and now you shall see
how their justice works out.' We are promised a mathe-
matical perfection of total recompense, where justice and
revenge are identical. From this point of view the human
beings who appear in Andrea's dream—the characters of the
play, scheming, complaining, and hoping—are not to be
taken by the audience as the independent and self-willed
individuals they suppose themselves to be, but in fact only as
the puppets of a predetermined and omnicompetent justice
that they (the characters) cannot see and never really understand. But *we* (watching the whole stage) must never lose
sight of this piece of knowledge.

The concern with justice in the opening scenes establishes
an ironic set of responses for the audience and an ironic
mode of construction for the play. The structure, indeed,
may remind us of a Ptolemaic model of the universe, one
level of awareness outside another level of awareness and,
outside the whole, the unsleeping eye of God.

The disjunction between what the audience knows and
what is known in the Spanish court is established straight-
away when the 'play proper' starts. The Spaniards con-

gratulate themselves on the late victory and stress the unimportance of the losses:

> All wel, my soueraigne Liege, except some few
> That are deceast by fortune of the warre.
>
> (I. ii. 2–3)

And again: 'Victorie, my Liege, and that with little losse.' *We*, seeing Andrea sitting on the stage, know that the 'little losse' can be too easily discounted and that the 'some few' may yet blemish the complacency of the court and the over-confident assumption that justice is already achieved:

> Then blest be heauen, and guider of the heauens,
> From whose faire influence such iustice flowes.
>
> (I. ii. 10–11)

We now see assembled before us the characters who are to be involved in the final demonstration of justice, centrally Don Balthazar, who is to die (we have been told) by the hand of Bel-imperia. But what we see in the opening scenes is no movement that can be understood as leading toward the death of Balthazar. What happens involves Balthazar with a variety of different kinds of justice, but the play is obviously more interested in exploring thematic comprehensiveness than in moving toward any narrative consequence.

The problem of deciding justly between competing claims to truth, which has appeared already in the dispute between Aeacus and Rhadamanthus, recurs in the contest between Lorenzo and Horatio, who dispute which of them, in law, has Balthazar as prisoner; and the king shows a Solomon-like wisdom in making a just decision:

> Then by my iudgement thus your strife shall end:
> You both deserue, and both shall haue reward.
> Nephew, thou tookst his weapon and his horse:
> His weapons and his horse are thy reward.
> *Horatio*, thou didst force him first to yeeld:
> His ransome therefore is thy valours fee; [etc.].
>
> (I. ii. 178–83)

Expectation is tuned into a competency of human justice that *we* know cannot finally be sustained against the meddling of divine justice in this human scene.

The next scene introduces the Portuguese episode so famous for its irrelevance to the main action. The first scene of the 'play proper' showed the Spaniards rejoicing over their victory and absorbing Balthazar into their court life. What the second (Portuguese) scene does is to show us the other side of the coin—the Portingales bewailing their defeat. And actually the Portuguese scenes serve as a continuous counterpoint against the earlier stages of *The Spanish Tragedy*, not only setting Portuguese sorrow against the Spanish mirth of the first scene, but later inverting the counterpoint and setting the viceroy's joy at his son's recovery against Hieronimo's cry of sorrow and demand for vengeance. Moreover, the long aria of grief put into the viceroy's mouth in I. iii gives the first statement of what is to become the central theme of *The Spanish Tragedy*, certainly the central and most famous impulse in its rhetoric—that frantic poetry of loss and sense of universal injustice which was to give Hieronimo his fame. We can see that, in spatial terms, the viceroy prepares the way for Hieronimo by living through the same class of experience—the loss of a son. Hieronimo makes this point quite explicitly when he says at the end of the play:

> Speake, Portaguise, whose losse resembles mine:
> If thou canst weepe vpon thy *Balthazar*,
> Tis like I wailde for my *Horatio*. (IV. iv. 114–16)

The viceroy does not weep at this point, when Balthazar is really dead, but the opening scenes and the speeches in which he bewails his supposed death sustain our sense of what Hieronimo is referring to. Moreover, the connection between national sin and individual sorrow which seems to be implied in the main story of Hieronimo and Horatio is quite explicit in the Portuguese episode:

> My late ambition hath distaind my faith;
> My breach of faith occasiond bloudie warres;
> Those bloudie warres haue spent my treasure;
> And with my treasure my peoples blood;
> And with their blood, my ioy and best beloued,
> My best beloued, my sweete and onely Sonne.
> (I. iii. 33–38)

But this scene of sorrow does more than prepare for the

second and central lost son, Don Horatio; it establishes an
ironic countercurrent inside the framework of the general
information that has been given us by Andrea and Revenge.
Not only is it deeply ironic to see the viceroy bewailing the
death of a son, who is at that moment involved in the murder
of another son, Horatio, and the bereavement of another
father (and we should note that this second bereavement is
one which cannot, this time, be avoided as if by a miracle
[see III. xiv. 34]). But more, the general framework of the play
tells us that it is ironic even when the viceroy changes from
lamentation to rejoicing; for *we* know that the relationship
with Bel-imperia which looks so auspicious from inside the
play will be the actual cause of his death.

The short fable of human fallibility and divine concern
which supplies the narrative (as against the thematic)
substance of the Portuguese episode—this feeds into the
main plot an expectation that '. . . murder cannot be hid: /
Time is the author both of truth and right, / And time will
bring this trecherie to light' (II. v. 58–60); it strengthens the
expectation which Revenge and Andrea arouse by their very
presence—that wrong must soon, and inevitably, be followed
by retribution. It is no accident that places the second Portuguese scene (III. i)—which shows Alexandro rescued from
death, as if by miracle, at the very last moment—immediately
after the death of Horatio and the first sounds of Hieronimo's
passion: 'What out-cries pluck me from my naked bed,
[etc.]' (II. v. 1) The discovery of Horatio is the centre of the
main plot, being the re-enactment in real life of the death
which began the action of the play; for Don Horatio is, as it
were, the living surrogate for the ghost Andrea. As he was
friend and revenger to Andrea on the battlefield, so he has
taken on the role of lover to Bel-imperia, and so too he falls
victim to Balthazar (and his confederates). And this is the
point in the play where the sense of just gods directing a
revenge on Balthazar is at its lowest ebb. As Andrea under-
standably exclaims to Revenge:

> Broughtst thou me hether to encrease my paine?
> I lookt that *Balthazar* should haue beene slaine:
> But tis my freend *Horatio* that is slaine,
> And they abuse fair *Bel-imperia*,

On whom I doted more then all the world,
Because she lou'd me more then all the world.
                                        (II. vi. 1–6)

The reinforcement of the justice theme at this point is,
therefore, particularly useful. Even if the Portuguese episode
had no other function, this one would seem to justify it.

Andrea was returned to earth by the just gods, to witness a
parable of perfect recompense, a parable which would
re-enact the story of his life, but cleared of the ambiguities
and uncertainties that had surrounded him. The death of
Horatio re-presents the death of Andrea, but presents it as a
definite crime (as the death of Andrea was not) and makes
Balthazar into a definite criminal (as in the battle he was not).
More important, the death of Horatio raises up an agent of
recompense who has the best claim to justification in his
action—the father of the victim and a man renowned for
state service, the chief judicial functionary of the court. Kyd
goes out of his way to show Hieronimo in this function and
to make the first citizen tell us that

> . . . for learning and for law,
> There is not any Aduocate in Spaine
> That can preuaile, or will take halfe the paine
> That he will in pursuit of equitie.
>   (III. xiii. 51–54)

Hieronimo is justly at the centre of *The Spanish Tragedy*
because he is constructed to embody perfectly the central
question about justice that the play poses: the question, 'How
can a human being pursue the path of justice?' Hieronimo is
constructed to suggest both complete justification of motive
(his outraged fatherhood) and the strongest advantages in
social position. And as such he is groomed to be the perfect
victim of a justice machine that uses up and destroys even
this paragon. Herein lies the truly cathartic quality of *The
Spanish Tragedy*: If this man, Kyd seems to be saying, fails
to find any secure way of justice on earth, how will it fare
with you and me? For Hieronimo, for all his devotion to the
cause of justice, is as much a puppet of the play's divine
system of recompense as are the other characters in the
action. He is stuck on the ironic pin of his ignorance; we

watch his struggles to keep the action at a legal and human
level with involvement, with sympathy, but with assurance
of their predestinate failure:

> Thus must we toyle in other mens extreames,
> That know not how to remedie our owne;
> And doe them iustice, when uniustly we,
> For all our wrongs, can compasse no redresse.
> But shall I neuer liue to see the day,
> That I may come (by iustice of the heauens)
> To know the cause that may my cares allay?
> This toyles my body, this consumeth age,
> That onely I to all men iust must be,
> And neither Gods nor men be iust to me.
> DEPUTY. Worthy *Hieronimo*, your office askes
> A care to punish such as doe transgresse.
> HIERONIMO. So ist my duety to regarde his death,
> Who, when he liued, deserued my dearest blood.
> (III. vi. 1–14)

He calls on heavenly justice; what he cannot know is that
his agony and frustration are part of the process of heavenly
justice. As his madness takes him nearer and nearer the
nightmare world of Revenge and Andrea, this mode of irony
is reinforced. Hieronimo tells us:

> Though on this earth iustice will not be found,
> Ile downe to hell, and in this passion
> Knock at the dismall gates of *Plutos* Court,
> . . .
> Till we do gaine that *Proserpine* may grant
> Reuenge on them that murd⟨e⟩red my Sonne.
> (III. xiii. 108–10, 120–1)

What he cannot know is that this is precisely what Don
Andrea has already done—indeed the explanation of the
whole action of the play up to this point. Again and again he
calls on the justices of Hell:

> Goe backe, my sonne, complaine to *Eacus*,
> For heeres no iustice; gentle boy, be gone,
> For iustice is exiled from the earth:
> *Hieronimo* will beare thee company.
> Thy mother cries on righteous *Radamant*
> For iust reuenge against the murderers.
> (III. xiii. 137–42)

> . . . thou then a furie art,
> Sent from the emptie Kingdome of blacke night,
> To sommon me to make appearance
> Before grim *Mynos* and iust *Radamant*,
> To plague *Hieronimo* that is remisse,
> And seekes not vengeance for *Horatioes* death.
>
> (III. xiii. 152–7)

But these infernal judges have already acted. All that Hieronimo can see is that he, the justice, the magistrate, the proponent of civil order, is living in a world where justice is impossible, where

> . . . neither pietie nor pittie mooues
> The King to iustice or compasion,
>
> (IV. ii. 2–3)

and where heavenly justice does not seem to be filling in the lacuna left by the failure of civil justice:

> O sacred heauens, if this vnhallowed deed,
> If this inhumane and barberous attempt,
> If this incomparable murder thus
> Of mine, but now no more my sonne,
> Shall vnreueald and vnreuenged passe,
> How should we tearme your dealings to be iust,
> If you vniustly deale with those, that in your iustice trust?
>
> (III. ii. 5–11)

The heavens are not asleep, in fact, but their wakefulness has a different aspect from that which mortals expect. Hieronimo knows the orthodox Christian doctrine of Romans 12: 19, which tells us ('Vindicta mihi, ego retribuam, dicit Dominus') to leave revenge to God:

> *Vindicta mihi.*
> I, heauen will be reuenged of euery ill;
> Nor will they suffer murder vnrepaide.
> Then stay, *Hieronimo*, attend their will:
> For mortall men may not appoint their time.
>
> (III. xiii. 1–5)

But no more than Andrea can he apply this knowledge or relate it to what is happening to himself and to those around him. Andrea feels that everything is going the wrong way:

I lookt that *Balthazar* should haue beene slaine:
But tis my freend *Horatio* that is slaine.
(II. vi. 2 ff.)

And when (in the next act) he finds that Revenge has actually
been sleeping while the wicked continued their triumph,
Heaven's conspiracy with injustice seems to be complete. But
Revenge is coldly contemptuous of these passionate human
outcries:

Thus worldlings ground, what they haue dreamd, vpon.
Content thy selfe, *Andrea*; though I sleepe,
Yet is my mood soliciting their soules.
. . .
Nor dies *Reuenge*, although he sleepe awhile;
For in vnquiet quietnes is faind,
And slumbring is a common worldly wile.
Behold, *Andrea*, for an instance, how
Reuenge hath slept, and then imagine thou
What tis to be subiect to destinie.
[*Enter a dumme shew.*]   (III. xv. 17–19, 22–27)

The menace and even horror of Revenge's outlook, for those
who are 'subject to destiny', needs to be stressed. The presence of a justice machine in this play is no more cosily
reassuring than in Kafka's *Strafkolonie*. For the irony of its
operation works against Andrea and Hieronimo no less than
against Lorenzo and Balthazar.

All in *The Spanish Tragedy* are caught in the toils of their
ignorance and incomprehension, each with his own sense of
knowledge and power preserved intact, and blindly confident
of his own (baseless) understanding, even down to the level
of the boy with the box (III. v). This episode—the only clearly
comic piece of business in *The Spanish Tragedy*—catches the
basic irony of the play in its simplest form. The boy's
preliminary explanation of the trap set up, and his key
sentence, 'Ist not a scuruie iest that a man should iest himselfe to death?' establishes the usual Kydian disjunction in
the levels of comprehension. Throughout the following trial
scene (III. vi) the boy stands pointing to the empty box, like a
cynical emblem of man's hope for justice; and yet the irony
has also (as is usual in the play) further levels of complexity.

For Lorenzo, the organizer of the ironic show which seals Pedringano's lips even while it betrays his body to the hangman, is himself a victim, not only in the larger irony of Revenge's scrutiny but also in the minor irony that it is his very cleverness that betrays him: It is Pedringano's letter that confirms Hieronimo's knowledge of the murderers of Horatio. Lorenzo, indeed, as Hieronimo remarks, 'marcht in a net and thought himselfe unseen' even at the time he was entrapping others.

Hieronimo prides himself on his devotion to justice and his thoroughness as a judge, but he serves divine justice by ceasing to be just at all in any human sense. The feeling of incomprehension, of not knowing where he is, in terms of the standards by which he has ordered his life—this drives him mad; but even here he reinforces the play's constant concern with justice by his mad fantasies of journeys into the hellish landscape of infernal justice.

> *Hieronimo*, tis time for thee to trudge:
> Downe by the dale that flowes with purple gore,
> Standeth a firie Tower; there sits a iudge
> Vpon a seat of steele and molten brasse, [etc.]
> (III. xii. 6–9)

His incomprehension is inescapable because it is a function of his humanity. His madness is a direct result of the collision of his human sense of justice with the quite different processes of divine justice; for it is a fearful thing to fall into the hands of a just God. The absorption of the human into the divine justice machine means the destruction of the human, and Hieronimo becomes the perfected instrument of Revenge only by becoming inhuman. He becomes part of the hellish landscape of his imagination. In the play of Soliman and Perseda that he organizes we have yet another re-enactment of the situation that began with Don Andrea. Bel-imperia (certainly resolute even if not certainly chaste) plays the part of 'Perseda chaste and resolute'. Balthazar, the princely lover who hoped to win Bel-imperia from her common lovers (Andrea, Horatio), plays the Emperor Soliman, who hopes to win Perseda from her common love. The crimes and killings in the play are organized by the Bashaw or Pasha, and this is the part to be played by Hieronimo himself. When asked, 'But which of us is to performe that parte?' he replies:

> O, that will I, my Lords, make no doubt of it:
> Ile play the murderer, I warrant you,
> For I already haue conceited that.
>
> (IV. i. 130–3)

The Spanish Tragedy as a whole has continuously set the marionette-like action of the man whose destiny is predetermined against the sense of choice or willpower in the passionate and self-confident individual. Continuously we have had actors watching actors but being watched themselves by still other actors (watched by the audience). *We* watch Revenge and Andrea watching Lorenzo watching Horatio and Bel-imperia; we watch Revenge and Andrea watching Hieronimo watching Pedringano watching the boy with the box; and at each point in this chain what seems free will to the individual seems only a predetermined *act* to the onlookers.

In the play within the play, in Hieronimo's playlet of Soliman and Perseda, this interest reaches its climax. The illusion of free will is suspended. The four central characters are absorbed into an action which acts out their just relationships *for them*. The net has closed, character has become role, speech has changed to ritual; the end is now totally predetermined. The play itself is a flat puppet-like action with a total absence of personal involvement; but as the characters intone their flat, liturgical responses to one another there is an enormous *frisson* of irony or disparity between what they say and what *we* know to be meant.

Hieronimo himself has become *instrument* rather than agent. *He* knows that his life has been absorbed into the ritual and that he cannot escape back into humanity, and he accepts this Hegelian kind of freedom (freedom as the knowledge of necessity) with a resolution at once noble and inhuman. At the end of his play he comes forward to speak his own epilogue:

> Heere breake we off our sundrie languages,
> . . .
> And, Princes, now beholde *Hieronimo*,

> Author and actor in this Tragedie,
> Bearing his latest fortune in his fist;
> And will as resolute conclude his parte
> As any of the Actors gone before.
> And, Gentles, thus I end my play.
>
> (IV. iv. 74, 146–51)

Commentators on the denouement of *The Spanish Tragedy* usually concentrate on the human *mess* which follows Hieronimo's failure to complete his life in ritual, noticing the break in the pattern rather than the pattern itself. But I think that the nature of the final actions is only kept in focus if we see them as measuring the gap between the dream of justice and the haphazard and inefficient human actions that so often must embody it. This is a recurrent interest of a writer like Seneca. When he describes the suicide of Cato Uticensis, his greatest hero, he is not content to relate his fortitude in doing the deed; he stresses the horror of Cato's failure to finish himself off in one clean blow. What he is concerned to show is the persistence of Cato's will to die, in spite of his own inefficiency.[5] And I think a similar concern to contrast the will to martyrdom with the *mess* of actual martyrdom can be seen at the end of *The Spanish Tragedy*.

A martyr is rather exceptional if his suffering is not prolonged and humanly degrading; a martyr whose soul had been antiseptically abstracted from his body would be rather unlike those whose histories thronged the Elizabethan imagination, whether from *The Golden Legend* or from its local equivalent, Foxe's *Acts and Monuments*. We should remember that it was not simply Zeno who anticipated Hieronimo by biting out his own tongue, but St Christina as well. Much ink has been spilled in sympathy for Castile, who is struck down at the end of the play, simply because he stands too close to the protagonist. But Castile is, of course, identified with the tormenters who seek to interrupt the ritual and prevent it from completing itself. It is Castile who sug-

---

5. An unnoticed borrowing suggests that Kyd's mind was moving in areas not very remote from these. In Act IV, scene iv, Hieronimo asks for a knife to mend his pen. It is with this instrument that he stabs Castile and himself. The device seems to come from the eighth book of Tacitus' *Annals* where 'Vitellius ... under colour of using it in his study, asking for a pen knife, lightly pricked a vein and ended his life with grief and anguish' (Greneway's translation [1598]).

gests that torture is still of use, to compel Hieronimo to *write* the names of his confederates. And the death of Castile confers another dramatic advantage: It transfers mourning to the highest personage on the stage. The king of Spain has hitherto been concerned with the miseries of existence only at second hand. Now, at the end of the play, he himself becomes a principal mourner, as is indicated well enough in the final stage direction:

The Trumpets sound a dead march, the King *of Spaine mourning after his brothers body, and the* King *of Portingale bearing the body of his sonne.*

In the final chorus we return to the justice of Hell, where the characters of the play now supply the classical examples of sin and wickedness with which the play began ('Place *Don Lorenzo* on *Ixions* Wheele,' [IV. v. 33]). A last judgement places everyone where he morally belongs,[6] but we would do less than justice to the complexity of this play if we did not notice that humanity has been sacrificed so that justice can be fulfilled. Revenge has been completed; we have seen what Fulke Greville describes as the mode of modern tragedy: 'God's revenging aspect upon every particular sin to the despair and confusion of mortality.'

6. See above, p. 191 and n. 6.

9

The heroism of Hamlet

The period 1599–1602 seems to show Shakespeare much interested in the nature of heroism. Comedies apart, the plays usually assigned to this time—*Henry V, Julius Caesar, Hamlet, Troilus and Cressida*—all raise a question about it in one form or another. And at the end of the period we have two plays, *Othello*, and *King Lear*, which show a new and markedly less cerebral handling of the qualities that make for greatness. It may be possible to regard these as the fruits of a preceding time of intense and restless searching (whose crown is *Hamlet*). It is my argument that this search can be seen as proceeding through the repertory of traditional kinds of heroism, seeking human values that will endure—endure, that is, against such forces as are represented by the corrosive cynicism of Thersites and the no less corrosive hedonism of Falstaff.

In any view of life (literary or non-literary) the *hero*, if he is able to make an important stretch of action meaningful to us, must seem to us to be (in himself) an important kind of person. Bowra sums this up very well when describing the epic hero:[1]

He gives dignity to the human race by showing of what feats it is capable; he extends the bounds of experience for others and enhances their appreciation of life by the example of his abundant vitality.

The tragic hero would seem only to be a special case of this generic kind of heroism. A. H. Thorndike provides a suitably simplified view of his function when he says that 'a typical tragedy is concerned with a great personality engaged in a

[First published in *Hamlet*, ed. J. R. Brown and B. Harris (Stratford-upon-Avon Studies, 5) (1963).]

1. *Heroic Poetry* (1952), p. 4.

struggle that ends disastrously'.[2] It is not true, of course, that all tragic actions revolve round the figure of a hero; but some awareness of responses to the created situation that are larger than the ordinary certainly seems to be required. Our lives are caught up into a larger and more violent course of action; the tragic hero conveniently focuses this for us because he is 'like us'; but he is also greater than us, an image of the fullness of human capacity, so that we cannot patronize his failure and his fall, cannot suppose that we would have done better. We become aware that even in this fullness humanity can only resist fate, not conquer it; but the vitality displayed in the struggle remains a magnificent extension of our own being, and we continue to respond to its vibrations, even in defeat.

But what qualities make a man seem 'important' enough to us to have this effect? Different actions as well as different ages involve different conceptions of heroism; the hero of the battlefield may be the fool of the council-chamber; the 'great personality' may be insufficient in terms of mere human understanding to impress us more than partially. In tragedy, we not only measure the heroism of the 'hero' (meaning protagonist) in terms of the challenges that the play itself puts forward, but all the time we are also measuring the adequacy of these challenges to represent the worst that life can offer. In the period of Shakespeare's writing around *Hamlet* it is the question of this general adequacy that seems to be at stake under the pressure of an increasingly vivid sense of evil. Three different traditions of heroism jostle for attention. These are (1) the power to command and control human affairs (leading to deserved social eminence), (2) goodness (however defined), and (3) force of personality. They may be recognized as being embodied typically in the king, the saint and the soldier. We may begin by examining how these modes of heroism appear in Shakespeare's work of the period 1599–1602.

The long concern with plays about English history (the most sustained effort of Shakespeare's lifetime) had made prominent in his world the virtue of the leader of men who, however limited in goodness (seen as a private virtue), knows

2. *Tragedy* (1908), p. 9.

how to preserve the well-being of the state. *Henry V* is obviously the climax of this interest and must have been designed to be so for a long time before it was written. It is clear enough from the two parts of *Henry IV* that Hal was intended to be a hero in the round (in contrast to the merely military Hotspur). Here was to be a generosity of interest: 'Sirrah, I am sworn brother to a leash of drawers and can call them all by their christen names', disciplined by self-awareness and proper reverence for his own destiny. As we all know, the resulting paragon is, however well prepared, strangely cold and hollow, and men have usually preferred the characteristics that bring defeat (in Falstaff) to those that give victory to Hal. And in spite of Falstaff's absence from the play of *Henry V* it remains difficult, even there, to give full assent to the heroism of a leader who is so much the puppet of his own propaganda. Henry tells us that it is not Ceremony that is the soul of kingship, but it is not clear what else is. One who wears the public mask as gracefully as this king is bound to make us suspect the reality of his face; it is hard to trust the man whose conquest of environment is unsupported by any suggestion of struggle against the baseness of his own human nature.

It would be tendentious to suggest that it was any sense of this limitation in England's paragon that sent Shakespeare to look through Plutarch's picture-gallery of antique heroes. But it is true that the ending of the English history cycle in *Henry V* coincides with a renewed interest in Plutarch. The Amyot/North Introduction makes it sound as if Plutarch's interest was in the external histories of successful statesmen like Henry V, relating (as it says) 'the speciall actes of the best persons, of the famosest nations of the world'. But if Shakespeare picked up the *Parallel Lives* with this in his mind he must soon have changed it, reading a passage like:

The noblest deedes doe not alwayes shew mens vertues and vices, but oftentimes a light occasion, a word, or some sporte makes mens naturale dispositions and maners appeare more plaine, then the famous battells wonne, wherein are slaine tenne thowsande men, or the great armies, or cities wonne by siege or assault . . . they must geve us leave to seeke out the signes and tokens of the minde only, and thereby shewe the life of either of them, referring you unto others to wryte the warres, battells and other great thinges they did. ('Life of Alexander.')

Plutarch's interest is in the very thing that was missing from *Henry V*—the inner shape of greatness—that form of which success is only the shadow, and which can exist without the outward evidence of success to support it. That Shakespeare was prepared to go straight to the heart of this view of heroism as an inner integrity, and set it against the public endorsement that pervaded *Henry V*, is implied by the choice of material from Plutarch for his next play, *Julius Caesar*. For Brutus is, of all the characters in Plutarch, the one who is most clearly admired for what he was rather than what he did, a man whose action was (pragmatically judged) disastrous, but who is redeemed by the ruthless sense of duty that drove him to it. Julius Caesar, on the other hand, is not only a transcendent Henry V, the master statesman of the Western World, but a sharper image of imperious self-ignorance than patriotism could allow in the paragon of English monarchy. Shakespeare is well known to have strengthened the contrast between the sublimity of Caesar, the vessel of *Imperium*, and the weakness of Julius, a body. He seems in fact to have sought to create in this play two contrary images of heroism, allowing them to compete with one another for our admiration, and our distaste. But the play does not seek to force a choice between these images; the ethical genius and the political genius face one another across a chasm of valuation that action, however violent, cannot bridge. That third kind of heroism that I have mentioned above (that of the soldier) appears here only in the figure of Antony, passionate, affectionate, powerful, but eventually (under the shadow of Octavius) morally unstable. But the play does not develop any action that can be seen as originating in the will of Antony, so that his heroism here remains potential rather than actual.

Shakespeare's concern with these varieties of human capacity appears even more clearly in the other antique drama which he wrote in this period, in *Troilus and Cressida*, which may be taken to reflect an appeal to the most celebrated fictional heroism (in the *Iliad*) as *Julius Caesar* to the most resounding historical one. In *Troilus* we meet heroism as integrity (Hector), heroism as passionate battle-prowess (Achilles), heroism as rational control (Ulysses) and, joined to these as reflector, the passionate and attractive inexperience of the lover-hero Troilus. And once again, the variety of heroic attitudes in the play points to an analytical rather than synthetic interest in this material; the play seems more concerned to set the attitudes against one another than to make any one central. *Troilus and Cressida* is closer to *Hamlet* than is *Julius Caesar* (largely because of the figure of Troilus, with his capacity to change or grow); but, like *Julius Caesar*, it lacks the essential focus of choice between its different conceptions of greatness. In *Julius Caesar* the different heroisms are left in separate (ethical and political) compartments; the play does not show us Brutus tempted to behave like Caesar, nor Caesar as envious of Brutus. In *Troilus* the values appear in a world which supports none of them, enclosed in a narrative which betrays them all. Choice between them is impossible, for each is presented as the delusion of an individual mind: Troilus' Cressida and Diomed's Cressida are different people, the products of different outlooks, and no compromise between them is possible.

But in *Hamlet* all the possibilities reflect back to the hero; we are asked to note not only the variety of potentially heroic attitudes, but also to consider their relationship within one mind, and the possibility of choice between them. *Hamlet* implicates us as readers or (even more) as audience, where *Troilus* can only intrigue us; for we feel ourselves caught, with Hamlet, by the currents of attraction and repulsion which the polarities of heroism exercise upon him. The yearning of the self-conscious mind to be other than it is, the potentiality of choice between personae, the doubt concerning choices made—all this catches us with a personal acuteness that the other plays cannot rival. The central focus which is lacking in *Julius Caesar* and *Troilus and Cressida* is here found in the mind of the prince; his self-consciousness (especially seen in the soliloquies) is the means by which Shakespeare is enabled to collate and compare modes of heroism which (objectively considered) are essentially disparate; for their fields of activity are here less important than the feelings about them in the central observing mind.

The range of potential heroism observed by Hamlet is, however, just what Shakespeare had measured in the other plays I have discussed. The same norms of success, integrity, and passion appear here, but not simply (as in the other plays) as separate figures—Fortinbras, Horatio, and Laertes in this case—but as figures whose meaning depends on their relationship inside the observing and discriminating mind of Hamlet himself.

Heroism of the Henry V kind, competence in the management of affairs, capacity to seize opportunity and skill to turn it to advantage, control over passion coupled with power of passionate display at precisely the right moment— these leader's gifts appear not only in Claudius (whose competence Hamlet can hardly be shown to envy) but also in Fortinbras, whose relationship to father and uncle enforces comparison with Hamlet. The admirable qualities in Fortinbras are focused in the final soliloquy, 'How all occasions do inform against me', and it is clear enough from this why Hamlet admires Fortinbras (or 'strong-in-the-arm'); but one can also see from it why Fortinbras cannot be the hero of this play. Even in Hamlet's praise there are ambiguities enough to start counter-currents in our minds. Fortinbras is presented as all air and fire, all aspiration, in Hamlet's image of

> a delicate and tender prince
> Whose spirit with divine ambition puff'd
> Makes mouths at the invisible event,
> (IV. iv. 48–50)

and this is admirable enough when set in opposition to the heavy sloth that Hamlet imputes to himself in *dull . . . sleep and feed, a beast, no more . . . bestial oblivion*. But what looks like 'divine' aspiration from this subjective point of view may look like culpable levity when seen objectively. The idea of *puff'd* is carried on in *egg-shell . . . straw . . . fantasy and trick of fame*, where the subjective valuation (*fame*) is seen as unrelated to the facts, and the aspiration begins to appear as the kind of expensive princely folly that Montaigne never tires of exposing. Shakespeare had made this undercut explicit enough, before the soliloquy began, in Hamlet's

> This is th' imposthume of much wealth and peace,
> That inward breaks, and shows no cause without
> Why the man dies. (IV. iv. 27)

But the prince's own mind does not take up this objective valuation. Rather he picks up the idea of fame and honour as the essential element in 'rightly to be great'; he presents 'greatly to find quarrel in a straw' as the natural corollary of 'capability and godlike reason'. This is a strange line of reasoning, though critics seldom question it, supposing that Shakespeare is wholly with Hamlet in his conclusion:

> My thoughts be bloody, or be nothing worth!

There is danger, of course, in imputing modern squeamishness to an Elizabethan play; but there is also the danger of suppressing Shakespeare's human responses lest they seem too humane. Tillyard has pointed out the close parallel between this soliloquy and the Trojan council scene in *Troilus and Cressida*, and, in view of the general relationship between the two plays, we ought to allow this to affect our view of Shakespeare's intentions in *Hamlet*. The Trojan scene shows Hector defending the reason that looks 'before and after' and deriding that subjective valuation of experience that makes 'honour' the key to right conduct:

> 'Tis mad idolatry
> To make the service greater than the god;
> And the will dotes that is attributive
> To what infectiously itself affects,
> Without some image of th' affected merit.
> (II. ii. 56)

The whole course of *Troilus and Cressida* supports this separation of subjective and objective valuation. And in *Hamlet* too, the Reason that controls the daylight world of action, and the Honour that means following one's dream, even one's nightmare, and accepting *its* logic—these are just as hard to reconcile. Hamlet wishes to reconcile them, of course, and the soliloquy suggests a short cut, an assimilation of Hamlet's mind and Fortinbras's action. But surely we are meant to see the discontinuity in this, even though Hamlet cannot. The prince's blindness should not blind us to the limitations of Fortinbras's heroic will. Henry V was presented in a play that showed off his capacities; Fortinbras appears in one mainly focused by individual self-scrutiny, and in this context his range of abilities is bound to seem shallow and opportunist.

He appears again, at the end of the play, knowing how to speak the proper consolations, but moving very quickly to matters more close to his heart:

> For me, with sorrow I embrace my fortune;
> I have some rights of memory in this kingdom,
> Which now to claim my vantage doth invite me
> (v. ii. 380)

We may feel satisfied that he will tidy up efficiently the re-maining uncertainties in Denmark. But the power to order what has been achieved and the power to live through and redeem the unjointed time are seen as quite different in dimension; and in the life of the play Fortinbras's efficient kind of heroism is fairly insignificant. In any case, as I have noticed above, the heroism of public success is already devalued in the play by the success of Claudius and his henchman Polonius. The rottenness of their rule lies pre-cisely in the divorce of public statement (or 'painted word' as Claudius calls it) from personal value; and Fortinbras has no equipment for combatting such corruption. We can hardly regret that Hamlet has failed to be like him.

In Laertes we meet other characteristics that Hamlet feels to be heroic, and absent from his own character. Laertes is a passionate young man whose passions carry him towards irrevocable action; and since his main action concerns revenge for a murdered father, we are obviously intended to contrast his behaviour with Hamlet's. Laertes (unlike Hamlet) is always ready with a passionate speech and a big theatrical gesture in response to emotional stimulus:

> To hell, allegiance! vows, to the blackest devil!
> Conscience and grace, to the profoundest pit!
> I dare damnation. To this point I stand,
> That both the worlds I give to negligence,

> Let come what comes; only I'll be revenged
> Most thoroughly for my father.   (IV. v. 128)

Hamlet is guiltily aware that he does not have this capacity. When he returns to Elsinore, to find the burial of Ophelia in execution, it is the sound of Laertes's passions that stimulates him to leave Horatio and the quizzical observer's role, and compete in rhetorical self-expression:

> I loved Ophelia: forty thousand brothers
> Could not, with all their quantity of love,
> Make up my sum. What wilt thou do for her?
> . . .
> Woo't weep? woo't fight? woo't fast? woo't tear thyself?
> Woo't drink up eisel? eat a crocodile?
> I'll do't. Dost thou come here to whine?
> To outface me with leaping in her grave?
> Be buried quick with her, and so will I:
> And, if thou prate of mountains, let them throw
> Millions of acres on us, till our ground,
> Singeing his pate against the burning zone
> Make Ossa like a wart! Nay, an thou'lt mouth,
> I'll rant as well as thou.   (V. i. 263)

But in the very act of competing, Hamlet reveals his awareness that this is absurd, and in the Hamlet-world such direct self-expression is bound to be absurd; nothing can be expressed by it. And that Shakespeare intends us to see this as self-evident seems to be indicated both in the career of Laertes and in the parallel situation of *Troilus and Cressida*. In *Troilus* the 'valiant ignorance' Achilles, and the 'beef-witted' Ajax, 'with too much blood [i.e. passion] and too little brain', are 'bought and sold among those of any wit'. The passion of Laertes is likewise the mere plaything of the magnificently competent Claudius. Within the space of some thirty lines or so, his rebellion has been scotched and he, the leader, has become principal agent in the king's own policy. It is clear that passion alone would not take Hamlet very far in the battle against such a 'mighty opposite'.

Hamlet's relationship to the passionate ideal of conduct is kept before our eyes in the middle scenes of the play by the further parallel of Pyrrhus engaged in revenging *his* father. The player's speech describing this passionate revenge

(proper enough for the son of Shakespeare's Achilles) gives
rise to Hamlet's longest single meditation on the attractive-
ness of the ideal—the soliloquy 'O, what a rogue and peasant
slave am I'.

As in the soliloquy facing Fortinbras, Hamlet here sees his
inaction only as sloth:

> yet I,
> A dull and muddy-mettled rascal, peak,
> Like John-a-dreams, unpregnant of my cause.
>   (II. ii. 560)

But the soliloquy as a whole hardly supports the view that
the power of passionate self-expression would give answer to
his difficulties. The words of passion come, but only in the
accents of a 'very drab', 'a stallion'. And if we call Laertes
'theatrical', what words shall we use for the first player?
The cue for passion that Hamlet hears is not to be answered
by simple violence of response. Hamlet's obliquity, his
hesitation, his awareness of complexity and ambiguity, argue
him fully human in a way that the two-dimensional propo-
nents of Passion can hardly be; and this, given that he carries
forward the struggle to realize his 'duty' as unrelentingly as
they do, argues him 'not less but more heroic'.

A norm that is more difficult to place in relation to Hamlet
is represented by Horatio,

> one, in suffering all, that suffers nothing;
> A man that Fortune's buffets and rewards
> Hast ta'en with equal thanks . . . not a pipe for fortune's finger
> To sound what stop she please.   (III. ii. 64)

Hamlet's praise of Horatio is warm and unqualified, and,
even more telling, is not accompanied by incredible self-
accusations (for sloth is the last quality anyone could impute
to Hamlet). It is clear that Horatio's virtue is close to Hamlet's own mind; they share that vein of University philoso-
phizing which looms out of the Wittenberg past and into the
disillusioning present. But the disillusioning present has
brought out differences between Hamlet and the standard
philosopher-hero which are important to any consideration
of his heroism. Horatio, on the other hand, remains well
inside the best Christian-Stoic tradition; he guards his

integrity with *apatheia* (what Charron[3] calls 'a courageous
insensibility in the suffering of injuries')—what enables a
good man to survive with his virtue intact even in the wicked-
est of times (under a Nero or a Domitian—or a Claudius of
Denmark). And this means, of course, that Horatio, like
other passive heroes, like the Stoic commentators in Jonson's
Sejanus, cannot move beyond the sidelines. He will not commit himself to the misrule of passion; but at the same time as
this makes him virtuous it renders him incapable of controlling any fate other than his own. 'More an antique Roman
than a Dane', he believes in the Stoic's final freedom, the
freedom to commit suicide; but even this is seen here as a
limitation; there are better things for a man to do:

> As th'art a man,
> Give me the cup: let go; by heaven, I'll have't.
> . . .
> If thou didst ever hold me in thy heart,
> Absent thee from felicity a while,
> And in this harsh world draw thy breath in pain,
> To tell my story.   (v. ii. 334)

Even while it is more violently disillusioned, Hamlet's
wider vision remains more freely optimistic about possible
success in action and the advantage of involvement. And this
is not simply because he is commanded to revenge and therefore has to believe that he is moving towards a climactic
action. The whole bias of his mind is towards the passionate
exploration of unknown modes of being, an exploration that
draws its impetus from Hope, a virtue unknown to Stoicism.

> He falls to such perusal of my face
> As he would draw it. Long stay'd he so
>   (II. i. 90)

says Ophelia, reporting her interview with the prince. It is
one of the principal ironies of the play that not only this but
every exploration is turned back upon himself; the more he
searches for external contact, the more he is driven into
isolation. But this is not the isolation of the defeatist; only
that of the frustrated man of action.

3. P. Charron, *Of Wisdom*, tr. S. Lennard (n.d.; entered S.R., 1606), III. xxxiv.

In 'to be or not to be' Hamlet begins by taking up the Stoic potentialities of his own situation; he begins (I suppose that he is here talking about action against enemies, not about suicide) by asking where true nobility lies—in passive endurance ('suffer the slings and arrows of outrageous fortune') or in action. But by line 4 he has left *apatheia* behind him; the rest of the soliloquy, however inconclusive, is concerned with the possible results of action against evil, not with the capacity to endure it.

The contrast between Hamlet and Horatio is neatly caught by the difference of their response to the ghost. The first we ever hear of Horatio is that he 'will not let belief take hold of him', and the first independent line he speaks is

> Tush, Tush, 'twill not appear.   (I. i. 30)

He is harrowed by the strangeness of it when he can no longer disbelieve it, but his rational mind soon encompasses the fear in explanation:

> But, in the gross and scope of my opinion,
> This bodes some strange eruption to our state.
> (I. i. 68)

It is an explanation which refers the apparition to the world outside the beholder's mind, limiting its power to disturb:

> A mote it is to trouble the mind's eye.

But Hamlet, though aware of its potential evil, strains towards involvement with the ghost ('would the night were come'); seeking not so much to explain it as to find in it an explanation of his own intuitions (or 'prophetic soul'). When he decides to follow it and (as it were) takes the experience into his being, Horatio can only suppose that he waxes desperate with imagination.

But Hamlet welcomes *strangeness* (as, later, *rashness*) where Horatio would avoid it:

HORATIO. O day and night, but this is wondrous strange!
HAMLET. And therefore as a stranger give it welcome.
> There are more things in heaven and earth, Horatio,
> Than are dreamt of in your philosophy.   (I. v. 164–7)

'Philosophy' here presumably means 'rational explanation'; the philosophical mind is presented as a closed or a reductive kind of mind, as in *All's Well* (II. iii. 1–5):

> we have our philosophical persons to make modern and familiar, things supernatural and causeless. Hence is it that we make trifles of terrors, ensconcing ourselves into seeming knowledge when we should submit ourselves to an unknown fear.

It is only the mind that is not philosophic (in this sense) that can bring a full response to the new categories of experience, the 'unknown fear' that divides Elsinore from Wittenberg.

Not only in the contrast with Horatio (though most obviously there) but throughout the play, Hamlet seems almost deliberately designed as a counterblast to the received figure of the Christian-Stoic hero. We meet him first in a situation that was the standard setting for philosophic 'Consolations'—that of a bereaved son. He is showered with standard advice:

> Fie! 'tis a fault to heaven,
> A fault against the dead, a fault to nature,
> To reason most absurd; whose common theme
> Is death of fathers.   (I. ii. 101)

Claudius's sentiments here are entirely within the gospel of the times. Charron has a long chapter (Bk I, cap. xxxi) on the enervating effects of sadness 'against nature':

> it polluteth and defaceth whatsoever Nature hath made beautiful and amiable in us, which is drowned by the force of this passion ... we go with our heads hanging, our eyes fastened on the earth, ... turned (as the Poets feign) like *Niobe* into a stone by the power of this passion. Now it is not only contrary and an enemy unto Nature, ... but a rash and outragious complaint against the Lord and common Law of the whole world, which hath made all things under the Moon changeable and corruptible.

In terms of these vulgate values Hamlet certainly stands condemned.

And there are more respects than this in which Hamlet is set against the Christian-Stoic ideal of the philosopher hero. The use of maxims or *sententiae*, and of a 'table-book' in which to record these and other moral matters, was standard practice for those who wished to arm themselves against the vicissitudes of fortune. But when Hamlet meets the ghost he throws away this armoury:

> Yea, from the table of my memory
> I'll wipe away all trivial fond records,
> All saws of books, all forms, all pressures past,
> That youth and observation copied there,
> And thy commandment all alone shall live
> Within the book and volume of my brain . . .
> O villain, villain, smiling damned villain!
> My tables, meet it is I set it down
> That one may smile, and smile, and be a villain.
> (I. v. 98)

As the power to speak 'consolations' is left to Claudius, so the power to dole out maxims is left to Polonius. What Hamlet writes down in his table-book is a paradox whose implications are so staggering that they make set advice irrelevant; it is indeed essentially the same paradox as confounds Troilus:

> If there be rule in unity itself
> This was not she. O madness of discourse,
> That cause sets up with and against itself!
> Bifold authority! where reason can revolt
> Without perdition, and loss assume all reason
> Without revolt.   (v. ii. 139)

In the world of experience that Hamlet must live through, appearance and reality, subjective and objective truth, have fallen apart; nay more, one thing may both be and not be at the same time, may be both 'the royal bed of Denmark' and 'a couch for luxury and damned lust', both 'man, how noble!' and 'this quintessence of dust'. One vision presents simultaneous 'school-fellows' and 'adders fanged', the 'fair Ophelia, nymph at thy orisons' and the archetypal wanton, 'you jig, you amble, and you lisp, you nickname God's creatures and make your wantonness your ignorance', simultaneous queen-mother and 'most pernicious woman'.

In this landscape of paradox the philosophy that is founded on the 'rule of unity', the assumption of coherence in experience and the capacity to generalize—this is bound to collapse. Troilus escaped from such 'knowledge enormous' into a subjective fury which really fulfilled Hamlet's:

From this time forth
My thoughts be bloody, or be nothing worth,
(IV. iv. 65)

but the play of *Troilus* presents this as escapism, as an un-
thinking anger which is more bestial than admirable, perhaps
heroic but certainly not fully human, and therefore not one
which could be counted a full response to the *Hamlet*
situation. A more painful and more difficult course of action
is laid out for Hamlet (native and indued to paradox as he
becomes—an innocent murderer and a sane madman); he is
asked by Shakespeare to retain a sense of divine ordinance,
of an objective meaning that validates experience, even amid
the ruins of his own world of meaning, and to act out of this
perilous intuition, to know and feel from this indescribable
centre. Shakespeare raises the idea of escape on several
occasions; the idea of suicide obviously attracts Hamlet;
but the continuing sense of supernatural sanctions, existing
and objective, forbids him to indulge his personal desires.
'Must I remember?' he asks at the beginning of the action;
and pat comes the answer in the ghost's 'remember me',
which Hamlet takes as his motto. It is, however, a motto for
a madman, for only in the added freedom of madness can
the mind 'distracted with contrariety of desires', as Dr
Johnson finely puts it, *remember* the blackness of the ghost's
vision while looking at the 'eyes assured of certain certain-
ties', the daylight simplicities of Claudius's Denmark. Of
course, even in the first soliloquy, placed strategically just
before he hears of the ghost, Hamlet is aware of the gap
between the inner landscape of his own mind,

Fie on't! ah fie! 'tis an unweeded garden,

and the outer world of efficient government and family
solicitudes. But this division is one which, however strongly
felt, cannot at this point be bridged by expression, let alone
action. 'I have that within which passeth show', he tells the
court; and this I take to mean not that it would be impolitic
to show his feelings, but that no expressive means of com-
municating them can be imagined—and again, at the end of
the soliloquy: 'But break my heart, for I must hold my
tongue.' This is one resolve whose non-fulfilment every critic

of *Hamlet* would agree about. For the ghost provides a language as well as a resolve; but it is the language of madness.

If the nightmare landscape of paradox requires the response of madness to carry the human mind through it, then we must recognize the madness as part of a heroic struggle—a struggle to remember the evil that interpenetrates our being, even while living in the ordinary world of action and anticipation. And this is a heroic struggle which none of the established modes of heroism could encompass. It is not enough for Hamlet to be *angry* (like Achilles), or self-contained, or competent, though he must remain aware of these as potentialities in himself. He must possess, and be seen in the play to exercise, a unique capacity to face and absorb into his purpose every experience that comes his way, however strange (or mad). What the Stoic would reject, the passionate man brush aside, the man of affairs organize out of existence, he continues to accept, modifying his consciousness to incorporate it, and struggling all the time for purposive mastery over the chaos of his perceptions.

I have presented Hamlet as a hero whom we admire because he keeps facing up to and (however desperate) maintaining some control over the flux of action that he stirs around him, though sometimes he maintains it only by the inner turbulence of madness. We admire him because he is never merely passive, or escapist or cowed in a situation which presses him all the time to be one (or all) of these. His will remains pointed in a single direction, though his movement is labyrinthine. He has integrity, but it is an integrity that depends on no exclusion of sympathies or passions, but on a fully human response to the implications of his deeds, so that he may say with Macduff:

> I shall [dispute it like a man] . . .
> But I must also feel it as a man.
> (*Macbeth*, IV. iii. 220)

He has passions, but the force of his feelings does not oversimplify the actions in front of him. He even has competence, but it is not competence that he is prepared to exercise in the service of an ideal that he has never examined.

His struggle is, in fact, a struggle to remain fully human, and yet capable of controlling a world that is out of joint. It is not (in spite of what the critics say) simply a struggle to bring himself to obey the ghost; but rather a struggle to act meaningfully, which means to *translate* the ghost's absurdly simplified command into the terms of daylight and responsible activities. He is presented by the play as caught between two equally impossible courses: to give in to the ghost's command, reverberating out of that region where truth is never less than absolute (and so lose control that way), or to give in to the world of social and political truth, meaning expediency, the world which has charge of all the sane language in Elsinore. The former alternative exercises a continuous and appalling pressure on his mind; but the latter is real, and all around him every day; and both would be equally destructive of his individual life.

It is this, far more than any strategy of revenge, that marks the difference between the play of Hamlet and such 'primitive' revenge plays, as Kyd's *The Spanish Tragedy* or Marston's *Antonio's Revenge*. In these, the hero's (and the audience's) sense of the difference between right action and wrong action is often obscured, but is never ultimately in doubt. Hamlet, however, is not allowed to go on drawing strength from the certainty of this distinction, which is lost among the competing formulations of his mind. In none of these plays is the revenge simply a matter of striking a blow; in all of them it involves moving into a position where the blow is most meaningful. In *The Spanish Tragedy*, however, the meaning is created around Hieronimo by the supernatural chorus, permanently on the stage. In *Antonio's Revenge* it is created, not so much by the ghost (whose supernatural authority has somewhat waned since the time of Kyd), as by the political image of Piero as a tyrant, against whom political retribution is inevitable. But Hamlet is deprived of both supernatural and political certainty; he has to create the sense of meaning in his action out of himself, out of his hard-fought-for personal grasp on what is right action and what is wrong. It is this absence of external standards that makes it so difficult to define the nature of Hamlet's heroism. Hamlet is immensely articulate; but the many words he expends, defining his relationship to the various representatives of heroic conduct in the play, are mostly words which separate him from these norms. Hamlet is defined less by his own actions and opinions than by his reactions to others—to the Queen, the Ghost, Ophelia, Claudius, Laertes, Fortinbras. And these reactions involve, in nearly every case, a complex response of attraction *and* revulsion; the play seems designed to prevent Hamlet from finding any external model or simple solution for conduct, driving him into a version of heroism which depends less upon acting or even knowing than upon *being*. And this is appropriate enough to a play which shows evil, for the first time in Shakespeare, and one of the earliest times in European literature, not as a class of activity but as a description of individual being. For the notice of what Claudius has done comes into the play only to confirm what is seen as logically prior—the kind of man he is. And for the rest—Gertrude, Polonius, Rosencrantz and Guildenstern —evil is something that hangs around them like a cloud rather than an activity they engage in.

But the play of *Hamlet* can only be seen as a study of Being if it is followed as an action. The continuity of the action cannot be ignored or subordinated, and it may seem that the formulation of Hamlet's heroism which I have given so far ignores the action by pursuing a line of interest that is largely complete before the enactment of revenge. If the central movement of *Hamlet* were a movement to acquire standards by which the final action could be meaningful, we would expect the revenge to stem from some advantage that these standards gave. And this is not at all evident. To quote Dr Johnson again, 'his [Claudius'] death is at last effected by an incident which Hamlet has no part in producing'. A gap would seem to be left between the inner history of Hamlet's mind and the outer development of the action, a gap that has often been used to prise the play apart, and could be used so again. But the sense that Hamlet is passive in the last act where he ought to be active, the victim where he ought to be the master of the situation, depends perhaps on a view of these polarities markedly simpler and very different from those of the Elizabethans. The age was well acquainted with the stories of martyrdoms; is the martyr passive or active, the victim or the victor? Eliot's St Thomas notes the complexities:

> Neither does the agent suffer
> Nor the patient act. But both are fixed
> In an eternal action, an eternal patience.

Even the allegedly 'simple' revenge play is marked by this complexity. Revenge plays very regularly move on to the plane of ritual for their final scenes; and ritual involves actions for which the person acting cannot be held entirely responsible. *The Spanish Tragedy* set the fashion; Hieronimo's fatal playlet of Soliman and Perseda formalizes and simplifies the relationships that the central characters have established in the main play.[4] We have the sense of each of these characters being absorbed into a pattern which acts out their just relationship for them, almost without their volition. In *Antonio's Revenge*, by a tissue of ironies, the murder is given the formal structure of a wedding masque; the ghost of Andrugio takes the role of Master of the Revels, and tells us,

> Now downe lookes providence,
> T'attend the last act of my sons revenge.

By vesting Hamlet's heroism in the fullness of his human response, Shakespeare has denied himself the opportunity to use this formula. Hamlet cannot, without loss of his kind of heroism, be absorbed into a framework of meaning outside himself; his personal quest for standards of being cannot be dropped and then replaced by an impersonal action; in any case, the moral relationships of *Hamlet* are too complex to be fulfilled by a simple plot of the 'Soliman and Perseda' kind. No more can he be allowed to make his exit as an explicitly Christian hero. The performance of his final actions as the accredited agent of God would remove the tragic element in his relationship to death. A similar reason can be invoked against a final appearance of the ghost; the point of the denouement must be not that the ghost is satisfied, but that Hamlet has fulfilled his destiny.

4. See above, pp. 225–6.

Shakespeare relies on none of these ways to create a fusion of active and passive responses. And yet few would deny that there are elements of all these in the final scene of the play. Hamlet is not made a Christian, and yet he is given sentences (the famous ones about the divinity that shapes our ends, and about the fall of a sparrow) which strongly suggest the patience of the Christian martyr, awaiting the blow. He does not foreknow the plot that is laid against him, and yet he is given an intuition of it, a kind of awareness, in 'the interim is mine' and 'but thou wouldst not think how ill all's here about my heart'. But these are not allowed to carry the action; they are overscored by the foolery with Osric and the merely courteous relationship with Laertes. Again, the sword-play with Laertes is far more formalized than we usually remember. The Q2 Entry should give us a lead: *A table prepared, Trumpets, Drums and officers with Cushions, King, Queene, and all the state, Foiles, daggers, and Laertes.* This, with the judges, the wagers, draughts of Rhenish, the kettle-drums braying and cannon sounding off, creates a ritualistic framework for the realism ('fat and scant of breath') of the fencing-bout itself. Hamlet himself shares some of this ambivalence. Throughout the act he has been rather like an actor waiting in the wings for the call that he knows will come. He does not know that it has come when the sword-play begins, but he is remarkably detached from his own interests, and when the moment of truth arrives, there is a notable absence of rant, shock, or exclamation. His mind seems well prepared for what has happened; he leaps forward triumphantly, and with overmastering wit, into the role he has so long been waiting for (allowing Claudius to discover the death he himself has devised):

> The point envenomed too!
> Then, venom, to thy work.
> Is thy union here?
> Follow my mother.
> (v. ii. 313)

And in the imperious eloquence of his speech from the throne,

> You that look pale and tremble at this chance,
> That are but mutes or audience to this act,
> Had I but time ...   (v. ii. 326)

with its self-conscious use of theatrical imagery, we may feel
that the personal and ritual roles, the active and the passive,
have at last, however momentarily, combined. This play, no
less than the Mousetrap, has become Hamlet's. Claudius may
have organized it, but it is Hamlet who has taken control of it
and make it his own. But even this, it is important to recognize, does not bring the play to rest in ritual or impersonality.
Horatio sees Hamlet's death as that of a Christian soul, but
twenty lines later Shakespeare, ambivalent to the last, makes
him express the course of events, not as due to Providence but
as 'accidental judgments, casual slaughters', as the production of chance.

It seems possible to see what Shakespeare is doing here, in
this final scene, in relation to what I have said about Hamlet's
heroism. He is, I suggest, doing everything in his power to
blur the merely personal responsibility of Hamlet for acting
or not acting, everything, that is, short of infringing his hard-
won individuality. In *Othello* and *Lear* he was to present a
different final battle, a battle against oneself and what one
has made of life, where both victim and victor are inside the
single heroic individuality. Never again was he to seek to
combine this battle, the struggle to absorb and transmute
evil, with the physical action to overthrow evil. Never again
was he to make the climactic tragic movement out of the
hero's battle against an external enemy. And one can see
why. *Hamlet* represents an enormous and convulsive effort
to move forward to the heroism of the individual, without
abandoning the older social and religious framework of
external action. And one cannot say that the effort failed,
though the length and complexity of the play are unparalleled.
If we feel disposed to regret that it has not the formal unity
and perfection of *Othello*, we should remember that without
the convulsion of *Hamlet* the later (and unique) Shakespearian kind of tragedy is unlikely to have come into being.

all of them are plays of exile in the *Timon* rather than the *Lear* sense, for in none does the individual hero succeed in creating a new world of value inside himself, finding the point of growth which will absorb and transmute the world as it is. The temporizing and compromising society is rejected, but the rejection leaves the hero maimed and incomplete.[4] There is no sense in which Lear (or Hamlet or Othello, for that matter) is diminished by his failure to accept integration into society; but there is a real sense in which this is true of the later heroes.

The whole behaviour of Timon shows the curious paradox of the man, superlatively endowed and favoured by Fortune, who thinks that it is his privilege to move through society like an earthly god:

> He moved among us, as a muttering king,
> Magnificent, would move among his hinds.[5]

He dispenses largesse with an open, undiscriminating hand; he refuses reward; he never counts the cost. It is certainly magnificent; but it is also inhuman. The word *inhumanity* is no doubt merely appropriate to a god, and can be seen as a proper part of his praise; but when used of Timon, a man, the word can only be pejorative:

> For bounty, that makes gods, does still mar men.
> (IV. ii. 41)

And this paradox applies equally in both halves of the play. For Timon the indiscriminate hater of men has the same hunger for the absolute as Timon the indiscriminate lover. If we recoil from the inhumanity of the former we must also recoil from the latter.

The censure that I see aimed at Timon's indiscriminateness seems to be paralleled by a similar censure aimed at the Senate. The Senate refuses to allow particular cases or to see

4. To this extent the thesis presented here is similar to that of Willard Farnham, whose *Shakespeare's Tragic Frontier* (1950) presents the heroes of the last tragedies as 'deeply flawed': 'each of these heroes has faulty substance reaching to the very center of his character'. Farnham's treatment is mainly concerned with this kind of judgement of individual character; he does not deal with the social aspects of the plays, which I take (in what follows) to be central to their meaning.
5. Wallace Stevens, 'Sunday Morning'.

any mitigating circumstances in the crime of Alcibiades's anonymous friend. With Angelo-like incapacity to discriminate law from justice, they rest on the assertion, 'We are for law', and banish Alcibiades for questioning this. But at the end of the play, when they themselves are the victims, they take an opposite view:

> We were not all unkind, nor all deserve
> The common stroke of war. . . .
> . . . All have not offended;
> For those that were, it is not square to take,
> On those that are, revenge: crimes, like lands,
> Are not inherited . . . Like a shepherd
> Approach the fold and cull th' infected forth,
> But kill not all together.   (v. iv. 21)

Alcibiades, and the play as a whole, accepts the plea; he makes his victory an occasion for compromise;

> I will use the olive with my sword,
> Make war breed peace, make peace stint war, make each
> Prescribe to other, as each other's leech.   (v. iv. 82)

But in the very same speech we have his appreciation of the magnificence of Timon who never learned to compromise. The paradox of an absoluteness which simultaneously exalts and maims the hero remains unresolved at the end of the play.

The life of Alcibiades, who fled and conspired against his country, provides a natural bridge between Timon, who forecast his career (as Plutarch tells us), and Coriolanus, who formed his Roman 'parallel'. Certainly Shakespeare's *Coriolanus* provides the obvious instance of exile and hatred to be compared with that in *Timon*. And, again, the speech spoken at the point of exile serves to focus the attitude of the hero:

> You common cry of curs, whose breath I hate
> As reek o' th' rotten fens, whose loves I prize
> As the dead carcasses of unburied men
> That do corrupt my air—I banish you.
> . . . Despising
> For you the city, thus I turn my back;
> There is a world elsewhere.   (III. iii. 122)

The gesture is magnificent, but the same reservation still applies: it is inhuman, or rather anti-human. The 'world elsewhere' of Coriolanus does not turn out to be in the least like Lear's world of introspective anguish and revaluation; it is only the same Roman political world, at a certain geographical remove, and equally resistant to the monomaniac individual. And however proud that individual, he continues to need a populace, a city, that accepts his dominance. *Coriolanus* makes quite clear what is only implicit in *Timon*: the political nature of the scrutiny to which these later heroes are subjected. The aspirations of Hamlet, Othello, and Lear relate centrally to their families; their principal effort is to comprehend and adjust the strains and tensions arising in that context; the wider sphere of politics is present only as a background.[6] But the difficulties of the later heroes involve organized society in a much more direct way: Macbeth, Coriolanus, Antony all feel the pressure to pursue a political course which runs against their natural individualities. Moreover the 'family life' of Coriolanus, as of Macbeth or Antony, is only a particular aspect of this general social pressure. Volumnia, the type of the Roman matron, sees home as a parade-ground for training in leadership; the pressure of her love is always exercised for a political end. Indeed the play shows a paucity of relationships which are entirely private in intention. One might indeed allow Virgilia to be unswayed by public interests; but it is notorious that Virgilia is the most ineffectual character in the play. There is no evidence that her love is any more listened to than that of Flavius the steward in *Timon*, who is dismissed as statistically meaningless, too exceptional to count; in the political or social contexts of these plays the humble and disinterested love of the private individual can exercise little power, for the careers of their heroes are too little attuned to such cadences.

A unique feature of these late plays is of relevance here. *Macbeth, Coriolanus, Antony and Cleopatra* has each as its

6. Brutus might seem to be an exception to the division being attempted here: he is an 'early' hero, whose dramatic life is concerned with politics and hardly at all with family. But Brutus cannot justly be assimilated into the later group of heroes: he is indeed made the opposite to Caesar, as a man whose real life remains obstinately 'private' even when he is caught up in political action. His private integrity is not threatened by his public failure.

deuteragonist a woman of mature years and of amply developed political instincts.[7] Each of these exercises on the protagonist a dominating influence which is eventually destructive of his life. In the homes dominated by these women the domestic emotions, love, loyalty, mutual comfort, thus become the prey of political ambition; and the mind of the hero is left with no counters to stake against the devouring claims of the political world.

The loss of a domestic scene whose values of trust and repose are believed by the hero to be distinct from those of the jostling political world, providing him therefore with an alternative vision of life—this loss is probably to be associated with a decline in the sense of an immanent sustaining metaphysical order, also characteristic of the last tragedies. In this respect, as in some others, *Macbeth* is obviously a transitional play. In the earlier tragedies—*Hamlet*, *Othello*, *Lear*—the political world is peripheral; the real conflict occurs inside the protagonist, whose struggle it is to absorb the assumptions of the world he lives in and transmute them into something metaphysically meaningful; the effect of Brutus, Hamlet, Othello, and Lear is to moralize through their sufferings the self-interested assumptions of those who live around them and have power over them. But Coriolanus and Antony do not try to make this effect; they make gestures of opposition to the world they live in, gestures towards apparent alternatives, but their opposition is more apparent than real; neither Corioli nor Egypt really exists on a different

7. It may seem strange that just before giving the world his picture-gallery of fresh and even extravagantly innocent heroines—Marina, Imogen, Perdita, Miranda—Shakespeare should have been lavishing his attention on ladies whose innocence is their least obvious characteristic. But I think that there is a fairly straightforward connection between the two sets of characters. The archetype of Snow-White, evident behind Imogen, requires the complementary archetype of the wicked queen; both the Queen in *Cymbeline* and Dionyza in *Pericles* carry on an already established line of plotting females. The change from Tragedies to Romances involves a general change in atmosphere, a recession of historical reality, so that character becomes caricature (or line drawing); as this change reduces the complexity of the ageing female figure, using her power to impose a selfish will on the commonwealth, so it gives new prominence to the innocent girl who is the natural victim of sophisticated guile, whose goodness owes much of its appeal to the situation of danger in which it lives, and who survives less through her own skill than by the good fortune that we suppose to have a natural attachment to innocence.

plane from Rome, nor does Timon's cave offer a meaningfully alternative life to that of Athens. These exiles make claims which have a metaphysical resonance, but the real effects in the play are determined on the lower plane of *Realpolitik*. In *Macbeth*, on the other hand, the two worlds of politics and metaphysics exist side by side in a state of almost perfect balance, where personal ambition is seen as a breach of both orders simultaneously, and escape from politics to metaphysics turns out to be no escape at all. Macbeth has an agonized knowledge of what a true domestic relationship ought to provide:

> Honour, love, obedience, troops of friends,

but, of course, he tries to act as if he did not know, as if the stuff of ambition were the stuff of life.

In these terms it is probable that *Timon* also should count as a transitional play, though in a less obvious or satisfactory way; and one cannot avoid the suspicion that 'transitional' here may be a mere synonym for 'unfinished'.[8] The possibility of political action in *Timon* is limited and complicated all the time by metaphysical assumptions about human nature. Timon sees man as either a blessed or an accursed creature, and this effectively prevents him from seeking to affect human life by leadership or any other political activity.

Lear's curses when he goes into exile ask the gods to intervene or at least to observe; Timon's only ask that the *human* observances of religion (seen as symptoms of order) should cease to exist. Coriolanus manages to curse his banishers without mentioning the gods at all. The gods are invoked constantly, of course, even in this markedly secular play. There is a notable example in Coriolanus's speech after his capitulation in Act v:

> Behold, the heavens do ope,
> The gods look down, and this unnatural scene
> They laugh at.   (v. iii. 183)

But the gods who appear out of Coriolanus's heaven are quite different from those who, in *Lear*, 'keep this dreadful

8. See U. Ellis-Fermor, '*Timon of Athens:* an unfinished play', *R.E.S.* xviii (1942), reprinted in *Shakespeare the Dramatist* (1961).

pudder o'er our heads'. Coriolanus's gods only reflect back
the human scene; most often, indeed, they appear to be the
mere conveniences of Roman political faction;[9] certainly a
gulf of irony separates them from involvement in the tragedy
of any one individual.

Their withdrawal from possible involvement further
isolates the hero, leaves him alone with his own standards
and the political urge to fulfil the sense of individual greatness
in terms of distinction from and dominion over his fellows.
Unfortunately for Coriolanus's fulfilment, the *distinction* and
dominion are not entirely compatible. He desires to be a
nonpareil, to behave

> As if a man were author of himself
> And knew no other kin.

He speaks of the people

> As if you were a god, to punish; not
> A man of their infirmity. (III. i. 81)

Like Timon, he denies reciprocity. 'He pays himself by being
proud', his wounds 'smart to hear themselves remembered'.
His condescensions are general, hardly at all concerned with
individuals. An episode, which seems to mirror Shakespeare's
desire to make this point obvious, is that in which we see
Coriolanus pleading for the exemption of a Volsci who had
once sheltered him—but he cannot remember his name. As
the bastard Faulconbridge tells us:

> . . . new made honour doth forget men's names:
> 'Tis too respective and too sociable.
> (*John*, I. i. 187)

Coriolanus's pretension to be a god takes him rather further into action than does Timon's, and this undoubtedly
reflects his greater involvement in politics, his interest in
leadership:

> He is their god; he leads them like a thing
> Made by some other deity than Nature,
> That shapes men better; (IV. vi. 91)

9. e.g. I. i. 191; I. viii. 6; I. ix. 8; II. iii. 142; III. i. 290; III. iii. 33; IV. vi. 36;
V. iii. 104.

But his involvement is also his destruction. To fulfil his distinction above other men he has to seek dominion over them; but he is bound to fail in this because the distinction is too great; he is too inhuman. Indeed the more godlike he seeks to be, the more *inhuman* he becomes. The play has very usefully been seen in relation to Aristotle's celebrated dictum: 'He that is incapable of living in a society is a god or a beast'; or (as the Elizabethan translation expanded it): 'He that cannot abide to live in company, or through sufficiency hath need of nothing, is not esteemed a part or member of a City, but is either a beast or a God.'[1] The ambiguity of Aristotle's remark is nicely adjusted to the ambiguity that I find in these last tragedies, the moral ambiguity of heroes who are both godlike and *inhuman*. The inhumanity of Coriolanus is conveyed to us in terms both of a beast and of a machine. Sometimes the two are combined as in the following:

he no more remembers his mother now than an eight-year-old horse. The tartness of his face sours ripe grapes; when he walks, he moves like an engine and the ground shrinks before his treading. He is able to pierce a corslet with his eye, talks like a knell, and his hum is a battery. He sits in his state as a thing made for Alexander. What he bids be done is finished with his bidding. He wants nothing of a god but eternity, and a heaven to throne in.

(v. iv. 16)

Coriolanus, like Timon, and like Macbeth, searches for an *absolute* mode of behaviour, and like them he finds it; but the finding it is the destruction of humanity in him, as it was in them. And as far as it concerns personality, the process is as irreversible for Coriolanus as for Timon or Macbeth; he can, however, avoid that final stage, where the absoluteness of the individual demands to be guaranteed by the destruction of his society. He is unable to sustain the absoluteness of 'Wife, mother, child, I know not'; but I do not think we should see the collapse before Volumnia as a great triumph of human love.[2] The play's judgement on the beast-machine nature of 'absolute' man stands unchanged. Only death can

1. See F. N. Lees, 'Coriolanus, Aristotle and Bacon', *R.E.S.* i (1950), 114–25.
2. It has been so represented by Bradley and (more ecstatically) by G. Wilson Knight.

chillingly enough satisfy the hunger for absoluteness; and the final scene in Corioli, with its ironic repetition of the political and personal pattern already set in Rome, makes it clear that nothing in Coriolanus has altered or can alter. Greatness is seen as a doubtful and destructive blessing; love is powerless to change that. And this would seem to be as true of *Antony and Cleopatra* as of the other plays considered.

Antony and Cleopatra is, of all the tragedies after *Lear*, the one which has least obvious connection with the line of thought pursued here. But the connections exist, I think, and to pursue them is to remove some of the difficulties of this 'most quintessential of Shakespeare's "Problem Plays" ' (as it has recently been called).³ Is Antony an exile? I suggest that he is, though only in a different sense from Timon and Coriolanus. He is an exile from a world that we never see in the play, which existed splendidly in the past and will never be recovered again, a world in which

> his goodly eyes
> . . . o'er the files and musters of the war
> Have glow'd like plated Mars   (I. i. 2)

and where

> his captain's heart
> . . . in the scuffles of great fights hath burst
> The buckles on his breast   (I. i. 6)

The play is remarkable in the sense it gives of living in a second age; it is full of references to the heroes of the recent past; Julius Caesar and Pompey the Great still overshadow the world of the present, whose major characters were then being formed. In the past it had seemed possible to be both glamorous and efficient, heroic and political. But Antony's 'heroic' gestures—challenging Caesar to single combat, seeking to fight again at Pharsalia—are seen to be quite inappropriate to the present in which he lives. The minor characters display this obviously enough: Ventidius, who knows how to avoid seeming to be a hero, is the real man of the time; Enobarbus tries to be, but fails miserably. Pompey indeed has the choice set before him more clearly than anyone

---

3. E. Schanzer, *The Problem Plays of Shakespeare* (1963).

else in the play, when Menas offers to cut the throats of the
triumvirs; but Pompey feels he cannot stoop to success:

> Thou must know
> 'Tis not my profit that does lead mine honour:
> Mine honour, it.   (II. vii. 74)

He 'will not take when once 'tis offer'd', and thus (as Menas
sees) he becomes (at that very moment) a man of the past.

It is in the contrast between Antony and Octavius, of
course, that this split in the world of the play is developed
most fully. Octavius suffers from none of the scruples which
affect Pompey; his treatment of Lepidus may serve to characterize his whole mode of proceeding:

> ... having made use of [Lepidus] in the wars 'gainst Pompey,
> presently denied him rivality, would not let him partake in the
> glory of the action; and not resting here, accuses him of letters he
> had formerly wrote to Pompey; upon his own appeal, seizes him.
>   (III. v. 7)

He is everywhere marked by the celerity and decisiveness of
his moves. "'Tis done already' and 'most certain' are his
typical locutions; when he fights, 'this speed of Caesar's /
Carries beyond belief'. There is no sense in which Caesar,
like the other major characters, is still living in the past. Time
is not for him a destroyer, but a whirlwind he rides to command the future.

Antony, on the other hand, is, as I have said, an exile from
a glorious past that cannot be recovered. As an 'ebb'd man',
time is not his to command. In Egypt he is becalmed in the
dramatic equivalent of Spenser's Lake of Idleness, Cleopatra
having the role of Phaedria:

> But that your royalty
> Holds idleness your subject, I should take you
> For idleness itself.   (I. iii. 91)

In this fertile and stagnant atmosphere of Nilus's mud, of

> The dull billows thick as troubled mire,
> Whom neither wind out of their seat could force,
> Nor timely tides did drive out of their sluggish source,
>   (*Faerie Queene*, II. vi. 20)

time has a function other than that of developing the future out of the present:

> Now for the love of Love and her soft hours,
> Let's not confound the time with conference harsh;
> There's not a minute of our lives should stretch
> Without some pleasure now. What sport tonight?
>
> (I. i. 44)

The deviousness of Cleopatra, the sense of time stopping when Antony leaves her, the impossibility of forecasting her actions, her capacity to say and unsay—all these are means to bend the time of action into a hoop of enjoyment, the time of thinking into the time of the heart:[4]

> And now like am'rous birds of prey
> Rather at once our Time devour
> Than languish in his slow-chapt pow'r.
> (Marvell, 'To his coy mistress', 38)

In this atmosphere it is easy enough for Antony to be 'heroic' (in the old, Herculean, sense of 'generous', 'large-scale'); but if heroism is to be more than sentimental self-indulgence, then it must allow also that every action, taken or avoided, is the moulding of the future. And this the play never allows us to forget, with its repeated reference to 'our slippery people' who constantly shift their allegiance to the newcomer, to the primal law by which

> This common body,
> Like to a vagabond flag upon the stream,
> Goes to and back, lackeying the varying tide.
> (I. iv. 44)

Antony himself knows that

> The present pleasure,
> By revolution low'ring, does become
> The opposite of itself.   (I. ii. 128)

4. In these respects the relationship of Cleopatra and Antony is very close to that of Falstaff and Hal. The characters of the queen and the knight are very similar in their power to tease the literal-minded critic; each is the impresario of his own performance, which he arranges to affect others rather than to establish any inner consistency. See my 'Shakespeare's politics and the rejection of Falstaff', *C.Q.* i (1959), 235.

But even Antony's capacity to break out of this Idle Lake where 'we bring forth weeds / When our quick minds lie still', and to return to the Roman world of action, cannot heal the schism in the world of the present. Critics often write as if it was open to Antony to choose a complete and satisfactory life as a Roman, married to Octavia and sharing rule with Caesar. But Caesar himself knows better:

> I must perforce
> Have shown to thee such a declining day
> Or look on thine; we could not stall together
> In the whole world. But yet let me lament
> . . . that our stars,
> Unreconcilable, should divide
> Our equalness to this.   (v. i. 37)

In the present of the play the partial life lived by Octavius, and the other partial life, lived to the full by Antony, are as incapable of fusion as time present and time past. Octavius and Antony are affected equally by this; but Octavius can hardly be called an exile from the completer world of the past, for he never belonged to it; his speeches move in the present and the future. But Antony is an exile and is aware that he is an exile, living on borrowed time in an inevitably hostile world. The idea is particularly well conveyed by the continuous play on the word *Antony* as representing not only the name of the man we see before us, but also the *Idea* of the man as he was once, and as he ought to be:

> Since my lord
> Is Antony again, I will be Cleopatra. (III. xiii. 186)

> He comes too short in that great property
> Which still should go with Antony. (I. i. 58)

> O my oblivion is a very Antony. (I. iii. 90)

> I dream'd there was an Emperor Antony—
> .. Think you there was or might be such a man?
> (v. ii. 76)

> yet t'imagine
> An Antony were nature's piece 'gainst fancy,
> Condemning shadows quite.   (v. ii. 98)

> she looks like sleep,
> As she would catch another Antony
> In her strong toil of grace. (v. ii. 343)

The magic of an image of *Antony* has the power to hold the
heroic past alive for the moment of the present; but the magic
is a kind of confidence-trick. Nothing in the present really
supports the idea; and as soon as the charm of immediate
power weakens (at Actium) the empire shatters like quick-
silver. The most telling of these *Antony* references comes in
his death-speech:

> Here I am Antony;
> Yet cannot hold this visible shape my knave.
> (IV. xiv. 13)

The effort to be *Antony*, to identify the actions of the present
with this heroic figure, is fully revealed in the necessity to die
for it, and so, by this means, to deny and defeat the reductive
currents of time and policy. Antony's choice here is as much
a choice of the absolute as is that of Coriolanus or Timon;
but the absolute is of the opposite kind. They choose detachment, hardness, inhumanity; he prefers the grand illusion of
an absolute magnetism, loyalty, love:

> The nobleness of life
> Is to do thus [*Embracing*], when such a mutual pair
> And such a twain can do it.   (I. i. 36)

This is magnificent, but it is undercut by self-indulgent
sentimentality as surely as are the 'victories' of Act IV. The
will to be godlike must have set against it the fact that 'the
god Hercules whom Antony lov'd' leaves him when his
fortunes decline. As in *Coriolanus*, the gods only reflect back
what human beings have made for themselves.

The later tragedies offer the alternative absolutes of exclusion and inclusion, of denying the world and of swallowing
it; death seals equally the opposite magnificences of Timon
and Antony; but in neither case does the play conceal the
price that has been paid for closing the uneasy gap between
the absolute and the real—abandonment of the good ordinari-
ness of a life lived among compromises, or the loss of a sense
of reverence for the unknown in destiny, a sense of submission to the immanence of higher powers.

The theme of exile, which bulks so large in these later tragedies, does not wither away when Shakespeare turns to the writing of the 'Romances'. Pericles, very obviously, lives his life around his exile; Belarius and Posthumus are exiled from the British Court; Perdita and Camillo live in banishment (though she does not know it); Prospero's exile provides the whole subject of *The Tempest*. The societies which exile these characters are all corrupt ones; but, as in the later tragedies, the corruption is viewed as something basic in human nature so that it has to be dealt with by compromise and acceptance rather than by extirpation. It is as if the figure of Timon were to be removed from the play that bears his name and the attitude of Alcibiades developed as the basis of the plot. The hero, whose quest for absoluteness has been scrutinized in these last tragedies and whose mode of life has been seen as inhuman, now ceases to be the magnetic centre of interest. *The Tempest* is rather exceptional in this respect and will be dealt with separately. Certainly *Cymbeline* and *The Winter's Tale* lack dominating central figures, whose developing feelings carry us along the main channel of the play's movement. In these plays (and in *The Tempest* and even *Pericles* as well) it is in terms of the social embodiment of virtue that the play develops, rather than towards the achievement of virtue in the individual conscience. We are less interested in the 'redemption' of Leontes or Posthumus than in the complex of interests and attitudes inside which their redeemed lives have to be accommodated. The state of exile is not here (as in *Lear*) an opportunity to discover the true quality of humanity; it is rather that the structure of society is seen as coming to recognize its need for the elements it has rejected. This is true of *Timon* and *Coriolanus* as well; but there our point of view remains closely attached to the exile himself; we see society's repeated offers of compromise from his viewpoint and we recognize that he owes it to his absoluteness to refuse them. In the Last Plays the individual is seen much more as an inextricable part of the social group, and his actions are followed from that standpoint. Alonso's need for Prospero's comfort, Leontes' for the friends and family he dispersed, and (most clearly of all) Britain's need for soldiers like Belarius and Posthumus, finds a natural

answer in a restoration of earlier social alignments. This does
not occur because the individual has changed in his exile; it is
not even that society has changed in any basic way. The mix-
ture of good and evil is much as it was; it is only that time
has brought the unchanged elements into a new arrangement.
Clearly we are meant to rejoice at this; but (the mode of
vicissitude so obvious in the construction of these plays
serves to insist) time will change all things again. Time himself tells us so when he appears before us in *The Winter's
Tale*:

> I, that please some, try all, both joy and terror
> Of good and bad, that makes and unfolds error
> . . . so shall I do
> To' th' freshest things now reigning, and make stale
> The glistering of this present.   (IV. i. I)

Mutability is not an important theme in *Lear*; but the heroes
of the last tragedies all live within its scope, though they try
to outface it; the Last Plays accept it as basic and inevitable,
and the natural result is a diminution in the scope of the
individuals who initiate action. The exiles of *Cymbeline* and
The Winter's Tale return, not to take any 'absolute' revenges,
but rather to accept again the society in which we first saw
them—the place to which they belong.

It is only thematically that the situations of these plays are
similar to those of the last tragedies. But in *The Tempest*
Shakespeare returns also to a plot-line which is parallel.
Prospero is exiled from political office, and exiled for an
absoluteness of temperament which made him too much like
a god and too little like a man. And the 'god' image is now
more than a metaphor; Prospero's magic gives him the power
to enact what the curses of Lear, Coriolanus, and Timon only
imagined:

> I will do such things—
> What they are yet I know not; but they shall be
> The terrors of the earth. (*King Lear*, II. iv. 279)

But here again (as, most notably, in *Coriolanus*) the power to
execute such threats can only be bought at the price of inhumanity; Ariel's sense of what is proper to a man reveals
the quality of the danger and Prospero acknowledges it:

Hast thou, which art but air, a touch, a feeling
Of their afflictions, and shall not myself,
One of their kind, that relish all as sharply,
Passion as they, be kindlier mov'd than thou art?
(*The Tempest*, v. i. 21)

Prospero's acceptance of *kindness*—the feeling of necessary
fellowship between one member of the human *kind* and the
rest of the species—implies the rejection of his earlier notion
that he could isolate himself:

being transported
And rapt in secret studies.
(*The Tempest*, I. ii. 76)

It also implies the rejection of his later delusion that he could
change mankind, or execute justice upon it. The recognition
here of the isolated individual's ultimate powerlessness picks
up what I take to be the central theme of the later tragedies.
The splendid self-will of the last tragic heroes existed in
defiance of this recognition; and, given their celerity in dying,
they may even be said to *defeat* it. For in death (and only in
death) they are able to fix the image of greatness they lived
by, and free it from the necessary decay of still-living things.
The last tragedies explore the *splendour*; the Last Plays
concentrate on the quality of the *living*; both groups of plays
accept that the two concepts will appear on opposite sides of
the dramatic conflict; and it is this that gives their worlds
their common and unique quality.

From the views advanced in this essay it follows that the
Last Plays have to be greatly simplified before we can see
them just as fables of reconciliation. Their relation to the last
tragedies suggests a different point of view; the capacity to
accept the world-as-it-is has had to be bought by a sacrifice
of heroic pretensions, by a loss of confidence in the heroic
individual. In reading the Last Plays we should feel the sense
of this loss even as we rejoice in the sweetness of their recon-
ciliations.

I I

A.C.Bradley's
Shakespearean Tragedy

A. C. Bradley's *Shakespearean Tragedy* stands on the bookshelves like one of the more ponderous and irremovable monuments of the late Victorian establishment, overshadowing what has followed it, and none the less resented for that. The clerihew in which Shakespeare sits for a Civil Service Exam, '. . . In which Shakespeare did very badly / Because he hadn't studied Bradley' / catches very well this image of the book as an Establishment synthesis,[1] making possible the absorption of Shakespeare into the higher educational system, long dominated by the Greats syllabus of Classics and Philosophy. Bradley himself, classicist and philosopher, was an obvious person to effect this sea-change in Shakespeare study.

As I suggest, most references to Bradley's book since the time of its publication have been either resentful of its influence or (alternatively) defensive about its virtues. I wish here to take up neither of these roles; but, accepting *Shakespearean Tragedy* as one of the classics of English criticism, to ask what kind of book it is, and how it came to possess the qualities that characterize it. This involves a look at its author.

Andrew Cecil Bradley was born in 1851 into the already extensive family of the Revd Charles Bradley, an Evangelical

[Given originally as a lecture at the Royal Shakespeare Theatre Summer School, September 1964, and first published in *Essays and Studies*, 21 (English Association), 1968.]

1. Cf. *The Times Literary Supplement*, 23 May 1936: 'the critic recognises . . . that in so far as he agrees with Bradley he is mature; and where he disagrees he has still a long road to travel. But he makes no doubt that the road will lead him to Bradley again, and bring him under that sign to the thrill of critical certitude, and the bliss of critical peace.'

clergyman of some fame as a sermon-writer. The Revd
Charles looks from this distance like a caricature of all that
we suppose Victorian clergymen to have been—forceful,
long-lived, dogmatic, a domestic tyrant,[2] whose first wife
'succumbed before the advent of her fourteenth baby'[3] and
whose second wife raised the total of his children to some
twenty-two. The children were moreover destined to spread
their competence over large areas of late Victorian intellectual
life. George Granville Bradley, the fourth son of the first
marriage, born some thirty years before Andrew Cecil,
became Headmaster of Marlborough College in 1858, and
Master of University College, Oxford, in 1870. He was to go
on to become Dean of Westminster in succession to Arthur
Stanley, whose life he wrote. His children were A. C.
Bradley's contemporaries; several of them (for example,
Arthur Granville Bradley and (Daisy) Margaret Louisa
Woods) became literary figures in their own right. The
atmosphere of the family may be gauged from the magazine
The Miscellany, which was edited by two daughters of G. G.
Bradley in the years 1867–73.[4] This had a list of subscribers
and of contributors that would be the delight of any modern
professional and metropolitan effort—including two that
Edith Bradley was later to call 'our father's brilliant young
step-brothers, the younger of whom was not only near my
own age, but a warm and close friend'.[5] The two step-
brothers were Francis Herbert Bradley, the Idealist Philosopher and valetudinarian Fellow of Merton, born in 1846, and
Andrew Cecil Bradley, whose contributions to *The Miscellany* are interesting supplements to the corpus of his
literary criticism. F. H. Bradley was at Oxford at the same
time as Andrew Bradley, moved in the same crucial circles;
they remained close enough for the younger brother to take
responsibility for the second edition of *Ethical Studies* in
1927.

This description of the family circle should not end without
the mention of one other member, Sir George Grove, civil

2. See G. R. G. Mure, 'F. H. Bradley', *Encounter*, xvi (1961), 28.
3. See Bodleian MS. Don. d 129, fol. 154.
4. Now in the Bodleian Library as Bodl. MS. Don. e 35, d 196.
5. Edith Nicholl Ellison, *A Child's Recollection of Tennyson* (1907).

engineer, musicologist, editor, founder and first Principal of the Royal College of Music. Grove had grown up in Clapham, that hotbed of Evangelical piety, where the Revd Charles Bradley had had a chapel (St James's, Clapham) built for him by his admiring flock; Grove married Harriet Bradley, and towards the end of the century he seems to have been close friend of Andrew Bradley; he published several signed articles by his brother-in-law in *Macmillan's Magazine* while he was its editor; Germanic and musical interests were among the bonds that tied the two men together.

By the time A. C. Bradley was born, the Revd Charles had moved from Clapham to Cheltenham, and it was at Cheltenham College (for boys) that Andrew was educated. What seems crucial in the formation of his intellectual position was, however, what followed the schooling.

Between school and Oxford (to which he went in 1869) Bradley had some free time; and it is in this period that Mackail[6] locates a spiritual crisis—'a strong, even violent reaction from the atmosphere of rigid evangelicalism in which he had grown up'. Much of his intellectual position in later years is to be explained by the rejection of this form of faith, with its emphasis on the literal truth of scripture, the need for a personal sense of sin and a personal path to salvation, its insistence on the miraculous, supernatural, and irrational quality of conventional religious life. The reaction against a dominant Evangelical father is a standard enough Victorian pattern which few intellectuals of the time seem to have avoided. The particular form the story took in the life of A. C. Bradley—a form that leads directly, I believe, to *Shakespearean Tragedy*—is to be explained by the influences he met when he carried his spiritual crisis to Balliol in 1869.

Fifty years later Bradley was to tell a friend that his soul had been saved by Thomas Hill Green.[7] Green, himself the son of an Evangelical parson, had come to Balliol in 1855, and he was elected Fellow in 1860. He became the centre of an Oxford attachment to German Idealist philosophy, but was perhaps even more influential as a living testimony to the ethical power possible outside supernatural sanctions.

6. 'Andrew Cecil Bradley', *Proc. B.A.* xxi (1935).
7. Ibid., p. 386.

Edward Caird says in the preface to Seth and Haldane's *Essays in Philosophical Criticism* (1883), a memorial volume by Green's former pupils:

To Professor Green philosophy was not a study of the words of men that are gone but a life transmitted from them to him—a life expressing itself with that power and authority which belongs to one who speaks from his own experience and never to 'the scribes' who speak from tradition.

Again, and even more extremely:

There are not a few among the Oxford men of the last fifteen years to whom . . . his existence was one of the things that gave reality to the distinction between good and evil.

But perhaps the most eloquent description of Green's effect on men of Bradley's generation is to be found in Mrs Humphrey Ward's *Robert Elsmere*, where Mr Grey represents T. H. Green. The young Robert Elsmere attends a lay sermon by Grey and is immediately bowled over by the force of this new call to self sacrifice:

How the 'pitiful earthy self' with its passions and its cravings sank into nothingness beside the 'great ideas' and the 'great causes' for which, as Christians and as men he claimed their devotion.

Shortly afterwards Elsmere describes Grey/Green's intellectual position more explicitly:

The whole basis of Grey's thought was ardently idealist and Hegelian. He had broken with the popular Christianity, but for him, God, consciousness, duty, were the only realities. None of the various forms of materialist thought escaped his challenge; no genuine utterance of the spiritual life of man but was sure of his sympathy.

To ardent souls brought up in the hectic atmosphere of Evangelical charity, but unwilling to accept supernatural sanctions, Green managed to suggest a new set of ethical imperatives, a new sense of guilt, a new call to the higher life. 'He gave us back the language of self-sacrifice', said one of his pupils, quoted by Mr Melvin Richter. The world was still full of evils that the good man had to fight; but the path of combat Green indicated did not lead to Rome; but to Stepney, to Toynbee Hall, to female emancipation and the University Extension Lectures Movement.

Bradley's debt to Green is quite explicit—he was one of the small inner circle of disciples—and he remained under the spell of Green's 'metaphysics of morality' for the rest of his life. The set of Gifford lectures he delivered in Glasgow in 1907—published in 1940 by his sister, Marian de Glehn, under the title *Ideals of Religion*—is still entirely Greenian in its devotion to the concept of God as the highest realization of the inner self. And in the same lectures we may notice the Greenian point that the universal good can often be achieved only by the surrender or sacrifice of individual happiness or prosperity—but then the sacrifice of individual goods is in the highest sense 'good'. The relation of this to the famous 'substance of tragedy' chapter in *Shakespearean Tragedy* is sufficiently obvious not to require further comment.

In 1915 Bradley gave a lecture in Bedford College, London, on 'International Morality: the United States of Europe'. The intellectual framework of his remarks here is still the same: Aristotle, F. H. Bradley, Green, Bosanquet, Green again. It is obvious that Bradley did not discover new allegiances in the second half of his life, but remained essentially a part of the Oxford circle (Bosanquet, F. H. Bradley, Nettleship, Arnold Toynbee, J. H. Muirhead, Edward Caird, Charles Gore, *et al.*) he knew in the 1870s. It is not really surprising that Bradley's mind remained dyed in Green's colouring. Not only was he devoted to him as a pupil and a colleague, but he was involved in publishing Green's *Prolegomena* after the latter's death in 1882. The editorial process is likely to render ideas indelible; but martyrdom leaves an even deeper impress; and Bradley seems to have suffered some kind of martyrdom in Oxford because of his devotion to Green. Benjamin Jowett, from 1870 onward the Master of Balliol, was opposed to Green's tendency to systematize and to gather disciples who believed in his system. Jowett thought of philosophy as a school of scepticism; and believed that the tutor should leave the pupil's mind free to form individual opinions. Green's younger disciples—Nettleship and Bradley

—seem never to have enjoyed the Master's confidence.[8] Bradley's teaching career in Balliol must have been frustrating. In 1875 he was offered a History lectureship if he spent two semesters in a German University.[9] Accordingly he went in 1875 to Berlin. But from another letter of slightly later date it appears that he is still suspect as a possible *proselytizer*. He says 'I must try to convince him [Jowett] that I can attend to grammar and I do not want to proselytize'. He *did* lecture on Aristotle's *Ethics*—some shorthand notes of his lectures survive—but the Master's opposition does not seem to have dissolved.

A letter from Green dated 23 June 1881 implies that about 1876 Bradley had been offered a lectureship at New College and that Green had persuaded him to stay in Balliol. Green goes on:

I did not then forecast the financial future of the College or the persistency of the Master's opposition—not as it is needless to say to you personally—but to that kind of teaching being given in the College in which you could be most useful.[1]

He mentions the possibility of Bradley applying for a Chair of literature in the new University College in Liverpool ('Enquire carefully about the climate'). Bradley pursued the Liverpool possibility ('So far as I was able to learn there is nothing very deterrent about the climate of Liverpool'), and states clearly enough his reasons for moving:

Some amount of collision with the Master will I foresee be inevitable if I stay. I do not think I can teach more with a view to the examination than I have.[2]

Bradley's move from philosophy at Oxford to literature at Liverpool was to prove a fortunate one for English scholarship, but it came about fortuitously enough. Two Chairs were available: one of Philosophy and Political Economy, another

8. Letter from J. A. Symonds to Mrs Green, cited in Melvin Richter, *The Politics of Conscience* (1964), p. 392, n. 22.
9. MS. letter from Bradley to Green (May or June 1875) in Balliol College Library.
1. MS. letter from Green to Bradley (dated 23 June 1881) in Balliol College Library.
2. MS. letter from Bradley to Green (27 September 1881) in Balliol College Library.

of Modern Literature and History. Bradley was puzzled to know which fitted him better (or worse). He had been, throughout his time at Balliol, a philosopher above all. In his application to Liverpool he said that 'during the last nine years I have worked most at philosophy, especially in its application to morals, politics and literature'.[3] His references (all twenty-eight of them!) are predominantly concerned with his philosophical abilities, which are described in terms not very different from those earlier applied to Green. For example, he is called 'a man . . . to whom philosophy is not a set of abstractions but a life'.[4] J. H. Muirhead describes the surprise of Oxford men of the time that Bradley should have obtained the Literature Chair and not the Philosophy one, while his Balliol colleague, John MacCunn, became Professor of Philosophy.[5]

Bradley had, in fact, displayed his literary leanings before this time. I have already mentioned his essays in *The Miscellany*. S. H. Butcher, in a reference written for him when he applied for the Merton Chair of English in 1885, says that he had known Bradley 'from the time when as a boy at school he already possessed a knowledge of English literature that was quite unusual at such an age'. Butcher goes on to tell us that 'in 1879 he was invited by the Committee of the Association for Promoting the Higher Education of Women in Oxford to lecture for them on English Literature'.[6] He had already contributed essays on Marlowe and on Beaumont and Fletcher to T. H. Ward's *Selections from the English Poets* (1880) and on Browning and on Mythological Poetry to *Macmillan's Magazine*. He tells us himself that in 1877 he was invited to meet Swinburne: 'Jowett was then Master, and I a young don whom he knew to be interested in poetry.'[7]

So began the career of lectures—we hear of Liverpool lectures on 'Socrates', 'Mazzini', 'The Study of Poetry',

3. Testimonials in favour of A. C. Bradley (*Applications for the English Chair at Liverpool*, 1881) in the Bodleian Library.

4. Letter of recommendation from R. G. Tatton, printed with the above.

5. J. H. Muirhead, *Reflections of a Journeyman in Philosophy* (1942), pp. 41, 48 f.

6. Testimonials in favour of A. C. Bradley (*Applications for the Merton Chair of English in 1885*) in the Bodleian Library.

7. E. Gosse, *Swinburne* (1917), pp. 296 f.

'Shakespeare', 'Cowper', 'Wordsworth and Coleridge', Tennyson's *In Memoriam*[8]—which carried him from Liverpool to Glasgow in 1889 and, after he had resigned the Glasgow Chair in 1900, through his stint as Professor of Poetry at Oxford, 1901–6. These finally emerged in publication as *Shakespearean Tragedy* and *Oxford Lectures on Poetry*. A last gleaning of his lectures appeared in *A Miscellany*—a volume of less sustained excellence than the other two. Subsequently, his retirement 'to devote himself to leisured critical work'[9] was not broken; it seems probable that the collapse of his Germanophile intellectual world in the First World War was answered by some decline in his intellectual powers.[1] He lived until 1935, but wrote no more (so far as we know), shielded from scrutiny by his sister, Marian de Glehn.

I have dwelt at length on Bradley's philosophical allegiances, for these are central, I believe, to an explanation of his literary criticism, and in particular to an explanation of the most sustained critical exercise of his life—*Shakespearean Tragedy*. Throughout his life he was proud to think of himself as a philosopher-critic. At the end of his Oxford lectures he defended his 'propensity to philosophize' with the credo that Oxford's 'best intellectual gift was the conviction that what imagination loved as poetry reason might love as philosophy'. Dealing with Shakespeare, Bradley seems to start from his imaginative response to the tragic power of his poetry; and the effort of *Shakespearean Tragedy* is then, in terms of this equation, to transmute this response into a rational and systematized account of what is there, without loss and without falsification.

But Shakespearian tragedy is no accidental resting-place for Bradley's critical powers. The world of these tragedies is remarkably apposite to the systems of thought to which he was most attached and to the mode in which his mind worked

8. Letters from Joshua Sing and H. C. Beeching, as above, p. 276, n. 6.
9. M. R. Ridley in *D.N.B.*, *1931–1940*.
1. 'The strain of the war on him was great and he never quite recovered from it' (Mackail, in *Proc. B.A.* xxi [1935], 391).

most fruitfully. M. R. Ridley had noticed that even among the diverse essays of the *Oxford Lectures* Shakespeare occupies a prominent place, and that the Shakespearian subjects seem to call out a fuller measure of critical power than do the others. We may make the same point in another way: certain subjects do not seem to have elicited Bradley's response. Of these the most notable, and I believe the most significant, is Milton. It is apparent from a sentence at the end of 'Shelley's view of poetry' that Bradley was offended by the explicit dogmatisms of *Paradise Lost*:

Milton was far from justifying the ways of God to men by the argumentation he put into divine and angelic lips; his truer moral insight is in the creations of his genius; for instance, in the character of Satan or the picture of the glorious humanity of Adam and Eve.

With this slender hold on the range of *Paradise Lost* we may feel that Bradley was well justified in his Miltonic abstinence. But we should further notice that Shakespeare possesses perfectly what Milton is censured for lacking, a world fraught with spiritual meaning, but never explicit, a world of 'modern' realities—and here obviously superior to Greek tragedies, as on the other 'spiritual' side it is superior to the world of the novelists.

A remarkable essay on 'Old mythology in modern poetry', published by Bradley in *Macmillan's Magazine*, vol. 44 (1881), when his brother-in-law George Grove was editor, indicates some of the reasons why Shakespearian tragedy was so perfectly appropriate to his philosophic interests. The essay is concerned with the relation between belief and understanding, between the religious and the aesthetic senses, and pursues the tendency of religious beliefs to turn into poetic mythologies. The final section of the essay deplores the tendency of modern poets to draw on remote mythologies:

Art had two great enemies, the dominion of theology and the prejudices of aristocracy: She has freed herself from both, and should look at life with open eyes. Why, most of all, not content with

Jove, Apollo, Mars and such raskaille,

should we interpose the shapes of eastern and northern myth-ology between ourselves and reality, and even attempt to preserve those portions of our own religious ideas, the disappearance of which we ought to welcome?   (p. 47)

If Bradley is asking here (as I suppose) that the mythologi-cal or poetic-religious perceptions of modern poets should refer to real life, it is interesting that he goes on to invoke Shakespeare as an exponent of this activity: '. . . they can appeal for confirmation of its dignity to the greatest name in all literature.' In the language of this article, Shakespeare's tragic world seems to have the powerful recommendation that it is both real and factual and, at the same time, to be employing its realities as a mode of mythology, as a way of telling us about the general truths of the universe. I assume that Bradley is drawing on the same nomenclature when in an obscure passage of *Shakespearean Tragedy* he tells us that fate in Shakespeare

appears to be a mythological expression for the whole system or order, of which the individual characters form an inconsiderable and feeble part.   (p. 30)

The tragedies as wholes have *meanings*, and the meanings far transcend the individual parts, the individual opinions of the characters; but this meaning is, like the meaning of a mytho-logy, only to be inferred from the surface facts; it cannot be proved to exist, but its effects can be felt and responded to, and in terms of the ideal critic 'loved as philosophy'.

'What a piece of work is man,' we cry; 'so much more beautiful and so much more terrible than we knew! Why should he be so if this beauty and greatness only tortures itself and throws itself away?' We seem to have before us a type of the mystery of the whole world, the tragic fact which extends far beyond the limits of tragedy. Everywhere, from the crushed rocks beneath our feet to the soul of man, we see power, intelligence, life and glory, which astound us and seem to call for our worship. And every-where we see them perishing, devouring one another and destroy-ing themselves, often with dreadful pain, as though they came into being for no other end. Tragedy is the typical form of this mystery, because that greatness of soul which it exhibits oppressed, con-flicting and destroyed, is the highest existence in our view. (p. 23)

The poetic power of the tragic world gives an especially cogent image of the human mystery that had faced Bradley from the time of coming up to Oxford. Moreover, it is an image of that world which rules out, by its nature, the orthodox religious answers that he had long ago abandoned as inappropriate. In the opening lecture he speaks of the basic question 'regarding the tragic world and the ultimate power in it' and then goes on to indicate some of the conditions involved in a satisfactory answer to this question:

It will be agreed, however, first, that this question must not be answered in 'religious' language. For although this or that *dramatis persona* may speak of gods or of God, of evil spirits or of Satan, of heaven and of hell, and although the poet may show us ghosts from another world, these ideas do not materially influence his representation of life, nor are they used to throw light on the mystery of its tragedy. The Elizabethan drama was almost wholly secular; and while Shakespeare was writing he practically confined his view to the world of non-theological observation and thought, so that he represents it substantially in one and the same way whether the period of the story is pre-Christian or Christian.[2] He looked at this 'secular' world most intently and seriously; and he painted it, we cannot but conclude, with entire fidelity, without the wish to enforce an opinion of his own, and, in essentials, without regard to anyone's hopes, fears or beliefs. His greatness is largely due to this fidelity in a mind of extraordinary power; and if, as a private person, he had a religious faith, his tragic view can hardly have been in contradiction with this faith, but must have been included in it, and supplemented, not abolished, by additional ideas.   (p. 25)

Green's call to a life of self-sacrifice in the pursuit of the 'higher self', and for the sake of the whole of society, or even of the Spiritual Substance, seems to find brilliantly poignant illustration in the worlds of these plays where our feelings, honestly recorded, are most firmly attached to the man who will lose, who will be defeated, but whose defeat we cannot but think is in the interests of a good greater than himself. We receive (says Bradley)

the impression that the heroic being, though in one sense and outwardly he has failed, is yet in another sense superior to the

2. I say substantially; but the concluding remarks on *Hamlet* will modify a little the statements above [Bradley's note].

world in which he appears; is, in some way which we do not
seek to define, untouched by the doom that overtakes him; and
is rather set free from life than deprived of it.   (p. 324)

The world of Shakespearian tragedy is then for A. C.
Bradley, a world of secular men whose lives yet embody and
display the deepest mysteries of our existence. If these plays
demonstrate the Hegelian image of a Universe 'animated by a
passion for perfection', and crushing the partial perfections
of individuals, our inquiry how this is so can be conducted
only by investigating the lives of Shakespeare's men and
women ('the highest existence in our view'). Hence, of course,
Bradley's famous insistence on treating the characters of the
plays as if they were real. I accept that this is a critical weakness; it is of course a common weakness in nineteenth-
century criticism; and I would only point out that Bradley
was as well aware of its dangers as are his critics:

To consider separately the action or the characters of a play . . .
is legitimate and valuable, so long as we remember what we are
doing. But the true critic in speaking of these apart does not
really think of them apart; the whole, the poetic experience, of
which they are but aspects, is always in his mind; and he is
always aiming at a richer, truer, more intense repetition of that
experience.   (*Oxford Lectures*, pp. 16–17)

The more important point is that his assumption of reality
in the characters is a pre-condition of the brilliant kind of
inquiry he is conducting. He approaches these crucial instances of the moral life (created with intensity, but without
prejudice and without preconceptions) in the same spirit of
search as had animated Wordsworth:

My question eagerly did I renew
How is it that you live, and what is it you do?

The tragic heroes, like the leech-gatherer, are crucial, for in
them the inquirer detects the 'hiding-places of man's power'.

It is particularly the mystery of the evil in the world that
seems to be hidden in these brief but brilliant lives:

Why is it that a man's virtues help to destroy him, and that his
weakness or defect is so intertwined with everything that is
admirable in him that we can hardly separate them even in
imagination?   (*Shakespearean Tragedy*, p. 29)

But, allowing Green's principle that evil comes only from evil, and that good always produces good, it is Bradley's business to prosecute precisely this separation of good and evil. And so he uses his powers to deal with questions of the kind 'How could Iago, so brilliant in intellect, have been so evil?' or 'How could Hamlet, with these gifts, have failed to do what he believed to be the will of Providence?' The action of these plays is a landscape in which the moral lives of the characters are unfolded, and at the centre of their lives lie these questions about the intertwining of good and evil:

What is the answer to that appeal of Othello's:

> Will you, I pray, demand that demi-devil
> Why he hath thus ensnared my soul and body?

This question Why? is *the* question about Iago, just as the question Why did Hamlet delay? is *the* question about Hamlet.

(p. 222)

The answer to such central questions must be sought, in Bradley's view, in purely human terms. He rejects the view that Iago loves evil simply because it is evil, because that 'makes him psychologically impossible'. He goes to great pains to reject any sense of demonic possession in *Macbeth*:

There is no sign whatever in the play that Shakespeare meant the actions of Macbeth to be forced on him by an external power, whether that of the Witches, or of their 'masters', or of Hecate. It is needless therefore to insist that such a conception would be in contradiction with his whole tragic practice.   (p. 343)

Macbeth, Bradley is arguing here, is 'perfectly free' to make moral choices, which are, in this respect, exactly the same as the moral choices made by real men in the real world. The lessons we may learn by investigating his case are precisely the lessons that need to be learned for ordinary ethical living. Hence the detail he lavishes on the establishment of the factual reality of the cases; allowances for dramatic vagueness are to be avoided, for they would imply a separation of the play's moral life and that of human beings. The famous series of notes (A–EE)—'Where was Hamlet at the time of his father's death?', 'Did Emilia suspect Iago?', 'When was the murder of Duncan first plotted?'[3] are concerned to close every possible loophole of vagueness. They are more extreme than the body of the text, but they spring from the same central passion that animates the book. Bradley's *Shakespearean Tragedy* could not be the classic work it is if it were not characterized by this tenacity of central viewpoint, accompanied (and critical tenacity is rarely so accompanied) by extreme fair-mindedness in the handling of evidence, and extreme honesty of self-analysis.

The twentieth-century success of Bradley's criticism is very remarkable, if my account of its background is correct. Long after Green's *Prolegomena* is forgotten, long after the Oxford Idealists have been demolished, *Shakespearean Tragedy* goes bowling along, reprint after reprint. Why should this be?

Mrs Warnock has recently remarked of Idealist or Metaphysical ethics that

The metaphysical pleasure precisely consists in . . . seeing familiar problems, such as the problem of how it is right to behave, somehow reduced, and also answered, by being shown to be a part of a total scheme of things. This kind of pleasure may be partially aesthetic; it certainly has very little to do with how many of the propositions contained in the system are actually true statements.[4]

We may imagine that Green's formulations are especially liable to attacks on their truth of statement. The spiritual power invoked in Green's system was so vague that both Christians and Freethinkers could regard him as of their camp. But this vagueness is a positive necessity in the world invoked by A. C. Bradley. A tragedy which explicitly and precisely invokes supernatural justice is bound to be, to that extent, the less tragic. (The sense of waste in *Dr. Faustus* can only be strong because Marlowe's Christian world is so animated by anti-Christian feeling.) And a tragic world without some sense of spiritual meaning is lamed and deprived, a body without a soul. Shakespeare's tragedies avoid both pitfalls; and what would be vagueness or evasion in a philosophic system is here a recognition that human life is

3. But not, of course, the out-Bradleying Bradley question Leavis proposed to L. C. Knights: 'How many children had Lady Macbeth?'.
4. *Ethics since 1900* (1960), p. 47, quoted in Richter, op. cit., p. 190.

involved in tragic mystery. *Shakespearean Tragedy* is able again and again to suggest the potential of explicit spiritual meaning in the tragic events before us; but is always careful to withdraw before improper definiteness is required. Thus,

> In *Macbeth* and *Hamlet* not only is the feeling of a supreme power or destiny peculiarly marked, but it has also at times a peculiar tone, which may be called, in a sense, religious. I cannot make my meaning clear without using language too definite to describe truly the imaginative impression produced; but it is roughly true that, while we do not imagine the supreme power as a divine being who avenges crime, or as a providence which supernaturally interferes, our sense of it is influenced by the fact that Shakespeare uses current religious ideas here much more decidedly than in *Othello* or *King Lear*.   (p. 172)

or again,

> ... the result is that the Ghost affects imagination not simply as the apparition of a dead king who desires the accomplishment of *his* purposes, but also as the representative of that hidden ultimate power, the messenger of divine justice set upon the expiation of offences which it appeared impossible for man to discover and avenge, a reminder or a symbol of the connexion of the limited world of ordinary experience with the vaster life of which it is but a partial appearance. And as, at the beginning of the play, we have this intimation, conveyed through the medium of the received religious idea of a soul come from purgatory, so at the end, conveyed through the similar idea of a soul carried by angels to its rest, we have an intimation of the same character, and a reminder that the apparent failure of Hamlet's life is not the ultimate truth concerning him.   (p. 174)

This is the closest Bradley ever comes to an explicitly Christian reference in Shakespeare. Usually he prefers the 'in some sense which we do not seek to define' strategy which may be noticed in the quotation from p. 324 given above (pp. 280 f.). Later, speaking of feelings evoked by the death of Cordelia, he again moves towards definition:

> It implies that the tragic world, if taken as it is presented, with all its error, guilt, failure, woe and waste, is no final reality, but only a part of reality taken for the whole, and, when so taken, illusive; and that if we could see the whole, and the tragic facts in their true place in it, we should find them, not abolished, of course, but so transmuted that they had ceased to be strictly tragic.   (p. 324)

But in a footnote he withdraws from any improper explicitness, any illegitimate extension of the actual experience of the play:

It follows from the above that, if this idea were made explicit and accompanied our reading of a tragedy throughout, it would confuse or even destroy the tragic impression. So would the constant presence of Christian beliefs. The reader most attached to these beliefs holds them in temporary suspension while he is immersed in a Shakespearean tragedy. Such tragedy assumes that the world, as it is presented, is the truth, though it also provokes feelings which imply that this world is not the whole truth, and therefore not the truth.   (p. 325, n. 1)

The culpable vagueness of Idealism is no longer culpable here, for it is vague at precisely the point where tragedy *has* to be vague if it is to remain tragic. The system of thought and the work to be analysed are splendidly at one. What the imagination has loved as poetry the critic has enabled us to love as system and as reason.

12

T. S. Eliot and the creation
of a symbolist Shakespeare

The most influential new movement in twentieth-century
criticism of English poetry—the criticism which begins with
Pound and Eliot and passes (through Richards and Empson)
into the hands of the 'New Critics' in America and the
'Scrutiny' Critics in England—can be seen to be closely
associated with the most powerful movement in the poetry
of the same time. The domestication of French Symbolism in
Yeats and Pound and Eliot and Stevens demanded a new set
of literary priorities; it required the upgrading of the 'Image'
—Hulme says that 'images in verse are not mere decoration,
but the very essence of an intuitive language' (*Speculations*
[Kegan Paul, 1924], 2nd edn, p. 135)—and the downgrading
of explicit and describable subject matter. Recent discussion
of the critical movement has tended to speak of it in terms of
a general shift in philosophical temper. Certainly the drift of
thought can be described as anti-Cartesian, the content/form
dichotomy in criticism being equated with the body/soul or
matter/spirit one in metaphysics; and at least one of its
principal figures, I. A. Richards, was explicitly concerned to
find a philosophic basis for criticism, of such a kind that the
pursuit of a paraphrased or abstracted content would no
longer be respectable. But this philosophic side of the movement seems to me to have received too much attention. The
instinctive reforming of boundaries which appears in the
fairly haphazard critical statements of poets and artists
writing at least a decade before Richards may offer less
precision to the historian of ideas, but I suspect that it gives

[First published in *Twentieth-Century Literature in Retrospect*, ed. Reuben
Brower (Harvard Studies in English 2), 1971.]

a more typical diagram of the way in which general critical attitudes come to be formed. Eliot argued in 'Tradition and the Individual Talent' that each new work of art alters the tradition it joins, by making us revalue the works that precede it. But Eliot was not willing to let his criticism work in quite so insidious a way; he sought deliberately to alter the landscape of the past by dynamiting some old reputations and building up others. The map of English literary history that the Romantics had drawn (for the similar purposes of their own time) was no longer useful. Not only did it fail to mention Yeats, Pound, Eliot; it did not even mark the highway as moving in their direction. A new road had to be designated the superhighway, a new tradition canonized. The general features of the new road are well known: it was drawn to bypass the now irrelevant capital cities of Spenser, Milton, Wordsworth; it gave importance to the underdeveloped area of the Metaphysicals; Ben and Samuel Johnson, Dryden, and Pope found themselves in an improved situation; Shelley, Swinburne, Tennyson, and the Georgians moved to the suburbs of displeasure. But what of Shakespeare? Too large to be ignored, too great to be dismissed, Shakespeare seemed also too antipathetic to be accommodated inside the Symbolist aesthetic.

From many points of view Shakespeare's mode of poetry seems to be at the opposite pole from that of *L'Après-midi d'un faune, Le Cimitière marin, Sunday Morning, Ash Wednesday,* or *Byzantium.* It is rhetorical, easily intelligible in general drift, powerfully expressive of large, extroverted emotions, unconcerned with the details or velleities of the poet's private emotional state, content to echo generalized assumptions about religion or patriotism and to stimulate a fair number of stock responses. He works along the line of an easily paraphrased content, and invites our response (in approval or condemnation) to men and women with clearly defined characteristics and lifelike social relationships. If Symbolism is concerned (as Arthur Symons said it was) with the attempt 'to evade the old bondage of rhetoric, the old bondage of exteriority' (*The Symbolist Movement in Literature* [1899], p. 8), then Shakespeare would appear to be anti-Symbolist.

In what may be called the heroic age of English Symbolist criticism (the late teens and the twenties) Shakespeare does not figure much in the critics' remaking of the map. When he does appear he is usually passed off with some degree of petulance or enmity. This was the period in which Eliot was writing his brilliant essays on the Metaphysicals and on Elizabethan drama, and in which he displayed an almost obsessive concern with the categories and limitations of poetic drama. These would seem to be concerns which would lead directly to a confrontation with Shakespeare; but this is, in fact, avoided.

Only two essays in this creative phase of Eliot's criticism are explicitly concerned with Shakespeare, the *Hamlet* essay of 1919 and the 1927 essay 'Shakespeare and the stoicism of Seneca'. The latter is a very interesting attempt to deal with what was obviously a central problem for Eliot, as it had been for Santayana and others, that Shakespeare's 'philosophy' is so second-hand and (it is implied) so second-rate, compared with the great exemplar, Dante. Eliot commits himself in this essay to the opinion that 'I have as high an estimate of the greatness of Shakespeare as poet and dramatist as anyone living; I certainly believe that there is nothing greater'. None the less the essay seethes with an ill-concealed irritation about all critical positions that may be adopted in relation to Shakespeare:

I propose a Shakespeare under the influence of the stoicism of Seneca. But I do not believe that Shakespeare was under the influence of Seneca. I propose it largely because I believe that after the Montaigne Shakespeare (not that Montaigne had any philosophy whatever) and after the Machiavelli Shakespeare, a stoical or Senecan Shakespeare is almost certain to be produced. I wish merely to disinfect the Senecan Shakespeare before he appears. My ambitions would be realized if I could prevent him, in so doing, from appearing at all.

(*Selected Essays* [Faber & Faber, 1932], pp. 128 ff.)

He refuses to accept the positions of Middleton Murry or Wyndham Lewis or Lytton Strachey. But he finds them preferable to the positions of Coleridge or Swinburne or Dowden, in the sense that new errors are preferable to old errors. Error seems to be all that he sees available: 'there are very few generalizations that can be applied to the whole of Shakespeare's work' (ibid., p. 131).

In so far as the hypothesis of Seneca's influence is applied to Shakespeare it seems purely destructive of what has traditionally been supposed to be the grandeur or effectiveness of his work. The famous passage in which Eliot describes Othello 'cheering himself up' in his final speech is presented as if it is praise: 'I do not believe that any writer has ever exposed this *bovarysme*, the human will to see things as they are not, more clearly than Shakespeare' (ibid., p. 131). But the praise undercuts the whole mode of the play—as is made more crudely obvious in F. R. Leavis's extension of Eliot's perception in 'Diabolic intellect and the noble hero'. One is reminded that Eliot had said in a footnote to the *Hamlet* essay of eight years earlier, 'I have never by the way seen a cogent refutation of Thomas Rymer's objections to *Othello*'.

The *Hamlet* essay itself is equally oblique in its attack on Shakespeare. Eliot had here the stalking-horse of J. M. Robertson's disintegration of *Hamlet*, and behind this he could shoot the arrows of his discontent. One can see the advantage to Eliot of Robertson's wholesale attribution of the machinery and theatricality of the play to other hands, for this enables him to say: 'We find Shakespeare's *Hamlet* not in the action, not in any quotations that we might select, so much as in an unmistakable tone which is unmistakably not in the earlier play' (ibid., p. 145). What is left after the Robertsonian deductions, the 'unmistakable tone', brings Shakespeare's work within the orbit of the Symbolist aesthetic; for unmistakable tone is what unifies the 'tone poems' of the Symbolists. It brings Shakespeare's *Hamlet* into direct comparison with the Hamlet of Eliot's poetic model, Laforgue. And in these terms 'the play is most certainly an artistic failure'. If what is Shakespearian in *Hamlet* is, as Robertson says, 'Utter sickness of heart, revealing itself in pessimism [which] is again and again dramatically obtruded as if to set us feeling that for a heart so crushed revenge is no remedy' (*The Problem of 'Hamlet'* [Allen & Unwin, 1919], p. 73), then Eliot is justified in assuming that 'the Hamlet of Laforgue is an adolescent; the Hamlet of Shakespeare is not, he has not that explanation and excuse' (*Selected Essays,*

p. 146). The play in this case lacks a unifying focus, a symbol. Such is the burden of Eliot's celebrated complaint that Gertrude fails to provide an 'objective correlative'. The function of a symbol is to mediate and 'objectify' the emotion which attaches to it; Gertrude fails in this for both Hamlet and Shakespeare: she is neither the Freudian mother nor the aesthetic symbol. Another way of saying the same thing is to point out that she is not the Amy of *The Family Reunion*. It is a pity she should be thought of as trying to be.

More positive light on Eliot's attitude towards Shakespeare is cast by the general essays on poetic drama he was writing in this period. He had been seeking, it is clear, to formulate a notion of poetic drama that would liberate him from the degenerate Shakespearian tradition which turned up in the plays of Tennyson or Browning or Swinburne, or in the more recent work of Stephen Phillips—plays in which the poetry is a padded overlay applied to a dramatic structure already sufficient in its prose meaning. The enemy here is not the degenerate poetry but, as for Arthur Symons and other Symbolist critics, the assumption that the prose meaning is the essential core of the poetic presentation: 'The great vice of English drama from Kyd to Galsworthy has been that its aim of realism was unlimited' (ibid., p. 111). 'Unlimited' here means not contained by any 'form or rhythm imposed upon the world of action' (p. 112), not controlled by any consistent stylization or convention:

Shakespeare like all his contemporaries was aiming in more than one direction ... It is essential that a work of art should be self-consistent, that an artist should consciously or unconsciously draw a circle beyond which he does not trespass ... an abstraction from life is a necessary condition to the creation of the work of art.   (p. 111)

Art defends its autonomy from the standards of the real world (the desirability of heroines, the just-like-me quality of heroes) by the strictness of its stylization. And lacking this discipline, 'a play of Shakespeare's and a play of Henry Arthur Jones's are essentially of the same type, the difference being that Shakespeare is very much greater and Mr Jones very much more skilful' (p. 114).

What is meant by 'the limitations of art' is, I think, well expressed by the plays of another Symbolist poet writing at the time these pronouncements were being made, W. B. Yeats. Yeats's 'plays for dancers', derived from the highly stylized 'noble plays of Japan', represent a mode cleanly separate from that of Henry Arthur Jones. Yeats had of course anticipated Eliot's discontent with a poetic drama tied to 'the daily mood' and, like him, objected to the sense of dramatic possibilities presented by journalist criticism:

One dogma of the printed criticism is that if a play does not contain definite character, its constitution is not strong enough for the stage, and that the dramatic moment is always the contest of character with character. In poetical drama there is, it is held, an antithesis between character and lyric poetry, for lyric poetry—however much it moves you when read out of a book—can, as these critics think, but encumber the action. Yet when we go back a few centuries and enter the great periods of drama, character grows less and sometimes disappears, and there is much lyric feeling.

('The Tragic Theatre' [1910], in *Essays and Introductions* [Macmillan, 1961], pp. 239 ff.)

Against the practices of the modern stage Yeats summons the image of a 'Byzantine' art: 'ideal form, a symbolism handled by the generations, a mask from whose eyes the disembodied looks, a style that remembers many masters that it may escape contemporary suggestion' (p. 243). Yeats's rhapsodic critical style hardly allowed him to formulate a general attitude toward Shakespeare. He recognized great moments (Timon's death) but he did not approach the larger problem of accommodating the actual plays to Byzantium. And his own plays are too far from Shakespeare to suggest any connection; they are too exotic in mode and too remote from any conceivable public.

The only play by Eliot which bears a direct relationship to these Symbolist ideals is *Sweeney Agonistes* (1926), the only play he wrote in the period when he was formulating the attitudes outlined above. The fact that the conventions of *Sweeney Agonistes* are derived from a popular area of entertainment should not lead us to suppose that Eliot has abandoned the purism of the Symbolist aesthetic. Bernard

Bergonzi has pointed out to me a revealing comment on the music hall made by Eliot in 1921. Writing his 'London Letter' in the *Dial* for 21 June, Eliot speaks of Ethel Levey,

> our best revue comedienne . . . She is the most aloof and impersonal of personalities: indifferent, rather than contemptuous, towards the audience; her appearance and movement are of an extremely modern type of beauty   . she plays for herself rather than for the audience.

Eliot's admiration for the music hall is obviously close to his admiration for the Russian ballet. Both demonstrate artistic impersonality in an art form which is screened from the destructive disorder of real life by rigid or ritualized conventions. *Sweeney Agonistes* is of course a fragment; but it seems unlikely that Eliot could ever have developed it into an easily accessible structure. It is typical of the Symbolist aesthetic that what is defined is the mask, the lyric mode, the circle of art, the unmistakable tone; what is undefined is the developing interest which might hold an audience in a theatre. Before Eliot wrote his first generally performable play (*Murder in the Cathedral*, 1935) he had modified—and we might think he had to modify—his sense of the aesthetics of the theatre and his attitude to Shakespeare.

In the Dante essay of 1929 we hear that

> we do not understand Shakespeare from a single reading, and certainly not from a single play. There is a relation between the various plays of Shakespeare, taken in order; and it is a work of years to venture even one individual interpretation of the pattern in Shakespeare's carpet.   (*Selected Essays*, p. 245)

Two new approaches to Shakespeare appear here together. One is the idea of the *oeuvre*, the whole life's work, which gives Shakespeare a weight comparable to Dante's. The other is the concept of 'the figure in the carpet', the sense of a unifying pattern below the level of explicit statement, so woven into the texture of the work that it cannot be extracted, but which need not disrupt a surface realism.

Both these ideas appear again, considerably developed, in the preface which Eliot wrote for G. Wilson Knight's *The Wheel of Fire* (Oxford University Press, 1930), an essay central to any view of Eliot's Shakespeare criticism. Here he explicitly disavows the 'pure prejudice' which had led him in the 1927 'Shakespeare and the stoicism of Seneca' to deny philosophical interest to Shakespeare. He corrects his earlier assumption by pointing to 'the pattern below the level of "plot" and "character"' with which Wilson Knight's 'interpretation' is concerned. The rag-bag surface philosophy of the Elizabethans can in fact be defended by invoking Henry James's figure in the carpet: 'they do seem, the best of Shakespeare's contemporaries, to have more or less faint or distinct patterns' (*The Wheel of Fire*, p. xiii). One play, however, he says of *The Revenger's Tragedy*, 'does not make a pattern . . . by work of art I mean here rather the work of one artist as a whole' (p. xv). There is also, we should notice, a switch of special attention to a new area of Shakespeare. The force of Wilson Knight's work (as of another book which anticipated him, Colin Still's *Shakespeare's Mystery Play*) is most obvious when we group the 'last plays' together, and then perhaps it is felt in *Pericles* above all. The 'important and very serious recurrences of mood and theme' (p. xvii) give to 'these strange plays' a meaning which is not at all discursive, but which is similar in its impersonal and non-realistic mode to the 'meaning' presented by a Symbolist poem. Eliot's own *Marina* (1930) reflects the same sense of the Symbolist potential of *Pericles*. *Marina* is not only concerned with the discovery of life and meaning at the end of search, but with the knowledge that such 'discovery' involves forgetting no less than remembering, the realization of a pattern which has always been there but which can never be isolated from the experience and given abstract formulation:

> I made this, I have forgotten
> And remember . . .
> Made this unknowing, half-conscious, unknown, my own

Pericles's recovery of the pattern which had always been there might almost serve as a symbol of Eliot's discovery of the Symbolist Shakespeare who had, in a sense, always been there.

The revaluation of the last plays as Symbolist masterpieces is one of the great achievements of twentieth-century Shakespeare criticism. But the mode of criticism which discovered the pattern of the last plays could not stop at this point. *The*

Wheel of Fire is concerned with 'Shakespeare's sombre tragedies', and it outlines a mode of reading which can be applied to all the plays. What Wilson Knight calls 'interpretation' derives from a more or less visionary response to the whole of the artist's work, the 'dominating atmosphere' of the plays rather than the mechanics of plot or character. At this level of response one's attention is guided by 'a direct personal symbol growing out of the dominating atmosphere'; to seek to resolve this vision into logic or motivation is the Bergsonian error of seeking to stop the process in order to look at its working. Wilson Knight's reconstruction of the plays is not along the lines of the 'temporal' structures of Ibsenite dramaturgy, but in the 'spatial' terms of Eliot's 'patterns below the level of plot and character', where all the material is simultaneously present, as that of an Imagist poem is said to be. These patterns have come increasingly to be understood as made up of recurrent imagery and thematic interests. Shakespeare criticism has, since the 1930s, been increasingly concentrated on this point. Of course factors other than the Symbolist concern for aesthetic autonomy are involved. The Freudian and post-Freudian demonstration of man's pattern-making capacities, at levels well below the conscious, pushes criticism in the same direction. But it is interesting to note how dominant the Symbolist concern has become. When Caroline Spurgeon prepared her card index of Shakespeare's imagery, it seems to have been her primary aim to discover hidden truths about the mind of Shakespeare rather than the image-structures of his plays. But so strong was the desire to find that Shakespeare's plays were Symbolist, like Noh plays—at least as Pound described Noh plays, 'gathered about one image'—that her work was at once taken over for aesthetic rather than biographical purposes. Cleanth Brooks has remarked: 'perhaps her interest in classifying and cataloguing the imagery of the plays has obscured for her some of the larger and more important relationships. At any rate . . . she has realized only a part of the potentialities of her discovery' (*The Well Wrought Urn* [Reynal & Hitchcock, 1947], pp. 30 ff.). The larger and more important relationships that Brooks refers to are those that might be judged to support and unify the plays.

The concentration on imagery is only the most obvious part of a new concern with poetry as the essential element in a Shakespeare play. But Eliot did not dwell on his perception long enough to develop this point. He was already, in his Harvard lectures of 1932–3 (printed as *The Use of Poetry and the Use of Criticism* [Harvard University Press, 1933]), moving to new explorations of his interests, and these bring him still closer to the actual theatre and the facts of social communication: 'The ideal medium for poetry, to my mind, and the most direct means of social "usefulness" for poetry, is the theatre' (p. 153). This means some compromise with those old enemies of the Symbolist position, the 'discursive' elements, plot and character; but eventually unification by 'unmistakable tone' inside 'the circle of art' is not irremediably lost:

In a play of Shakespeare you get several levels of significance. For the simplest auditors there is the plot, for the more thoughtful the character and conflict of character, for the more literary the words and phrasing, for the more musically sensitive the rhythm, and for auditors of greater sensitiveness and understanding a meaning which reveals itself gradually (p. 153).

In these terms Shakespeare's plays are rather like Eliot's own plays, a point made obvious by the passage following. Both authors accept a theatrical mode already available in contemporary entertainment (in Eliot's case the drawing-room comedy, in Shakespeare's the revenge play, the romance, and so on). But the real power lies not in the inherited mode but in 'something else', in 'a pattern below the level of plot and character': 'The genuine poetic drama must, at its best, observe all the regulations of the plain drama, but will weave them organically . . . into a much richer design' (introduction to *The Wheel of Fire*, p. xviii). Shakespeare is now 'the rarest of dramatic poets, in that each of his characters is most nearly adequate both to the requirements of the real world and to those of the poet's world' (ibid., p. xviii). Eliot seems to be concerned, in this phase of his criticism, to find a way of describing Shakespeare which will make his plays anticipations of the yet unwritten *Family Reunion* and *Cocktail Party*. He is thinking in terms of an actual society and an actual theatre, not in terms of analyses which will take the reader through the text of a Shakespeare play. Here the mainstream of modern Shakespeare criticism has failed to follow him. For, as they have succumbed to the Symbolist image of Shakespeare, critics have moved further and further away from a language appropriate to the theatre. Wilson Knight has, throughout his life, been deeply involved in theatrical enterprises, but his mode of 'spatial' interpretation belongs especially, perhaps exclusively, to the student's *reading* of a text, comparing different effects of minute detail, going backwards in order to check relationships. In the New Criticism the plays have become poems, approachable by the method now considered particularly appropriate to poems—close stylistic analysis.

It is a further point that most critics who have dealt in this revaluation of Shakespeare have been concerned with pedagogic method. Eliot was not. He remained content to use the Symbolist vocabulary of 'meaning', 'pattern', even 'secret' without defining what these implied about particular plays. Others have felt the need (for the sake of their pupils) to be more precise. If what unifies plays is a pattern below the level of the explicit, one is likely to be asked to show this pattern in operation, to trace or define it, and even to say what it tells about the content of the play. Those who refuse this demand are likely to seem evasive; those who succumb to it probably betray the aesthetic they derive from. For the aesthetic Image does not 'stand for' a meaning, it only evokes it. If the critic is too explicit he will hear that 'generations have known this about Shakespeare without card-indexing his images'; if he is more evasive he will be told, 'these patterns are not really there; they are not in the play; they are only in the over-heated brain of the critic himself'. This latter has been a common response to Wilson Knight; for Knight has on the whole avoided anything other than the vaguest outline of a system. He himself has said: 'The finest commentary will always leave the work of art more mysterious than it was before' (*Essays in Criticism*, iii [1953], 390). His sense of the need to avoid abstraction from the work itself led him to write: 'An imaginative interpretation will always be interwoven with numerous quotations. By the number of such quotations all interpretation must, to a large extent, be judged' (*The Imperial Theme* [Oxford University Press, 1931], p. 19). But he has himself indulged very little in the detailed reading that this would seem to imply.

L. C. Knights, Derek Traversi, John Crowe Ransom, and Cleanth Brooks have sought to avoid both abstraction and realism and what, on the other hand, might be thought the irresponsibility of Wilson Knight by a more purely inductive method. In *How Many Children Had Lady Macbeth* (Gordon Fraser, 1933), L. C. Knights describes the ideal procedure:

> How should we read Shakespeare? We start with so many lines of verse on a printed page which we read as we should read any other poem. We have to elucidate the meaning (using Dr Richards's fourfold definition) and to unravel ambiguities; we have to estimate the kind and quality of the imagery and determine the precise degree of evocation of particular figures; we have to allow full weight to each word, exploring its 'tentacular roots,' and to determine how it controls and is controlled by the rhythmic movement of the passage in which it occurs. In short, we have to decide exactly why the lines 'are so and not otherwise.' As we read other factors come into play. The lines have a cumulative effect. 'Plot,' aspect of 'character,' recurrent 'themes' and 'symbols'—all 'precipitates from the memory'—help to determine our reaction at a given point . . .
> (reprinted in *Explorations* [Chatto and Windus, 1946], p. 16)

Such an inductive approach seeks to protect the play's explicit subject matter from extra-aesthetic responses, by starting at the point of maximum aesthetic engagement and only subsequently taking up the discursive elements. But it is very doubtful if a *play* can be so protected. Even when we only read it—and this is the only kind of response with which Knights is concerned—it is doubtful if close attention to lyric-length passages will by itself take us very far. We rely on stage directions, on our past experience of the real theatre, on the counterpointing of the silent figures against the speaking ones, to tell us what is intended, what kind of listening is appropriate. Otherwise we shall never come from the texture of the trees to the shape of the forest. F. R. Leavis offers an interesting parallel attempt to deal inductively with characters. In his essay 'The criticism of Shakespeare's late plays' (1942) he tries to defend his preference for Florizel and Perdita by pointing out that 'Florizel and Perdita are not merely two individual lovers; they are organic elements in the poetry and symbolism of the pastoral scene, and the pastoral scene is an organic part of the whole play' (*The Common Pursuit* [Chatto and Windus, 1952], p. 181). This is however very much an ex post facto induction; it defends the critic from the charge of deserting his system; but it does not correspond to anyone's process of exploring a play, in the theatre or even at home.

The antitheatrical prejudice of the New Critics stems not only from their desire to work, or seem to work, inductively, but also from their tendency to think in terms of the *oeuvre*. This habit has sometimes been presented as a method of rescuing plays which might be thought failures when considered in isolation, such as *Pericles*, or *All's Well*, or *Timon of Athens*. The rescue is, however, a somewhat double-edged process. Inevitably a critical consensus working in this way widens the gap between any performance of a play (and what a theatre critic might say about it) and its literary criticism. It also, I suspect, gives rise to greater directorial tyranny over the very plays it is claiming to rescue. Since what the critics have had to say often seems irrelevant to any theatrical possibilities, the theatre has been left to fashion-crazed inventiveness. The plays have been made 'good' (that is, successful) by methods that have as little to do with their actual dramatic structures as have the critical efforts to extract 'significance'. Shakespeare has had to pay a high price for admission into the Symbolist club.

On the other hand this may be the inescapable price for admission into the modern world. Opposition to the Symbolist Shakespeare has been vociferous, but it has hardly been successful in projecting an alternative that seems more than reactionary. The historical approach to Shakespeare does not escape the charge that its historiography belongs to the nineteenth century. Stoll and Schücking clearly believed that they were escaping from the subjective sentimentality of Victorian attitudes to character into an objective and 'real' world of Elizabethan dramaturgy. But of course they were doing nothing of the kind; the emphases of their 'Elizabethan' world are their own, and often designed in antithesis to what they dislike in their own real world. The final standards they apply are those of their own time, and in particular of their own theatre. Shakespeare's 'primitive' dramaturgy is set in a pattern of progress towards a 'modern' dramaturgy, which is in fact only that of the late nineteenth century. Now, in the age of *Endgame* and *The American Dream*, the theatre of illusion no longer seems a relevant norm for measuring Shakespeare's skills. The theatre of Schücking's 'episodic intensification', of surface brilliances rather than psychological depths, is no longer a historical supposition, but rather a social reality; and in this light it looks very different, not at all primitive, not in the least folksy.

The relationship of Eliot to the other critics discussed in the second half of this essay is rather interesting. At one point (in the *Hamlet* essay of 1919) Eliot takes up a position close to that of Stoll. But whereas Stoll remained fixed in the same polemical attitude throughout his long critical life, Eliot displayed an artist's flexibility and uncommitedness. He moved through a series of attitudes and responses, and virtually invented the twentieth-century Shakespeare in a collection of asides. The academic and systematic critics are still largely engaged in dotting the i's and crossing the t's of what he said in the early thirties. And even at that time he was picking up another, more theatrical, phase of Shakespeare criticism. Certainly the current state of this trade could do with a more theatrical bias. Perhaps even now we may catch up with Mr Eliot's further creative insights and reduce those too to system and teachability.

STRUCTURES

13

Henry IV and the Elizabethan two-part play

Critics who wish to discuss 'unity' in the two parts of *Henry IV*[1] come up against two major difficulties which seem to be inherent in the subject. The first difficulty derives from the historical nature of the material: the critics cannot argue from incompleteness in the story of one history-play and a tendency to point forward to events which may appear in later history-plays; they cannot use this to show a design of relationship between several plays, for history is necessarily incomplete and the dramatist is entitled to point forward to events which his audience knows about, even when he does not think of dramatizing them. This limitation is obvious enough in a general way; Professor Shaaber has already made the point[2] and I shall not elaborate it here. Less obvious is the second inherent difficulty, which derives from the complex nature of the word 'unity'. Critics seem to assume that the 'unity' of *Henry IV* must be a unity such as we find in a long novel, a unity based on continuity (Dr Dover Wilson actually calls it 'unity and continuity'),[3] in which character and/or events develop steadily, moving through incidents which

[First published in *The Review of English Studies*, v (1954).]

1. See the list in the New Variorum *2 Henry IV*, ed. M. A. Shaaber (1940), pp. 558–63. I am concerned here more especially with work done since 1940; i.e. with J. Dover Wilson, *The Fortunes of Falstaff* (Cambridge, 1943), pp. 4, 90 f.; New Cambridge *1 Henry IV*, ed. J. Dover Wilson (1946), pp. x ff.; E. M. W. Tillyard, *Shakespeare's History Plays* (London, 1944), pp. 264 ff.; M. A. Shaaber, 'The unity of *Henry IV*', *Quincy Adams Memorial Studies*, ed. J. G. McManaway *et al.* (1948), pp. 217–27; H. E. Cain, 'Further light on the relation of *1* and *2 Henry IV*', *Shakespeare Quarterly*, iii (1952), 21–38. I am indebted to Mr J. C. Maxwell for supplying me with this last reference and for pertinent criticism of the whole paper.
2. Shaaber, 'The unity of *Henry IV*', p. 219.
3. *The Fortunes of Falstaff*, p. 4.

derive their importance from the contribution they make to this development—the unity of *Clarissa* or *Anna Karenina*. The presupposition that the unity of *Henry IV* could be of this kind does not, however, seem to be justified, and both Mr Shaaber and Mr Cain have demonstrated that the 'unity and continuity' which Dr Dover Wilson and Dr Tillyard find in *Henry IV* is based on inadequate or illusory evidence. The points made by Mr Shaaber and Mr Cain bear, however, against 'continuity' rather than 'unity'; the sensitive reader who continues to detect 'unity' in *Henry IV* can be justified if 'unity' can be found to have a meaning (appropriate to Shakespeare) which is dissociated from the untenable 'continuity'.

It has been demonstrated in a number of recent studies[4] that the 'unity' of a large number of Elizabethan plays is a 'unity of theme' rather than a 'unity of story': scenes and acts do not lead on from one another as they do in Ibsen; rather they are organized to reveal different levels of the theme, shuttling back and forward in time, and by repetitions of phrases, scenes, and episodes illustrating the interpenetration of single vision and diverse experience. I contend that the connection between the two parts of *Henry IV* formalizes a unity of this kind: the unity of the play is that of a diptych, in which repetition of shape and design focuses attention on what is parallel in the two parts.

The use of such features to unify a two-part play does not seem to have found any justification in the critical theory of the Elizabethan period, but appears to have been conscious to the extent that we can find a technique and a history attached to the form, and it is with these that I shall be concerned in the rest of this paper. Mr Shaaber is quite correct in pointing out that the greater number of surviving two-part plays of the Elizabethan period are not unified in any way.[5]

4. See the articles by R. A. Law, in *S.P.* xxiv (1927), *P.M.L.A.* lx (1945), *Texas University Studies* (1929); cf. H. T. Price, 'Mirror-scenes in Shakespeare', *Adams Studies* (Washington, 1948), pp. 101–13, M. C. Bradbrook, *Themes and Conventions of Elizabethan Tragedy* (Cambridge, 1935).

5. In the case of historical chronicles like *If you know not me* or *The troublesome reign of John, King of England* (perhaps Shakespeare's *Henry VI* should be placed here, as far as structure is concerned), mythological chronicles like Heywood's *Silver Age* and *Brazen Age* (which Henslowe calls 1st and 2nd parts

There is, however, one small group of Elizabethan two-part plays which have a method of unification in common. If we examine these plays, we uncover an approach to the construction of *Henry IV* which, though it does not tell us anything about Shakespeare's original intentions, does give us information about his later view of the completed structure.

In examining this group it is well to start with the play which shows the form at its most exact (though the text we have is mutilated)—Chapman's *The Conspiracie and Tragedie of Charles Duke of Byron, Marshall of France. Acted lately in two playes, at the Black-Friars . . . 1608.* The two parts seem to have been designed together; they share one prologue which covers both parts. The French ambassador, recording his intervention and the subsequent ban, refers to the matter of the two plays under one heading: 'the

of Hercules) and moral chronicles like *Promos and Cassandra*, the only justification for the second part would seem to be that given by Whetstone: '. . . this Discourse of *Promos* and *Cassandra*; which for the rarenesse (and the needeful knowledge) of the necessary matter contained therein (to make the actions appear more liuely) I deuided the whole history into two Commedies, for that, *Decorum* vsed, it would not be conuayed in one.' In these cases the different parts represent successive episodes (or series of episodes) in a history, without any real attempt to give each part a separate point or centre. The simplest form of continuation which does involve this would seem to be that which shows the rise of some great person in Part One, and his downfall in Part Two. This formula is frequently used, however, without giving anything like unity to the parts. Thus Heywood shows the rise to power of Mrs Shore in Part One of *Edward IV* and devotes Part Two to her downfall, but Mrs Shore does not in fact appear till the fourth act of Part One, and there is no parallelism in the episodes. In Chettle and Munday's *Downfall and Death of Robert, Earl of Huntingdon*, the reconciliation at the end of Part One would allow the dramatists to renew a parallel conflict in Part Two, but the renewed conflict and the death of Robin Hood is in fact completed by the end of the first act of Part Two, and the second part is in fact concerned with the history of Matilda, for which a separate exposition is provided. In Dekker's *The Honest Whore* we find a two-part play which is more nearly unified than any of these: Part One shows Bellamira converted to virtue by Hippolito and eventually settled in virtue by her betrothal to Matheo; in Part Two we find Hippolito trying to reverse the conversion. There are some structural similarities between the two parts—both plays end in places of imprisonment (Part One in Bedlam, Part Two in Bridewell) where the plot is untied and the inmates paraded before the nobles—but there is, in *The Honest Whore*, nothing of the detailed parallelism of the plays I discuss below. Sometimes the connection seems to be ethical rather than structural, as between Chapman's *Bussy D'Ambois* and *The Revenge of Bussy D'Ambois*, where we find traditional 'noblesse' set against Stoic 'noblesse'. Clermont D'Ambois is, of course, a parallel figure to Bussy, and the course of his career—temptation, ambush, and death—is much the same. There is little or no parallelism of structure, however, to set forth the ethical parallel.

history of the Duke of Byron', i.e. as a theatrical unit. If in *Byron* we have a play designed as a two-part unit, how did Chapman organize his material to produce an effect of unity? The means can be seen most clearly in a tabular presentation:

Byron I	*Byron II*
ACT I	
Byron is presented as the coming man in a future of treason. Henry is shown (banishing Lafin) as still struggling to consolidate his monarchy. His lack of an heir is emphasized.	Henry is presented as the coming man in a future of peace and security. He is shown as confident, expecting Lafin, now spying on Byron. The Dauphin is brought in to emphasize Henry's grip on the future.
Byron (in Brussels) is tempted into treason by Picote.	Byron is tempted into mock-treason by Henry's spy Lafin.
ACT II	
Byron is further implicated in treason by Lafin, acting as Savoy's agent. Henry, hearing of the temptation in Brussels, seeks to temporize by sending Byron to England; drawn by Savoy, he contributes to the breach by praising himself rather than Byron.	Henry, hearing of Byron's treasonable moves from his agent Lafin, sends for him in order to prevent his plots. *A masque is staged showing the conflict between Temperance (Henry's queen) and Liberality (his mistress).*[6]
ACT III	
Byron decides to revolt; Lafin brings him to Savoy, who encourages his treason with flattery and by describing Henry's dispraise.	Byron preaches treason; sent for by Henry he at first refuses, but is persuaded to go by Lafin's assurances.
Byron consults an astrologer and is warned of his coming execution. He refuses to accept this prophecy.	Byron is warned of the danger but insists on returning to court. Henry tries to make him confess his treasons, but in vain.

6. The italicized portions of the synopsis refer to scenes which seem to have been altered or abridged.

ACT IV

It is reported how Byron's pride and ambition were rebuked in England. He is reported to have accepted these rebukes.	Byron is advised, implored, and commanded to humble himself and confess his treasons; he refuses and is arrested.

ACT V

Not parallel.

The method on which Chapman relies to secure unity of effect is obviously a method of parallelism. Though the text we have is mutilated, it is clear enough that Part Two is designed to repeat the main outlines of Part One, though now the movement is one of descent and deprivation, not (as in Part One) of ascent and aggregation. The character of the aspiring hero remains the same, but circumstances have altered: in Part One he was able to have things go the way he wanted them; in Part Two circumstances do not yield to him in the same way; he struggles against odds and eventually is brought to nought. The play thus works out a tragic pattern of achievement and defeat in ten acts. It brings an essentially unstable situation (in which irreconcilables are opposed) to a point of rest at the end of Part One, so that the audience can leave the theatre with some kind of resolution in their minds. This resolution, however, suggests a truce rather than a ratified peace-treaty; the conflict is suspended, not ended. Part Two also can stand by itself; it is provided with a separate exposition in which the relevant facts from Part One are summarized; the two parts, however, combine to form a more complete and coherent unit than either part in isolation.

This structure in *Byron* Chapman may have developed from the more rudimentary form of the same thing that is found in Marlowe's *Tamburlaine*. If this were so it would certainly fit in with what we know of Chapman's discipleship to Marlowe. Like Byron, Tamburlaine is an aspiring man who drives all before him in Part One, so that the peak of glory, conquest, and stability is achieved at the end of Part

One. I accept Professor Duthie's suggestion[7] that the psychological battle against Zenocrate's beauty in the First Part of *Tamburlaine*, Act v, scene ii, is the greatest of Tamburlaine's battles. Having reconciled the warring and ultimately incompatible principles represented by Zenocrate and himself, peace and war, beauty and valour, he achieves the kind of stability that Chapman represents in the more political atmosphere of *Byron* by the reconciliation of Byron and the king: the audience can go home with some kind of resolution in their minds.[8] Part Two is then integrated with Part One by means of a structure which repeats many of the main features of Part One:

Tamburlaine I	*Tamburlaine II*
ACT I	
Confusion of the Persian monarchy shown. Tamburlaine, in contrast, is resolute and dignified—his first successes.	The enemies of Tamburlaine make sensible and dignified plans to oppose him. The corruptness of one of Tamburlaine's guards and the effeteness of one of his sons is shown.
ACT II	
Tamburlaine takes advantage of the confusion in the Persian court to seize the crown.	Tamburlaine's enemies triumph over treason. Zenocrate dies.
ACT III	

Preparations for the battle against Bajazeth. Zenocrate confesses her love for Tamburlaine.
    Tamburlaine defeats and captures Bajazeth.
	Preparations for the battle against Bajazeth's supporters. Zenocrate is buried.
	    Battle is joined against Bajazeth's supporters.

7. G. I. Duthie, 'The dramatic structure of Marlowe's "Tamburlaine the Great", Parts I and II', *Essays and Studies*, London, 1948, pp. 101–26. I find that many of my remarks on *Tamburlaine* have been anticipated by Professor Gardner in *M.L.R.* xxxvii (1942).

8. In this connection the wording of l. 2311 is notable: 'For Tamburlaine takes *truce* with all the world' (my italics).

ACT IV

Tamburlaine exults over Bajazeth. The Soldan and Arabia march against him.	Tamburlaine defeats and exults over the Turkish kings. He stabs his son.

ACT V

Tamburlaine reduces Damascus. In love with both Zenocrate and valour he defeats her father and then spares him. He prepares to marry Zenocrate.	Tamburlaine reduces Babylon. He defeats Callapine while fighting at the same time against death. He dies.

As in Chapman, the parallel placing of incidents is used here to unify a structure which reverses its direction in the second part. The stability (psychological and territorial) which Tamburlaine built up in Part One is destroyed; he is never again so happy or so secure; the initiative passes to others; his battles are now defensive battles, but he cannot defend his family or himself against the power of Death.

I am aware that critics have normally regarded the second part of *Tamburlaine* as only vaguely related to the first part; the prologue to Part Two suggests a catchpenny origin for the sequel:

> The generall welcomes Tamburlain receiu'd,
> When he arriued last vpon our stage,
> Hath made our Poet pen his second part,

but it does not follow that Part Two is a botched job. Marlowe has certainly constructed his Part Two in such a way that he has produced a two-part play which is unified in structure if not always in effect—the megalomania of Tamburlaine is not made as clear as was his *virtù*; the defeat of Part Two does not balance the achievement of Part One. The parallel of *Byron* suggests that the structural excellencies of *Tamburlaine* did not pass unnoticed in its own day, and that in this, as in so many other matters, Marlowe was the grand original of the later dramatists.

One other two-part tragedy of the period shows traces of the same structure (derived probably from *Tamburlaine*)— Marston's *Antonio and Mellida*. *Antonio and Mellida*, like the two plays I have already considered, shows a feud between two opponents, ultimately incompatible, in this case the dukes of Venice and Genoa. Part One, amid a great deal of satirical comment on court life, shows the triumph of Piero Sforza, Duke of Venice, over the Genoese ducal family; in Act v a sudden reconciliation is achieved, and Antonio, the heir of Genoa, is betrothed to Mellida, Piero Sforza's daughter. Part Two has a structure parallel to that of Part One, dealing again with Piero's persecution of the Genoese family, this time by 'policy' instead of arms:

Antonio and Mellida I	*Antonio and Mellida II*
ACT I	
The Genoese having been defeated by the Venetians, Piero triumphs and Antonio despairs.	Having killed Andrugio and dishonoured Mellida, Piero triumphs while Antonio despairs.
ACT II	
Antonio, disguised as an Amazon, reveals himself to Mellida; they plan to fly.	Antonio meets the imprisoned Mellida and resolves to fight Piero by dissimulation.
ACT III	
Andrugio, exiled, with a price on his head, puts his trust in stoical fortitude. Antonio and Mellida flee from the court.	The ghost of Andrugio commands Antonio to revenge. He charges him to fly from the court.
ACT IV	
Passion and stoical resolve alternate in both Andrugio and Antonio. Mellida is recaptured by Piero. Andrugio plans to recoup his fortunes by a final act of stoicism.	Antonio, disguised as a fool, contrasts his passion with the fool's invulnerability. Mellida is condemned by Piero and (by error) dies. Antonio and others plan a final revenge on Piero.
ACT V	
Reconciliation in a masque.	Revenge achieved in a masque.

Here, as in *Tamburlaine*, the first part culminates in betrothal to an enemy's daughter, while Part Two shows this lady taken away from the hero by death. The structure is, however, less clear-cut than in Marlowe (let alone Chapman) since there is no single figure whose rise and fall dominates the play. What Marston seems to have attempted is to fit the *Spanish Tragedy* kind of revenge intrigue into the framework of *Tamburlaine*; and the result cannot be said to be very happy. *Antonio and Mellida* provides a good example of the bastard unity which results when the method of parallelism is handled ineptly. Unity of character is not obtained, not so much because of any change of characterization between the first and second parts, but because the characters are never realized distinctly. Unity of plot is damaged by clumsiness (typical of Marston) in handling the transition from Part One to Part Two. The difficulty of transition need not, however, lead to the conclusion of Mr H. Harvey Wood:

Although the two plays were entered and published together, it is necessary to postulate a considerable interval between their composition; an interval sufficient to allow for a complete change in the author's conception of the plot and characterisation. *Antonio and Mellida* ends with an accumulation of spectacular postures and devices, on a note of extravagant happiness and reconciliation. The opening lines of *Antonio's Revenge* betray a grim revision of the situation. There is nothing in the last scenes of *Antonio and Mellida* to suggest that the magnanimity of Piero is feigned, or the reconciliation insincere. But the opening lines of the *Revenge* reveal a whole tangled network of intrigue and rivalry. . . .[9]

The evidence does not seem to justify this. The two prologues answer one another as masks of comedy and tragedy, so that we need not presume any 'grim revision'; they are constructed on somewhat parallel lines so that the 'wreath of pleasure, and delicious sweetes' of the one is answered by 'the rawish danke of clumzie winter' in the other, the 'woorthlesse present' by the 'waightie passion', the 'That with a straine of fresh invention / She might presse out the raritie of Art' by the 'That with unused paize of stile and sense, / We might waigh massy in judicious scale'. Again, the transition from

9. *The Plays of John Marston*, ed. H. Harvey Wood (Edinburgh, 1934–9), I. xxii.

Part One to Part Two in *Antonio and Mellida* is not basically different from that in *Byron*. At the end of Part One of *Byron* there is nothing to suggest that Byron's reconciliation is feigned, nor would any such suggestion be theatrically justified. The play ends on a note of equanimity: 'With him go all our faults and from us fly / With all his counsel, all conspiracy', though the beginning of Part Two reveals a new network of intrigue: 'Byron fall'n in so trait'rous a relapse, / Alleg'd for our ingratitude.' There is in both plays equally an unexpectedness about the reconciliation which ends Part One; this unexpectedness is the sole excuse Chapman uses to justify the new beginning of Part Two; there is no reason to presume that this results from any 'considerable interval' between the parts of *Byron*, and there is no need to presume that it springs from any such cause in Marston. Where Marston does differ from Chapman is in the brusquerie of his invention. He allows no impression of time passed to soften the transition from comedy to tragedy, since only the time of the wedding arrangements can be allowed to divide the two parts; hence the beginning of Part Two gives the impression of a morning-after-the-night-before and not the desired effect of a tragic reopening of the old conflict. Finally we should notice that the one induction to the two plays refers to both of them:

... I have heard that those persons ... that are but slightly drawn in this Comedie, should receive more exact accomplishment in a second Part: which, if this obtaine gratious acceptance, meanes to try his fortune.[1]

This suggests that though the second part was not originally billed to follow Part One, it was written, or at least planned, at the time Part One was first staged. No more than a suggestion can, of course, be derived from such evidence, but there seems to be a sufficient number of small points to make it probable that Marston's failure to achieve in *Antonio and Mellida* the unity of *Byron* is due to an impatience of technique rather than to any different conception of the relationship between the parts.

We are now in a position to see that such unity as we can

1. *Antonio and Mellida* (Malone Society Reprint), ll. 148–52.

find in Elizabethan two-part plays depends on a parallel setting-out of the incidents rather than on any picking-up of all the threads of Part One. The plays we have examined all use this method, with a greater or lesser degree of success, and it is the only method I have been able to find. Does Shakespeare use this method in *Henry IV*,[2] or is that play unique among Elizabethan two-part plays in possessing a different or more complex organization of its parts?

It was pointed out as long ago as 1877 by Dr König and more recently by Mr Shaaber[3] that the two parts of *Henry IV* are built up on parallel lines, but neither author has noted the full extent of this parallelism, so I shall set out the two parts to illustrate this:

1 Henry IV	*2 Henry IV*
ACT I	
Sc. i. The disruption of peace by rebellion is hinted at.	News of Shrewsbury is given, with news of a second rebellion—in the north.
Sc. ii. Poins details the plan of the Gadshill robbery; Poins and Hal plan a comic defeat for Falstaff.	Falstaff prepares to join the army; he is rebuked by the Chief Justice.
Sc. iii. Turned off by the king, Hotspur, Worcester, and Northumberland plan their revolt.	The Northern conspirators meet and plan their revolt.
ACT II	
Sc. i. Preparations are made for the Gadshill robbery.	Falstaff is arrested at the instance of Mrs Quickly, but manages to escape.
Sc. ii. Falstaff robs the travellers; Hal and Poins prepare the fun of II. iv by their counter-robbery.	Hal and Poins plan the fun of II. iv.

2. Dover Wilson refers to 2 and 3 *Henry VI* as a 'two-part drama' (New Cambridge *1 Henry VI*, p. xv), but I do not find any structural similarity of the kind I am discussing here between any of the *Henry VI* plays.

3. W. König, 'Shakespeares Königsdramen, ihr Zusammenhang und ihr Werth für die Bühne', *Shakespeare-Jahrbuch*, xii (1877), 245 f.; Shaaber, 'The unity of *Henry IV*', pp. 221 f.

Sc. iii. Harry Percy and his wife discuss the revolt; he sets out.	Northumberland and his wife discuss the revolt; he flees to Scotland.
Sc. iv. The big comic scene: in the Eastcheap tavern the prince mingles with the drawers. Falstaff is discovered in lies, but jests his way out of the discovery. At the end of the scene the outer world breaks in upon the fun.	The big comic scene: in the Eastcheap tavern Falstaff swaggers and blusters till Hal and Poins (disguised as drawers) discover him; he jests his way out of the discovery. At the end of the scene the outer world breaks in upon the fun.

ACT III

Sc. i. The conspirators seal their bonds and prepare to fight.	
Sc. ii. The king reproaches Hal, who promises to amend.	Sc. i. The king mourns his unquiet reign.
Sc. iii. Falstaff quarrels with the hostess, prepares for the war.	Sc. ii. Falstaff recruits in Gloucestershire.

ACT IV

Sc. i. Rebellion suffers setbacks: Northumberland will not join and Glendower cannot.	Northumberland will not join the rebels, who are tricked and defeated.
Sc. ii. Falstaff, on his way to the battlefield, expatiates on the tricks he has employed in recruiting.	(Modern sc. iii—but I take modern scenes i and ii to be continuous.)[4] Falstaff captures Coleville while on his way to the battlefield; he expatiates on the virtues of sack.

Thereafter the structure is not parallel.

Here we find, as in the plays already examined, a structure which shows the relationship between two incompatibles—Rebellion and Order, in the state and in the mind of the

---

4. See the discussion of this point in New Variorum 2 *Henry IV*, pp. 306 f.

prince; the first is subordinated to the second at the end of Part One, but by showing us the preparations of the Archbishop of York and by resurrecting Falstaff from his sham death, Shakespeare keeps his conclusion from being irretrievably final. The incompatibles clash again in Part Two and a final conclusion is only produced when one is destroyed by the other. Both parts have the same design, but in the second we have a change of direction and a different atmosphere. In Part One the prince seems to be fighting through his environment—even if we allow the 'I know you all' soliloquy its fullest force, the general misunderstanding, the preference of Hotspur, not to say Falstaff, remains—so that the process of self-education and self-revelation is a genuine and dramatic struggle. Part Two is more than a feeble repetition of this: though the design is the same, the focus of interest is different. In Part Two the chance of victory by Disorder, either in the state or in the prince's mind, is much more remote; the misunderstandings are less deep-seated and more easily dispelled. In this part there can be little or no doubt that Hal is the hero of a golden future—his defection or ineffectiveness is never a possible feature of the second revolt.

This change of environment can be seen clearly enough if we compare the conclusion of Act II, scene iv, in Part One with the corresponding passage in Part Two. In both parts the fun at Eastcheap is interrupted by news from court; in Part One Hal seems unwilling to respond; he appears to be subdued to the element he works in; he allows Falstaff to dispose of the messenger while he himself continues to unravel the Gadshill plot. His thoughts of Shrewsbury are as near burlesque as they are to the heroic:

> I'll to the court in the morning. We must all
> to the wars, and thy place shall be honourable.
> I'll procure this fat rogue a charge of foot;
> and I know his death will be a march of
> twelve-score. (II. iv. 525–8)

In the environment of Part Two the 'low transformation' from a prince to a prentice is obviously an interlude. As soon as news comes from court Hal translates himself back into his true element:

By heaven, Poins, I feel me much to blame
So idly to profane the precious time,
When tempest of commotion, like the south,
Borne with black vapour, doth begin to melt
And drop upon our bare unarmed heads.
Give me my sword and cloak. Falstaff, good night
(II. iv. 348–53)

The struggle of Part Two is not the struggle of coming-of-age, nor indeed a personal struggle of this kind at all. Its interest is that it draws from the interaction of Rebellion and Order in court and country (the same framework as in Part One) a more abstract and meditative view of kingship. The first part may be said to deal with the question: 'What is the relationship between the princely mind and the common disorder of experience?'; the second part raises a rather different question: 'What is the cost of kingliness in a world of duties rather than achievements?' In most respects the kind of development from Part One to Part Two which Shakespeare devises for his hero is very different from that of Marlowe or Chapman, but the sense of difficulty in sustaining a role achieved at the end of Part One in a world more searching and more severe is the same in all these plays.

In the treatment of national affairs we can see the same pattern of rise and fall we noticed in *Tamburlaine* and *Byron*, things seeming to go well with the rebels in Part One (at least up to Act IV), buoyed as they are by the vigour and youth of Hotspur, but going dubiously and sluggishly against a tide which is never favourable in Part Two. This change is perhaps most obvious in Shakespeare's handling of II. iii in the two parts. In both parts we meet the Percy household here, but in Part One the tone is confident: Hotspur is setting out and is not to be deterred; in Part Two it is Northumberland who is setting out; the tone is lachrymose and backward-looking, and woman's counsel is all too able to deter him from battle.

Falstaff's career also follows the two-part play's normal design of rise and fall; the zenith of his success is reached at the end of Part One, his claim to have killed Hotspur being allowed by the prince. Though his career in Part Two does not show anything like a steady decline, he is never again able to enjoy such prestige and security. He performs a similar feat in Part Two—the capture of Sir John Coleville—but John of Lancaster is a different kind of person from Hal, and the action does not yield similar results. In general he is kept apart from the prince in Part Two, and even when the comic culmination of the play brings them together (in II. iv) he is not allowed here to impose on the prince, to parody the court, or to escape the normal duties or punishments. At the end of Part One his grossest presumption (that he has killed Hotspur) is allowed to pass, but no similar indulgence accompanies his intrusion into high life at the end of Part Two—he is dismissed with contumely. I do not think that an audience which sees the two parts played continuously ought to sense that Falstaff is a different kind of person in Part Two, but certainly it ought to notice that the temper of the world he lives in has become less amenable to his methods. Very different though Byron and Falstaff may be, the comic presumption of the *miles gloriosus* can be treated structurally in much the same way as the ὕβρις of the overgreat servant. Byron and Falstaff are alike in their inability to change their ways, and both proceed directly and blindly through a repetition of the acts of Part One to a purgation by death or dismissal at the end of Part Two.

Though there may not be any exact continuity in *Henry IV*, we see that the word 'unity' can be applied to it, in the limited sense of 'diptych-unity'; that is, the form of the play depends *primarily* on a parallel presentation of incidents (as in the other two-part plays examined here) and only secondarily on a preservation of traits of character or strands of the plot. An absence of continuity in such features cannot be used to prove a lack of unity, for the 'unity' of *Henry IV* does not depend primarily on these factors. There can be no doubt, of course, that the diptych-unity disciplines a greater complexity of material in *Henry IV* than in any of the other 'unified' two-part plays—a sub-plot which merges into the main plot, and a wide range of principal characters—but the methods employed are, in general, the same; it follows that the justification of the word 'unity' must be the same.

The evidence that we have been examining here does not tell us anything about the genesis of *Henry IV*. We see that

Marlowe, in what was presumably a catchpenny sequel, and
Chapman, designing a two-part play from the beginning,
both used the methods of 'unity in duality' to link together
the two parts of their plays. The fact that Shakespeare used
the same methods does not tell us whether he should be
associated with Chapman or with Marlowe. Some of the
arguments used by Shaaber and Cain—'setting the clock
back' at the beginning of Part Two, the unstable conditions
of Elizabethan production, for example—apply to *Byron* not
less than to *Tamburlaine*; therefore they cannot be used to
weigh the evidence either for or against any idea that
Shakespeare planned *Henry IV* from the beginning as a two-
part play. This is not to say that all the evidence advanced by
these scholars must be discounted; indeed I would allow that
enough evidence remains[5] to establish their view that Shakespeare composed *1 Henry IV* without any intention of
composing its sequel. Nevertheless, it seems to me that in pro-
pagating this truth they allow (and so propagate) a false
corollary—the view that the natural alternative to 'unity and
continuity' is 'two plays linked by catch-as-catch-can
methods'.[6] It is as important to see Shakespeare in these plays
as an artist painstakingly concerned about the 'unity' which
was possible and significant within the terms of his art as to
avoid seeing him with intentions he is unlikely to have
possessed.

5. I would single out two points as especially cogent: (1) Cain's argument
from the original entry in the Stationers' Register ('Further Light . . .', pp. 23 f.);
(2) Shaaber's remarks about the two uses of the name 'Bardolph' (Variorum
2 Henry IV, p. 3).
   6. Shaaber, 'The unity of *Henry IV*', p. 226.

14

Shakespeare's earliest tragedies
Titus Andronicus and *Romeo and Juliet*

It is commonly accepted that Shakespeare's earliest essays in
tragic form are *Titus Andronicus* and *Romeo and Juliet*[1]—
accepted, that is, among those who allow that Shakespeare
was responsible for *Titus Andronicus*. But few critics, even
among the accepters, seem willing to go beyond the merely
chronological point to take up the critical consequence:
that we might expect to be able to analyse here an early but
characteristic Shakespearian mode of tragedy.[2] The two plays
are so obviously unlike one another that it is hard even to
think of adding them together to make up any description of
a unified mode. Whatever the reason, it is a clear critical fact

[First published in *Shakespeare Survey* 27 (1974).]
1. The exact chronology of these early plays is too uncertain to bear any
weight of consequential argument. It is worth noticing that modern scholarship
(following E. K. Chambers) has tended to keep the two tragedies within two or
three years of one another; so there is nothing on this side to impede the idea of
a close relationship. I have not included *Richard III* among the 'early tragedies',
though it certainly has a tragic dimension. I have excluded it because I see its
historical content and its role in completing the stretch of chronicle begun in *1
Henry VI* as impediments which effectively prevent it from being regarded as a
straight example of Shakespearian tragic invention. That level of the play which
is not dominated by historical sequence is largely concerned with the dominant
personality of Richard himself. The creation of dominant personalities is not, of
course, to prove uncharacteristic of Shakespeare in his tragic mood; it is, however, an over-tilled field, and in any case is not that with which I am here concerned.
2. The obvious exception to this blanket statement is Nicholas Brooke
(*Shakespeare's Early Tragedies* [London, 1968]). Professor Brooke's brief is,
however, much larger than mine; he includes *Julius Caesar* and *Hamlet* (also
Richard III and *Richard II*) within his survey. Brooke's sense of 'the mode of
tragedy' is also rather different from that pursued here, so that the question of
'early tragedy' can, I believe, be rehandled without culpable repetition.

that these plays are not normally considered together, or even apart, in a description of Shakespearian tragedy. Shakespeare, it is implied, had to throw away this dispersed prentice work, set it against experience rather than achievement, when he began to compose the sequence of truly 'Shakespearian' tragedies beginning with *Julius Caesar* and growing out of the political interests of the English history plays.

These prejudgements bear more heavily against *Titus Andronicus* than *Romeo and Juliet*, for *Romeo* has, whatever its generic implication, the refuge of being a 'well-loved' play, where *Titus* can only be called 'much disliked'. I begin, however, by assuming an equality of interest and importance, taking it that in both plays Shakespeare was writing as well as he knew how. The subsequent reputations of the plays may be thought to tell us more securely about audience preferences in the period between Shakespeare and the present than about the author's intention. My concern in this paper is not with differences of valuation but with the formal similarities and relationships that can be established between the two tragedies.

In making this point I am not, of course, forgetting that *Titus* is the most horrific of Shakespeare's tragedies. To some minds this implies that it is exceptional and that its evidence about Shakespeare's tragic mode is out of court. The idea that true tragedy is essentially about the mental suffering of noble natures, and therefore unbloody, is, however, probably a delusion, based on the social assumptions of a post-Enlightenment society which has shown itself incapable of writing tragedy. The Victorian sub-genre, 'the tragedy of blood', invented to deal with plays like *Titus Andronicus*, offers us, as I have noted, a pointless tautology: the *Oedipus Rex*, *The Bacchae*, *King Lear*, *The Duchess of Malfi*, are all blood-spattered and horrific; but who would be so bold as to confine such plays to a sub-genre?

That Shakespeare when he wrote *Titus* was under the influence of classical exemplars must also be allowed; but this does not mean that his mind can be cleared of responsibility for it. Shakespeare was no doubt like other artists, and achieved his own voice by working through aesthetic enthusiasms and derivative exercises, and in this *Titus* is no different from other early plays. Like *Lucrece* and its comic counterpart, *Venus and Adonis*, *Titus Andronicus* is deeply indebted to Ovid's sense of human mutability, the frailty of man's happiness and of his capacity for reason. In a similar way *The Comedy of Errors* is indebted to Plautus, *The Taming of the Shrew* to Italianate comedy, *Romeo and Juliet* to the atmosphere and conventions of the Italian novella. The real difference between *Titus Andronicus* and *Romeo and Juliet* seems to emerge not from the derivativeness of the one and the originality of the other, but from the different implications of the genres used. If *Titus* is exceptional among Shakespeare's tragedies in its devotion to a hysterically bleak view of human potential, *Romeo* is exceptional also, in its general sunniness, its closeness to comedy. It is, of course, particularly close to the kind of comedy that Shakespeare was writing in these years, 'Italian', courtly, exploring the romantic sensibilities of well-bred youth. It goes without saying that we are the better able to understand *Romeo and Juliet* because we know these cognate comedies.

The distinction I have so far made between the two plays suggests that Shakespeare's first move in tragedy was to seek to delimit the space within which he could operate, marking out the extreme polarities of his tragic range. He was never again to pursue the image of man's bestiality with the single-mindedness he showed in *Titus*. And likewise he was never, after *Romeo*, to write another tragedy which was so clearly a diversion by malign fate of materials that would normally form the basis of comedy. From time to time hereafter he will, of course, come close to one pole or the other, but always in a manner which invokes the presence of its opposite. *King Lear*, for example, can be regarded as in some ways a reworking of themes from *Titus Andronicus*. We have the same grieved and deprived father, hounded from dignity into madness by a malignant group whose authority comes from his gift, and rescued in the end by a foreign invasion led by his loyal child. We have the same pervading image of man as a beast of prey, the same contrast between extremes of female rapacity and female innocence, the same overlapping of lust and political ambition. But the role of the family in

society is very different in the two plays. In both, the good
and evil quickly sort themselves out as opposing forces. But
in *Titus* the social gap between the two groups is what is
emphasized: on the one hand we have the barbarian out-
siders, on the other the Andronici, the pious Roman family.
In *Lear*, however, the opposition of good and bad emerges
from the matrix of a single family. Among the sufferings of
Titus the fact that Saturninus betrayed the favour he received
does not bulk large; but for Lear the ingratitude of the
daughters is the central agony. Thus the social rituals through
which the conflict is expressed in *Titus* (feasting, family
reading, the birth of a child, etc.) must give way in *Lear* to
more unstructured domestic confrontations, and in these the
side of Shakespeare's tragic vision represented by *Romeo*
re-emerges. Something of Old Capulet's irascible absurdity
survives into the very different world of Lear and his daughters.

Not only in *Lear* but throughout Shakespeare's mature
tragedies the ritual of *Titus* is complemented by the domes-
ticity of *Romeo*, the hieratic flanked by the familiar. Shakespeare achieves his later tragic centrality not only by diluting
the unreality of *Titus* but also by making more remote and
overpowering the cosinesses of Verona. Among the later
tragedies *Antony and Cleopatra* is probably the one that
most closely resembles *Romeo and Juliet*: in both plays the
poetic power is centrally involved in projecting the love
emotions of a socially significant couple, whose relationship
defies the prevailing political and ethical assumptions of
their society. Both are plays whose minor characters (Nurse,
Mercutio, Enobarbus, Charmian, Alexis) are much given to
comic routines. The lovers are finally united by quasi-
sacrificial deaths; their deaths open the way to a unification
of their society; and they are memorialized by joint tombs of
exemplary splendour. But *Antony and Cleopatra*, in spite of
its high comedy, does not in any sense give us a comic world
wrenched by fate to a tragic conclusion. The characters are
not like us; they are colossuses, and their laughter shakes the
world. Here there is no private sphere into which lovers can
escape from the pressures of other men's expectations. The
love gestures of Antony and Cleopatra, all made in the

world's eye, have to have the ritual quality of great public occasions. Their quarrels mirror the clash of alternative moral systems, Roman severity and barbarian self-indulgence. And in these respects the play may be seen to be closer to *Titus Andronicus*, or at least to the pole of tragedy it represents, than to *Romeo and Juliet*.

I have been arguing for a relationship between *Titus Andronicus* and *Romeo and Juliet* and between these two and the rest of Shakespeare's tragedies in terms of the polar characteristics of tragedy they exhibit. But *Titus Andronicus* and *Romeo and Juliet* are not related only as opposites. As one might expect with a playwright finding his way into his craft, similar structural skeletons serve for both plays, though the flesh hung on top of them is very different. We may note how the two plays open:

Flourish. Enter the Tribunes and Senators aloft; and then enter below Saturninus and his followers at one door, and Bassianus and his followers at the other, with drums and trumpets.

The scene that follows fleshes out the diagram thus established: first Saturninus (the elder) speaks, claiming his right to the crown, derived from primogeniture; then Bassianus (the younger) repeats the speech, claiming the crown as his right, derived from election. Then

Enter Marcus Andronicus aloft, with the crown.

Marcus tells us that the *populus Romanus* has chosen Titus Andronicus as its representative to take to himself the issue being contested. The contenders then leave the stage to allow Titus to enter in his *triumphus*.

The opening diagram of the forces in *Romeo and Juliet* is extraordinarily similar:

Enter [at one door] Sampson and Gregory, of the house of Capulet ... Enter [at the other door] two other Serving-men, Abraham and Balthazar [of the house of Montague] ... Enter [at one door] Benvolio [a nobleman of the house of Capulet] ... Enter Tybalt [a nobleman of the house of Montague] ... [they fight] ... Enter an Officer and three or four citizens ... Enter [at one door] Old Capulet ... and his wife ... Enter [at the other door] Old Montague and his wife ... Enter [? above] Prince Escalus with his Train.

In both plays the opening movement establishes discord against rule. The formalized stage-pictures set one competitor for power against another, the greater social range of the representatives of faction in *Romeo and Juliet* measuring the variety of social experience that play will draw on, the more concentrated concern with political power in *Titus Andronicus* marking that play's range of significant action. In both cases power is denied to the competitors. A central justice in the possession of power is demonstrated, and the establishment of this central authority over the brawling factions leads to their departure from the stage at the end of this dramatic phrase or movement.

In both tragedies, however, the remedy for discord which this opening diagram displays is a matter for display rather than acceptance. The failures in acceptance are, of course, very different. In *Romeo and Juliet* the Prince remains throughout the action an objective and unsubverted guarantor of order. The discord that persists is, in political terms, a hole-and-corner affair, dealt with by easy penalties. In *Titus Andronicus*, however, the supreme authorities of the opening, Marcus and Titus Andronicus, the representatives of the citizens and of the army, quickly lose their central position *aloft*. Titus is soon self-subverted and then hounded into grotesque subservience and madness. Astraea leaves the country; justice and order cease to have a political dimension. The movement by which moral order vanishes from Rome is, of course, without parallel in *Romeo and Juliet*. But the process by which Titus, in his wrong-headed and high-principled choice of Saturninus, his abject surrender of all rights to the new Emperor, falls from arbiter to suppliant does not end by breaking the parallel with *Romeo*. It ends, in fact, by re-forming the opening diagram of strife into a more stable and more exactly parallel shape.

The central conflict of *Titus Andronicus* stabilizes itself as the story of two family groupings, whose conflict destroys (or threatens to destroy) the civilization represented by the city. The opening chorus of *Romeo and Juliet* can easily be adapted to fit the other play:

Two households, both alike in dignity,
In Rome's fair city, where we lay our scene,

From early grudge break to new mutiny,
Where civil blood makes civil hands unclean.

It must be confessed, of course, that the 'two households' of *Titus* are less obvious than those of *Romeo*. By the middle of Act II, however, it is clear that the action is going to hinge on the conflict between the Andronicus family and that alternative 'household' of Saturninus/Tamora/Aaron with Tamora's assorted children, Chiron and Demetrius (later joined by the black baby). That this latter grouping can only be called a 'family' by a radically deformed definition does not reduce the significance of the parallel; indeed it strengthens it. The family ties of the Andronici suggest the strength of the family unit as the basis of all social order, and particularly that of Rome, demonstrating loyalty, mutual support, and above all *pietas*, drawing on the dutifulness of the past to secure the dutifulness of the future. The household of husband, lover, and assorted children that clusters round Tamora suggests the opposite: a dreadful burgeoning of uncontrolled nature into a rank and unweeded plot, where parental love cannot compensate for the various disorders and mismatings that result. Within a short time we are shown the wife over-ruling the husband, the mismating of Emperor and enemy, of Empress and slave, of white and black, the mother encouraging the sons to rape and murder, the brothers ready to kill one another until reduced to 'order' by the black lover (acting as surrogate father). Finally we have the black baby itself 'as loathsome as a toad', the complete image of instinctual wickedness.

In the two plays the conflicts of the households are handled, of necessity, in very different terms. In *Romeo and Juliet* the conflict between Montagues and Capulets has little political reality. It exists to maintain a certain pressure on what the play presents as more real—the personal emotions of the two lovers. In *Romeo and Juliet* evil exists only in so far as the traditional conflict exists. It is not presented as a facet of the normal human will (even in the case of Tybalt); stability and concord are always possible, as a result of spontaneous human action, and we are always aware that peace is only a hand's breadth away. The narrow distance between tragedy and comedy is of course one of the principal effects of the play. But in *Titus* the political conflict remains central and cannot possibly be evaded. It arises from the fact of being human, from the need to resist destruction, the imposition of chaos, the reduction of civilization to appetite, and man to beast, all of which here grows out of a personal will to evil, deeply implanted in human nature, and requiring for its neutralization every energy and every resource available in the play. Here no aspect of life can be thought of as merely personal and private, and so exempted from the struggle. The loves of Aaron and Tamora, the rape of Lavinia, are political as well as moral offences. There is no Duke to intervene; the conflict is not simply a relic of past bitternesses, but a monstrous burgeoning of manic energies; death or flight are the only alternatives to absorption into the system.

And in the end, flight is not possible either. The world of the play demands a return to the scene of the struggle. This is equally true of both tragedies: the two plays are (uniquely among Shakespeare's tragedies) tales whose significance is expressed in terms of single cities, though *Rome* has, of course, a very different civic resonance from *Verona*. Verona suggests to us, when we hear that it is in 'fair Verona, where we lay our scene', that we should expect Italian passions, Italian family honour, the hot blood stirring in the sun, balconies, friars, domestic luxury and homely social display, a cosy familiarity of masters and servants, a world poised between the bourgeois and the aristocratic; though we must try to beware of finding in the play too much of the 'Italianism' which entered English literature through *Romeo and Juliet*. Rome on the other hand suggests *ab initio* a military civilization, severity, self-conscious masculinity, stoical self-denial, the inexorable rule of law—that collection of ethical icons that long dominated the European sense of culture: Horatius defending the bridge, Mutius Scevola burning off his right hand, Regulus returning to Carthage, Lucretia preferring death to dishonour, Manlius Torquatus killing his son for disobedience, etc., etc.

It appears in consequence that the two cities are well chosen by Shakespeare as points of focus, for a love story on the one hand, and on the other hand for a story of civilization and its enemies, concerned with fortitude and brutality. In both plays the city walls measure the limit of the ordered world.

> There is no world without Verona walls
>
> (III. iii. 17)

says Romeo with what might seem merely adolescent exaggeration; but the exaggeration is in fact quite close to truth. Meaning does not exist for the play outside Verona; the only non-Veronese of whom we hear is the Apothecary, who is death's emissary:

> Famine is in thy cheeks,
> Need and oppression starveth in thy eyes,
> Contempt and beggary hangs upon thy back,
> The world is not thy friend, nor the world's law . . .
>
> (v. i. 69–72)

The balance of love and hate, of personal life and public reputation, the context within which meaning exists—this can be found only in Verona.

In *Titus*, very similarly, the play's meaning can only be brought to focus inside the walls of its city. Of course the focus is very different, the city being so different. We are here concerned with self-sacrifice and self-indulgence, rule and disobedience, with suffering and cruelty, with the destructive will to chaos, set against personal commitment to justice as the only meaningful basis for society. Only in Rome, it is implied, can the victory of cosmos or chaos be fully significant; Rome is seen as the hub of things, where final decisions are made and known to be final. This is why at the end of the play:

> As for that ravenous tiger, Tamora,
> No funeral rite, nor man in mourning weed,
> No mournful bell shall ring her burial;
> But throw her forth to beasts and birds to prey.
>
> (v. iii. 195–8)

Rome is here finally returned to the status appropriate to it, a status it has seemed to lose in the course of the action, when the city came to seem no different from the barbarism outside. When, as Titus tells us,

> Rome is but a wilderness of tigers,
>
> (III. i. 54)

when Lucius has to flee to the Goths to raise an army 'to be revenged on Rome and Saturnine', Rome clearly has forgotten how to be Roman. It takes a political convulsion and a blood-bath to re-establish the city as different from the wilderness of tigers. In the meantime Titus is required to carry the role of Rome's speaking conscience, when Rome cannot speak for herself. Where is Astraea gone? Why do the gods not answer, or not listen? Such questions keep continuously before our minds a sense of meaning in the city which is elsewhere out of sight. Meaning cannot be given to the world again, it is implied, till the mind of Rome and the mind of Titus are at one, when Moors and Goths know their place outside the walls and Roman *severitas* rules all within.

The only locale established in *Titus Andronicus* outside the walls of Rome is the forest of Act II where the major crimes are committed. It is to be noticed that those who are at home and effective here are Aaron and Tamora, Chiron and Demetrius. For Tamora everything in the forest 'doth make a gleeful boast':

> The snakes lie rolled in the cheerful sun;
> The green leaves quiver with the cooling wind
> And make a chequer'd shadow on the ground;
> Under their sweet shade, Aaron, let us sit . . .
>
> (II. iii. 13–16)

For Lavinia, however, the forest scene is, like Aaron, dark and evil:

> let her joy her raven-coloured love;
> This valley fits the purpose passing well.
>
> (II. iii. 83–84)

Aaron is skilful in the use of forest pits and stratagems; his energy sprouts at the thought of them. The young Andronici, however, grow uncertain and dim of sight:

QUINTUS. My sight is very dull, whate'er it bodes.
MARTIUS. And mine, I promise you; were it not for shame,
  Well could I leave our sport to sleep awhile.
. . .

QUINTUS. I am surprised with an uncouth fear;
A chilling sweat o'er-runs my trembling joints;
My heart suspects more than mine eye can see.
(II. iii. 195–7, 211–13)

Within the dim light of the forest meanings change at the whim of the observer; this is no place for the hard clear minds of the Andronici. It is, however, a natural context for Tamora's Gothic deceptions and shifts of role. At one point the forest is for her, as noted above, a place of love and repose. It is also Tamora, however, who expresses most eloquently the idea of the forest as a place of horror—without even the excuse that it is 'another part of the forest':

A barren detested vale you see it is:
The trees, though summer, yet forlorn and lean,
Overcome with moss and baleful mistletoe;
Here never shines the sun; here nothing breeds,
Unless the nightly owl or fatal raven.
(II. iii. 93–97)

This description, like the previous one designed to encourage Aaron to acts of love, is, of course, not organized as a scientific account of a place actually there, but presents a rhetorical backdrop, appropriate in this case to murder, rape, and mutilation. When Titus asks for 'proof' that his sons performed the murder he brings a Roman attachment to the rules of evidence to a Gothic dream of total personal fulfilment, where the world becomes what the dreamer desires it to be. At the end of Act II when the night-world of the forest is giving way again to the daylight clarities of Rome, Marcus Andronicus sees the nightmare figure of his niece; he remarks:

If I do dream, would all my wealth would wake me!
If I do wake, some planet strike me down,
That I may slumber an eternal sleep! (II. iv. 13–15)

Henceforth in the play, however, such nightmare shadows have to be allowed as part of the daylight population of Rome. The ghosts are only laid, the shadows of the forest dispelled, when nightmare and truth have faced one another in Tamora's last disguise—as Revenge, the mother of Rapine and Murder ('A pair of cursed hell-hounds and their dam' as Titus puts it)—so that mutilators and mutilated can perish together in a shared universe of absurdity and Rome be restored to rule and the daylight processes of justice.[3]

At the centre of the city, as its soul you may say, stands the family of the Andronici, and at the centre of the Andronici's sense of themselves stands one essential object, which the stage-picture should surely highlight—the tomb. The structural use of the family vault or tomb provides another point of correspondence between *Titus* and *Romeo*. We are shown the tomb of the Andronici very early in the play: when Titus first enters in his Roman Triumph, bearing the Gothic family into Rome among his prisoners, the first action he undertakes is the burial of the dead in the family vault:

> Romans, of five and twenty valiant sons . . .
> Behold the poor remains, alive and dead!
> These that survive let Rome reward with love;
> These that I bring unto their latest home,
> With burial amongst their ancestors . . .
> Make way to lay them by their brethren.
> There greet in silence, as the dead are wont,
> And sleep in peace, slain in your country's wars.
> O sacred receptacle of my joys,
> Sweet cell of virtue and nobility,
> How many sons hast thou of mine in store
> That thou wilt never render to me more!
>
> (I. i. 79–95)

And it is the tomb that stimulates the first statement of the conflict that will dominate the play. Lucius demands, in what is clearly part of a controlled ritual:

> Give us the proudest prisoner of the Goths,
> That we may hew his limbs, and on a pile
> Ad manes fratrum sacrifice his flesh
> Before this earthly prison of their bones,
> That so the shadows be not unappeas'd,
> Nor we disturb'd with prodigies on earth.
>
> (I. i. 96–101)

3. In these terms *Titus* looks like a tragic version of the city–forest–city pattern found in *A Midsummer Night's Dream*—a play which also has close affinities with *Romeo and Juliet*.

Shakespeare seems here to be dramatizing a clear conception of the religious basis of the Roman way of life; there is no suggestion that he is criticizing the system. The dead citizen-warriors claim the right to be returned to their family place within the city. There they will rest in peace, provided the appropriate honour is paid to them; and the appropriate honour is that the living should hear their claim for the propitiatory sacrifice of 'the proudest prisoner of the Goths', and be absolutely obliged to fulfil this claim.

Against this Roman ritual Shakespeare sets the personal plea of Tamora:

> Victorious Titus, rue the tears I shed,
> A mother's tears in passion for her son.
>
> (I. i. 105–6)

Modern readers naturally feel more sympathy for the more personal position taken up by Tamora and argued by her with eloquence and passion. But the play hardly supports the view that these Roman rituals are in themselves barbarous, or that Tamora is in some sense 'justified' in taking up revenge against the Andronici. The stern suppression of self in the interest of family, community, or state is certainly presented in an extreme form, but it is the extreme form of a value-system consistently preferred in the play before subjective passion or individual emotionalism. The military dead are represented as an essential part of the living family and of the national destiny; they cannot be fobbed off with something less than their right. As in other military civilizations, the valiancy of the living is preserved by the promise that they, too, in their turn will have the right to enter the family tomb, to join the honoured bones of their ancestors and be rewarded with reverence and with sacrificial victims. This is why the tomb becomes the primary focus again at the end of the play. The new conqueror and paterfamilias, Lucius Andronicus, throws out the tiger Tamora for birds to peck at; Aaron is treated very similarly—half buried in the earth and left to the mercies of a Nature that 'swallows her own increase'. Both are replaced in the extramural world of unhallowed appetite. But

> My father and Lavinia shall forthwith
> Be closed in our household's monument.
> (v. iii. 193–4)

Interment in the tomb validates the efforts of the life preceding, and ensures the continuity of past, present, and
future under the same standards of civilization.

The parallel importance of the tomb in *Romeo and Juliet*
suggests that the Andronicus 'household's monument' reflects
more than Shakespeare's study of Roman antiquities. It
implies that Shakespeare found the tomb property a convenient expression of his sense of the tragic importance of
family and social continuities. The Capulet family monument
is not, of course, a military symbol. But the choice of it as the
most appropriate final setting for the tragedy brings out the
structure of significances this play shares with *Titus Andronicus*. It is entirely appropriate that the 'public' wedding-bed of
Romeo and Juliet (as against their previous private bedding)
should be placed in the Capulet tomb, for it is there that
Romeo may be most effectively seen to have joined his wife's
clan, there where their corporate identity is most unequivocally established:

> Where all the kindred of the Capulets lie,
> (IV. i. 112)

> Where for this many hundred years the bones
> Of all my buried ancestors are pack'd.
> (IV. iii. 40–41)

The rash and personal passion of Romeo and Juliet can
hardly claim a truly tragic significance if it cannot be caught
up in the corporate and continuing life of Verona. Here, as in
Titus Andronicus, the presence of the tomb assures us that
the extreme acts of tragic individuals contribute to the past
and future as well as to the brilliant present of personal
assertion, here where they join the confluence of acts that
make up social continuity.

In both plays a woman as well as a man is placed in the
tomb at the end of the action. One might have expected the
Andronicus tomb to exclude women; but Lavinia is clearly
said to be Titus's companion in death. I do not think, however, that this implies any weakening of the military signifi-

cance of the family monument. Lavinia, too, has like a soldier triumphed over her enemy. The battle has, of course, been a strange and even a grotesque one. The code of military ethics does not provide much guidance for dealing with a wilderness of tigers; and the cunning ploys of the mad Titus are only marginally 'Roman'. But it is worth noticing that the appeal to Roman precedent and tradition returns at the moment of Lavinia's death:

> Was it well done of rash Virginius
> To slay his daughter with his own right hand,
>   (v. iii. 36–37)

asks Titus, and, being told by the Emperor, 'It was, Andronicus', he stabs and kills her. This is often seen as yet another senseless butchery; but in the light of the precedent explicitly established one may prefer to see it as the restoration of truly Roman or meaningful death. To have killed Lavinia earlier would have been an act of despair, for the standards by which such an act might be justified seemed to have vanished. To have enclosed her in the tomb then would have devalued the generations of soldiers already inhearsed. Now, with the mutilators mutilated, and with Tamora and Saturninus securely within the grasp of punishment, the practical possibility of justice reappears, the tomb can reopen and receive the honourable dead. Their presence there can now give meaning to the continuing efforts of the living. The persistent *Romanitas* of the family is spelt out in Marcus's submission of the 'poor remainder of Andronici' to the will of the Roman people:

> Now have you heard the truth: what say you, Romans?
> Have we done aught amiss, show us wherein,
> And, from the place where you behold us pleading,
> The poor remainder of Andronici
> Will hand in hand all headlong hurl ourselves,
> And on the ragged stones beat forth our souls,
> And make a mutual closure of our house.
>   (v. iii. 128–34)

On the contrary, of course, the people exalt the family and the family, in its turn, must exalt the dead. It is in this context that Lavinia (whose name is, after all, that of the inheritrix through whom Aeneas established his claim to found Rome) becomes something like a Roman tutelary deity, raped, mutilated, rendered incapable of crying out against these invasive barbarisms, but, by virtue of family *pietas* and unflinching self-sacrifice, enabled to take up her niche in the household monument and to represent to later ages a mode of tragic experience appropriate to a meaningfully 'Roman' world.

15

Five-act structure in *Doctor Faustus*

The original and substantive texts of Marlowe's *Doctor Faustus* (the Quartos of 1604 and 1616) present the play completely without the punctuation of act division or scene enumeration. This is common enough in the play-texts of the period. Indeed it is much the commonest form in plays written for the public theatres.[1] Shakespeare's *Henry V* and *Pericles* are without divisions in their quarto texts, but we know that they were written with a five-act structure in mind—the choruses tell us that.

What is exceptional in the textual history of *Doctor Faustus* is not the lack of division in the original texts; it is rather the reluctance of modern editors to impose an act-structure on the modern texts. This is curious, but it seems possible to discern why the reluctance exists and a survey of the modern editions of *Faustus* throws some interesting light on critical attitudes to the subject matter of the play.

Marlowe (like other Elizabethan dramatists) was 'rediscovered' by the educated English public in an atmosphere which played down his specifically dramatic and theatrical powers. Charles Lamb's *Specimens of the English dramatic poets who lived about the time of Shakespeare* (1808) established him primarily as a poet. This, as I say, did not distinguish him from other dramatists of the period. But the attitudes implied by Lamb's volume were more difficult to shake off in the case of *Doctor Faustus* than in other

[First published in *Tulane Drama Review*, viii, no. 4 (1964).]

1. W. T. Jewkes notes that 'of the 134 plays written for the public stage [*and printed before 1616*], 30 are divided, as against 104 undivided'. (*Act Division in Elizabethan and Jacobean Plays, 1583–1616* [Hamden, Conn., 1958], p. 96.) See, however, my 'Were there act-pauses on Shakespeare's stage?' in *English Renaissance Drama*, ed. Henning, Kimbrough, Knowles (1976).

·Elizabethan plays; for here they were reinforced, later in the century, by a second wave of anti-theatrical (or at least a-theatrical) influence. In 1887 the young Havelock Ellis (then a medical student) suggested to Henry Vizetelly, well known in 'advanced' circles as a courageous though rather *risqué* publisher, that he should put out a series of unexpurgated (key word!) texts of the Elizabethan dramatists—the famous 'Mermaid' series. The *Marlowe*, the first volume in the series, was edited by Ellis himself, and may be taken as a manifesto of the whole new movement. It bore proudly on the title-page the legend *Unexpurgated*, not simply because the usual casual indecencies of clown conversations were preserved, but rather because an appendix carried the full testimony of the informer Richard Baines 'concernynge [Marlowe's] damnable opinions and judgment of Religion and scorne of Gods worde', to which Ellis added the even more offensive comment that such 'damnable opinions . . . have, without exception, been substantially held, more or less widely, by students of science and the Bible in our own days'. To say this of remarks like 'Moses was but a juggler', 'that Christ better deserved to die than Barabas', etc., was to push Marlowe into the front line of the late Victorian battle against bourgeois values. Marlowe appears as a social rebel and religious freethinker (like Ellis himself) and this comes to reinforce the earlier view that he was primarily a poet. The two attitudes join together, in fact, to suggest that he was a poet *because* he was a freethinker, rejecting social conventions in order to achieve his individual and personal vision. He becomes the morning-star of the 1890s, a harder and more gem-like Oscar Wilde.

In order to preserve the image of Marlowe as a cult-figure of this kind it is necessary to discount the theatrical, and so popular, provenance of his work. If he was the laureate of the atheistical imagination, he must have stood at a considerable distance from his rudely Christian audience; and this assumption presses especially heavily upon *Doctor Faustus*, whose hero is himself a freethinker and (by implication at least) a poet. It is not surprising therefore to find Ellis saying in his headnote to *Faustus*: 'I have retained the excellent plan introduced by Professor Ward and adopted by Mr. Bullen, of dividing the play into scenes only; it is a dramatic poem rather than a regular drama.' In the face of this critical assurance, and with the *Zeitgeist* exerting the kind of pressure that I have described, the earlier editorial practice of presenting the play in five acts, derived from the 1663 Quarto by Robinson (1826) and continued in Cunningham (1870), Wagner (1877), and Morley (1883), withered away. It was not until the bibliographical breakthrough[2] of Boas, Kirschbaum, and Greg (1932, 1946, 1950) that the play reappeared in the five-act form. Even after their labours the old attitudes persist. The edition by Kocher (1950) is divided into scenes only, and the recent replacement of Boas by the 'Revels' edition of J. D. Jump (1962) avoids the act divisions: 'Neither A1 [1604] nor B1 [1616] makes any attempt to divide the play into acts and scenes, so no such distribution is given prominence in the present edition' (xxxv). It may be sufficient reply to this to quote the recent comment of W. T. Jewkes, who has analysed the act structure of all the plays in the period:

The plays of the 'University wits', however, appear both undivided and divided. On a closer inspection it was evident that the clearly divided texts from this group were those which showed least sign of playhouse annotation, while those which retained fragmentary division, or none at all, showed signs of adaptation for performance. It is evident then that these dramatists divided their plays originally, but that adaptation for the stage resulted in either the total or partial loss of act headings.[3]

This argument might well be augmented, in the particular

2. I mean the perception that the 1616 text must be the basis of any modern recension. In this text the nature of the structure is much clearer; and it was, in fact, the reading of Greg's *editio minor* that first made clear to me the precision with which the play moved. Greg himself, however, hedges his bets. He finds the act division 'convenient in discussing the construction of the play' (parallel text edition, p. 153) and so presents it to the reader; but he confides to us in a footnote that 'I see no reason to suppose that any act division was originally contemplated' (p. 153, n. 5). His argument is that there is too great a disproportion between the numbers of lines to be found in the different acts for these to make just divisions. A rereading of *The Winter's Tale*, in which Act IV is two and a half times as long as Act III, ought to convince us of the peculiarity of this mode of assessment. It may be, of course, that Shakespeare also ought to be presented without act-division. But no editor has yet had the courage to present his text in this way.

3. Op. cit., p. 97. Cf. my article cited above, p. 335, n. 1.

case of *Doctor Faustus*, by reference to the choruses which mark the beginnings of some of the acts, or by repeating Boas's observations about the material taken from the Faustbook. But it is not my purpose here to argue in detail the textual or theatrical probability that *Faustus* is in five-act form. I rather wish to look at the developing movement of the play to see if the act divisions accepted by Boas and others correspond to anything in the inner economy of the work, marking progressive stages in an organized advance through the material. Since Goethe remarked, 'How greatly is it all planned' in 1829,[4] many have been found to repeat his encomium, but few to justify it. I would suggest that the play *is* planned greatly, even precisely, in five clear stages (or acts), moving forward continuously in a single direction. I am assuming, when I say this, that the text as we have it in the 1616 Quarto is the product of a unified organizing intelligence. Marlowe *may* have had a collaborator, but I do not believe that we can detect his work—and a stroke of Occam's razor makes him disappear.

The first point I should like to make is that the action (I deal only with the main plot at the moment) moves through clearly separable stages. Act I is concerned (as is usual) with setting up the situation and introducing the principal characters. Here we learn the nature of Faustus's desires, set against the limiting factor of his nature; we meet Mephistophilis and the contrast between the two is made evident. Act II begins with a preliminary reminder (found before each act of the play) of the stage at which the action has arrived:[5]

> Now Faustus must thou needs be damned,
> And canst thou not be saved.
> What boots it then to think on God or heaven?
>
> (II. i. 1–3)

In Act I, the temptation to think of heaven is hardly present; but the subject here announced is the warp on which much of the main-plot action of Act II is woven. The conflict is now entered upon in real earnest. The introductory note to Act III

---

4. Recorded in the *Diary* of H. Crabb Robinson, for 2 August 1829.

5. Text and line numbers of quotations from Marlowe are taken from Irving Ribner's text (1963).

is more obvious, being handled by the 'Chorus'. He tells us that 'Learned Faustus', having searched into the secrets of Astronomy, now is gone to prove Cosmography. He is in fact completing his Grand Tour when we meet him, having taken in Paris, Mainz, Naples, Venice, and Padua, and is newly arrived in Rome, 'Queen of the Earth' as Milton's Satan calls it,[6] and the summation of worldly grandeur. Mephistophilis describes the sights, and then conducts his master into the highest social circles in the city, and so in the world.

Act III is spent in Rome; Act IV in the courts of Germany. The introductory Chorus makes clear the distinction between 'the view / Of rarest things' which is the substance of Act III and the 'trial of his art' which is what we are to see in Act IV. The introductory speech to Act V is spoken by Wagner, Faustus's servant, who is confused in one text with the Chorus, and who is exercising here what is clearly a choric function. His first line marks the change of key: 'I think my master means to die shortly.' Act V is concerned with preparations and prevarications in the face of death.

It is obvious enough, I suggest, that each act handles a separate stage in Faustus's career. But it is not obvious from what I have said that the stages move forward in any single and significant line of development. To see that they do requires a fairly laborious retracing of the action, seen now in the light of what was more obvious to Marlowe and his audience than to us—the supposed hierarchy of studies.

The opening lines of the play show us Faustus trying to *settle his studies*; the opening speech, with this aim in mind, moves in an orthodox direction through the academic disciplines, beginning with logic, here representative of the whole undergraduate course of Liberal Arts, through the *Noble Sciences* of Medicine and Law and so to the *Queen of Sciences*, Divinity. So far, the movement has been, as I say, completely orthodox, and a frame of reference has been neatly established. But, having reached Divinity, Faustus still hopes to advance, and can only do so in reverse:

6. *Paradise Regained*, IV. 45. Cf. William Thomas, who calls Rome 'the onelie jewell, myrrour, maistres, and beautie of the worlde' (*Historie of Italie* [1549]).

> ... Divinity, adieu!
> These metaphysics of magicians
> And negromantic books are heavenly[7]
>   (I. i. 49–51)

At this point he passes, as it were, through the looking glass; he goes on trying to evaluate experience, but his words of value (like 'heavenly') now mean the opposite of what they should. The 'profit and delight ... power ... honour ... omnipotence' that he promises himself through the practice of magic are all devalued in advance. By embracing negromancy he ensures that worthwhile ends cannot be reached; and the rest of the play is a demonstration of this, moving as it does in a steadily downward direction.

The route taken by Faustus in his descent through human activities was, I think, intended to be easily understood by the original audience, and again I suggest that it is the structure of knowledge as at that time understood that provides the key. Divinity was, as I have noted, the 'Queen of the Sciences'. Not only so, but it was the discipline which gave meaning to all other knowledge and experience. Hugh of St Victor expresses the idea succinctly: 'all the natural arts serve divine science, and the lower order leads to the higher'.[8] In Marlowe's own day the same point is made, more elaborately, in the popular *French Academy* of La Primaudaye:

> What would it availe or profit us to have and attaine unto the knowledge and understanding of all humane and morall Philosophy, Logicke, Phisicke, Metaphisicke, and Mathematick ... not to bee ignorant of any thing, which the liberall arts and sciences teach us, therewith to content the curious minds of men and by that means to give them a tast, and to make them enjoy some kind of transitory good in this life: and in the meane time to be altogether and wholy ignorant, or badly instructed, in the true and onely science of divine Philosophy, whereat all the rest ought to aime.   (Preface to Book IV)

But if one rejects the final cause here supposed, what

7. I preserve the original form *negromantic*, though most modernizing editors change it to *necromantic*. This seems to me to be a greater change than is warranted by a licence to modernize. It is the 'black art' in general that Faustus is welcoming, not the power to raise the dead.

8. *De Sacramentis* (Prologue), in Migne's *Patrologia Latina*, vol. clxxvi, col. 185.

happens to the rest of knowledge? This is the question that the play asks and pursues. In what direction does the Icarus of learning fall when he abandons the orthodox methods of flight? The order of topics in the medieval encyclopaedias gives one some clue here. These regularly begin with God and divine matters. Vincent of Beauvais' *Speculum* starts from the Creator, then moves to 'the empyrean heaven and the nature of angels', then to 'the formless material and the making of the world; the nature and the properties of things created', then to the human state and its ramifications. The *De Rerum Natura* attributed to Bede and William of Conches's *Philosophia Mundi*[9] have the same four-book order. Book I deals with God; Book II with the heavens; Book III with the lower atmosphere; Book IV with the earth, so down to man and his human activities. The *Proem* to Book IV (identical in both works) gives a fair indication of the nature of the movement assumed:

The series of books which began with the First Cause has now descended to The Earth, not catering for itching ears nor loitering in the minds of fools, but dealing with what is useful to the reader. For now is that verse fulfilled: 'For the time will come when they will not endure sound doctrine; but after their own lusts shall they heap to themselves teachers, having itching ears.' (2 Timothy, iv, 3). But since the mind of the honest man does not turn after wickedness, but conforms itself to the better way, let us turn to the remaining subjects, in the interest of a mind of this kind, estranged from wickedness and conformable to virtue.

In Marlowe's own day this order of topics appeared in works as popular as the Baldwin–Palfreyman *Treatise of Moral Philosophy* (innumerable editions from 1557 to 1640), in Palfreyman's companion *Treatise of Heavenly Philosophy*, and in William Vaughan's *The Golden Grove* (1600, 1608). *The French Academy*, which Marlowe has been supposed to have known, uses the same organization of topics but treats them in reverse order, upwards from (1) 'the institution of manners and callings of all estates', through (2) 'concerning the soule and body of man', and (3) 'a notable description

9. The first is to be found in *P.L.* xc, cols 1127 ff., and the second (attributed to Honorius Augustodunensis) in vol. clxxii, cols 39 ff. I am indebted to Dr Hans Liebeschütz for pointing these out to me.

of the whole world . . . Angels . . . the foure elements . . .
fowles, fishes, beasts . . . ' etc. to (4) 'Christian philosophy,
instructing the true and onely meanes to eternall life'. It
seems reasonable to suppose that Marlowe knew this system
of knowledge; and it is my assertion that he used it to plan
the relationship of the parts of *Doctor Faustus*.

When Faustus has signed away his soul, the first fruits of
his new 'power . . . honour . . . omnipotence' appear in the
knowledge of astronomy that he seeks. Astronomy is a
heavenly art, no doubt—it appears early in the encyclopaedias—but it is one that is not obviously dependent on divinity.
Yet here it leads by the natural process that the encyclo-
paedists describe to the question of first cause. If the heavens
involve more than the tedium of mechanics ('these slender
questions Wagner can decide') then astronomy leads straight
back to the fundamental question: Who made the world?
But, under the conditions of knowledge that Faustus has
embraced, this basic question cannot be answered, for it is
'against our kingdom'. The trap closes on the pseudo-scholar
and forces him backwards and downwards.

This is the movement—backwards into ever more superficial shallows of knowledge and experience—which continues inexorably throughout the whole play, as it must,
given the initial choice. Baulked in Act II from the full pursuit
of astronomy, in Act III Faustus turns to cosmography, from
the heavens to the earth. But the charms of sightseeing pall,
and a magical entrée even to the 'best' society in the world
involves only a tediously superficial contact. Marlowe's age
had serious doubts about the importance of cosmography (or
geography) as an object of human endeavour. *The French
Academy* treats it under the heading of 'curiosity and
novelty', as a destructively unserious pursuit. The drop in the
status of Faustus's activities is nicely caught by the change of
tone between the Chorus at the beginning of Act III and that
introducing Act IV. The first tells us that

> Learnèd Faustus
> To find the secrets of astronomy
> Graven in the book of Jove's high firmament
> Did mount him up to scale Olympus' top.
>   (III, Prol. 1–4)

We seem here still to be dealing with a genuine search for knowledge. But in the later chorus we hear only that:

> When Faustus had *with pleasure*[1] ta'en the view
> Of rarest things and royal courts of kings,
> He stay'd his course and so returnèd home.
>
> (IV, Prol. 1–3)

The emphasis is no longer on the search after knowledge, with discovery, presumably, as the aimed-for end, but with what is more appropriate to the diabolical premise ('that is not against our kingdom'), with pleasure taken and then given up, without reaching forward to the final causes. Faustus's merry japes among the cardinals are enjoyed by the protagonist, and are clearly meant to be enjoyed by the audience; but nothing more than pleasure is involved, and given the giant pretensions of the first act, the omission is bound to be a factor in our view of the Roman scenes.

Faustus not only views Rome. He also dabbles in statecraft, rescuing the Antipope Bruno and transporting him back to his supporters in Germany. The step from cosmography to statecraft is similar to that from astronomy to cosmography. In each case we have a reduction in the area covered, and an increasing remoteness from first causes. The panoply of state is not here (as it usually is in Shakespeare) an awesome and a righteous thing. It is not approached through the lives of those who must live and suffer inside the system, but via the structure of knowledge, so that it is the relationship to divinity rather than the power over individual lives that is the determining factor in our attitude. The ludicrous antics at the Papal court have usually been seen as a simple piece of Protestant propaganda, pleasing to the groundlings and inserted for no better reason. Yet one can see that this episode (placed where it is) has its own unique part to play in the total economy of the work. It is proper to start Faustus's descent through the world from the highest point, in Rome; it is equally proper to begin his social and political descent with the Vicar of Christ (and so down to Emperor, to Duke, and back to private life). By turning the conduct of the papal court into farce Marlowe devalues *all*

1. My italics.

sovereignty and political activity in advance. Bruno (and his tiara) are saved; but there is no suggestion that *he* has any more virtue to recommend him; he has no real function in the play except to reduce the title and state of the Pope to a mere name.

There is no suggestion in this act that Faustus himself is aware of the startling discrepancy between the actual happenings and the promises he made to himself (and to us) at the beginning of the play. The audience, however, can hardly forget so soon; and our memory is reinforced in the papal palace by the ritual threats of damnation uttered by the Pope and friars. It is no doubt comic that the Pope should be boxed on the ear and exclaim, 'Damn'd be this soul for ever for this deed', but we should not fail to notice the sinister echo reverberating behind the horseplay; the curse is comic at this point, but sinister in the context of the whole action.

Act IV carries the descent of Faustus one more clear step, by still further reducing the importance of the area in which he operates. I have mentioned the social descent to the secular courts of Emperor and Duke of Vanholt. At the same time there is a descent in terms of the kind of activity that the magic procures. Faustus's anti-Papal activities can be seen as political action of a kind, and this aspect would be more obvious to the Elizabethans than it is to us (involved, as they were, in the kind of struggle depicted). But in Act IV he is presented quite frankly as a court entertainer or hired conjurer. In the court of Charles V, of course, there is still some intellectual dignity in his activities. Charles's longing, to see 'that famous conqueror, Great Alexander, and his paramour', is a kingly interest in a paragon of kingship. But when Faustus goes on to the court of the Duke of Vanholt he is reduced to satisfying nothing more dignified than the pregnant 'longings' of the duchess for out-of-season grapes. At the same time his side activities are brought down by a parallel route. At the court of the Emperor he was matched against the disbelieving knights, Frederick, Benvolio, etc.; at Vanholt his opponents are clowns, the Horse-courser, the Hostess.[2]

2. I find that this general point has been made by Kirschbaum in his paperback *The Plays of Christopher Marlowe* (New York: Meridian, 1962):

The last act of *Faustus* is often thought of as involving restoration of dignity and brilliance to the sadly tarnished magician. In terms of poetic power there is something to be said on this side; but the poetry that Faustus is given in this act serves to do more than simply glorify the speaker. The fiery brilliance of the Helen speech is lit by the Fire of Hell (as has been pointed out by Kirschbaum[3] and others). The imminence of eternal damnation gives strength and urgency to the action, but the actions that Faustus himself can initiate are as trivial and as restricted as one would expect, given the moral development that I have described as operating throughout the rest of the play. There is no change of direction. In Acts III and IV we saw Faustus sink steadily from political intrigue at the Curia to fruit-fetching for a longing duchess. The last act shows a consistent extension of this movement. It picks up the role of Faustus as entertainer, but reduces the area of its exercise still further; it is now confined to the enjoyment of some 'two or three' private friends, and as an epilogue to what Wagner characterizes by 'banquet . . . carouse . . . swill . . . belly-cheer'. Helen appears, in short, at the point where one might have expected dancing-girls.

The nature of the object conjured in Act v, no less than the occasion of the conjuring, shows the same logical development of the movement in the preceding acts. Charles V had longed to satisfy an intellectual interest; the Duchess of Vanholt longed for the satisfaction of a carnal but perfectly natural appetite; but the desire to view Helen of Troy is both carnal and (as the ironic word *blessed* should warn us) reprehensible, and leads logically to the further and final depravity of:

> One thing, good servant, let me crave of thee
> To glut the longing of my heart's desire—
> That I may have unto my paramour
> That heavenly Helen which I saw of late,

'Surely Marlowe means to stress the magician's continuing degradation by showing him first playing his tricks with the spiritual head of all Roman Christendom and then ultimately declining, to play them with the clowns' (p. 119).

---

3. 'Marlowe's Faustus: a reconsideration', *R.E.S.* xix (1943).

Whose sweet embracings may extinguish clear
Those thoughts that do dissuade me from my vow
And keep mine oath I made to Lucifer.

(v. i. 90–96)

The circle in which Faustus conjures has now shrunk from the *urbs et orbis* of Rome to the smallest circle of all. When the dream of power was lost, the gift of entertainment remained; but even this has now faded. The conjuring here exists for an exclusively self-interested and clearly damnable purpose. The loneliness of the damned, summed up in Mephistophilis's cryptic '*Solamen miseris socios habuisse doloris*'—this now is clearly Faustus's lot. Left alone with himself and the mirror of his own damnation[4] in Helen ('Her lips suck forth my soul: see where it flies!'), he is in a situation that cannot be reached by either the Old Man or the students. His descent has taken him below the reach of human aid; and there is a certain terrible splendour in this, as the poetry conveys, but the moral level of this splendour is never in doubt; it is something that the whole weight of the play's momentum presses on our attention, moving steadily as it does, through the clearly defined stages of its act-structure, away from the deluded dream of power and knowledge and downward, inevitably, coherently, and logically, into the sordid reality of damnation.

I have sought to show that the movement of the main plot of *Faustus* is controlled and splendidly meaningful. It moves in a single direction (downwards) through a series of definite stages which it would be wilfully obscurantist not to call acts. Indeed it conforms, by and large, to the strict form of five-act structure which was taught in Tudor grammar schools, out of the example of Terence. The structural paradigm was, of course, concerned with comedy, and especially the comedy of intrigue, and could not be applied very exactly to a moralistic tragedy like *Faustus*. But it is easy to see that Act I of *Faustus* gives us the introductory materials, Act II the first moves in the central conflict (Faustus versus the Devil), Acts

4. See W. W. Greg, 'The damnation of Faustus', *M.L.R.* xli (1946).

III and IV the swaying back and forward of this conflict, and Act V the catastrophe.

What is more, these stages of the main plot are reinforced or underlined by a parallel movement going on simultaneously in the subplot. The general relation between the two levels of the plot, the level of spiritual struggle and that of carnal opportunism, is one of parody—a mode of connection that was common in the period. And I should state that by 'parody' I do not mean the feeble modern reduction of characteristics to caricature, but rather that multiple presentation of serious themes[5] which relates them both to the man of affairs and to the light-minded clown.

It is not only in the detail of individual scenes that the subplot parodies the main plot: the whole movement of the subplot mirrors that social and intellectual descent that I have traced in the career of Faustus. The first subplot scene concerns Wagner, a man close to Faustus himself. The second comic scene involves Wagner and *his* servants, Robin and Dick. The third and subsequent scenes show Robin and Dick by themselves, Wagner having disappeared (he reappears— though not as part of the subplot—in v. i). It has been argued that this very descent, and the disappearance of Wagner, 'suggests a different hand' [*not Marlowe's*] for the Robin and Dick scenes.[6] This provides an interesting parallel to the assumption that Marlowe cannot be responsible for the main-plot scenes in the middle of the play. At both levels the action descends to trivialities, and the critics close their eyes in dissent. But if the movement is deliberate at one level it seems likely that it is so at the other level also.

Even more impressive than this general movement in the subplot is the accumulation of details in which the action of the subplot scene mirrors that of the contiguous main plot. Thus Act I, scene i, shows us Faustus using his virtuosity in logic to deceive himself. Scene ii shows us Wagner as no less able to chop logic and so to avoid the plain meaning of words. As a development from this we see Faustus raising Mephisto-

5. See G. K. Hunter, *John Lyly* (London: Routledge and Kegan Paul, 1962), pp. 135–40. The significance of the parody in *Faustus* is denied by Jump (op cit. lix–lx).
6. *Doctor Faustus*, ed. F. S. Boas (London: Methuen, 1932), p. 27.

philis and arranging that he should be his servant. The following scene shows us Wagner trying to control Robin, who would not 'give his soul to the devil for a shoulder of mutton', unless it were 'well roasted, and good sauce to it, if I pay so dear'. Wagner too has learned how to raise spirits and makes Robin his servant by a parody compact, promising to teach him 'to turn thyself to a dog, or a cat, or a mouse, or a rat, or any thing'. It may be noted that the general effect of this and the preceding comic scene is to reduce in status and to 'place' for us Faustus's pretensions to have conquered a new art by the force of his learning, and to have gained important new powers. When such as Wagner can raise Banio and Belcher, and all for the sake of terrifying Robin, then neither the means nor the ends of magic can be considered sufficient, by themselves, to make the magician a hero.

In Act II, scenes i and ii, Faustus signs his pact with the Devil and has the first fruits of his 'new' knowledge. In scene iii we meet Robin again. The power of raising spirits has declined from Faustus's servant Wagner to Wagner's servant, Robin. He and his fellow, Dick, plan to use one of the conjuring books to get free drink. In Act III the first two scenes show Doctor Faustus surveying the great cities of Europe and conjuring at Rome. The third scene shows Robin and Dick enjoying *themselves* in their own clownish way; but it is not now a way that is so remote from that of Faustus. He 'took away his holiness' wine', 'stole his holiness' meat from the table', 'struck Friar Sandelo a blow on the pate'; they steal the Vintner's cup, and when pursued for it they rely (as Faustus does) on magic as a rescue from their scape.

The play began with Faustus and Robin at opposite ends of the spectrum. One was 'glutted . . . with learning's golden gifts', powerful and renowned; the other was ignorant, 'out of service', and 'hungry'. But the process of logical development in the main plot, as I have described it, has by the end of Act III brought Faustus down through the diminishing circles of his capacity to the point where his powers and Robin's are no longer incommensurate. Up to this point, of course, Faustus and the clowns have never appeared together in any one scene. Such a conjunction would be unthinkable at the beginning of the play. But by Act IV Faustus has himself sunk to the level of a comic entertainer. His relationship to Frederick, Martino, and Benvolio is entirely without dignity or intellectual pretension, and the intrusion of the clowns, Robin, Dick, Carter, Horse-courser, Hostess, into the court of the Duke of Vanholt marks a natural and inevitable climax in the downward movement of the main plot. The comic 'Doctor Fustian' is now all the figure that Faustus can cut in the world; the 'success' that he has bought so dearly is to be the leader of a troupe of clowns.

There is no doubt a *frisson* intended between the last line of Act IV and the first line of Act V—between the duchess's appreciation of Faustus's powers: 'His artful sport drives all sad thoughts away', and (set against that) Wagner's 'I think my master means to die shortly'. The contrast between the two lines catches much of the movement from Act IV to Act V. Act IV is the climax of the subplot interest. Almost the whole act is taken up with triviality of one kind or another, and it ends with the confrontation of main plot and subplot characters, reducing them to one level. Act V, on the other hand, is without comic relief; and one can see why, in the terms I have outlined, this should be so. Through Act IV we see Faustus's life enmeshed in the triviality that was inherent in the original stipulation of 'any thing ... that is not against our kingdom'. Act V, as it begins with the mention of death, so continues to move in the shadow of a tragic conclusion. Faustus has now fallen *beneath* the level of the clowns and horse-courser:

> Why wert thou not a creature wanting soul?
>
> . . .
>
> Ah, Pythagoras' *metempsychosis*, were that true,
> This soul should fly from me and I be changed
> Into some brutish beast. All beasts are happy,
> For when they die
> Their souls are soon dissolved in elements.
>
> (V. ii. 169. 171–5)

The movement of the subplot helps to confirm this view of the general direction of Faustus's development. The constant looming presence of the clownish common man, with his attention set on immediate comforts, serves as a norm against which we may observe and judge the splendours and the miseries of the overweening intellectual.

Index

356

moral comparison of England and,
22, 24, 113
number of Italians living in
England, 21
political structures of, 21–22, 24,
112
relation to England, 22, 23, 112
religious aspects of, 112
Romantic image of, 111, 112, 113
Shakespeare's use of, 111
social comparison with England,
22, 23, 113
sophistication of, 113
vice plays set in, 110, 111–12,
117–18, 122–6
Webster's, 123–6

Jack Straw, 16
Jacob and Esau, 167n2
Jacquot, J., 161, 176n4
James I, King, 25, 190
James IV, King of Scotland, 35n6,
39n5
James, H., 15, 53
Jefferson, T., 39–40n5
Jew, The, 65n2
Jewkes, W. T., 335n1, 337
Jews:
absence of contact with, 26, 67
adversus Judaeos tradition, 64–70,
74
as an idea, 27, 28
as a norm, 28, 66–67
as anti-Christ, 64–65, 71
as a term of abuse, 26, 26n2, 66
association with Islam, 26, 67
association with Turks, 26, 28, 87
association with usury, 28, 74,
75n2, 94
'blaspheming', 24, 26n3
colonies of, in London, 67n9
Elizabethan image of, 26–27, 64–68
Jew figure:
Haughton's, 16n4
Marlowe's use of, 24, 28–29, 30,
66
Shakespeare's use of, 24, 26
Jewishness as a moral condition,
64–68
Judas tradition, 64, 74, 74n8
Lombard, 27
medieval image of, 26, 27, 65–67
racial view of, 27–29, 65–66, 67, 73

representing infidel forces, 26, 27,
66–67
Shakespeare's treatment of, 24, 26–28
social conduct of, 24, 26
stage portrayal of, 16n4, 30
the sin of, 27–28
villainy of, 28, 28n4, 111
Job, 70–74
Jodelle, E., 8
Johnson, R., 169
Johnson, S., 244, 247
Jones, H. A., 290–1
Jonson, Ben, 30, 41, 63, 103, 104,
105–6, 114, 115, 116, 121, 138,
141–2, 144
Every man in His Humour, 28n4,
105
Every man Out of His Humour,
103, 104–5, 121
Magnetic Lady, 115
Sejanus, 106, 114, 115, 240
Volpone, 23–24, 41, 63, 70, 75, 87
Jowett, B., 274–5
Jubinal, A., 92
Judas, 64, 74, 74n8, 83n9
July and Julian, 167n2
Jump, J. D., 337

Kafka, F., 225
Kalender of Shepherdes, The, 94
King Leir, The Chronicle History of,
29n8, 173
Kipling, R., 47
Kirchmeyer, T., *Pammachius*, 65n5
Kirschbaum, L., 60n2, 63n7, 337, 345
Kisch, G., 66
Klein, J. L., 148n9
Knight, G. Wilson, 261n2, 292–5,
296–7
Knights, L. C., 297
Knolles, R., 10n3
Kocher, P., 96n3, 99, 337
König, W., 313
Kyd, T., *The Spanish Tragedy*,
106–9, 110, 121, 122, 160,
163n6, 165–6, 173, 186, 187,
191, 192, 194, 195, 196, 199,
202, 203, 204, 214–29, 246, 248

Laforgue, J., 289
Lamb, C., 335–6
Lancaster, J., 40